LAZARO CARDENAS

Mexican Democrat

by

William Cameron Townsend

With a Foreword by
Frank Tannenbaum

INTERNATIONAL FRIENDSHIP

Waxhaw, North Carolina

1979

LÁZARO CÁRDENAS

Mexican Democrat

Copyright 1952, 1979 by
W. Cameron Townsend

Second edition, 1979, with six additional chapters

ISBN 0-935 340-00-9

Printed in the United States of America

Foreword

It is difficult for anyone who has known General Cárdenas to write about him dispassionately, and this interesting book by Mr. Townsend will suggest why. His mere presence stirred enthusiasm. One always thinks of him as surrounded by people. Wherever he went, crowds gathered and pressed themselves about him, tried to get close to him, to touch him. This seems always to have been so, not merely during the six years when he was President of Mexico; it is still that way. He attracts the common folk, and they follow him about, sit all day long for a chance to speak, or just to see him. His life has always belonged to others, mainly to the poor peasants, the laborers, and especially to the Indians. They have always known that, and they have loved him for it.

The quality of this relationship has a uniqueness perhaps unequalled in any other instance in the Western World. For the relationship has always been personal, intimate. Each individual seems to have a special place of his own. Cárdenas seems to know their names and understand their needs, and they never wear out his patience or dull his sympathy.

I once remarked on the almost complete merging of the President of the country with the common folk, and he replied, "They need so much, at least patience I can give them." This quality of patience, of self-abnegation, of endless devotion to the poor of Mexico has the element of saintliness. It is not political. I have seen him, while President, stand for many hours leaning against the door of a building, on a busy street in a large city, listening to each grievance, each petition, with unchanging equanimity.

In some ways the people are part of him, they are life itself. It was perfectly consistant with his character and temperament to attend a party in a little hut with a bare floor, in some little village in the mountains, after a long and difficult day that would have worn most men with sheer weariness. I recall one such instance, when after a long tiresome trip we attended a town party until four o'clock in the morning, and as the sun began to rise we departed

v

from the little town with all the people following us to the station, and waving goodbye as long as the train was visible. Cárdenas wasn't just the President. He was the personal friend and companion. He belonged to the people of Mexico, and they were part of him. The American reader will find this hard to understand. But that is the way it was—and is, for Cárdenas has remained unchanged.

This character is all of a piece. He carried the patience and the sense of friendliness into politics, into the army, into the revolution, into government administration, and into the personal friendships that are his. He is, in fact, everyone's friend, and probably has no personal enemies—a strange and incredible thing in any country for a man who has been a soldier, a general, and president of his country, but especially incredible in Mexico. For the remarkable thing about Cárdenas is that he could live this kind of life, and have this kind of career in Mexico. The Mexican milieu is difficult, recalcitrant, and impenetrable. The bitter history of Mexico has left its imprint upon the Mexican people.' Their memories are filled with stories of betrayals, political murders, promises unkept, and of indifference to the public weal. The people of Mexico have learned from bitter experience that in politics and government the game is played at great hazard, and that the spoils of victory go to the hard, the ruthless, and to those who are callous of the lives of their opponents. The remarkable thing about Cárdenas is that he could grow into an integrated, gentle, and selfless public servant in so difficult a world.

How this miracle was accomplished I do not know. It is clear that Cárdenas is deeply rooted in the Mexican soil. He is part of the earth itself, and he is timeless. Many books will be written about him, for he has influenced Mexico in many ways. He has in fact made a different Mexico from the one he found—in politics, in economics, in government, in international relations, in land ownership, in the place of the Indian and the worker, and in the role of the foreign investor. But the most lasting imprint upon Mexico, and what will make him timeless for the Mexicans, is his quality of simple faith in the Mexican people. He trusts them, believes in them, and loves them. The new sense of dignity and courage by the common folk of Mexico is the result of this acceptance by Cárdenas of the mass of the people. In some ways it is comparable to what Ghandi did for the masses of India, and the Mexican milieu was probably the more difficult for such an accomplishment.

The record of Cárdenas's career as President has been written in indelible ink upon the pages of Mexican history. He fulfilled the promise of land distribution for the peasants, and the old plantation system is gone forever. Whatever the future of Mexico, it will not be controlled by the hacienda. The Mexican workers and trade unions are closer to a responsible relationship with industry and government than was the case before. He has greatly strengthened the rural community. The expropriation of the oil industry gave the Mexican people the kind of lift in self-confidence and in national courage that has permanently changed the character of the nation. Mexico discovered its freedom in proving to itself that it was stronger than the foreign oil companies.

In international relations Cárdenas has asserted the equal dignity of the small nation with the large, and has greatly strengthened the Pan American system by proving that the United States and Mexico can work together as equals in the cause of international peace and justice. He has given the Mexican Church relief from public oppression for the first time in many a year, and to the Mexicans the opportunity to worship God without fear.

Cárdenas stimulated and carried through large and important public works. He established for the first time the principle that the government belonged to the people, and he took it to them in person. He laid it down that government officials are public servants who ought to devote themselves to the general good. He proved that a man can be in office and remain honest, and retire poor. He demonstrated what seemed the impossible: that a president could retire, and refrain from trying to dictate the future politics of the nation.

I recall talking about this with him one day. I expressed my doubts. It had never been done before, and probably could not be done. He said, "I will teach the people that a president can retire." "How?" I asked. "I will have a police man in the town, and arrest all of my friends who come to see me, and put them in jail." "Will you arrest me?" "Yes," he replied, "unless you promise to talk about the Peruvian, but not about the Mexican Indians."

Cárdenas has proven that it could be done. More significant is the example he set of not keeping himself in office, and by asserting the principle that it is better to permit an unpopular government to stay in power for its alloted time, has discouraged revolutions. The peaceful transmission of the office of the presidency is the greatest single political gift that he has given to Mexico. His mere presence is an assurance that there will be no revolution against the government in power, and no re-election. If that becomes a tradition Cárdenas will have permanently changed the character of Mexican politics.

But more important than any of these specific things that we have enumerated, and many others left unmentioned, is his contribution to the sense of dignity and self-respect of the Mexican people. He made the humblest man equal to the president. He never knew the difference between the great and the lowly. Each of them was a man, and each human being was equal in dignity and deserving of the same consideration as the President himself. This is the great lesson he taught the Mexican people, and the one for which they will always cherish his name.

To achieve this required a complete selflessness and courage. One day I remarked upon the indifference to personal danger with which he exposed himself to a possible enemy. He replied: "It is better to lose one's life doing good than to do evil in order to live."

Frank E. Tannenbaum
Columbia University
1951

Contents

General Lázaro Cárdenas, President of Mexico from 1934 to 1940, was a great statesman and a remarkable person in every way. I have known 40 presidents of ten different republics including the U.S.A. and not one of them approached his stature. The world needs to know about his remarkable character as well as his exceptional accomplishments. In this book I have tried to present him in all the aspects I observed over a period of 34 years. In April 1946 he and his beloved wife, Amalia, consented to stand up with Elaine and me at our wedding, but he was careful to make it known at the banquet that followed that he had consented to be our "best man" not because of our ties of friendship but because of the services we were performing for the many Indian groups of Mexico through the scores of dedicated linguists of the Summer Institute of Linguistics. He had found that these groups, numbering over 3 million, lived like foreigners in their own fatherland because of linguistic barriers. These barriers, he realized, would be broken down more rapidly as the government applied the findings of our linguists to national programs of bilingual education. Cárdenas invariably subordinated his personal desires to the interests of others.

The first 35 chapters, written in 1951, have been reprinted in this present edition. The remaining chapters were written after the death of Cárdenas in 1970.

William Cameron Townsend
Founder
Summer Institute of Linguistics

Waxhaw, North Carolina
February 1979

To

MEXICO

Realm of exploitation yesterday
Land of vision and struggle today
Commonwealth triumphant tomorrow

General Cárdenas, step by step you are carrying out with valor your destiny as an American, going into danger with the fatalism of our aborigines, respecting the weak, pardoning the enemy, protecting the needy, and always avoiding useless bloodshed between Mexicans. Reserved and discreet, you go about the working out of your destinies tranquilly, tirelessly and with tremendous force of will. Simply with your virtues as an untainted man of our Americas, you are gaining without seeking it, the most difficult of all the prizes that a statesman can attain, the goodwill of all the Hemisphere.

— Alfredo Sanjinés, Minister of Bolivia in Mexico
June 5, 1938

I

A GLIMPSE BEFORE THE STORY

RAINLESS AIR held a withering hand over the wretched little village of Tetelcingo. The villagers, seeking surcease from the scorching sun in the meager shade cast by adobe walls, cactus borders, and sparse foliage, were taking what *siesta* the oppressive heat would allow them.

There was little apparent activity—some of the men were, of necessity, working for their few *centavos* in the surrounding fields —others were, by preference, spending their few *centavos* to sate their thirst at the local *pulqueria*—some of the women were bent over their *metates* grinding *masa* for their *tortillas*. But for the most part, the heat had lulled the town to sleep. Only the red ants, whom the barefoot Tetelcingans superstitiously worshipped because of their power to destroy crops and vegetation, went about their vicious work with any energy.

The village seemed almost vacated—except for an astounding phenomenon. There, before the schoolhouse, amidst the squalor of the stone-strewn alley that served as "Main Street", were parked two elegant automobiles. Their presence was of sufficient rarity and incongruity with the surroundings to attract the attention of several of the villagers. In fact, Tetelcingo woke up, and was drawn en masse to the magnet.

About that time, a curious woman known in the village as "The Talking One" noticed the gathering crowd. Passing by the schoolhouse door she asked an important looking person, "Who's in there?"

"Why, haven't you heard? He's the Chief Ruler of the nation."

"Quit your lying to me," snapped the blunt inquirer, "not even the ruler of this district comes out here to see us. That man is probably some second-rate secretary."

3

"No, *Señora*," reassured the official, "that is none other than the President of the United States of Mexico."

"I don't believe you!" was her churlish reply.

"See for yourself," said the aide.

The woman brushed past him, pushed her way into the room, and waited for a pause in the proceedings. Then fixing her still incredulous eyes on Lázaro Cárdenas, and taking complete advantage of her unexpected encounter with the nation's chief executive, she broke out into a scathing denunciation of local officials, including her own brother, the boss of the village, who was away on a journey.

The president listened patiently to her ranting, though several times he raised his hand in a courteous effort to calm her. When her cup of bitterness was finally emptied, he turned her complaints over to an investigating officer, and went on to exhort the people to seek harmony among themselves.

My own first encounter with President Cárdenas had been less personal. It was in August, 1935, at the opening of the Seventh American Scientific Congress in the Palace of Fine Arts in Mexico City. There at the presiding officer's desk sat a man just past forty with dark curly hair crowning a high receding forehead, large kindly eyes, a short bushy mustache, a physique radiating energy, and a serious military bearing. Speaking to an international group of scientists stilted with learning, President Cárdenas looked uncomfortable. With the perfunctory opening over, however, he marched off in a stride which I realized was taking him places. And the celebrities, including a former president, followed in a way which showed that they knew who was leader.

Mexico City, however, was not the best place to observe President Cárdenas. He was away from his capital so much that humorists would say, "Where is the president? Oh, he is out in the mountains teaching the Indians how to raise lettuce."

Actually, the best place to see Cárdenas in action *is* in a rural community. The second time I saw him was several months later on the occasion of his visit to Tetelcingo in Morelos, the miserable Indian village of our anecdote where Mrs. Townsend and I were studying the Aztec language. We had parked our house trailer in the square between the town hall and one of the seven Catholic churches for a protracted period, since beautiful Aztec is not learned in a day. Around our simple shelter we had planted vegetables and flowers, and between one of the churches and the public school we had laid out a little park for the sleepy town. The outside world, only a few miles away, never disturbed us. Even the tax collector seldom came around.

One afternoon, however, we heard two motor cars making their way into the village. Glancing around a corner of the trailer, we soon saw half a dozen men cross the square in the direction of the school teachers' living quarters. The man in front led with a stride I had seen before. It was President Cárdenas!

There was no time to change my gardener's clothes. I was anxious to see this circuit-riding ruler hold court in a village schoolhouse. Crossing the square I presented myself, work clothes and all, where he stood talking with the teachers who were still gasping from surprise.

"Mr. President," I said, as I extended my hand, "I am glad that you are a friend of the peasants, for you have found me one today."

It did not seem to displease him to find that his large family of *campesinos* had been increased by a slim blonde from California, but the lobes of his large well-set ears turned red, and his prominent cheek bones tinged the same color. I thought to myself: "This man does not enjoy meeting strangers any more than I do." He quietly accepted my invitation to visit our trailer home as soon as he had finished his inspection, and then went on asking pointed questions of the teachers.

His large hazel eyes, serious but not stern, looked intently from beneath heavy dark brows, drinking in the details of the classroom. There were the teachers, each with eighty or more pupils, and not a book in the schoolhouse—the small blackboard in the front of the room—the students each carrying a notebook and a pencil with which to copy the alphabet, arithmetic problems, and other information from the blackboard—the long benches on which the students sat and wrote on the plank that was fastened to the bench in front of them.

As the president spoke to them I noticed that his chin did not stand out with the prominence the remaining features called for, a detail seeming to suggest a weakness of character which his acts belied. I had puzzled much over that chin in portraits and was glad to notice now that it was backed up by a massive jaw indicating a driving force which would be hard to stop. That jaw was supported by a powerful neck. In conversation, the jaw and chin vibrated with quick, decisive movements, while the heavy lips opened only sufficiently to let out a deep mellow voice which articulated so rapidly and quietly that bystanders had to listen closely to get all the words.

Wanting to tell my wife that the president would pay us a call, I asked to be excused. "Don't go yet. I will accompany you soon," was the reply. And I, like others, obeyed the voice willingly.

Ours was a pleasant visit with the president who, never failing to manifest interest in anything, paid close attention to our linguistic work as we explained it to him. He expressed appreciation for our efforts, and referring to some of my newspaper and magazine articles on Mexico which he had seen, said, "We welcome inspection and criticism, but we object to reports based on hearsay and prejudice. We are endeavoring to help the poor people who have suffered so long, and are glad to have foreigners come and see what we are trying to do, especially when they lend a helping hand." With that he launched into a careful explanation of his agrarian program.

Before returning to the schoolhouse he questioned Mrs. Townsend solicitously about the inconveniences of living in an Indian community, and then evinced great interest as she showed him the handy features of the trailer.

Meanwhile the villagers, who had been either in the fields or taking *siestas,* gathered to the call of the town criers. "What help do you fellow citizens need from the government which the Revolution has placed in power?" the president asked a crowd of unkempt, barefoot, surprised Indians. The women, wearing their hair in long black braids, were dressed in dark blue woolen costumes, and the men in pajama-like muslin outfits which had once been white. "We want to give you land," he continued, "on which to make a living, and schools equipped to teach you how to do your daily tasks better. Are there any special needs to which you would like to call my attention?"

Two or three men huddled together and conferred among themselves in melodious Aztec, after which the oldest straightened himself, cleared his throat, and spoke for the rest in Spanish:

"Mr. President, we need pipe to bring drinking water into the part of our town which is on the other side of the gully. Furthermore, most of our people have not received enough land to take care of their absolute needs, and in the third place, we have long desired a bridge on which to cross the dangerous stream which separates our town from the lands you have already given us."

Another voice piped up: "We need cement to repair the schoolhouse floor." All these petitions and others were granted until the puzzled Indians began to feel that they had only to ask in order to receive (at least in promise—since four centuries of deceit at the hands of outsiders had taught them never to put much stock in promises). Finally convinced that the President would not refuse anything, a wizened old man called out, "Won't you give us paint with which to paint our biggest church building?" This was the only request not granted.

"One of the most interesting figures in the world, confronted by one of the most difficult tasks in the world" is the way Ambassador to Mexico, Josephus Daniels, had described General Lázaro Cárdenas. Part of that difficult task was to try to lift the burden of ignorance, poverty, vice, and exploitation which kept such large numbers of his countrymen, including the Tetelcingans, in numb stupor, contributing nothing to the life of their nation.

Later the president backed up his promises by sending to the little town shipments of cement, fine nursery stock, thoroughbred cattle, a grant of more farm land, thousands of budded orange trees, and new tanks and pipe for the supply of drinking water. And his visit also initiated an extensive improvement program which resulted in a new industrial school and an elaborate irrigation system.

Tetelcingo was only one of over 70,000 villages in Mexico that President Cárdenas yearned to help and one of thousands that he did help. It happened to be one of the most needy, however. To some who criticized his doing more for it than he could do for the average community he said:

When there is someone like this American couple living in a village with the know-how and enthusiasm to help personally in the improvement projects, that's where the government can put forth special effort with more assurance of adequate returns on its investment.

It is true that thousands of Mexican homes still exist where men, women, and children live without having their most elementary needs satisfied. These conditions of misery are an inheritance from the past that cannot be liquidated in a short period of struggle and effort. Far from condemning the Revolution, however, they justify it and stimulate its march . . . .

— Lázaro Cárdenas to the Nation —
December 9, 1938

II

CHILDHOOD AND YOUTH

MOST CHILDREN in rural Mexico, and all too often in the cities as well, get their first glimpse of the world in one-room abodes where the whole family eats, sleeps, entertains visitors, and shares space with chickens, pigs, and inevitably a dog or dogs. Little preparation is made for the new arrival and modern medical science has nothing to do with his reception.

Lázaro Cárdenas, however, had a real home in which to be born. Not that his parents were well-to-do. On the contrary, their income was very small. In fact, had Lázaro arrived a few months earlier, he would have been welcomed, like his two older sisters, to small rented quarters; but his mother's aunt, Ignacia Mora de Torres, the widow of a prosperous citizen, had bequeathed a comfortable though modest home to her niece, Felícitas del Río de Cárdenas, and there the future president was born and reared.

The long dry season had ended, and the daily showers which share in the half-year rule of the trade winds had begun to turn the hills south and west of Jiquilpan green when, on the twenty-first of May, 1895, Dámaso Cárdenas proudly walked to the town hall and announced the birth of his first son, Lázaro. Regrettably, the birthplace was torn down in 1937, for it stood just where the engineers wanted the international highway from Arizona to Mexico City to pass, and President Cárdenas refused to make his birthplace an exception of the rule to clear away all buildings in the path of new arteries of travel.

The apparent similarity of Jiquilpan to other towns of the area is misleading, for this town has some striking distinctions. Old mounds and graves have yielded archeological remains that indicate the presence in the past of a people quite unique on the American continent. Clay figures of men and women show enormous straight noses and high pompadour hair dresses held in place by elegant

9

combs. Jiquilpan is unusual, also, because it is the only town in Mexico that has produced two presidents.[1]

Wonder of wonders, in a land where infant mortality has for centuries approached or exceeded 50%, Lázaro's parents, Dámaso and Felícitas Cárdenas, lost none of their eight children in infancy. This should not be taken as indicative of more favorable conditions in Jiquilpan than elsewhere, though its mile-high elevation does give it a more healthful climate than that of the hot malarial regions of lower Mexico. Nor does it mean that the town had better hospitals. Outside of the state capitals there simply were no hospitals, and few communities even had a doctor or the minimum of medical services.

Jiquilpan had no hospital, but could boast of a part-time resident physician. From such a one, and from books, Dámaso Cárdenas picked up many ideas on how to treat the sick, and gained quite a reputation for his cures, especially among the poor. Naturally, the boy Lázaro was deeply impressed as he watched him, unprepared, and single-handed, battle against disease. Nor was the father's lesson lost on Lázaro, for when he came to national prominence, he built hospitals and established medical units far and wide, and also created a special bureau of government to combat infant and maternal mortality.

Dámaso Cárdenas did not earn a living from his medical practice. It was just an impromptu response to the emergency need around him, and he was fully as solicitous when the patient could pay nothing for his services as when he was rewarded with a *peso* or two, a chicken, or a basket of fruit. Dámaso's father, Francisco Cárdenas, and his maternal cousin, José María Pinedo, were weavers. Indeed, even today many a humble home in Jiquilpan has its loom and dyeing vat. The ordinary thing would have been for Dámaso to have followed the same trade and, in turn, bequeath it to his oldest son, Lázaro. Dámaso, however, had been ambitious for something different. The weaving business yielded only a very poor income, for the rich wool blankets and the gay *rebozos* when sold brought little more than the cost of the materials. Furthermore, it was too confining to sit at a foot-loom

---

[1]The first citizen of Jiquilpan to become president was a conservative, General Anastasio Bustamante, back in the first decade of Mexican Independence.

all day long monotonously tossing the long wooden shuttle back and forth. Don Dámaso had too much life in him for that, and there was also a streak of ambition in him which cried out for a vocation which would give him more standing in the community.

After trying his hand at running a little village store he turned to a relative on the Pinedo side of the family who had opened a soap factory, and Don Dámaso joined him in business there about the time he married the gentle and industrious Felícitas del Río. Then billiard halls became popular and somehow Don Dámaso secured a table and started what he called "The Reunion of Friends". It became a rather much-frequented place for men to while away their time.

Don Dámaso seems to have kept the tone of his place above what is commonly expected of billiard halls, but at best it was not a likely atmosphere in which to rear a president and much less a reformer president. Liquor and tobacco were not lacking among its attractions, and Lázaro as a child would reach up to the counter when his father was not looking and take cigarettes wrapped in corn-husks and packed in little bundles to give as barter for stories from a blind neighbor. If he ever smoked one himself it must have been frightfully strong, for he turned against the weed for life. In the "Reunion of Friends" there was doubtless also profanity and smutty talk (though Don Dámaso was considered rather stern about such matters), and general loafing ever and always. The reaction of the boy was unsympathetic to the whole atmosphere of the hall—loafing, profanity, tobacco, liquor, and dice—and as president, he threw his entire influence against them.

Dámaso's income from his business was about fifteen *pesos* a month, and that, together with what little was made from the practice of medicine and Felícitas' sewing, was sufficient to keep the family clothed and to maintain the home in respectable circumstances. Then, too, Dámaso usually owned a cow or two, so that there was milk to sell when it was not all needed at home.

More fortunate than most homes in Jiquilpan, the Cárdenas home also had a well in the *patio*. Dámaso had also installed a pump so that it was not necessary to go to the river at the edge of town to take a bath and to put out the family wash. As president, Cárdenas engaged in an intense crusade to pipe drinking water into hundreds of towns all over Mexico, for as a child he had observed how neighbors came from all around to draw water at his father's well and blessed the man who had installed the pump.

Grandfather Francisco Cárdenas did not spend all of his time at the loom. Over week-ends and on festival-days he would visit surrounding towns to peddle his handicraft, and from time to time would ride his pony out to a small plot of ground on a hill south of town where he did a little farming. His Indian ancestry prompted him to do this, for poor indeed was the Indian who had absolutely no land to till, though thousands had already come to this deplorable condition. Often Lázaro would climb up onto the pony behind his grandfather and ride out to the "rock pile", as he now refers to the stony plot on the hill, and help coax some verdure from the sterile soil. From his point of vantage there he would view the broad fertile valleys below him and wonder why they all belonged to one man, while the many had to farm the hillside. His gaze surveyed the miles and miles of productive fields clear to the far rim of the valley where his Del Río uncles and cousins were wresting a living from the soil, in semi-slavery to the owner of that broad expanse. He could see no justice in the picture.

Sometimes his mother would take him to visit the Del Río relatives and on such occasions he was looked upon as the typical city cousin only partially informed of animals, farming, and the like, just as they were uninitiated to his classroom talk. However, the day was to come when he would master not only many of the technical points about farming, but would also return all that broad expanse of land to the descendants of its original Indian owners. His "rock pile" experience was not in vain.

Jiquilpan had two schools, even in those days. Prior to the Revolution coeducation was frowned upon so that towns that believed in educating their girls had one school for boys and another for girls. In many towns the latter was lacking as unnecessarily progressive. The boys' school in Jiquilpan was presided over by a hard-working, serious-minded man of dignified bearing named Fajardo. It was his task to teach, single-handed, one hundred and fifty boys. He was stern. There was no time for disobedience or horseplay. He ruled with an iron hand. The boy Lázaro was serious-minded himself and adapted himself readily to the situation, but at heart he rebelled against such undemocratic tactics in halls of learning.

Young Cárdenas applied himself to his studies with a real sense of duty and with plenty of brains. He played little with other boys, not that he was in any sense snobbish or unappreciative of companions, but because he was generally too deeply absorbed in his own thoughts. Perhaps even there he rebelled. Certainly there was plenty against which to rebel—not so much against what they did as what they did not do. There were no playgrounds. There were no athletics. Is it any wonder that during Cárdenas' term as president, Jiquilpan was to receive an athletic field?

Once in awhile Lázaro would join the youngsters in playing *juego de avas*, a game of keeps, out on a hill where they often resorted for their good times, but perhaps Lázaro lost, for he became soured on gambling for life. This dislike was accentuated under the influence of his first military commander, General García Aragón, who was strongly opposed to games of chance.

Dámaso Cárdenas was very strict and would not permit his children to play on the streets. Lázaro once tried playing hooky by hiding in the *guayaba* trees at home. Professor Fajardo sent word of the boy's absence from school and his father caught him and administered a thrashing. The father's disciplinary generosity is attested to by the fact that on the same occasion he gave a whipping to Lázaro's companion in truancy in spite of the fact that the neighbor lad remonstrated vociferously saying, "I'm not *your* boy!"

The red-letter days of childhood in Jiquilpan, as in all Latin-American towns, came when the annual town festival was held in honor of the patron saint and when the whole countryside gathered for three days of barter, street dances, fireworks, and gossip, as well as religious ceremonies. Mother Felícitas was a pious soul, having both a first and second cousin in the priesthood, and in spite of her husband's coolness toward the Church, saw to it that her children attended mass from time to time, especially when festival days came around. Lázaro, however, had a hard time separating in significance what he saw of religion itself from the recreation and vice which accompanied it. The recreation it afforded laborers was to his mind a redeeming feature of the religious system.

Lázaro's favorite diversion was to get the philosophical old tailor, Modesto Estrada, to tell him stories in his spare time. The old gentleman was full of adages and quaint wisdom so that the boy received much to think about. But even more than that he enjoyed the tales of battle and military campaigns in which Don Modesto either had taken part personally or had heard so much about that he could tell of them as though he had been present himself.

On the hill just west of town a battle against the French invaders had taken place in 1865. Having listened to Don Modesto describe the engagement, the boy would climb the gentle slope to the broad top, perch himself on a rock beside a clump of cactus, and reenact it all in his mind. He could picture the Mexican troops assembling on the hill from different directions, the French Zouaves charging in the early morning, the firing of muskets, the clash of sabres, and the falling of brave defenders, but he could not understand the flight of the Mexicans. Then he recalled that though the Mexican troops had defeated the French very seldom in open engagements, they had won out at the last, and he resolved that when he became a soldier he would never give up just because of reversals at the start. He did not. His unfailing tenacity is known to all. Some call it stubbornness. However, often the only distinction between tenacity and stubbornness is the viewpoint of the observer.

Cárdenas received his first taste of military drill when eleven years of age. One of the few outstanding leaders whom President Porfirio Díaz permitted to bask long in the sunlight of popularity was General Reyes. He organized a national militia in 1905, and companies of reserves were formed, far and wide, especially in the schools. The movement hit Jiquilpan, and squads of boys were seen every Saturday drilling near town. A manual was published for the use of these reserves, and Lázaro learned it almost by heart. He mastered it so well and his serious bearing commanded such respect that he was often called upon to take charge of a squad even though many of the boys were larger than he.

The Jiquilpan school took him through only six grades. Then it was a case of either looking for a job or else applying for a scholarship at the Catholic *Semanario* in Zamora, a day's journey away, where his mother's cousin, the distinguished canon Manuel Sandoval, was very influential. The normal or preparatory school far away at Morelia, the capital of the state, seemed out of the question although Professor Fajardo, who had prophesied that some day Lázaro would rise to be governor, would have done his best to have obtained a scholarship for him.

As Don Dámaso was not contemplating the priesthood for his son, he took him instead to his friend, the local revenue collector, Donaciano Carreón, where Lázaro was put to work as a clerk. The office of jailer which was vacant was also assigned to Lázaro, though his actual work was in the revenue office as a bookkeeper and a writer and filer of legal papers.

The revenue collector was a liberal in political thought, and favored the movement which Francisco Madero was organizing to overthrow Porfirio Díaz and institute democratic reforms. He would lend liberal literature to the young men who worked under him. Young Cárdenas enjoyed particularly the books on the French Revolution in which he saw that things could be changed when the people were aroused to do it. The seed thoughts of revolution had been sown in Lázaro's mind and were to yield an abundant harvest.

From his point of vantage at the collector's office Lázaro could observe the injustices handed out to the common man by the Díaz regime. The federally appointed *Jefe Político* had a small squad of soldiers under his command and was more powerful than the locally elected mayor. He was generally very arbitrary and could commit the rankest injustices with impunity as long as he kept order and rapidly executed the commands of higher authorities. Cárdenas was riled to see his fellow men kicked and cuffed around like dogs. On one occasion he watched a commission of peasants from a nearby village come to ask redress of a grievance against a rich landholder, and his cheeks flushed red, though he had to remain passive, when he saw the *Jefe Político,* who had been previously bribed, drive them away. Later he learned that in reward for their temerity they had been torn from their homes and sent off as "volunteers" for service in the army.

The serious youth in the collector's office began to grow restless at the desk, a trait which he carries with him to this day. He decided to approach an influential friend and ask him to put in a word for him with the commanding officer who was about to appoint a lieutenant for the local squad of troops. It was in vain; the commander merely sneered at the thought of such a youthful officer in his ranks.

Señor Carreón and some of his friends decided to form a co-operative association and start a printing business. A very simple foot press was purchased and Lázaro Cárdenas was made typesetter and pressman. A liberal periodical was started with a high-sounding name. It was not a great success from the financial viewpoint, but it was immensely successful as a preparation for a future president. Madero's movement had triumphed and for the first time in decades the press was no longer throttled by Díaz, and men could write what they thought. As young Cárdenas would set up the articles letter by letter, he had time to meditate upon their revolutionary contents.

Jiquilpan had been little affected by the military movements leading to the fall of Díaz. The fighting had taken place far to the north in Chihuahua and off to the south in Morelos. Furthermore, Jiquilpan was off the beaten path in those days. To get to Mexico City from there, it was necessary to ride horseback to the shores of Lake Chapala, the largest lake in Mexico. Near the town of Sahuayo one embarked in a launch for the other shore. From there it was a horseback ride of several hours to the railroad where one could take the south-bound Guadalajara-Querétaro train and ride for a day and a night to the capital. In such isolation, the infiltration of new ideas proceeds very slowly. Had the cooperative press continued, the process would have been more rapid, but the printer felt the call to arms after a brief year and a half. Soon after he had gone, the business closed.

Cárdenas had been raised under stern authority and it is doubtful if he would have exchanged the printer's tools for a rifle as young as he did without his father's consent. But the year that Díaz fled for Spain, Don Dámaso died of pneumonia. Billiard cues could no longer provide a livelihood, and so Doña Felícitas had to take in more sewing and the older children sought work. The main responsibility fell upon Lázaro, just seventeen years of age, who accepted the burden without flinching. Doña Felícitas found that she could lean heavily on the strong shoulder of her quiet but loving son. Together they toiled early and late to keep the needs of the growing children supplied, neither of them realizing that soon the hand of destiny would separate them and not permit another affectionate embrace until the day before Doña Felícitas was to breathe her last.

I am aware of my obligations and I do not forget my origin. I belong to the same class that you do. Before I became a public servant I was a laborer in a small shop. Being loyal to my class, the class that elevated me to the presidency, my program of government seeks by legal means the emancipation of the masses of day laborers and peasants.

— Lázaro Cárdenas—to the peasants at a town in the state of Guanajuato, March 31, 1936

III

YOUTHFUL FIGHTER

"OH, TO MARCH at the head of twenty-five men!"

This dream of his youth was expressed not to his mother, teacher, or partners in printing, but to some humble neighbors, Pilar Medina and her blind brother, Pancho. Lázaro Cárdenas has throughout his life often saved his special confidences for unassuming friends who have no claims upon him.

Blind Pancho and Pilar had such love and admiration for the young visionary that even the blind man could "see" the realization of the dreams as vividly as Lázaro himself. It was not unusual for the young man to go around the corner to the Medina home after printing hours and the evening meal where he would find Pancho on a little log stool by the wall and Pilar on a mat in the doorway picking over some beans. He would take his place in a comfortable *equipal*, designated as "Lázaro's chair". It stood on the little porch which looked out over a small *patio* to a stone wall. In it, Lázaro would sit and give way to dreams which leaped over that wall with far greater ease than he himself was to do a year or two later as bullets whined around him. Out in the Mexico beyond the wall, the Mexico which had yet to be thrown open to her ambitious but penniless sons, his dreams placed him at the head of twenty-five men.

Perhaps the taste of military drill he had had in school, or maybe the tales of battle told him by Modesto Estrada, had provoked that vision. But foremost was the call of duty. When the news reached lovers of democracy all over Mexico that their idol, Madero, had been assassinated and the country had fallen into the hands of another dictator, there were cries of alarm from every direction. With the army backing the usurper, Victoriano Huerta, patriots found that they could make their opposition effective in no other way than by taking arms in rebellion.

19

To lead twenty-five men in the cause of constitutional government, the young Jiquilpan printer had to secure a gun. This problem seemed insurmountable in a section of the country where the government had seen to it that there were no arms available. Sometime later, though, Lázaro had his chance. A few marauders, possibly bandits, made a surprise attack on the small Jiquilpan garrison and quickly routed it. The intruders exacted funds from well-to-do citizens and then marched off to do the same in the more prosperous city of Sahuayo. When the report was circulated that they were about to return to Jiquilpan, an indignation meeting was held in the town hall at which a call was issued for volunteers to defend the town. Guns were offered to all who would go. Lázaro, together with nine other daring young men, responded.

The squad was organized, firearms distributed, and off the stalwarts marched down the dusty road toward Sahuayo. At a strategic point where stone fences lined the road they took their stand. Soon a cloud of dust indicated that the enemy was approaching and the command was given to make ready. The squad left the road, clambered over the stones, and leveled nine barrels in the direction of the dust. The moment was tense for the impromptu soldiers, their breath came haltingly, and no one missed the tenth volunteer. Then the cause of all the dust emerged—a group of harmless peasants, jogging along on their burros. Relaxed laughter broke out in the brave detachment and they looked at one another with relief.

But where was Lázaro Cárdenas? Had he run? No! This foolhardy one had planted himself right in the middle of the road, crouched on one knee, his pistol resting on the other. What an easy mark he would have been for the bandits. But Cárdenas appears to be devoid of all sense of fear. Although his companions chided him for unnecessary exposure to a threatening menace on the Jiquilpan-Sahuayo road, he was unconcerned, as though by daring danger he had dispelled it. And what was more, he now had a gun!

The printer returned to his tiny press and galleys of type, but while his fingers set up the ambitious but insignificant little magazines, *Myosotes* and *El Caballero Vallardo,* or the job printing that came his way, his mind and heart were with the scattered bands of citizen soldiers who wanted "lands and liberty".

The first to take up the struggle had been Zapata. One of his lieutenants, General García Aragón, had quarreled with him, and to avoid the otherwise inevitable liquidation, had marched away from the state of Morelos across Guerrero to the hot lowland section of Michoacán where he began to work independently against the federal forces of Huerta.

Reports of what was taking place soon reached Jiquilpan and especially the Cárdenas household. One of Lázaro's uncles, José María del Río, had acquired a farm near Apatzingán, and as this city had fallen into the hands of García Aragón, the young eighteen-year-old made plans to go there.

He was pushed to this decision by his own carelessness in having left on his desk in the town hall a copy of a rebellious protest he had printed for private distribution. When Lázaro learned that the pamphlet had fallen into the hands of officials and that trouble was brewing for him, he enlisted a faithful Indian friend from a neighboring village to go with him at once to Apatzingán in the spirit of armorbearer. Ignorance of the true purpose of the trip made the farewell easier for the widowed mother who thought that it was just for Lázaro to live and work with her brother until his indiscretion had been forgotten. But the youth dreaded the accusation which some might bring that he was shirking his duty to his mother.

The evening before reaching the uncle's farm, an enraged man, mistaking their identity, attacked them where they had retired for the night, killing the friend. Thus bereft of armorbearer and without a gun, which had exploded in his hand during the scuffle, the young crusader presented himself at the Del Río's farm disappointed, but unwavering in his determination.

His uncle's son-in-law, a Texan named Leonard Neill, had planned a trip the following day to Apatzingán to see General García Aragón about a demand the latter had made upon him for several saddle horses, steers, and five hundred pesos to help the revolutionary cause. Making few explanations, Lázaro Cárdenas went along, offered himself for service, and was assessed by the keen-eyed general at such worth that he cancelled the demand he had made upon the youth's American cousin for money.

Young Cárdenas rapidly gained the confidence of his superiors through his extraordinary trustworthiness. Then again, his experience at the desk in the collector's office made him doubly useful to the growing little army. He was promoted to the rank of captain and made paymaster and secretary to the commander, who soon felt that his band had grown sufficiently to warrant an invasion of the highlands. But the result was disastrous. After a few skirmishes with Huerta's troops his forces were routed at the Battle of Purépero.

Captain Cárdenas, with a detachment under the command of Colonel Cenobio Moreno, returned to Apatzingán, but even there the pressure from the federal troops was so great that this remnant was dispersed. Moreno himself was wounded in a skirmish but continued to fight from the saddle as his little band retreated. Finally, in utter exhaustion, Moreno fell to the ground in a rocky place from which his followers, at his command, escaped by letting a rope down over a precipice. His pursuers finally found him, shot his head wide open, strapped his mangled body over a saddle with the top of the skull dangling down from the rest of the head, and paraded it in glee right past the Moreno home in Apatzingán to horrify the wife and children. Then they tied the body to the big cross before the church in the central plaza and called out the band to play before it in festive celebration. This was just one of countless ghastly scenes so common from one end of Mexico to the other during the turbulent days between 1913 and 1920.

With the dispersal of Aragón's "army", Cárdenas found himself alone and hunted like a criminal. He knew what had happened to Moreno. The only prudent thing to do was to get away, to run, but this did not appeal to him. He lingered around his uncle's farm until news of his presence reached the federal commander, who arrived to take him prisoner. Fortunately someone saw the troops approaching and Cárdenas was warned in time to take hiding in a clump of lemon trees. It was dinner time, and so the commander was diplomatically invited to dine. The fugitive captain, from his retreat, watched the meal proceed as long as his healthy appetite could stand it, and then he slipped around to the kitchen some fifty feet from where the table had been set and ate a hearty meal. In consternation the uncle saw him from where he sat, and sent him an urgent plea to get back to his hiding place.

When the commander finally left the uncle rebuked the youth

for his temerity, loaned him a horse and guide, and sent him by a private trail through the coffee bushes to another farm. There he was told that he had better leave immediately, that troops had been searching for him only a few minutes before. He returned the horse and guide to his uncle and made his way through the brush alone to a peasant's hut off the beaten path. The farmer and his wife took him in, for they did not know who he was. That evening, however, the man went to town and upon his return reported that everyone was talking about the hot chase that the federal forces had been giving a rebel named Lázaro Cárdenas. (Years later Cárdenas gave a farm to the couple who had befriended him that night.)

Huerta's troops failed to catch him, and within a few days a weary, crestfallen rebel lad, sick of the bloodshed he had seen, slunk into his Jiquilpan home. Doña Felícitas was rejoiced by the return of her son, but grew anxious when he informed her that he would have to remain in hiding. Nor was it safe for him to spend much time under his own roof. Sometimes he would hide away with one neighbor and then another. The Medina home was one refuge. As the days and weeks went by, it seemed that the local authorities had forgiven his fault and would let him settle down at home where his help was badly needed. He decided to take a chance and be seen out in the open.

One day a sentinel perched in the tall tower of the church spied him in a field on the southeast side of town, his head buried in a book. The *Jefe Político* was quickly informed and two policemen were dispatched to take him into custody. His capture was inevitable and the ignominious march to jail and certain execution began. It led past the Medina home and Cárdenas halted to knock on the door.

The impatient policeman said, "What are you doing? Come along!"

The youth calmly replied, "Surely you will let me ask for a drink of water, won't you?"

The door opened and Pancho and Pilar shrank back in alarm as they realized what had happened. The prisoner quickly stepped within the portal, but the policeman vociferously ordered him out.

"Oh, no," replied the youth, "I'm within a private home now, and you must remember that the Constitution prohibits your entering a home without a warrant."

The two policemen did not know what to think of that argument, and one left to report the situation to the *Jefe Político* while the other kept his eye and gun on Cárdenas. Suddenly the latter made a dash for the *patio* and the wall which divided it from a neighboring yard. The policeman followed, but Pilar and blind Pancho blocked the way. They grappled, and by the time the policeman could disentangle himself, his prisoner had scaled the wall and was about to jump to the other side. He fired his pistol, but the shots went wide of their mark. Thus, once again, the *Jefe Político's* unrelenting opposition forced the youth to continue the struggle. (In later years when the tables had turned, Cárdenas came to think of this as a kindness in disguise and, much to the disgust of some of his friends, he rewarded the old *Jefe Político* with favors to his sons.)

News from the north told of the victorious advances of Carranza, Obregón, and Villa. Soon one of their allies, General Zuñiga, marched into Jiquilpan on his way north to join them in Guadalajara. Captain Cárdenas came out of hiding and marched down the street to Zuñiga's headquarters with military stride, his broad-brimmed campaign hat, rifle, and cartridge belt attracting the attention of old friends and neighbors. Zuñiga welcomed this addition to his forces and within a few days Cárdenas had the opportunity to show his mettle in the Battle of *Hacienda del Castillo* where Huerta's forces under General Mier were dispersed.

The triumphant advance on Mexico City gave an unusual opportunity to get acquainted with the country along the line of march. Troop trains were scarce, and furthermore, Obregón, the commanding officer, had a prejudice against entraining his men. He preferred to have them ready for action at any time, the cavalry in their saddles and the infantry on the ground. He had had trouble once disembarking his troops to fight off a sudden attack. He kept his troops on the ground after that, and they learned their geography. Thus provincials awakened to a big Mexico.

The great capital with its new sights and influences, city influences to which many a revolutionist has succumbed, were not to be Cárdenas' for long. Victory brought strife between the leaders of the Constitutionalist cause, and soon Cárdenas, now a lieutenant colonel, found himself on the long march back to the north, ordered there by superiors who had embraced the cause of General Pancho Villa. He was to participate in the attack on Agua Prieta, where General Plutarco Elías Calles, one of Carranza's partisans, had been bottled up.

Cárdenas was personally inclined toward Carranza as opposed to Villa, for Carranza represented constitutional government. He persuaded his regimental commander, Colonel Morales, that they should take the first opportunity to join the Constitutionalists. The old colonel agreed, and left Cárdenas to continue the march north and across the Rockies while he himself went alone by a circuitous route to join Carranza in Vera Cruz. Cárdenas and his six hundred men traversed the long canyon *del Pulpito* between Chihuahua and Sonora and made camp near the forces that had laid siege on Agua Prieta. When night fell, instead of reporting to Villa, Cárdenas went alone to where Calles was entrenched and offered himself and his troops. Early the next day he lifted camp and marched into the beleaguered little city embracing a cause which at that time seemed certain to lose.

All the state of Sonora was in the hands of Villista forces except the cities of Agua Prieta in the north and Navojoa in the south, and these had been undergoing long sieges. Military importance was attached to towns planted right on the United States boundary, for they could be surrounded only in a half circle, thus offering a sure source of supplies as well as a way of escape should the enemy prove too strong. Otherwise, Agua Prieta would hardly have been worth fighting for. As it was, however, the squalid little city attained great prominence in the revolutionary movement. General Calles had built formidable trenches and had animated his troops with a do-or-die spirit.

Within the city things savored of a new order, for Calles had set up new laws and what he called the "Republic of Agua Prieta". Experiments were being made, too, with legal and social reforms. Saloons had been closed and vice of all forms was combatted. Everything centered around the energetic administrator and ardent reformer, General Calles, only slightly known then, but who was to become President of the country ten years later.

When on March 27, 1915, Cárdenas marched into town with his dust-covered soldiers, Calles welcomed his new recruit with some distrust. There was something about the youth, however, which inspired confidence, and Calles assented to his simple request, "Give me a chance to show my loyalty in battle." Loyalty, dash, and daring were demonstrated by the young officer as he led his soldiers in sally after sally against the powerful besiegers. As the lad of twenty demonstrated his ability and valor not only in the defense of Agua Prieta, but also in a series of engagements which pushed the Villista troops back in every direction, the name of *El Chamaco* (The Kid), as Calles affectionately came to call him, brought courage and confidence to the soldiers of Calles' army and to the citizens of Agua Prieta and neighboring towns.

An unusually strong friendship grew up between the dynamic leader and his young follower. The older gave the younger many an opportunity to show his worth and the latter never failed. Of Cárdenas' part in those early campaigns Calles reported: "The troops of Cárdenas conducted themselves admirably, and I was congratulated more than once, and justly so, upon their exemplary conduct, administering blows which the enemy did not expect, and very especially due to the rapid, almost instantaneous measures taken against the liquor traffic, prostitution, and gambling." General Calles also cited his young officer's "well known valor, discipline, and zeal in carrying out commissions delivered to him."

It is urgent to define what measures should be taken and what procedures should be followed in order that there may be more respect for human life. A way must be found to avoid the numerous cases of bloodshed that occur in the country. We need also to study means, establish norms, and put in play enforcement measures that will be effective in making the public administration honest, efficient, economical, and in keeping with our category as a poor nation.

— Lázaro Cárdenas—to Congress
September 1, 1938

IV

SOLDIER AND PEACEMAKER THROUGH CHAOS

AT THE TIME of Cárdenas' birth in 1895, Porfirio Díaz had already been ruling the country more than fifteen years, except for a short interim, and was to continue to rule for about fifteen years more. Mexico had experienced four centuries of injustice and exploitation at the hands, first of avaricious conquerors, clericals, and colonists from Spain, and later at the hands of their descendants and foreign investors. The chief objects of exploitation had been labor in general and the Indians in particular. An astute old dictator in Central America, when asked how it was that he could maintain his financial credit abroad in spite of the dreadful poverty of his nation, replied, "God gives the resources, and the Indian does the work." Thus he truthfully explained what had been the general procedure for four centuries in most of Latin America.

The Indians were made peons or semi-slaves, and the successful planter was the man who could work them most effectively. If, as was generally the case, the landlord was an absentee, living in luxury in some large Mexican city or in Europe or the United States, his plantation manager, seeking to send him the most money possible with the least expenditure of effort on his own part, avoided spending money on improving methods of farming, and sought to increase profits by paying the peasants the least possible for their labor.

Most of the important uprisings of the last century in Mexico were struggles between liberals and conservatives as far as political philosophy was concerned. The liberals sought to oust the Church from political and financial domination; to establish the public school system in the place of the parish school which had been more interested in teaching the catechism than the three R's; and to reform the economic and social abuses of the country. The conservatives consistently fought for the status quo in opposition to all these reforms. In the struggles which resulted from this basic difference in philosophy, the liberals had as their battle cries: liberty of worship, liberty of the press, and more extended suffrage.

The old liberalism, even when in power, had accomplished little for the lower classes, so that even before the fall of Díaz a new political philosophy, socialism, had been cropping up.

Lázaro Cárdenas was only sixteen, though doing the work of a man, when Francisco Madero revolted and ousted Díaz. Madero was an apostle of democracy, and he offered that system as a panacea for Mexico's ills. He formed his government from elements of the old regime in temporary coalition with reformers of his own following, and then held his hand lightly upon them. He failed to realize that the Mexican peasants knew little about democratic rule, and that the old Díaz army which he had taken over was not inclined to let them learn. Many of his followers who had made a study of socialism, whether during exile or through books smuggled into the country, clamored for a complete revolution. Failure was inevitable. Four revolts broke out during the sixteen months that he was president (October 1911 to February 1913).

Finally, the head of his own army, General Victoriano Huerta turned traitor, took Madero prisoner, forced him to resign, and then either ordered or permitted his assassination. Democracy was stillborn. Huerta tried to re-establish the old dictatorship. He secured help from the Church by promising to protect it from the rising tide of anti-clericalism. He lined up behind himself the old political machine of Porfirio Díaz by offering it a continuance of manipulated elections. To the army he held out the dream of dominance in peace. To make matters worse, he himself was a drunkard.

But Mexico was in no mood to tolerate a suppression of her craving for political liberty. Leaders of the type of the fallen Madero were appalled at the audacity of the usurper Huerta. Rebels rose up like mosquitoes in the jungle, and it became increasingly difficult for Huerta to get men to fight his battles. In some cases he resorted to conscription.

The Aztec Indians of Tetelcingo, a village about sixty miles from Mexico City, tell how it was done in their case. Their ancestors had no doubt been fighters at the time the Aztecs had fought so valiantly against Cortéz. But following the Conquest their little world had become a monotonous round of drudgery. Their quaint costumes, their melodious Aztec language, their superstitions, habits of thought, and ways of doing things were the same as had prevailed in the village for centuries. They tilled the soil as their fathers had done, planted the same crops on the same calendar dates, drank and danced in honor of the same images, and had the same distrust toward outside influences which had been instilled in the bosoms of their forefathers.

Upon this quiet town a force of Huerta's troops swooped down to make recruits. They searched the homes for able-bodied men and then carried their human loot off to barracks in Mexico City. There the Indians were stripped of their leather and wool costumes, and while these ascended to oblivion in smoke, their bewildered owners struggled awkwardly into the army uniforms which had been issued to them. Once outfitted, armed, and drilled, the unwilling recruits had been rushed to the north in freight cars and in ships to fight—for what? They knew not. Many never returned, and the ones who did found their village razed and their wives and families scattered far and wide.

Among those strongly anti-Huerta elements were students, political thinkers not of the privileged classes, a nascent middle class, and the labor agitators who had arisen in the cities. However, they were unable to cope with the regular army, and the cause of democracy was dependent for the most part on untrained peasant soldiers to fight her battles. But novices such as Zapata, Obregón, Villa, Calles, the Cedillo brothers, and many others of lesser fame soon became experienced fighters and popular chiefs. Zapata had been first a peasant and then cowboy; Obregón had run a chicken farm in the north before he took up arms; Villa had been just an abused peasant turned revengeful bandit; Calles had been a school teacher; the Cedillos had been peasants.

Carranza, with his government experience, force of character, and dogged determination, soon came to be generally recognized as the commander-in-chief of most of the forces fighting against Huerta, but he was not a soldier by training nor a leader who could harmonize his followers. Nevertheless, he succeeded in ousting the usurper because he was on the side of the people against the insidious causes of unrest. For this same reason youthful Lieutenant Colonel Cárdenas had joined Carranza's Constitutionalist Army even when the cause seemed hopeless.

Triumph was far from final with the fall of Huerta. Carranza, in victory, inherited an almost hopeless task, that of conciliating the unleashed ambitions of his power-drunk lieutenants. Soon open strife broke out between them. Where Madero had not been able to satisfy Zapata's demand for land, Carranza sought to appease him by enacting a law providing for the granting of lands to the peasants. But the executing of land grants proceeded far too slowly, and Zapata, as well as that strange soldier-bandit Pancho Villa, revolted.

Against such formidable opposition Carranza was obliged to go all the way with the people, at least in theory. Hence, he called a constitutional convention to rewrite the fundamental laws of the land in such a way as to do away once for all with the causes of popular unrest. The constitution that was written by the convention and accepted by Carranza in May, 1917, was a radical document—as radical as that of the United States had seemed when Jefferson and his colleagues first formulated it.

Some of its provisions were that 1) Every rural family in Mexico should have land on which to make a living; 2) The government should take acreage from excessively large plantations and distribute it among the landless wherever that was necessary; 3) All lands in Mexico were placed in the status of a public utility which could be commandeered when the welfare of the people called for it, and individual property rights were valid only within certain fixed limits; 4) Sub-soil wealth was declared to belong to the nation—oil and mining rights acquired prior to the new constitution not exempted; 5) The right of labor to strike with official protection was established; 6) Houses of worship were made properties of the nation, and other measures calculated to check the power of the Church were adopted.

Cárdenas was engaged at the time in combating Villa in the State of Chihuahua, and so had nothing to do with the formulation of the new constitution, but it was to become his task eighteen years later to put many of it most radical provisions into operation. Hence, he got the lion's share of the blame from people who had been able to maintain unconstitutional privileges up until he came into office.

The Mexican Revolution in its early phase cost the nation dearly. Railroads, bridges, wharves, sugar mills, farm buildings, and dwellings suffered to the amount of millions and millions of pesos. Soldiers on the march would shoot cattle and even birds just for the fun of shedding blood. The state of Chihuahua was left almost without a steer or sheep after having had, at the beginning of the struggle, about two million head of cattle. A wave of blood-thirstiness inundated the land. Postcards were on sale in all the cities picturing hangings and executions or the mutilated bodies of chieftains killed in battle. Rotting cadavers were to be found here and there, too numerous perhaps to interest even the buzzards who preferred to feed upon the corpses of captives who had been strung up more conveniently to the limbs of trees. Plantations in states like Morelos were abandoned by their owners and their manor houses reduced to charred ruins. Non-combatants hid in caves or back among the hills where they could conceal a few pigs and chickens and a little corn from the eyes of marauding parties. Small farmers, after losing one or two crops to foragers, were sorely tempted to abandon their own little farms and make an easier livelihood from pillaging.

Through all this reign of terror the soldier Cárdenas kept his head. His troops were always under strict control. His austere spirit never gave way to the excitement of the moment. His devotion to the Cause and faith in the ultimate triumph of right increased as he grew older. Come what might, one thing stood out before him—the fulfillment of duty—a trait which in ever growing proportion became the ruling passion of his life.

After Pancho Villa's forces had been driven from the state of Sonora in 1915, General Calles sent his dashing young cavalry officer, Lázaro Cárdenas, to help stifle the ire of the Yaqui Indians who were incensed over the fact that Obregón, for whom they had fought, had failed to keep promises he made to them, and that some of his military subordinates were dealing high-handedly with them.

The democratic Yaquis are tough fighters, having fought for centuries against the encroachments of outsiders. Porfirio Díaz conquered them by deceit and force of arms and marched a big portion of the tribe off to Yucatán to get rid of them, but those who survived made their way back like "drowned" cats. Some of the tribe fled over the border into Arizona and formed a settlement near Tucson from where they kept up their tribal dues and served the remnant at home by purchasing rifles and ammunition and smuggling them back over the border into Sonora by "underground" trails known only to the Yaquis.

General Obregón could speak the Mayo language, which is as closely related to Yaqui as Portuguese is to Spanish. (The Mayo Indians of Sonora are not to be confused with the Maya tribe of Yucatán to whom they are not related). He succeeded in getting large numbers of Mayos and Yaquis to join him in the Revolution. They formed the contingent upon which he could depend the most. Some of them became able generals and were detailed to points in the Republic where absolute fidelity and utter fearlessness were required.

In his experience with the Yaquis Cárdenas saw the futility of fighting the Indians in a military way. He was not yet in a position, however, to determine policies and had to spend nearly two years at the distasteful task. This young soldier, who in his first encounter with the Yaquis had chafed under the orders to subdue a foe he admired, was relieved of duty in Sonora and called to Chihuahua in 1917 to take up the fight against Villa where General Pershing had left off.

The year before Villa had become angry because the United States no longer permitted guns and ammunition to be shipped to him. On the night of March 8, 1916, he crossed the border and attacked the military garrison and town of Columbia, New Mexico. By the time he was driven off seven men of the U. S. forces, and eight civilians had been killed. About two hundred and fifteen of Villa's men were killed, a sizeable percentage of his estimated force of five hundred to one thousand men. General Pershing was ordered to capture him, and for most of a year he and his troops searched. In January, 1917, they were recalled, and it was then that Cárdenas once again led his troops through Pulpit Canyon, this time from west to east.

Several engagements were fought, one of which was the Battle of San Fermín, October 18, 1917. Though the number of soldiers engaged was not large, it was a rough and tumble affair and illustrated the difference betwen Villa's and Obregón's style of fighting. With only three or four thousand mounted soldiers, Villa was a brilliant leader, but he never mastered the art of maneuvering a whole army and would depend to excess upon dashing cavalry attacks.

Obregón, on the other hand, would have his mounted soldiers get down on the ground in rough terrain where they could cover up behind rocks or trees and present a difficult mark to the enemy, and also shoot more accurately too. Cárdenas had learned these principles and though he himself commanded cavalry troops, he was always ready to convert them into infantry. He, however, would remain on his mount, riding up and down the lines directing and encouraging his men. One of the Medina brothers of Jiquilpan who took part in the engagement tells how he and his comrades were encouraged as they saw their commander dare death by continuing in the saddle the better to supervise the contest.

Letters from old friends and relatives in Michoacán told Cárdenas of a lamentable situation there. Three reactionary leaders, Chávez, Cíntora, and Altamirano, had opposed the revolutionary cause and become a dreaded scourge to the towns and smaller cities. Chávez was the most feared and earned this primacy by deeds of valor, military prowess, and unspeakable cruelty. Everywhere he went, he murdered, burned, stole, and raped. Villagers who might have abetted him otherwise were forced to fight to save their homes from utter ruin. At last, after the campaign against Villa had ended and Cárdenas had returned to Sonora, General Calles gave him fifteen hundred men and a commission to go to Michoacán and combat Chávez and his fellows.

On the twentieth of June, 1918, Lázaro Cárdenas rode into Guadalajara at the head, not of twenty-five men, but of sixty times that number. During the five years that had elapsed since he had given his mother a parting kiss to ride off to the lowlands to take up arms, he had risen from an unknown printer lad to an army officer of repute. But he was not concerned now with how the home folks would take note of his success. *El Chamaco* had no thoughts of triumph that day as he entered Guadalajara, for he had just been informed that the mother whom he had left well and strong, was now dying in a local hospital. Though life

flickered in her decimated frame, it was not for long, and the
following day, surrounded by daughters and sons including Lázaro, Doña Felícitas de Cárdenas, to whom her Jiquilpan neighbors still refer as a *"saint"*, made her departure from this world.

The campaign against Chávez, Cíntora, and Altamirano was
no easy task. In it Cárdenas fought one of the hardest engagements of his career, the Battle of Los Naranjos, July 24, 1918.
With seventy troopers he suddenly came upon an enemy of eight
hundred men sprawled about eating. Without hesitation he ordered
the attack, thinking that the unpreparedness of the enemy would
more than offset the inequality of numbers. Consternation spread
through the camp of unsuspecting soldiers when their meal was
interrupted so abruptly by bullets. At first they thought that a
large force was striking due to the way Cárdenas had detailed his
troops, but soon they discovered how greatly they outnumbered
their attackers. With confidence, born of this discovery, they pressed the battle so that victory quickly turned to them.

Cárdenas himself was knocked down in close range fighting.
He rolled over several times, and finding himself out of the line of
action, scrambled to his feet and made off through the thicket
toward the railroad where he knew a freight train would be
passing soon. When it came he ordered the engineer to put on
full steam in a dash to the city of Morelia for reinforcements. A
trainload of soldiers was quickly secured and taken back to the
scene of battle where they arrived about four o'clock the next
morning.

The enemy, in full possession of the field, was resting con-
fidently after its victory, little realizing that a large force of fresh
fighters was about to fall on them. They were unequal to the
new encounter and were driven from the field, many of their
number remaining behind dead, wounded, or captured. Cárdenas' own captured troops who were to have been executed at
sunrise were all released. Even with that lesson, however, Cárdenas
had not yet learned completely that caution is as necessary as
valor in a commander.

In the capital, Venustiano Carranza was coming to the end of
his term in office. A semblance of order had been restored. The
government had taken over the railroads at a time when the
foreign owners had given up, for during the years of turmoil

they had found the railroads unprofitable. Somehow Carranza had managed to replace the torn-up tracks, repair the rolling stock, and hold the bandits in check. Foreign conductors, engineers, and construction crews were replaced with Mexicans. Once more the trains ran, and it was the Mexicans themselves who ran them. This success gave the people new confidence in their own country. Nationalism became basic in the reconstruction program. Effort was made to utilize Mexican brains and brawn in all enterprises.

Carranza had been a strong leader and could not resist the temptation of picking a successor through whom he might continue to rule. Obregón, his most successful general, had a different idea. For expressing it, he was thrown in jail, but escaped, while his friend Adolfo de la Huerta, backed by Calles, led a revolt to block Carranza and pave the way for Obregón himself to become president. Carranza could not stand up against the opposition and abandoned the capital in May, 1920. He was betrayed and shot in cold blood as he tried to escape through the mountains of the State of Vera Cruz. It was Lázaro Cárdenas who captured the betrayer and escorted him to Mexico City where, far from being punished, the betrayer was promoted in rank. Not until Cárdenas became president was that particular officer penalized by being expelled from the army.

Adolfo de la Huerta, not to be confused with Victoriano Huerta, became provisional president and governed the six remaining months of Carranza's unexpired term. It was he who, in agreement with Obregón, promoted Colonel Lázaro Cárdenas to the rank of brigadier general. Cárdenas was only twenty-five years old at the time and thus became one of the youngest generals in Mexico's military history. It was de la Huerta, too, who appointed Cárdenas to be provisional governor of Michoacán for three months.

Alvaro Obregón became president in November, 1920. His was a firm hand and the people welcomed it. Banditry waned. Foreign relations were patched up, though not without sacrificing some of the nationalistic objectives toward which Mexico had been struggling. The army was reorganized. Obregón encouraged the labor union movement and accelerated the distribution of land to the peasants. Perhaps his greatest contribution to his country was the founding of a federal school system through which emphasis was placed on the education of the masses. Mexico was being rebuilt for the plain people, and the fiber of the forgotten peasant was to be prepared for weaving into the national fabric.

Then Obregón, like Carranza before, tried to pick a successor. Adolfo de la Huerta again revolted against this growing tendency of the man in office to choose his successor. Because of the chronic undercurrent of dissatisfaction he was able to take half the army with him, and the loyal forces who were left with Obregón were hard pressed. De la Huerta's forces were advancing on Mexico City so rapidly from the east that Obregón had to withdraw some of his troops from the northwest in order to defend his position on the eastern side. That move so weakened the northwest sector, that to divert the attention of the advancing rebels in that direction General Cárdenas was ordered to attempt an impossible flanking movement through the mountains of Michoacán and Jalisco toward the Colima-Guadalajara railroad.

Only twelve hundred light cavalry troopers could be spared for the task, but considering the ability of his young general, Obregón felt that the flying column would be able to reach a certain point where Cárdenas was instructed to wait in a menacing attitude. The movement, involving many minor engagements, was carried out brilliantly and so rapidly that when the point designated for stopping was reached, the intrepid leader felt that he should push on. He defends this move by saying that to stop at the point indicated would have been as dangerous as to advance, but some critics deny this. The advance brought fatal consequences, for it permitted an overwhelmingly larger force of five thousand men in close contact with their base of supplies to mass against him and attack at a spot where he was put at further disadvantage.

Even so, in this battle of Teocuicatlán, December 26, 1923, he and his men fought until their ammunition was exhausted, Cárdenas himself falling with a bullet wound near his heart. The second in command had been killed. Cárdenas was given medical treatment and taken to Guadalajara. There the commander of the western zone of the rebellion, General Enrique Estrada, endeavored to persuade his young captive that, wounded as he was, he should declare himself in favor of the de la Huerta revolt, or suffer the consequences. Cárdenas never wavered and told his captor that he preferred the firing squad to betraying what he believed was the cause of the people. One morning at three o'clock he and his fellow captives were awakened and ordered up. Although Cárdenas had expected something better than execution of kindly General Estrada, he merely smiled and got dressed as best he could in his crippled condition. If his time had come, it had come.

Fortunately, the move was to the railway station instead of to the cemetery, for General Estrada was abandoning Guadalajara in the face of advancing loyal troops. The captives were taken to Colima and on the twentieth of February, 1924, the revolt having failed, Cárdenas was set free, placed in charge of the local troops, and tendered the surrender of Estrada and his companions. Cárdenas thanked them for not having shot him, and without giving Obregón time to order their execution, put them on a steamship in Manzanillo, secured money for them to live on till they got settled in exile, and shipped them off to California. Estrada was to come back and participate in another rebellion in 1929, but even so, when Cárdenas became president, he invited him to return once more and gave him a good position. Later, under Avila Camacho, Estrada became general manager of the railroads, a position he held with credit until his death.

The Teocuicatlán engagement had taught General Cárdenas once and for all to look out for the safety of his troops (a lesson which Villa never learned). Regarding their welfare in other ways, he had always been solicitous. He has discouraged drinking and gambling among them. While in charge of military operations in the Isthmus of Tehuantepec during 1922, he erected a soldiers' hospital, an unusual thing indeed for that period when the years of turmoil and destruction had accustomed the soldiers so thoroughly to hardship and suffering that even barracks were luxuries.

The man who had been chosen by Obregón to be his successor was Plutarco Elías Calles, the country school teacher who had become a hard-hitting general and the visionary leader of the short-lived "Republic of Agua Prieta". As president, Calles increased considerably the number of schools. His administration built some roads and balanced the budget. As big boss he did not hesitate to take on a fight with the big land owners, big business, and the Church. Foreign priests and nuns were deported. Churches were closed, first by the priests themselves who went on strike, refusing to hold services as a protest against Calles' enforcement of the anti-clerical laws.

In reaction against Calles' attitude toward the Church, groups of peasants and Indians calling themselves *cristeros* (partisans of Christ the King) arose in many places. In some parts the revolts were put down easily, but in Coalcomán, a mountainous area of Michoacán, the *cristeros* prevailed. In desperation the government forces burned homes and scourged the countryside generally but to no avail. The ardently religious mountain folk, under the leadership of a brave priest, held out against all attack.

Then Cárdenas was placed in command of the government troops, and he determined upon a new strategy. As soon as he had captured a few of the *cristeros* he gave them good rifles in place of the old muzzle loaders they had been using, and told them to return to their homes and use their new guns and ammunition, not for shooting people but for hunting game. The surprised men returned to their headquarters and told their story to the priest commander. The latter, utterly confounded, said that he would like to meet the man who had followed such strange procedure. One of the proud possessors of a new rifle took this message back to Cárdenas who accompanied him *alone* to the rendezvous of the priest. Once together, the zealous priest who saw his Church endangered and the equally zealous patriot who saw his country endangered, agreed on terms of peace. The Coalcomán campaign was thus won without casualties to either side, and without leaving coals of bitterness to smoulder in the breasts of the vanquished.

While Pancho Villa and other commanders executed thousands of prisoners during the turbulent years of internal strife, Cárdenas never consigned a captive of his to such a fate. Even as a young general, Cárdenas followed the policy of winning the good will of his enemies, dreaming always of an era in which all Mexicans could live together in peace.

It has been my belief that public tranquillity can be maintained only when due attention is paid to the spiritual and economic needs of the Mexican people, most of whom have lived in extreme poverty and neglect. It is for that reason that my government has dedicated special attention to the agrarian and labor problems and even more so to the Indian problem.

— Lázaro Cárdenas—May 18, 1938

V

THREE YEARS IN THE LAND OF BLACK GOLD

General Cárdenas and his aide, General Piña Soria, strode round and round the plaza of the little town of Cuauhtémoc near Tampico in the state of Tamaulipas. Restless, geared for action, Cárdenas seldom stood still while he talked. "I'm going to leave the army!" Another turn around the square, and he continued, "It's time the promises of the Revolution be converted into tangible deeds. All of us who believe in the ideal of the Revolution should put it into constructive and energetic action. Each one to the measure of his ability should do, do, do."

And Cárdenas was prepared to *do*. It wasn't that he was tired of army life by that year of 1925. Nor was it that after twelve years in military service he now wanted to go into business for himself. Rather, he was convinced that Mexico needed builders more than fighters.

But his superiors decreed a wait, and Cárdenas felt that, as a part of either a political or military machine, he must be an obedient cog. Though his personal inclinations were to enter government service immediately, he acquiesced in the desire of his commanders that he stay at his post in Tampico. In spite of the fact that he would have preferred a more active part in the reconstruction of his country, those three years in Tampico were invaluable as preparation for days to come. For it was there that Cárdenas became acquainted with the oil men and oil business.

Among other things his task in the military administration of the area included the handling of the labor problem. Unions had been formed among the oil workers. The oil interests tried to combat them by forming other unions and also, it is said, by hiring gunmen to cause trouble. Cárdenas disarmed the gunmen and then proceeded to protect both the labor unions and the oil companies. Other military commanders had winked at the gun-

43

men and the efforts of the oil interests to break up the labor unions. Perhaps it was expected that Cárdenas would do the same.

Soon after the general had taken over the post, a newspaper reporter seated himself at the table in the restaurant where Cárdenas usually ate. When he came in and took his place at the head of the table, the reporter greeted him cordially and then asked him how he liked his new post. Cárdenas answered that it was all right, that army officers could not be particular about where they were sent. "O," said the reporter somewhat cynically, "I mean, how do you like it financially?" "What are you driving at?" demanded the general. "Why, it is well known," went on the reporter, "that the oil companies here in this region are very solicitous about the financial welfare of you army officers." Cárdenas gave the table such a shove that it startled the diners and splashed the soup from their plates. "Don't be an ass!" he exploded, and stormed out of the room. The usually even-tempered Cárdenas simply could not restrain himself on that touchy subject.

Not that attempts were not made to bribe him. General Piña Soria tells a story of one of the many futile efforts which were made to buy Cárdenas' favor. He relates that when Cárdenas became military commander of the Tampico region, he took along an old Hudson with obviously only a short lease left on life. One day a representative of one of the powerful oil companies drove up to the general's office in a beautiful Packard sedan. Brand new, and glistening, it was a fortune on four wheels. The representative presented himself to Cárdenas and then said, "Sir, the company which I represent considers it a high honor and proof of its high esteem and respect toward you, to be permitted to offer you the automobile which is at the door and which is yours without reserve."

Through the office window could be seen the elegant and aristocratic car standing beside the ancient and decrepit Hudson. Cárdenas looked at the Packard for a moment and then replied courteously, " I beg to express to your company my appreciation for the gift which I decline irrevocably. I have brought an automobile with me which is sufficient for my needs. Many thanks." His manner indicated that the incident was closed, and the company's representative retired in graceless confusion.

Sometime later, the Hudson gave out completely and Cárdenas was without a car and sufficient money to buy one. The offer of the Packard still remained. A temptation? Maybe. But Cárdenas commissioned one of his aides to buy him a Dodge on time which he paid for in 100-peso-a-month installments.

There was much in the management of the oil industry which caused the young general deep concern. He said little, but drank deeply at the pool of observation even though the waters were bitter. When he arrived in Tampico, Cárdenas found that the foreign employees of the oil companies ate in a different dining room from the Mexican clerks and bookkeepers. At first it seemed that the difference was one of language, but later he noticed that the officers from his own staff who happened to be on the grounds at meal time, were invited to share the foreigners' table. When he was convinced that it was only to show deference to his staff that they had been invited to the other table, he ordered his men to eat with their fellow Mexicans.

He observed that when a foreigner and a Mexican performed identical tasks, the former received twice as much pay and was provided with better living quarters than the latter. He found that the oil companies took no interest in the welfare of the community whose sub-soil they were exploiting. He noticed, and did not forget, that one time some peasants asked the company whose water-main traversed their village, to install a hydrant at that point. The company refused, and the people had to go on carrying their water up from the river.

If the petroleum administrators had spent the same amount of money aiding the villages as they showed they were willing to spend in offering luxurious automobiles and other personal considerations to Cárdenas, the history of oil in Mexico might have ended differently than it finally did.

The three years spent by Cárdenas in Tampico were not just in the oil camps. The general's life was a very busy one. Piña Soria describes one of the expeditions which he took with Cárdenas in the year 1925. They had gone to Tuxpán to inspect the troops there, and were about to leave when Cárdenas was called to the telephone. Without telling his companions what the message was, he ordered thirteen soldiers to get into a boat and follow his own launch.

They traveled along one of the natural canals which parallel the sea coast between Tuxpán and Tampico. Occasional small craft were going back and forth carrying passengers and produce. On the banks here and there, were tiny clusters of huts belonging to the people who made their living by fishing, raising cattle, farming, or cutting timber. After a short distance the expedition put into shore, and Cárdenas ordered two of the soldiers to take the boats to a certain designated point and the rest to disembark. Then he informed his companions of the message he had received. A certain bandit leader, who had surrendered a short time before, had his home in that area. For awhile he had lived peaceably, but now he had gathered together sixty men and was planning an attack on one of the oil camps. Cárdenas had come to take him by surprise. Thirteen men against sixty? The soldiers were not too pleased, but there was nothing to do but follow.

Cárdenas led the way through the jungle, and in about two hours they arrived at the clearing where the bandit lived. By then they were all drenched with perspiration. Cárdenas waited a moment while they caught their breath, then he divided the men into three groups and gave instructions as to where they should meet if defeated. Then leading the smallest group out of the thicket, he crossed the clearing while the others circled around.

Cárdenas approached rapidly, but without the appearance of an attack. He and his group would have made an easy target as they walked the hundred yards from the thicket to the house. His pistol remained in the holster, and a small riding quirt was all he had in his hand. Without hesitation he knocked at the door and the bandit fearfully opened it. Cárdenas talked to him about the weather, the crops, and then asked for a drink of water. Finally he told him of the report he had heard. The bandit denied it vigorously, but Cárdenas asked him if he would accompany him to the oil camp, thereby demonstrating that the rumor was false. Fearfully the man went. His wife called after Cárdenas, "Sir, you will not kill him will you?" She knew that such things had happened often. The general looked back in kindly surprise and said simply in a tone of interrogation, "I?"

Perhaps this habit of taking the quiet means for accomplishing a desired end is based not only on his desire for peace but also on his dislike of ostentation. Ramón Beteta, as a young man on

his way to the University of Texas, visited the Tampico camp
where his brother Ignacio, now a general, was then serving as
a captain in Cárdenas' forces. Ramón was invited to attend a
program where the soldiers staged an exhibition of acrobatic
skill. One of the acts included a human pyramid. The soldier
at the pinnacle, in order to attract attention and heighten the
interest of the crowd, made grotesque faces and motions to indicate that his was a difficult task. Beteta tells how, from the
grandstand, Cárdenas dispatched an aide to order the soldier to
perform his stunt with dignity and not like a clown.

As Cárdenas waited his chance to leave the army and turn his
energies to rebuilding his country, he didn't overlook the opportunities at hand. Mexican soldiers, all during the Revolution
and even for years after that, took their families and assorted
belongings with them wherever they went. Constantly traveling,
the children missed any chance they might have had for schooling.
There in Tampico in 1925 Cárdenas started the first school for
"Children of the Army". He sent messages to all other commanders of military zones suggesting that they do the same, but it
wasn't until he himself became president that "Children of the
Army" schools sprang up all over the country, and the army
went all the way in an effort to eliminate illiteracy among the
soldiers and their families.

It was also in Tampico that Cárdenas remembered his large
farm that he had rented and placed in the care of an administrator.
He knew that he could begin right then to carry out some of his
socially benevolent ideas on his own farm. A good bit of Cárdenas'
thinking was done in the saddle as he traveled the jungle trails
from one post to another. It was after one particularly long day
on the trail—a day in which he had been reflecting on the needs
of peasant farmers all over Mexico—that he set about doing what
he felt should be done about his own farm.

He called his secretary and dictated a letter to the administrator. General Piña Soria, resting with his companions near by,
overheard the dictation and remembered it more or less as follows:
In view of my conviction that land and what it produces should benefit
those who cultivate it, give the laborers who live on my farm plots of land
which they may cultivate for themselves free of rent. Supply them with
seeds and loan them without charge the implements and horses they need
for working it. Farm the remaining land and pay the laborers sufficient

wages to allow them and their families to live as human beings who are worthy of just treatment. Whatever the lands cultivated by the management produce is to be used first to pay for the rent and costs of administration. If anything is left over it is to be used for projects of collective benefits such as schools or roads. I am sorry that I am not able to do more to bring about the immediate realization of one of the longings of my life—the emancipation of the peasants and laborers of Mexico.

It must be remembered that for centuries this Mexican peon had not been a free man. The plantation owners, priests, military officers, civil officials, storekeepers, and professional men had been able to order him about ever since the Conquest. Some might treat him with more consideration than others, but all saw to it that he kept the inferior place which had been his allotment. He could be abused with impunity. His very person was not immune to impositions and much less his property. Perhaps he had planned to plant corn on a certain day or call on a sick relative, but an order would come for him to perform some servile work for a petty official or pack some luggage for a traveler, and he would have to give up his own plans and go. If the official or traveler cuffed him about or insulted him, there was little or no redress.

The Mexican peon's badge of serfdom was the *mecapal,* the rawhide band which was fastened by a rope to the load on his back and then placed over his forehead to support the load. His outlook was the ground. Today, though still poverty-stricken, he can stand up straight and look out upon his narrow world as an independent creature, so independent, in fact, that it is not possible to force even progress upon him. He will take it if he likes it; but do not coerce him. He now enjoys a freedom he never knew before. Too often he fails to benefit by it, but he had to become free before he could ever hope to learn to use his freedom for progress.

Mexico itself had made considerable advance while Plutarco Elías Calles was president. The educational movement that had been started in the early twenties by Obregón with the help of his extraordinary Secretary of Education, José Vasconcelos, had forged ahead with still more help from Calles. A new day was dawning even though trouble still brewed.

Calles had exerted pressure upon the National Congress and the Mexican states to secure an amendment to the Constitution. Accordingly, a man could serve more than one term as president providing that he did not succeed himself. This was very objectionable to the rank and file of those faithful to the Revolution. They had tired of re-election succeeding re-election during the domination of Porfirio Díaz, and now it didn't require much imagination to see Obregón succeed Calles and vice versa in a vicious circle. It was also objectionable to the Church which felt that Obregón was as anti-church as Calles, and that he would continue those obnoxious measures which had been enacted by the Constitution and put in force by Calles.

Incensed over the attempt to get Obregón re-elected, Generals Arnulfo Gómez and Francisco Serrano decided, in 1927, to run for president. They were accused of sedition, captured, and executed. With those two candidates safely out of the way Obregón was re-elected president in June, 1928, but he never served. He was shot and killed in a restaurant in a suburb of Mexico City by a fanatic on July seventeenth of that same year.

People watched to see if Calles would not take advantage of the situation to prolong his own term in office. Instead, he decided to keep a firm hand on the affairs of the nation from behind the scenes. He let it be known that he favored a nonmilitary man, Emilio Portes Gil, for the post of provisional president, being always aware of the fact that in case of trouble he himself would be needed. As a second means of indirect control he planned the formation of a nation-wide political party through which he could make his influence felt effectively.

Up to the end of 1927 Cárdenas had waited in Tampico, wanting to serve his people and believing that it could best be done in some elective office. Still, he was reticent to seek it knowing that some might accuse him of merely being ambitious to rule. Therefore he hesitated to push himself forward in any way, or to pull strings with the right people. He had such a strong belief in destiny that he was able to bide his time with the utmost unconcern. His faith that an opening for service would come was almost fatalistic. It was the same fatalism that enabled him, and other Mexicans, to dare death so recklessly.

He had hoped, he explained to a fellow-officer, to return to Jiquilpan and run for mayor. There he would institute a municipal government which would conform to the ideals of the Revolution. As it turned out he had not aimed high enough, for in the fall of 1927 some of his friends went to Tampico and asked him to run for governor of Michoacán. Cárdenas hedged, being wary of friends who tried to push him forward. When they intimated that it would be a calamity to the state if he refused, he warned them, "Mine shall be a government *of* friends, not *for* friends". In order to obtain an unbiased opinion of the people's true desire, he sent his secretary to Michoacán, whose report convinced him that his wait was over, and the time for action had come. He announced his candidacy for the governorship on the tenth of January, 1928.

In his platform he declared himself in favor of carrying out the agrarian reforms called for by the Constitution in an orderly but decisive way. He expressed a desire to open more schools with a practical program of instruction. He promised to dedicate his efforts to developing agriculture, industry, highways, and "every enterprise that tends toward the betterment of the laboring classes and the progress of the state." In conclusion, he assured the voters that he would not take any prejudices with him into the governor's chair.

Regarding the financing of his campaign he said, "It is my determination not to bother any person or organization with requests for contributions to conduct my campaign. Although I do not have funds of my own to dedicate to political activities, I believe that I do not need money to ascertain the will of the people." As it turned out, this quixotic declaration about funds was well-founded after all. There was no opposition. The other two candidates withdrew as soon as they learned that he was going to run. This was due not so much to his popularity with the people as to his favor with the higher powers. His old friend Calles was still in the presidency, and had no qualms of conscience about announcing his preferences. Few politicians cared to risk a race against a Calles favorite.

That summer of 1928 was a time of crisis in the nation. Ex-president Obregón had been elected president again by the skilful manipulations of Calles. Idealistic Cárdenas disagreed with this breaking with the traditions of the Revolution. He as much as said so in the campaign address in which he told the people of Michoacán: "I shall keep my hands off political matters, for I shall not have candidates; the ones who should have candidates are the people."

If Calles knew of that rebuke he paid no attention. He knew that he could count on the fidelity of Cárdenas to his chief and to the political machine. About the same time that Cárdenas was elected governor, Calles appointed him to be *General de División,* the highest rank in the Mexican army. Then he sent him to the mountains to pacify those of the *cristeros* who still continued in arms. With this assignment Cárdenas was far from Mexico City when Obregón was assassinated.

That fall, in September of 1928, General Lázaro Cárdenas took office as Governor of Michoacán.

It was my conviction that in a country like ours where for various historical reasons there had been a hangover of a semi-feudal system, it was indispensable to break those moulds and go directly to the masses, especially the Indians, to impart confidence, teach them their rights and obligations, and to instil optimism and a spirit to work and cooperate with one another.

— Lázaro Cárdenas—to the laborers
November 25, 1940

VI

GOVERNOR OF MICHOACAN

LAZARO CARDENAS was only thirty-three years of age, a novice in politics and an inexperienced idealist in statecraft when he became chief executive of his native state. What had Michoacán to hope for from such a governor? Doubters consoled themselves by saying that he would at least be honest and maintain order. Few thought that he would meet with such success that his state administration would be interrupted with calls to serve the nation.

He had been governor for only a little over four and a half months when, on the twenty-first of January, 1929, he was called again to command the troops in the *cristero* campaign. These fighting Catholic peasants had taken up arms because the federal government had demanded that the priests either register or quit functioning. The clerics, refusing to comply, had gone on strike. Religious services in the churches stopped. Babies went unbaptized. The only marriage service was the civil ceremony.

Since 1926 Michoacán, one of the most ardently religious states of the Republic, had been in turmoil over the affair, and Cárdenas determined to bring peace. He let it be known to the *cristeros* that he was in their midst not merely as military commander but also as their governor. As the latter he was ready to listen to the complaints of any and all.

Little by little the people discovered that he meant what he said, and then they surrounded him in droves. Not only the *cristeros* but other peasants came, and not only from Michoacán but from bordering states as well. From morning until night petitioners and malcontents besieged his headquarters seeking favors or redresses. And Cárdenas, who believed that government, while being *of, by,* and *for* the people, should also be *among* the people, who believed that the people should have a chance to see what the governor looks like, listened to them all.

53

The task was so great that one of his staff, General Pizá Martínez, playing the role of Jethro, advised him to let someone else
hear part of the complaints. But Cárdenas, the modern Moses of
Michoacán, said, "No, this is my duty. The people have come a
long way to tell me their problems and would be disappointed if
I referred them to an aide. Even if I can't always help them, it
will make them feel better to have talked to me personally."

American opinion will always be sympathetic toward the man
who clings to his religion in spite of the State, but it cannot favor
the man who uses religious sentiment as a pretext to dam up
the stream of progress. In one section of Michoacán a religious
zealot by the name of Cortez had gathered together several hundred men. Cárdenas with his superior forces could have crushed
him, but it would have taken time and cost lives. Cortez had the
sympathy of the faithful, and it may have been that he was sincere
in really thinking he was fighting for God. Cárdenas determined
to find out by talking the matter over with him.

He made the arrangements secretly and then invited the highest
officer under his command to go for a ride with him. The officer
asked no questions, but entered the car and at Cárdenas' order,
the chauffeur drove into the territory controlled by Cortez, who
met him with fifty armed men. However, when he saw that
Cárdenas had only one officer and a chauffeur he ordered all but
a small bodyguard to retire.

Then Cárdenas and Cortez stepped off to one side where their
conversation could not be overheard, and the general explained to
the zealot why it was that the federal government wanted the
priests to register, and how far he as governor would go in carrying
out the decree. Quietly, and without loss of dignity, he pleaded
with the *cristero* to put down his arms. It was a confidential appeal
to the enemy's reason. And logic backed up with trust and human
sympathy won him over.

Cortez informed his men that he would accompany the governor,
and would send them orders as to what they should do. Within a
few days that particular *cristero* band ceased fighting. On June
29, 1929, the clergy called off the strike, and the church bells
rang again in Mexico. Cárdenas had handbills dropped from an
airplane broadcasting the news that President Portes Gil had come

to a compromise with the Church leaders, and once again peace settled over Michoacán.

That first year in which Cárdenas was governor he was called from the state capital not only to deal with the *cristeros* but also to aid the federal government against the last big revolt Mexico has had. The provisional president, Emilio Portes Gil, who had been elected by Congress upon Obregón's assassination, was a lawyer; and Cárdenas and others felt that government-by-civilians should have a chance to succeed. Therefore when Generals Escobar, Manzo, and other ambitious or reactionary militarists revolted, Cárdenas cooperated with the government. The opposing militarists carried a big portion of the national army with them, and at the height of the revolt they were in control of most of northern Mexico.

Cárdenas as divisional general was in command of one of the three columns which converged upon the forces of the militarists and forced them to surrender. The three generals in charge of the federal columns were each allowed a million pesos for the expenses of the campaign. It was expected that much of this money would go toward buying the support of the army officers, but Cárdenas neither took his allotment nor passed any on. He whose loyalty could not be bought astounded the Treasury Department by returning seven hundred thousand of the million pesos which had been at his disposal for the campaign. A former staff officer complained to me that not merely frugality but outright stinginess with his friends had enabled the general to do it.

The revolt lasted about two months, collapsing in April, 1929. Then Cárdenas was able to return again to Michoacán. During the four years that he was governor he was called outside the state on three occasions totalling over a year in time. Two other times he was within the state, but absent from Morelia, the capital. However, when not there he developed a technique for overseeing the affairs of the state by telephone, telegraph, and correspondence. He kept in close contact with the capital, though often by remote control, and always considered himself responsible for the acts of the government.

Because peace had come to Michoacán at the end of his first year in office he was subsequently free to devote most of his energies to gubernatorial duties. He had placed Professor Celso Flores

Zamora at the head of the educational system, and together they worked out plans for building new schools and improving the old. In all, one hundred new doors of learning were opened by his government and three hundred more were opened by the plantation owners, obligated by law to do so for the children of their employees. The normal school was made coeducational; industrial institutes were started with emphasis on practical instruction; and the State University was made more democratic. Schools far and wide received visits from the governor. He went to inspire and to help, and also to inspect. But he went, too, to get the viewpoint of teachers and pupils and to strengthen his own hope for the future. And who knows but that personal disappointment at having had only six years of schooling himself exerted its own pull toward the classroom?

Previously teachers' salaries had frequently been withheld for one reason or another. Cárdenas gave strict orders that they should be paid promptly. When an administrator of revenue used the money set aside for a teacher's salary in some other way, he was immediately dismissed. Cárdenas felt that the teachers and their needs were of primary importance. In this and other ways he demonstrated the depth of conviction with which he had said, "The Fatherland will become strong, and men will attain their freedom only when culture becomes the heritage of the masses."

Another problem claimed as much or more of Cárdenas' attention than the schools. It was the age-old problem of making a living. His argument was simple. You cannot inspire parents to send their children to school when they are too poor to put clothes on their backs. As a result landless peasants were given small plots to till, some credit was provided for small farmers and home factories, a minimum wage was set, flood lands were drained, roads constructed, and other enterprises undertaken which would improve living conditions.

Cárdenas encouraged the formation of labor and peasant organizations. He considered them as schools for democracy, and as such he listened with great satisfaction to the animated discussions at their gatherings. He tried to link the peasant and labor organizations together, showing them that they had interests in common and that they would stand or fall together. He met informally in the coffee houses with the school teachers and university students, showing them how their interests too were linked with the laboring classes.

While he was governor the three groups—students, laborers, and peasants—presented a united front for reform. Their organizations remained democratic, each person having a chance to express his opinion as long as Cárdenas was overseer. But after he was gone the groups split apart and petty bosses or leaders took control. The organizations had mushroomed so quickly that the ordinary peasant and laborer had not grown with it, and became easy prey for unscrupulous leaders. Perhaps a practical solution might have been to organize with small units of not more than ten peasants or laborers each so as to guarantee to every member an opportunity to enter into discussions and to get actual practice in democratic procedure. However, Cárdenas the laborite had been so interested in the regiment and column, that he had neglected to organize the squad. Mexican agrarian leaders in general seem to have been blind to this lack, and the blunder stands as a great hindrance to true democracy in rural Mexico.

"Land!" had been one of the main issues of the Revolution, and its redistribution had been authorized by the constitutional mandate of 1917. Cárdenas, one of the most agrarian-minded Mexicans since the days of Zapata, told the Michoacán voters in 1928, "I am in favor of the agrarian policy both because it is in the program of the Revolution, and because to solve the land question is a national need."

Emilio Portes Gil had gone into office as provisional president at about the same time as Cárdenas became governor. He was to serve only until the people could formally elect a president to fill out Obregón's term. By February, 1930, Pascual Ortiz Rubio was inaugurated, and Portes Gil went out of office. Therefore it was President Ortiz Rubio whom Cárdenas called on for help in settling a land problem which he had contemplated as a boy from the hill above Jiquilpan.

For years most of the land of the region had been used for the benefit of one man. The peons who worked it were driven by overseers and cowed by gunmen. Their lives were miserable; even the firewood used in cooking their meals could not be gathered on the plantation unless paid for. Rather than risk the *hacienda* jail which would be their fate if caught, they walked long distances to find wood, and then lugged it home on their backs.

At last, in spite of the danger of excommunication from the Church and in spite of the gunmen, a few of the brave peons asked the government that the large holdings of the plantation, *La Guaracha,* be broken up in accordance with the Constitution and the agrarian law. A riot resulted, and in an effort to daunt the landless peasants into submission the plantation managers ordered their homes destroyed.

A few days later Governor Cárdenas and President Ortiz Rubio appeared on the plantation. In a meeting which brought the recalcitrant managers face to face with the timorous peasants, the former were told that the land would be taken from the plantation and given to the peons who were dependent upon it. The peons became alarmed; only a few of them had dared ask for redistribution, and the rest were scandalized at the thought.

"Oh, no," they protested, "that would be sin, and the priest would punish us severely."

"All right," answered the governor, "but think it over. If you refuse to accept that which the law decrees to be yours, we will bring in landless people from other neighborhoods and give it to them. The criminal action of its present holders has made it imperative for us to act at once."

The peons accepted the land, and began to run the sugar mill by a cooperative association of farmers who planted and harvested the cane. The proud mansion of the owner which used to function with regal splendor became quiet, though the ornate chapel continued to be used, and a secret Catholic school functioned in one wing of the building.

"Unjust!" cries our American respect for the inviolability of individual property rights. Yes, it is unjust if you forget the peasant homes that had been burned down, the seventy lives that had been taken prior to this because they had dared to petition for land back in 1915 and later, and the chicanery through which title to much of the land had been secured by the Spanish conquerors and their successors. Of course two wrongs do not make a right. But perhaps it is both good logic and good ethics to say that that wrong is nearer right which brings the greatest good to the greatest number.

Let us have a new science of government. Let us take politics to mean the intimate and exact knowledge of the collective needs of the people and measures directed toward satisfying those needs.

— Lázaro Cárdenas — to the
Seventh American Scientific Congress, September 9, 1935

VII

IN NATIONAL POLITICS

WITHIN TWO AND A HALF YEARS after his first hesitant embarkation into political waters, Cárdenas found himself nominal helmsman on the ship of national politics. The P. N. R. (*Partido Nacional Revolucionario*) had been formed in May of 1929 by General Calles with the express purpose of making permanent the ideals of the Revolution. By accepting the chairmanship Cárdenas was, theoretically at least, head of the national party. However, Calles was referred to either as "the strong man" or *Jefe Máximo* (Supreme Chief) of the Revolution, and in this unofficial capacity exerted an overwhelming influence. As a personal friend of both "strong man" Calles and President Ortiz Rubio, Cárdenas was able to function well in his new position.

Nation-wide political parties of the kind that exist in the United States had not been known in Mexico. Only local or municipal political groups could live under the Díaz regime; with the advent of Madero, an Anti-Re-electionist Party came into being; under Carranza, a Constitutionalist Liberal Party was organized, only to disintegrate into a Nationalist Party. These groups depended upon the men at the helm to give them national prestige, and when these leaders lost control of the reins of government the party dropped out of sight. Toward the end of Carranza's administration a Labor Party was organized, and with impulse from Russia a Communist Party was also formed. These polled very few votes. There was need of an organization built around ideas rather than men, and of stronger stuff than the prestige of some prominent leader.

The P. N. R. at the time Cárdenas took over was new and undisciplined, and still dependent upon the renown of General Calles for a voice of authority. With idealistic Cárdenas at its

61

head the party was immediately put to work on activities not usually considered political.

Through the P. N. R., athletics were promoted and a temperance campaign sponsored; and when a tremendous earthquake laid the city of Oaxaca and surrounding towns in the dust Cárdenas led the new party into relief work. As active chairman of the relief committee he himself went to the scene of disaster; but he kept his balance on the political tight-rope by appointing two honorary chairmen, one President Ortiz Rubio, the other General Calles.

There in Oaxaca he found the people composed and carrying on their work in spite of the spectacle of desolation that surrounded them. He took occasion to tell them of his admiration. "In the homes I have observed the exemplary Oaxacan dignity with its optimism, and in the fields the undeniable courage of this race which goes on about its regular tasks with the same constancy now as in normal times."

This trace of optimism which had been apparent in the earthquake-stricken people was one which Cárdenas admired wherever he found it. Just a few weeks before, he had told the P. N. R., "The vicissitudes of fortune which have befallen us in the past should be used for the lessons to be learned from them—never as a cause for discouragement." Cárdenas himself, cognizant as he was of the problems and difficulties that obstruct the march toward a greater and better Mexico, approached every constructive undertaking with enthusiasm.

Party funds were drawn upon to help the homeless Oaxacans, but even in this Cárdenas demonstrated his customary tact by stating that the thousands of pesos which the committee was going to administer would not be given out as a dole in cash, but rather as supplies. It was done this way, he explained, "in order not to wound the high self-respect of the Oaxacan public." This same tact, backed with sincerity and purpose, was what permitted Cárdenas to manage the party without making enemies, while at the same time accomplishing work for the nation.

While Cárdenas was away in Oaxaca, Luís Cabrera, a highly respected lawyer who had been Secretary of the Treasury under Carranza, published a series of attacks on the work of the Revolution. Cárdenas, whose political equanimity was seldom ruffled,

had a stinging reply for this former colleague turned critic. First
he pointed out why such men as Cabrera acted as they did:

The reason that moves these men to disturb the tranquillity that reigns in
the Republic this year is the longing to reconstruct political situations that
would be favorable to the influencing of the public mind, and win for
themselves a political following.

Then with cold facts he defended the cause of the Revolution.
Concerning the army which Cabrera had criticized, Cárdenas
retorted:

Señor Cabrera is willingly ignorant of the social service that the army is
carrying out at this very time. Troops have laid aside the rifle in this hour
of peace in order to take up pick and shovel and build highways, help
construct dams, and place their energies at the service of every constructive
enterprise.

Cabrera had admitted the praiseworthiness of the educational
program of the Obregón Administration but gave all credit to the
Minister of Education, José Vasconcelos. Cárdenas defended
Obregón by pointing out that,

. . . in a type of government such as we have in Mexico, no cabinet member
can carry out a program unless the president is in accord. The work, then
that Vasconcelos did is Obregón's work, too . . . Díaz sought to build up
cultural centers in the capital of the Republic, but neglected the education
of the masses of the nation. The Revolution under Carranza is to be censured
in that it did away with the Ministry of Public Instruction . . . and entrusted national education . . . to the municipal and state governments. It
was General Obregón who first sponsored an amendment to the Constitution
making possible the creation of a Ministry of Education with nationwide
jurisdiction . . . The work begun during the administration of President
Obregón was intensified during the administration of President Calles,
special attention being paid to the rural centers of the land . . . This
tendency to raise the cultural standard of the masses . . . is characteristic
of the present administration's program.

Concerning financial matters Cárdenas contrasted the government finances of that day with the situation as found in the day
when Cabrera himself was in charge:

While Attorney Cabrera was head of the Treasury it was impossible, due
perhaps to the rough-and-tumble character of the Revolutionary movement
at that time, to properly organize the administration of funds and much
less to restore national credit. The pernicious habits of bribery, various other
dishonest practices, and unjustified expenditures were generalized. No one
even thought of tackling the problem of credits. It was not until the administration of General Calles that it was possible to establish severe discipline for those who handled public funds, to organize systems of control
to do away with leaks from the Treasury, to establish a balanced budget on
a sound basis, and to introduce a policy of efficiency and democratic modesty.

It is now, then, that effort is being concentrated upon the solution of all the problems inherent to recuperation in the finances of both the government and the country at large.

The document went on to answer Cabrera concerning labor and agrarian problems as well as the matter of public works and concluded with this challenge:

In conclusion, I wish to say once more that the P. N. R. would be highly pleased if conservative groups or those who are frankly reactionary would decide to organize politically and match their strength all along the course of our national life with the political organization of the Revolution.

Cárdenas remained at the head of the P. N. R. for about ten months. During that time he started a system of primary elections to name candidates of the party, and succeeded in bringing about a certain degree of recognition of the civilian president as an authority of the party to be reckoned with. A break, however, was inevitable, and Cárdenas decided to let it come over a rather insignificant matter.

On the first of September, 1931, President Ortiz Rubio was to give his report to Congress. Instead of the customary presentation of the report in the Hall of Congress he wanted to have that august group meet in the stadium where a large crowd of people could be accommodated. Cárdenas, as head of the national party, agreed to give him support in the matter, but Congress refused to leave its own halls even for that one occasion. Cárdenas chose to take this as a lack of confidence in himself, and therefore resigned from the chairmanship of the P. N. R.

Immediately President Ortiz Rubio appointed him to his cabinet as Minister of Government. Less than two months after that, a political crisis arose which was solved only by the elimination of all high army officers from the cabinet. Cárdenas as well as three other divisional generals who held portfolios resigned. General Calles seemed to have determined that the rule of the civilian should stand upon its own merits or not at all.

After months of governing in absentia Cárdenas returned again to Morelia, where among other things the idea occurred to him to build a statue of the great patriot Morelos, hoping that it would become Mexico's counterpart of the Statue of Liberty. Morelos is one of the most beloved and admired heroes of Mexican history. He was first a muleteer, then a priest, and then the daring and able leader of the army that fought for independence from the Spanish back in 1811. It was because of his part in this fight that he was excommunicated from the Church. He was devoted not only to the ideal of political independence, but also to agrarian and social reform. He was a forerunner of the Revolution of 1910.

As Morelos was a native of Cárdenas' own home state of Michoacán, the governor ordered a gigantic statue of the patriot to be erected on an island in Michoacán's watery gem, Lake Pátzcuaro. Stone was quarried, and soldiers were put to work building a figure higher than the Statue of Liberty. Clothed in churchly robes, the Morelos that is visible for miles in every direction is not the military commander but the priest, until one comes near enough to see that the facial features are not those of a theologian, but of a general. On the interior of the figure, over the spiral stairway, beautiful murals were painted depicting the life of the great Mexican.

As a work of art the statue cannot be called an outstanding success. Nor has it yet struck very responsive chords in the hearts of patriots as a temple of national devotion. Some day, however, it may, and in the meantime tourists seek it out as a sight not to be missed.

On the mainland facing the island and near to the city of Pátzcuaro stood the home of Lázaro Cárdenas. The original dwelling had been built for him by friends about the time that the statue was begun, but later it was superseded by a better structure. This in turn was donated by the general in 1950 for a continental teacher training school under the supervision of UNESCO. It stands on a knoll, and from its high porch one looks with uninterrupted vision across the water into the fearless, stern, and visionary face of Morelos. For Lázaro Cárdenas wants the students who will come from all parts of this hemisphere to study in the school located in his old home to find in Morelos a source of inspiration to serve their respective fatherlands with unabating consecration.

At the time when Calles was president an amendment to the Constitution had changed the presidential term of office from four years to six. For this reason Ortiz Rubio should have remained in office until December 1, 1934. But he had had trouble and opposition from the very day of his inauguration, when someone had attempted to assassinate him. At last on September 2, 1932, Ortiz Rubio resigned. As he presented his resignation to Congress he pointed out that the lack of stability in the government, its constant uncertainty, and its series of political reverses had not resulted from disagreement in policies between him and the party which had placed him in power, but was due rather to differences of a personal nature which he preferred not to discuss.

With subtle irony he mentioned the generous suggestion made by General Calles that the presidency change hands in a peaceable way. It was evident that he had received a strong ultimatum from the *Jefe Máximo*. Ortiz Rubio alluded to the control that Calles was maintaining behind the official scenes, and then threw into the face of Congress the statement that democracy and the high ideals of the Revolution could be attained only when Congress itself so desired it.

With this historic resignation Mexico's experiment in government-by-civilians took a recess for fifteen years. Ortiz Rubio left the country.

Cárdenas, in Michoacán, received a telegram directly from the "Supreme Chief" Calles, a man to be obeyed, requesting him to go immediately to Mexico City to become Minister of War in the provisional cabinet which was about to be set up. Cárdenas considered. He had always insisted that, for the sake of constitutional government, the duly elected president should be supported to the end of his term. If he acquiesced, and became part of the cabinet which was to replace that of Ortiz Rubio, to all intents and purposes he would be participating in his overthrow. On the other hand, the post to which he had been invited was the most important in the cabinet. To the Minister of War would fall the lot of expending the lion's share of the budget and of organizing and improving the army to which Cárdenas had dedicated most of his life.

With the problem still before him he put on his hat, left the governor's office, and walked down the hall to the Director of Education, Professor Flores Zamora, and called, "Would you like to come with me to visit a school?" Delighted, the professor followed him to the car. While riding along the governor silently drew Calles' telegram from his pocket and handed it to his companion.

As Zamora returned it he said, "I'm sorry about this. The state can hardly spare you with so many unfinished projects needing your attention."

"I'm not going," said Cárdenas nonchalantly. Calles was later to find out the real force of character behind this man who dared answer an unhesitating *"No"* to his command.

About two weeks later, in the middle of September, 1932, Lázaro Cárdenas completed his term as governor of Michoacán.

No one can deny that our working classes have suffered inordinately from the scourge of injustice and the consequences of neglect and privation. It is urgent that they be given an opportunity to become full members of our civilization. We aspire to a civilization in which there will be a just distribution of wealth and of the benefits of culture.

— Lázaro Cárdenas — to University Students
March 21, 1935

VIII

MARRIAGE; POLITICAL ADVANCEMENT

WHILE CARDENAS was still governor he attended an outing in a park near Tacámbaro, Michoacán, where he met Amalia Solórzano, a school girl yet in her teens, but tall and womanly. She was beautiful and graceful with a winning smile and innate dignity. Immediately he was attracted to her, and Amalia, in turn, found the general's gracious though military bearing to be pleasing. Amalia's parents, a highly respected and well-to-do family of Tacámbaro, were staunch Catholics, and as such looked upon the general, who was keeping in line with the federal government's anti-Church policies, as an enemy of their faith. Hoping to prevent any further development between Cárdenas and Amalia, they hurried her back to the convent school in Mexico City where she had been studying and gave the nuns special instructions to watch her closely.

Convent schools were and are prohibited by law in Mexico. Thus, for the nuns to have a general and governor interested in one of their students, almost drove them to distraction. They were afraid that Cárdenas would learn too much about them and close their school. Perhaps he could have, but all he did was persist in sending gifts and letters in to Amalia who knew of the nun's apprehension and cleverly used it to her advantage. Whenever they were too strict with her she had only to say, "I'll tell the general!" and immediately she got her own way. In despair the nuns asked her parents to take the girl out of school.

With Amalia at home in Michoacán the Solórzanos were at a decided disadvantage in opposing the governor of their state, and a year or so later the couple became engaged. Since the Revolution, only the civil ceremony is the legal marriage ceremony. Church rites are permitted, but not recognized by the government. The general, in accordance with the laws of the country, felt the

69

civil ceremony to be sufficient, but on Amalia's account he submitted to a religious one as well. Shortly after the conclusion of his gubernatorial term in the fall of 1932, Lázaro Cárdenas and Amalia Solórzano were married. A humble priest of peasant origin performed the religious ceremony with only one other couple present.

Their honeymoon was spent at Cárdenas' rustic little cottage in a valley between two mountains that meet at the shore of Lake Pátzcuaro. At the time of their marriage the home was small and with bare surroundings. Fifteen years later that first house had been replaced by a larger one, and even that was almost hid by sheltering trees and flowers, behind which was a full orchard. Cárdenas, the lover of trees, had seen to it that his own home was surrounded by them.

In 1923, nine years previous to the honeymoon, General Cárdenas and a group of friends were crossing Lake Pátzcuaro in a launch. Some distance from what is now the Cárdenas home at a point between the island of Janitzio and the shore, the launch capsized. The general, after helping a number of his friends to land, became too exhausted to save himself. An Indian saw his plight and came to his rescue, helping him into his canoe and taking him to land. Cárdenas did not forget the act, and in 1932, when he was able, built for the Indian a small but substantial brick home. He also gave him a picture of himself on which he had written, "To Benicio de la Cruz who helped me to shore with his canoe when our launch sank, in November, 1923." He signed it "L. Cárdenas", and added, "Eréndira, Pátzcuaro, November 1, 1932."

In 1937 I saw the sequel to the story of Benicio and his canoe. I was on that same lake with some men, one of whom was a trusted friend of Cárdenas' and who knew of the incident. As we approached the wharf below the mountain slope and the little brick home, we saw a Tarascan girl of about ten years of age. Her head was a most repulsive sight, a mass of infection. We had heard of smallpox in the area, and at first hesitated to land. Our companion, the close friend of Cárdenas, got out and examined her head and said that it bore an infected wound.

By that time people had gathered on the shore and he questioned them about the little girl, finding out that she was the granddaughter of Benicio de la Cruz. Her father in a drunken spree had laid open her scalp with a long *machete*. As we looked at the sick, dirty little miss, our friend said, "I know what General Cárdenas would do if he were here, and I'm going to do it for him." Then he told the child's relatives that her father had forfeited his right to his daughter, and that he was going to take her to *Tata Lacho* (the Tarascan term of affection for Lázaro "Lacho" Cárdenas). He lifted little Chabela into the launch, and off we went. Once ashore, he took her to the train and directly to the president's home.

Sometime later I met Chabela on her way to school with eight other youngsters whom President and Mrs. Cárdenas were bringing up with their own boy. A long scar ran from her forehead back into her hair. "Chabela", I asked her, "do you remember me?"

The Indian lassie smiled as she looked up at me and said, "Yes, sir, I do."

"Are you happy, Chabela?"

"Very happy, I'm going to school." And off she ran.

The honeymoon of Lázaro and Amalia was neither very long nor very expensive. Within a month of the time his term as governor had expired Cárdenas was back in the army serving as military commander in the state of Puebla. The general had given away so much, including that brick dwelling to his Indian rescuer, that according to General Manuel Nuñez he had to borrow money to make the move from Eréndira to Puebla.

After the resignation of Ortiz Rubio, General Abelardo Rodríguez was elected by Congress to fill the unexpired term, and was inaugurated as president on September 5, 1932. On January first, 1933, he appointed General Cárdenas, then in Puebla, to become Minister of War. This was a manifestation of utmost confidence, for should the man in that post turn traitor he was in a position to take the whole army with him. A strong and trustworthy man was needed for the post, especially preceding and during a presidential election, since the records showed that it was during this time that most revolutions had occurred. A new election loomed on the horizon eleven months hence, and the nominating convention of the P. N. R. had already mentioned several candidates.

Reorganizing his department at a rapid pace, Cárdenas brought

to the War Department a practical attitude toward the utility of
the armed forces in peace time. As the news daily, *El Nacional*,
put it a few days after his appointment to the post:

Whoever has lived near to the new minister of war knows that one of
his predominant ideas, in so far as the function of the armed forces is
concerned, is that of linking up their existence with the daily life of the
nation. Instead of the soldier isolating himself in the barracks, General
Cárdenas tries to make each soldier feel that he is a man who keeps on
being a citizen, and that he should give his cooperation to whatever
enterprise involves the public welfare. In this way the army, even in times
of peace, can never seem like an onerous institution. Rather, it takes the
role of the strong arm of the country that, besides freeing it from disorder,
is capable of extending its help toward attaining new heights of material
progress and social renovation.

The promotion into the important position in the cabinet
brought Cárdenas into the limelight. It was not long before he
himself was being mentioned as presidential timber. He did not,
however, use his place as head of the army to further his chances;
rather, his associates discovered that it nettled him for them even
to mention the possibility of his becoming president.

However, the need in the P. N. R. for a strong standard-bearer
became more and more apparent. That year of 1933 was one of
radical fomentation. The ever-present agrarian troubles were being crowded into the background by the religious issue. More and
more restrictions were being enacted against the Church not only
by the federal government but also by the individual states. Since
any religious restriction pleased General Calles, the various state
governors seemed to be vying with one another to gain the
"Strong Man's" favor by adding their efforts to his in an attempt
to stamp out religion.

A campaign was extended over the whole nation to amend the
third article of the Constitution in such a way that the Catholic
Church and all religious bodies considered it to be a disastrous
encroachment upon their rights. The talk of the amendment—to
make socialistic education compulsory—so alarmed the people
that they were more concerned about the proposed constitutional
change than they were in who would be president.

At the same time trouble brewed in the homes over the efforts
of the Department of Education to implant sex education in the
schools. The people were disturbed, too, by the disconcerting belief that the regime was shot through with graft and corruption.

On top of all this, radical propaganda bearing the earmarks of Russia flooded the land.

As time went on the clouds of discontent became more ominous, but there was still no abatement of radical zeal. The extreme leaders were determined to go the limit. With the silent but evident favor of General Calles, they determined to take control of the party convention to be held in November and write a radical platform. Then they would nominate a loyal, respectable, level-headed man to placate the public wrath.

In the meantime Cárdenas kept his head. He saw the danger and was anxious to avert any trouble that would jeopardize the cause of reform. It was this potential threat to the revolutionary cause that made him willing to undertake the place of supreme responsibility, although at first he had been reluctant. Therefore, when more and more sentiment focused upon him as the choice for president, he consented. On May 16, 1933, he resigned from the cabinet as Minister of War in order to dedicate his attention to securing the nomination.

General Calles may not have wanted him as president. Some say that the radical wing forced the candidacy of Cárdenas upon him. If that is true he took it with utmost grace. Others say that as the political leaders came to settle upon Cárdenas as the best choice, Calles felt he would lose prestige if he insisted upon someone else. Whatever Calles' preferences may have been at the start, he consented to Cárdenas' candidacy before the convention met. If he hadn't, Lázaro Cárdenas would never have been nominated, Calles' authority being final in party circles.

The convention of the P. N. R. was held in the historic old city of Querétaro, and on the sixth of December, 1933, with "Strong Man" Calles' blessing, Cárdenas was nominated for the presidency on the first ballot.

A school that will form better men, better because more just; unselfish men who put the interests of the collectivity above their own; men who will form a new Fatherland, a Fatherland that will be to its offspring a true parent and not a step-parent; that is the ideal of our Revolution as regards education.

— *Lázaro Cárdenas* —
Quoted by Antolín Piña Soria in Rutas, Mexico, D. F. 1939

IX

SOCIALISTIC EDUCATION: THE MAIN CAMPAIGN ISSUE

For months committees had been working in preparation for the convention. They had investigated the needs of the country and had selected the most urgent projects for an extensive building and development program. They had gone over the projects presented by the various ministries of the government and had laid down a program to be followed out by each one. The time alloted for the work to be carried out was the ensuing presidential term, and for that reason the platform was called the Six Year Plan. The committee, probably in consultation with Calles, had done their work so thoroughly that the convention made few changes.

In Cárdenas' speech of acceptance for the presidential nomination he manifested his accord with the plan. He also said that he would look to the party leaders for counsel, but that he himself would be responsible for all his acts. The people who heard him generally took the first statement to mean that he would continue to let Calles rule from his exalted, though indefinable, position as "Supreme Chief of the Revolution", while they interpreted the latter as a puppet's effort to save face. As it turned out, all could see that Cárdenas meant exactly what he said—he, not Calles, was responsible. And because of that, trouble was to ensue.

The part of the convention that the public was most interested in was the endorsement of the proposal to amend the third article of the Constitution. Its provisions and purposes as cited by Beteta were:

Education imparted by the State . . . shall combat fanaticism and prejudice, and to this end the school will organize its teaching and activities so as to permit the creation in the young of a rational and exact conception of the universe and of social life.

The government had the exclusive right to direct both primary and secondary education and that private schools could be established only if they accepted the ideas, text-books, and non-religious attitude of the government . . . It was thought that the merely negative principle so far established was not enough. The Church had a certain philosophy of life, well-defined economic ideas, and well-known methods. The government should likewise establish and teach its ideology, preach and defend the ideas of the Revolution, and forbid the breeding of a class of enemies whose continuous efforts from the time of the Independence had been directed towards getting control of the government to foster their own privileges. This reform is known in Mexico as the establishment of "socialistic education".[1]

By rabidly anti-religious leaders this amendment was regarded as a legal means by which to bring anti-religious propaganda into all the schools, both public and private. As it was endorsed at the convention, it was accompanied by tirades of oratory against the Church and religion. The haranguing gave the public the impression that "socialistic education" was of necessity "anti-religious education", and the people's consternation was great.

The long struggle between the Church and the State had begun more than a century before. Dr. Beteta told its history to an American audience in the University of Virginia about seven months after the initiation of the Cárdenas administration:

It is pertinent to point out that there has never been in Mexico a "religious question" in spite of the struggle just mentioned. That is to say, the government has never attempted to change the dogma, ceremonial, or ethics of the Catholic Church. The immense majority of our population are professing Catholics . . . and it would be an impossible task for any government to attempt any change in that respect. . .

When the movement of Independence started (in 1810) it was a Catholic priest who led it. He chose the Virgin of Guadalupe as the symbol of the insurgent movement, which, rather than a war against Spain, was a true rebellion against "the bad Government". Yet the hierarchy immediately declared itself against the Independence movement and had the leaders excommunicated first, and executed later . . . From that time on the struggle between Church and State has not ceased in Mexico, and education is one of the points over which the fight has been most bitter. . .

It was not until 1857 that an effective attempt was made by the government to secure liberty in education. The constitution of that year made primary education compulsory, free of charge, and non-religious, when imparted by the government schools.

In accordance with such a system Mexican children were automatically divided into two groups—those attending the public schools, who were brought up in a liberal environment and taught to accept the separation of Church and State; and the other group composed of those children who attended private schools where they learned that the government was

[1]*Economic and Social Program of Mexico*, p. 164. Published in Mexico City, November, 1935, by Ramón Beteta.

wicked, the constitution atheistic, and the laws of the country contrary to the Catholic faith and not to be respected. . .

When the Revolution of 1910 was eventually crystallized in the Constitution of 1917, it tried to face the situation. Knowing that this duality in education had brought evil results, it went a step further than the Fundamental Law of '57 and provided that all primary schools, both official and private, should impart non-religious education . . . But in spite of the discussions brought about by the Constitution of 1917, conditions remained as they were before. Religion was taught in the private schools where children were again informed about the immorality of the government. They were told that the Labor Laws were outrageous and that the Agrarian Reform was nothing short of rapine. . .

This explains why, in a desperate attempt once and for all to control primary education, the Constitution was amended in 1934.[2]

The Catholic Church, however, saw in the amendment the scheming of its more rabid enemies and denounced it bitterly, not only in Mexico but in the United States. The Rev. R. A. McGowan, assistant director of the Department of Social Action of the National Catholic Welfare Conference, stated to the same audience at the University of Virginia:

This article of the Constitution is persecution of religion in the highest degree. It violates the right and duty of parents to educate their children in the manner they see fit. It violates the right of the Church and of religious organizations to conduct schools. It gives to the State the monopoly of something which it has no right to possess as a monopoly. It tries to establish a naturalistic and anti-spiritual interpretation of life as the official philosophy of the Mexican people. It inculcates hatred of religion.[3]

Back in the 1920's there had been a nationalistic movement in the Catholic Church. A Mexican Catholic Church had been started with the approval of the government. It endorsed the Revolution's reform measures and protested against the Roman hierarchy's opposition to it. Had the Mexican Catholic Church prospered, the fanatical anti-religious phase of the Revolution might never have developed.

As it was, the country was in turmoil. The clergy warned the parents against sending their children to school and in some places classroom attendance was cut fifty percent. Had arms and leadership been available, there may very well have been a general uprising. One priest talked to me bitterly against United States Ambassador Josephus Daniels. But for Daniels' support of the

[2]*ibid.,* pp. 140, 156, 158, 160, 162, 164.
[3]*ibid.,* p. 126

government's ban on importing arms, the priest claimed, they could have obtained arms and had a rebellion.

At times the situation became ludicrous. A mother told me that in the city of Monterrey a sound truck had raced through the streets advising the citizens: "Parents! Alarm! Rush to the schools and take out your children. General Calles has given orders that they all be branded in their foreheads with the letters P. N. R. If you don't want your offspring to become property of the devil and of the National Revolutionary Party, take your children out of school before it is too late." The mother had believed the warning and hurried to the schoolhouse dragging her children out of danger. The teacher looked on with amazement while many other parents took like action.

Not only the Church but all conservative elements fought the measure. Mass meetings were held in protest. Conservative newspapers published editorials against the proposed amendment. Even some of the members of the P. N. R. had argued that the measure was an encroachment upon the liberty of worship. But opposition or no, the amendment passed, for Calles had so decreed.

Protestant circles had not assumed the belligerent attitude that the Catholic Church did. Indeed, they were so far in the minority that it was very easy to overlook them. They seem to have done nothing to incur the wrath of the reformers, and often their work had met with official favor. Early leaders such as Madero, Carranza, and Obregón had regarded the evangelical forces as allies in democratic and social reform. Calles himself had contributed to the support of the Young Men's Christian Association. During this crisis the various denominations submitted to the requirements of the government. The titles of their church buildings were transferred to the State. Most of their schools were closed. Their ministers were compelled to register and in some instances pay a special clergyman's tax. Their foreign ministers were prohibited from functioning as pastors.

The Protestants did become alarmed, however, and with reason, for the Calles machine gave the bitterly anti-religious leaders a free hand. In various states Protestant churches were closed and the ministers expelled. Children were placed under agnostic influences at school. Occasionally congregations almost disappeared as weak believers denied their faith to gain favor with the authorities. But for the most part, Protestant denominations continued to struggle along and some actually grew. This was particularly true in the state of Tabasco where the evangelical forces were stronger after than before the bitter persecutions of Governor Garrido Canabal.

The Masonic Order found itself in a difficult position. Many high government officials and revolutionary leaders, including General Cárdenas, were among its ranks, and pressure was brought to bear to cut loose from its declaration of belief in the Supreme Being. A number of lodges tacitly did this.

Some anti-religious leaders tried to purge the educational system of teachers who were connected with any church or who did not support the amendment. Many teachers who refused to march in parades demanding the enactment of the amendment were dismissed. In some states the directors of education obliged their teachers to sign statements denying religious beliefs. Among those who refused and consequently lost their jobs were some of Mexico's finest instructors. Some, however, were not fired, for their directors admired their courageous stand. In certain sections of the country it became popular and almost obligatory to deride all concept of God in the classroom. A professor in one of the large cities told me that he himself had rebuked a girl who had written the letters Q. D. M. A. (Spanish equivalent for "May God Help Me") at the top of her examination paper.

Before the amendment was actually ratified the high-water mark of the anti-religious movement was reached by Garrido Canabal. He had such control over Tabasco that he was able to expel all clergymen, both Protestant and Catholic. His expulsion of the priests was legalized by the enactment of a law which prohibited all unmarried clergymen from officiating in the state. He closed all churches—they were either torn down or converted into museums, social centers, or schools. The icons of the churches and even from some of the homes were taken and fed to bonfires in the public squares. Even a humble peddler of Bibles was seized, imprisoned, and later ignominiously thrown into a public water tank.

The amendment was ratified by the twenty-eight states of the Mexican Republic and became law before Cárdenas was inaugurated as president. With its ratification, the tactics of Garrido Canabal were extended to other states. Thousands of churches throughout Mexico were closed. Articles appeared in official and semi-official periodicals and especially in educational magazines that battered away not only at ecclesiastical practices but often at the Church's creed as well. One group of school teachers and laborers in Matamoros even made the suggestion that all priests be executed as enemies of society. Such bearbaiting tactics were smiled upon, both figuratively and literally, by the implacable Calles.

One keen politician expressed the view to me that he was convinced that the main purpose which General Calles had had in mind in giving the anti-religious twist to the amendment was to fasten upon the Cárdenas administration a difficulty so great that the young president would not be able to handle it without resorting to his old friend for help. Whether this was true or not, Cárdenas as candidate declared that he was in favor of that part of Article III which called for the elimination of the clerical influence not only from the public schools but from private as well:

If the people make me president of the Republic I will not permit the clergy to intervene in popular education in any way, for this is exclusively a faculty of the State. The Revolution cannot tolerate the clergy's continuing to utilize the youth of the country as instruments with which to divide the Mexican nation. Nor can it tolerate their converting the rising generation into enemies of the working classes. The clergy is not sincere when it speaks to the youth of the land. Why does it today ask liberty of conscience when yesterday it condemned it, yesterday when it exercised a dictatorship over the soul of the Mexican people? The clergy asks for liberty of conscience merely to make for itself a new instrument of oppression and to keep down and to subdue the just desires of the people for liberty.[4]

Undoubtedly, Cárdenas was enthusiastic about the socialistic school. He said as much while still campaigning in 1934:

Only with the socialistic school, together with the suppression of idolatry and the liquor traffic, shall we be able to secure the material and moral emancipation of the people.[5]

Cárdenas pointed out that private schools would be required to use text books authorized by the government and that the teachers employed must hold the socialistic view decreed by the new amendment. Because of this view some church schools closed.

---

[4]*La Jira del General Lázaro Cárdenas,* Chap. IV, p. 93
[5]*Cárdenas, Apuntes para una Semblanza Espiritual,* p. 88

Some went deeper underground than ever. Others, especially seminaries, went north of the border. After Cárdenas became president it was said that as many as five hundred Mexicans were in Texas training to return to Mexico as priests.

Cárdenas outlined his interpretation of socialistic education in an address he gave on January 1, 1935, about a month after he became president:

The mission of the Ministry of Education is to teach that the socialistic way of living, in its moral aspect, presents the means of attaining true individual liberty, and in its economic aspect, implies a system which will put an end to exploitation by means of adequate limitations on the accumulation of private property . . . It should diffuse instruction in a way that will capacitate our peasants and laborers to improve their conditions of living and their methods of work. It should direct the activities of our people during their hours of idleness toward athletic and artistic activities that will improve and strengthen our race.

The immediate effect of the amendment upon education was disastrous. Some of the most conscientious teachers either resigned or were dismissed. The pedagogical ministry of the classroom became secondary to the new mission of uprooting "fanaticism", which to the more rabid leaders meant any belief in God. The fine crusading spirit of Mexico's great movement for rural education, one of the most interesting and ambitious of this century, went off on a tangent while many of its builders wept over the situation.

In the meantime Cárdenas was trying to focus public attention upon the constructive phases of his educational program. To him, the school teacher was to become the front rank soldier of the Revolution, for upon the success of the teacher depended the full fruition of the Revolutionary movement.

Cárdenas kept continually before the people the following program: 1) Money designated for public education was to be increased until by 1939 it was to consist of twenty percent of the national budget—an increase of more than fifty percent over what it had been the five previous years. 2) New federal schools were to be built—11,000 of them—an increase of over one hundred percent. 3) The problem of illiteracy—fifty-nine percent of the total population at that time—was to be attacked with vigor. 4) The rural night schools which were giving simple instruction to the working classes were to be increased. 5) Many more normal and Indian boarding schools were to be founded. 6) In

order to improve the country schools and help the poorly prepared teacher, teacher institutes were to be conducted even in
the most remote areas. 7) In order to unify methods of teaching,
the state and city schools were to be brought under federal control as rapidly as possible. 8) In spite of its unpopularity with
the upper classes, Cárdenas insisted logically on a broadening of
the educational system at its base by placing greater emphasis
upon elementary education for children of city laborers and
peasants rather than to heighten its pinnacle by providing a dis-
proportionate number of schools of higher learning.

The Six Year Plan as outlined by the convention indicated
that the sincere leaders of the Revolution were at least conscious
of the needs of the people. To them, religious organizations as a
whole seemed cold toward the pitiful situation of the masses and
the economic needs of the country. That was why Felipe Carrillo
Puerto, the great socialist of Yucatán, said to the peasants:

If the Revolution is of the devil, as our priests would have us believe,
then give me the devil, for the Revolution seeks to make us free men,
to give us lands and schools, and to redeem us from the bondage of
ignorance and superstition.

It was useless to talk of government by the people and for the people when the producing classes lacked lands, security in their work, and schools for their children, and when they were taken to the polls only to give the appearance of popular origin to the oligarchies made up of big landlords, capitalists, and intellectuals.

— Lázaro Cárdenas — to the Nation — December 9, 1938

X

A UNIQUE CAMPAIGN

WITH THE P. N. R. behind him, Cárdenas could undoubtedly have won the election with no campaigning whatever. But he chose to cover the nation from Mexicali to Yucatán, from Matamoros to the Guatemalan border, appealing for the confidence of the voters. In the seven months between his nomination and election, campaigning against a phantom opposition, he traveled a total of 17,119 miles: 7,331 by air, 4,522 by rail, 4,514 by car, 456 by launch, and 294 by horse. Big cities, small towns, villages hidden among the mountains—there seemed to be no end to the places this energetic candidate chose to go. And he went with a purpose; as he himself said, it was to "draw near to the people and to get acquainted with the needs of the country."

As governor, Cárdenas had advocated government *among* the people. He was just as convinced of that principle as presidential candidate. In fact, in order to establish a closer contact between the rulers and the people, and in order to train the common citizen to rule, he proposed a circuit-riding system of government:

The executive authorities, from the president of the Republic and the governors of the states down to the most humble village mayor, should travel constantly over the regions for which they are responsible. Only in that way can they themselves know the needs of the people, solve their problems, secure their cooperation, and bring justice to the remote corners of the country.

He also advocated large conventions to be held at a common rendezvous where the peasants and rulers could meet together and mutually participate in the formulation of policies. Perhaps, too, he was well aware that the more people he contacted, the stronger would be his position as president—a support he would sorely need if he were not to be eternally under the thumb of his supervising friend, General Calles.

On several occasions Calles joined Cárdenas on his journeys, ostensibly to help, but doubtless to counsel and watch as well. Always friendly in public, the older man may have had forebodings lest his own glory be eclipsed by a younger leader whose popularity was rapidly ascending. Whenever Calles addressed the people it was in a way that incited and disturbed them. Cárdenas undoubtedly sensed trouble, for it is said that he told a friend that his term of office would be composed of one year of trouble, another of reorganization, and four years of constructive endeavor.

Cárdenas as president desired to set up a government not of the army, though he had its support; not of the politicians, though he was able to manipulate them successfully; not primarily the artisan branch of the labor movement, though he worked in close harmony with it; but as far as was possible, and in an unprecedented way, a government of and for the peasants and day laborers. Time and again he urged them to rally around him. "I consider it very difficult," he said, "to carry out the program stipulated by the Six Year Plan if I do not have the full cooperation of the laborers and peasants in a properly organized, disciplined, and unified front." This was an extension of his earlier gubernatorial policy of proletarian participation in government.

Concerning economic problems, candidate Cárdenas came out strongly in favor of cooperative enterprises. Associations of laborers were to take over idle factories and operate them under government supervision, aided by government loans:

I consider that it is contrary to social justice that productive machinery be found inactive. This in itself constitutes a right for the state to intervene. If I am elected president, all those factories which have been closed and whose owners are not able to operate them shall be rented and turned over to laborers organized into cooperative associations.

Cárdenas lamented the fact that the country's mines were in the hands of foreigners:

The mineral production of our country has been fantastic. For the period dating from 1521 to 1930 the total production of metals is estimated as follows:

> 310 tons of gold;
> 37,678 tons of silver;
> 220,911 tons of copper;
> 539,499 tons of lead;
> 41,050 tons of zinc;
> 413 tons of mercury;

7,738 tons of antimony;
18,506 tons of graphite.

And these enormous riches—have they perchance served to help our lower classes? Have they even created Mexican millionaires? Have they helped better the living conditions of the ones who, for foreign companies, produce this untold wealth? We shall no longer, through an increase of concessions, entrust to foreign capital the exploitation of the subsoil.[1]

. . . Neither should we delude ourselves with hope of securing the prosperity of Mexico on the basis of foreign interests.

This was stating the situation in pretty strong terms. However, the statement was qualified a little later by the following explanation:

The nationalistic spirit of our political philosophy does not mean an attitude of the closed door, or of hostility toward such national or foreign capital as endeavors to organize its efforts toward making our country greater, utilizing our natural resources, just as long as it lines itself up in perfect accord with the laws which the Revolution has enacted, respects our government, and resorts for protection only to the securities which our Fatherland offers it, establishing homes here, and likewise enjoying its wealth here, while sharing with us our destinies.

Then the idealistic candidate got down to what he felt to be realism and hopefully stated what was destined to be the greatest weakness of his regime and the cause of most of its failures. "On you yourselves," he told the laborers, "will depend your welfare and betterment."

For many years Cárdenas had such faith in mankind that he viewed laborers through lenses so rosy he could hardly imagine that any among them were predatory. Wherever he met with them he would either hear only the side of the leaders, due to the reticence of the rank and file to face the dangers of retaliation by speaking out against them, or his own irresistible optimism would so take hold of the gathering of laborers that grievances were buried beneath banks of hope. He has since learned, however, that the dangerous parasite of "bossism" is not only prolific but also ubiquitous.

Concerning the land problem, Cárdenas said:

If I am elected president, there will be no one who can stop me until the peasant has received the best lands and the State has given him all financial, moral, and material aid possible . . . On the banners of the Revolutionary movement in which we have been fighting and in which I have had a

[1]*La Jira del General Lázaro Cárdenas*, p. 82

personal part since 1913, it is written that lands and schools shall be given to the peasants. To these must be added credit, the implantation of modern systems of cultivation, and the development of new products, as well as campaigns against alcoholism and fanaticism. With these the Revolution's agrarian program will be complete.

To some sections of the country where tillable land was insufficient or unavailable, he promised irrigation systems to make the soil more productive; to others he promised industries to provide other means of livelihood; to others he promised that he would move the people whose need of land could not be met to regions where the natural resources were more abundant. The time limit of only six years in which to finish the ambitious program seemed utterly insufficient, but he prophesied, "The needs of all our villages for lands will be completely satisfied during the presidential term for which I am seeking election."

It was inevitable that he should be accused of communism. Not denying his radical purposes, he pointed out that they were not communistic:

The Revolution continues its march toward socialism, a movement . . . which draws away from individualistic liberalism, because this was not able to bequeath to the world more than exploitation of man by man when it turned over unreservedly the natural sources of wealth and the means of production to the selfishness of individuals. Likewise it shies clear of communism because the adoption of a system which would deprive our people of the full enjoyment of the fruit of their efforts is not in keeping with their temperament, nor do we desire that the old sysem of capitalistic overlords be substituted by an overlordship of the state.

Seeking to wean the peasant from his age-long submission to the dictates of the Church, candidate Cárdenas entered a large temple in a village of Oaxaca, from the roof of which a priest had been making antagonistic gestures at the political gathering in the plaza below. The black-robed *padre* had come down off the roof and had fallen to his knees before an image as he counted the beads of his rosary. Within the church building the candidate began to address the populace loudly enough for the priest to hear:

The Revolution desires that the priests adjust themselves completely to the law and also that by means of education, the conscience of you peasants may be enlightened. When have you been spoken to here in this church concerning your rights? When has it been told you that you are the owners of the soil and should reap its benefits? The Revolution took the soil from out of the hands of the overlords because it belongs to you, and now we are restoring it to your hands. When has it been said to you within the

churches that you should unite in labor unions in order to be strong and
to defend yourselves? Have you ever been told here that you should take
direct measures against the vice of alcohol? To the contrary, the advice
which you have received has been that you maintain an attitude of obedience,
of submission, that you fall upon your knees and kiss the hands of those
who render you no service whatever. . .

The P. N. R., by whom Cárdenas had been nominated, functioned handsomely. Demonstrations led by bands and accompanied
by fireworks were held in all the important towns. Not a mountain village nor a jungle hamlet was left without placards portraying the official candidate. His picture adorned the walls of
out-of-the-way school houses, town halls, post offices, and private
dwellings from Yucatán to Laredo.

The one thing lacking for a real contest was freedom for the
opposition, of whom General Antonio Villareal was the most popular candidate. Some of the men who stood behind him were
Luís Cabrera, the prominent lawyer; the poised and learned Professor Manrique; and another lawyer and eloquent orator, Soto
y Gama, whose favorite and sincere battle cry was, "If I must
choose between Lenin and Christ, I take Christ." Many thought
that this was the real issue before the country, though Cárdenas
sought to draw people's attention to other matters. Issues did not
seem to matter much, however, with the *Jefe Máximo* and his
machine in perfect control.

Villareal would probably have been permitted to go ahead
with his campaign, but his followers made too good use of the
few opportunities they had to attack Calles. Cárdenas himself
went almost ignored in the tirades, his clean political record being
acknowledged—after all, they thought, he is just a puppet. Several
outspoken little weeklies such as *El Hombre Libre* and *El Tornillo*
denounced the avarice, corruption, ambition, and general wicked-
ness of what they called the Calles "dictatorship".

When the machine fought back, animosities were aroused which
resulted in bodily assaults upon the opposition candidates, whose
supporters were helpless to retaliate. Cárdenas tried to hold his
hounds in check, and upon reading in the press of a nasty attack
by his followers upon the opposition, he wired to the president
of the P. N. R., "I beg of you to give orders to our state and
municipal committees that they instruct all my supporters to
maintain an attitude of sobriety before all the provocations of

Villareal and his fellows, in order that said opponents may enjoy the protection of our friends, leaving it to public opinion to pass judgment upon the personal insults which they are injecting into the campaign." Through the press he pleaded for a gentlemanly campaign, saying, "I have counselled my partisans to combat the opposition with ideas."

But Cárdenas as yet was merely a cog in the machine and his plea went unheeded. Calles was not at all squeamish in making it difficult for opposition candidates to expound their views. Villareal and his supporters found it impossible to continue in the open. Some of them emigrated to Texas, a few went into hiding, and others pretended to forget politics outside of their own homes.

Right to the end Cárdenas went ahead visiting communities everywhere, making speeches, shaking hands with laborers, and eating beans and *tortillas* with the Indians. He was particularly earnest in his appeals for harmony. He defined a fatherland as "a territory whose natural wealth the people enjoyed in common." To this end he declared that "Nothing can justify the shedding of blood due to differences of political opinions." He called for an era of good will, a goal which seemed impossible at that moment so rife with animosity.

While others, including General Calles, came to disown parts of the Six Year Plan, Cárdenas took the entire program seriously. For him it stood as the yardstick of endeavor, though he realized when president that some of its stipulations went far beyond all possibility of realization, especially since the struggle with the oil trusts crippled the country's finances. The nominee's personal expressions often seemed impossible to attain, but they outlined the course of action Cárdenas was to follow as president to a degree of accuracy not often carried over from campaign talk to execution in office. Even the most difficult measures, with the exception of prohibition and one or two other items, were attempted in a dogged way that knew no discouragement.

July 4, 1934, was election day. 2,268,567 votes were reported cast for Cárdenas; 24,690 for Villareal; 15,765 for Tejeda, Governor of Vera Cruz; and 1,188 for the candidate of the Communist Party.

In addition to these, there was one vote cast for Garrido Canabal, the radical dictator of Tabasco, by none other than Lázaro

Cárdenas. We shall see from later developments that it was the vote of an insufficiently informed enthusiast. Leaders other than Cárdenas, however, had also been impressed by the Tabascan tyrant. Obregón had said that Tabasco, under Canabal, marched at the head of the Revolution. Calles also considered him an asset to the Revolutionary cause. He and Cárdenas had visited Tabasco to see him in action. In spite of its swamps, malaria, and intense heat, they had come away with the feeling that the state, under the colorful Garrido Canabal, was a little paradise for socialism. It was a place where the most radical doctrines of the Revolution were put into practice without fear or compassion.

Cárdenas cannot be defended for the way he was taken in by the little dictator, but the things that appealed to him can be pointed out. First, there was the democratic way in which Garrido Canabal rubbed shoulders with the populace, and required all state employees to do likewise. (A school teacher who danced with a dapper young man, but refused to do so with a barefoot Indian, was summarily dismissed.) Second, Cárdenas admired the ardor and ability with which the Tabascan enforced prohibition. Canabal taught the liquor-loving inhabitants of the state the evils of alcohol, and then demanded that its manufacture, importation, and sale stop. Bootlegging there was a serious offense. The first transgression was punished by a year's imprisonment; the second by expulsion from the state; the third, it was said, by death from the firing squad. There were not many third offenses, everyone knowing that Canabal was not to be trifled with. Beer was the only liquor that could be secured legally. Drunks were arrested and fined for the first offense and given long terms of imprisonment for the second. No favoritism was shown to either friends, relatives, or foreigners. Garrido Canabal's own father was given the choice of giving up drink or leaving the state. (He left.) In Villa Hermosa, the capital of Tabasco, I met an American foreman of a banana plantation who was cautiously preparing to get privately drunk on beer in his room. He had learned from experience some weeks before that being publicly drunk resulted in a heavy fine and a jail sentence.

With the election over Cárdenas obediently went to pay his duty call on the Supreme Chief of the Revolution, General Calles, who was on his sugar plantation in the state of Sinaloa. At the time of Cárdenas' arrival he was playing poker with two other generals who would manage to lose a sizeable sum to him since they were courting his favor. His aide assumed that the arrival of the president-elect was important enough to interrupt even a poker game.

Calles, however, merely said, "Have him wait till I'm through here!" It was an affront that clearly showed the president-elect that he was expected to be subservient to the *Jefe Máximo*.

Politically, the young "puppet" waited ten months. But then Cárdenas dealt a joker that finished Calles once and for all as one to be reckoned with in the affairs of state.

The Reforma and Constitution of 1857 made the civil government free from the Church. That ecclesiastical body had been sharing the State's vital functions for centuries. Since 1857 the struggle between Church and State has had only one reason: to prevent the meddling of the clergy in political, juridical, economic, and civic affairs . . . either personally or collectively.

The activities of the Church in Mexico during the colonial period and also subsequent to Independence retarded the social and economic development of Mexico. The social organization of the Colony in which the Church was the predominant factor depressed the Indian in his personality and sentiments . . . Apart from the beneficent service of certain illustrious missionaries who protected the Indians, the work of the Church in Mexico only helped to maintain the position of the privileged class. It served the exploiting class by taking control of education, charities, and credit.

— *Lázaro Cárdenas*

It is an error to try to fight against religious fanaticism with an anti-religious fanaticism.

— *Lázaro Cárdenas* — *1935.*

XI

THE NEW PRESIDENT TAKES OVER

FIVE MONTHS elapsed between election and inauguration. While Cárdenas spent them making final arrangements for the organization of his government, Congress under Calles' domination decided to place certain limitations upon him in the choice of colleagues. A law was passed demanding that all high officials have a "clean revolutionary record."

The dictator Calles' political machine was at the zenith of its power, and decided that it was strong enough to enact inquisitorial measures to discipline its members, as well as to safeguard against some young converts Cárdenas had made and whose influence was feared. The spirit of Torquemada has been carried over into the blend of Iberian and Indian bloods in Latin America to a marked degree, showing up as a desire to bridle or annihilate all opposition. It was the spirit manifested by Garrido Canabal and many more like him in fanatically opposing the fanaticism of religion and all that savored the least bit of it.

A committee of senators and congressmen was formed to which accusations might be made concerning political errors in the past on the part of any public official. Once accused, an investigation was to be instituted and the person, if found guilty, was to be expelled from the National Revolutionary Party and hence from public office.

Such tactics were not in keeping with either the spirit of moderation inherited by Cárdenas from one of the less cruel of the Indian tribes, the Tarascan, or with the liberal-minded environment of Jiquilpan in which he had been reared. But the Calles machine ruled, and added this dangerous political liability to the heavy load it was about to turn over to the president-elect. Add to this a nascent rivalry between the partisans of Calles and those of Cárdenas presaging a disruption in the ruling household,

plus general unrest in the country over the serious questions of
socialistic education, the closing of the churches, and the distribution of lands. Any man other than so confident an idealist
as Lázaro Cárdenas would have felt very uneasy as he launched
his ship of state. With such dark clouds threatening at any moment to whip the sea ahead into a furious storm, most observers
prophesied that he would have to lean heavily upon the strong
arm of the "Supreme Chief."

Guerrilla warfare did break out in different sections of the
country, especially in the north. President Abelardo Rodríguez,
however, backed by the "Strong Man", was able to hold down
the lid and turn over the reins of government to General Cárdenas on the first of December, 1934, in comparative peace.

Cárdenas attended the stately ceremony dressed in street clothes
and then nonchalantly took a half day's leave of absence on his
little farm, *Palmira,* a few miles below Cuernavaca, where he
donned farmer's attire and planned with his old friend and neighbor, General Mujica, how to utilize a water-fall between their two
places for light and power. No inaugural ball for him!

Chapultepec Castle, the stately residence where former leaders
and presidents had held court and wined and dined the rich and
noble, was thrown open to visitors. President and Mrs. Cárdenas
continued to live in their own modest dwelling, and later at Los
Pinos, a large residence near the castle.

The president came and went among the people in a most
democratic fashion. This unostentatious leader silenced the bugles
which had always blown a presidential salute as former heads of
State had driven to the National Palace in the heart of Mexico
City each morning. He preferred to go to work like any other
laboring man without frills and fanfare. The laborers, however,
soon noticed that the lights in his office often burned till late
hours of the night. The leader who was endeavoring at every
opportunity to reduce their hours of work and secure for them
higher wages was himself working sixteen hours a day, while
cutting his own salary in half, that there might be more money
for welfare projects.

I recall a certain amount of relief in middle and upper class
circles when the names of Cárdenas' cabinet officers had been
announced. Though bad enough, people had expected something

worse. There had been some fear that the rabidly anti-religious leader from Tabasco, Garrido Canabal, would be given the principal post, but to everybody's relief he was placed in the Department of Agriculture, where it was hoped that his anti-clericalism could do little harm (a hope that proved ill-founded).

The man most responsible for the attempt to implant sex education in the schools was put over the Treasury, where his radical ideas along those lines would have to be shelved, while he dedicated his outstanding talents and reputed honesty to the coldly conservative facts of *pesos* and *centavos*. One of the "Strong Man's" sons, Rodolfo Calles, also an ardent anti-religionist, was given the portfolio of Communications, a branch of the government which in Mexico includes the Post Office Department, the telegraph, telephone, and radio networks, railways, civil aviation, and highways. Ex-President Portes Gil, seemingly a permanent member of presidential cabinets, having belonged to three already, was given a portfolio as a matter of course. His reputation for being opposed to communism and being somewhat conciliatory toward the Church, pleased the people, though they had no high esteem for what they called his political opportunism.

New posts were created on the cabinet, one of the first being that of the re-forestation program to which Cárdenas was pledged. It is surprising to anyone who has thought of Mexico as a land of dense forests and jungles to see how barren of trees are her northern plains and the central plateau. Climatic conditions and the lack of irrigation facilities account for the dearth of trees in much of the north, but elsewhere it is due to excessive cutting down and insufficient re-planting.

It is a common thing to fell and burn trees to permit a crop to be sown. The land may be poor for farming so that after two or three crops are harvested, the clearing is abandoned and many years go by before the forest covers it again. In lowland regions such as Yucatán, the recovering process is more rapid, but in other sections it is very slow. Some villages in the highlands have been left virtually without firewood or timber. As regards fruit trees the situation is more critical, for a land which can grow almost any kind of fruit still imports apples, peaches, pears, grapes, and prunes from the United States.

Cárdenas, the lover of trees, extended his tree-planting mania, for it is almost that, to take in the whole country. He distributed 485,848 fruit trees among the peasants and farmers. To the incipient silk industry he gave out 3,635,092 mulberry trees. Most of the fruit trees were imported from the United States, but he established twenty-nine nurseries throughout Mexico where 2,014,-916 more trees were planted, many of which were used for beautifying highways, railroad beds, and reforestation.

It was natural that there would be some criticism. However, a great deal of permanent good was accomplished, although unfortunately a large percentage of the trees have died for lack of care subsequent to planting, and the mulberry trees have not been utilized to any great degree. Public opinion needs to be aroused all over Mexico to give proper support to the far-sighted and very important project of restoring her forests and supplying her with her own orchards, both of fruits and nuts, to enable her to export them rather than to continue importing them at exorbitant prices.

Patience had to be a necessary part of the program. Once Cárdenas sent a shipment of high-priced fruit trees to an island town in Lake Pátzcuaro. Later he visited the island and found the trees in a pile all dried up. He asked the Indians why they had not planted them. They replied, "You did not send anyone to dig the holes." He persuaded them to dig holes for the next shipment and now the town has plums and apples. In another town he had distributed orange trees among the peasants. A few days later someone came saying that so-and-so was selling his allotment of trees. The local authorities wanted to arrest the Indian, but Cárdenas said, "No. So-and-so must need the money or else he would not sell the trees. We do not want the money, but rather to see the trees distributed where they will be used. That man is distributing them, so leave him alone."

Although the Irrigation Commission was theoretically under the Department of Agriculture, Cárdenas gave the Executive Secretary, Francisco Vásquez del Mercado, authority and responsibility almost equal to that of a cabinet member. His job was not only building dams and irrigation systems but training Mexican engineers as well. He hired well-qualified American engineers to supervise the large projects, and surrounded them with bright young Mexicans who learned on the job.

With a large corps of civil engineers the extensive projects undertaken during the Cárdenas regime have proved to be but the beginning. Since then the great Papaloapan and Tepalcatepec projects of the Alemán administration have expanded the irrigation program which will need emphasizing for years to come. If the work Cárdenas started is but continued over a long period of years, Mexico can duplicate Southern California or the irrigation triumphs of Utah many times over.

Physical Education was also given cabinet ranking. The purpose was not merely to convert Mexico into an athletic country or to improve the physique of her people. Cárdenas believed with other leaders of the Revolution before him that athletics would be of great value as a means of combating drunkenness and of developing the moral fiber of the people. He also looked upon the movement as a means of weakening clerical influence by giving people forms of "recreation" other than that which they received at Church fiestas.

In the annual parade held each November in Mexico City commemorating the outbreak of the Revolution, as many as forty thousand men and women in athletic attire march through the streets of the capital past the president, his cabinet, and some of the diplomatic corps. Nor is it only in the capital and large cities that athletics are being developed. There are basketball and soccer teams back in out-of-the-way villages. One morning in a small Indian town buried in the mountains I was surprised to meet a runner dressed in trunks out for his daily practice. An Indian community where I have lived, where for centuries the only pastime for adults was drunkenness and mock bull-fights, today possesses a basketball team which has defeated teams from surrounding cities. The games have become a part of the social life of the townspeople.

For various reasons Cárdenas was not satisfied with the set-up of the Supreme Court and decided to change it, also making the tenure of office for the justices to coincide with that of the Chief Executive. He asked for and obtained the resignation of the Justices, whereupon he appointed new men upon whose backing he could depend in the program he had planned. It was a drastic move, but caused hardly a ripple on the surface of public opinion in Mexico. One cannot help wondering, however, if it was not noticed by Franklin D. Roosevelt with some feeling of envy.

The Agrarian Department, which had been created almost a year before Cárdenas took office, received special attention and might be considered as his pet branch of government. He placed one of his most trusted associates, the lawyer Gabino Vásquez, in charge and proceeded to back him with full moral support and all the funds that could possibly be spared. Thus equipped, he goaded the department steadily toward the goal of land promised for every peasant by the time his term would expire.

To expedite its fulfillment two banks were established. One reason for this very necessary measure was the practice of a heartless type of usury in the towns and smaller cities where the laboring classes found no other credit available. It is no uncommon thing for private money lenders to charge as much as six per cent a month. Among Indians I have known cases where the farmer would give one-half of his crop for the use of a yoke of oxen to plant and cultivate it. The poor person who runs out of corn by the month of September and so has to borrow from some well-to-do neighbor is obliged to pay, when the harvest comes in November, two pounds for every one pound he borrowed previously. The government banks which Cárdenas founded still have a long way to go to handle the problem in its entirety. Yet as regards the purchasing of implements and the planting and harvesting of crops as well as the fostering of small cooperative industries, the facilities they offer are a tremendous aid.

Actually, the first official act of the new president had been to close the gambling dens of the country, including the notorious Foreign Club of Cuernavaca. The public mind had been forewarned somewhat by anti-gambling propaganda distributed at theaters by two of Cárdenas' aides. The reform pleased the rank and file and gave them something to talk about besides socialistic education. On top of this came a presidential decision to exclude all police news from the P. N. R.'s daily newspaper, *El Nacional*. For several years it was one important daily you could read without learning anything about murders, suicides, burglaries, divorces, and the like.

Many reforms were attempted, though the public heard little about some of them. As an example of unpublicized temperance endeavor, I found when touring the Palace of Fine Arts that a beautifully furnished barroom was no longer in use. Turning to a friend for an explanation, I was told that as soon as Cárdenas became president he ordered it closed. Formerly, gay after-theater parties had been held there, parties that Cárdenas considered typically bourgeois and unworthy of the Mexican Revolution. I had never seen either complaints or commendations in the press. The general liked to do such work without publicity. The upper-class frequenters of the elegant theater realized that there was no use in complaining, for the reformer in the president's chair cared little for their aristocratic tastes.

Cárdenas' own way of life was even more strict than that which he fostered for the public. As long as he was president no liquor was served at his table or on the presidential train, "The Olive Branch". Since leaving the presidency he has been freer about serving light wines, for he does not feel that his example is so important. People in official circles respected his wishes enough that they seldom smoked or drank in his presence. One of his secretaries told of the time he had found on his desk a note written by Cárdenas. It had stated that smoking was noxious and that he did not appreciate having his office smell of tobacco. The young man did not pay much attention to the note and three months later another was on his desk, "It is not my job to try to change your habits, but if you must smoke, please go outside to do it."

Cárdenas never went to bull-fights, and he would not allow his little boy to dress like a *matador*, those heroes of the bull-ring to many a Mexican lad. His wife seldom played bridge because of her husband's objection to it, although since he is out of the presidency he has relented somewhat.

In quick succession came one measure after another calculated to bring popular support to the new regime. An order was issued that between the hours of twelve and one o'clock any person in the land, even the lowliest peasant, could notify the president of any grievance or need by telegraph free of charge. Cárdenas also wanted the people to know that he was just one of them, placed in a position of responsibility. To a peasant or Indian far back in the mountains of Mexico, it means very little that there is someone whom he has never seen, in a great city far away which he has never visited and cannot visualize, and who looks after interests of which he has no conception, in behalf of a nation to which he is said to belong but which is beyond the grasp of his imagination. To him, that someone called president has been little more than a glorified spectre, the "big boss" to whom visiting politicians and the boss of his local town refer when they have some special axe to grind.

With Cárdenas in the president's chair this spectre took on flesh and blood and turned out to be a friend who visited villages far and wide, listening to grievances with utmost patience and sympathy, and leaving in his wake new school houses, drinking water, grist mills, something or many things to let the people know that a president is worth having.

On one of his trips to the Otomí country I was there to see this flesh-and-blood president in action. The Otomís of that region suffered from lack of water, and Cárdenas had ordered that a well be drilled near the new school house. When we arrived we found that the drilling had stopped, and the rig was on the point of being moved back to the capital. The engineer in charge had come to the conclusion that water could not be found in the area—besides, with all the big dams and irrigation projects going on, what did one little well matter? But to Cárdenas that single well was of extreme importance. Those unspeakably poor Indians had as much right to drinking water as other people had to the irrigation water that dams would provide. He was deeply provoked, though his manner evinced the fact only to those who knew him.

When one of the local citizens told Cárdenas that they themselves had found water not far from there, he asked to be shown. The peasants led us over the hot dry ground, through cactus and sage brush for a distance of two or three miles. There a well had been dug to the depth of 120 feet. Providence arranged to have a stolid Otomí and his wife there drawing water when we arrived. What devastating and conclusive proof! Cárdenas requested his engineering companions to turn the windlass for the Indian couple, and took a drink of the cool clean water that was drawn. The Indians with pick and shovel had accomplished more than the engineers with their modern machinery.

The presidential party moved on and later in the day was joined by the engineer who had ordered the project to be abandoned. On meeting him Cárdenas inquired about the well, and was assured that there was no water in the region. (He had not heard of the trip to the hand-dug well.) When Cárdenas asked him if he had seen it, he said no, but that he would visit it the next day. "No," said the president, "I want you to visit it today! Come, *now.*"

Our whole party had to reverse our trek back down the road to where the trail took off through the cactus. The car stopped and Cárdenas sat in silence that was replete with disgust while an aide showed the engineer the way to the well. Profanity is foreign to the president's vocabulary, but on this occasion he did not even scold. Not a disparaging word was said about or to the engineer. But when that hapless fellow returned, the president asked, "Did you *see* it?"

The incident had taken nearly an hour extra of his time, but Cárdenas had promised those Indians water, and in order to fulfill his promise he had to convince the engineer that it was there for the digging.

About this time Calles was obliged to seek the aid of surgery and went to Los Angeles to get it, even though there were excellent surgeons in Mexico. This freed his friends in the cabinet and other high posts from the necessity of running to his home in Cuernavaca every few days for consultation. People smiled sardonically when they read in the papers that the great enemy of the Church was being cared for in a Catholic hospital. Cárdenas went ahead busily with his plans for speeding up the distribution of land among the peasants, building new highways, constructing schools, and pushing forward the many projects called for in the Six Year Plan.

The religious problem, however, shackled his hands to a great extent. Garrido Canabal refused to remain in the pigeon-hole assigned him in the Department of Agriculture. He saw no reason why agriculture and attacks on religion could not be mixed. As governor of Tabasco he had done so, expanding and improving agriculture while simultaneously kicking the Church. Among other things, he had imported some fancy stock from the United States. In the lot had come a thoroughbred bull and a large jack about twice the size of the ordinary *burros* which cover the trails of Mexico. He had dubbed the bull "Bishop" and the ass "Pope". He would exhibit these animals at the agricultural fairs which he held frequently during his administration, invariably giving them places of honor in the opening parades. The crowds would be regaled as the brass band played and heralds cried out, "Hats off to the 'Pope' and to the 'Bishop'!"

Now that his sphere of activity had been enlarged to embrace the whole nation, Garrido Canabal sought more effective means of fighting religion. He filled the offices of the Department of Agriculture with his Red Shirts (they wore black trousers so as to complete the labor union colors of red and black) who were followers from Tabasco. He made it plain to all the other employees of the Department that to retain their positions they would have to cooperate in propaganda against "fanaticism". He organized what he called "Red Saturday Nights" in the Palace of Fine Arts in Mexico City and ordered the same practice established throughout the nation. On those evenings orators would defy God to prove His existence or rail against the beliefs and practices of the Church. One demagogue tried the trick of challenging God to cause the large beautiful dome to fall in upon them. (Some of the audience were struck with fear and ran out.) Every employee of the Department of Agriculture was expected to attend these gatherings.

The Red Shirts which Garrido had organized to keep him in power in Tabasco began to harass church worshippers in Mexico City as opportunity offered. The new regime was hardly under way when the "massacre of Coyoacán" took place. The Red-and-Blacks went out to that suburb of the capital early one Sunday morning to expound their views in the square across from the Catholic Church where a special service was being held. The irritated worshippers replied with abuse and threats, and before long bullets began to fly. The fact that several worshippers were killed and wounded seemed to indicate that the Red-and-Blacks had done most of the shooting. Before an angry mob they had to take refuge in the police station. Soon after they had fled from the scene, one of their fellows, a late arrival, ignorant of what had taken place, put in his appearance wearing a blazing red shirt and black trousers. Here was the opportunity for the crowd, now become a mob, to give vent to its fury, and they tore him limb from limb.

The country was horrified and apprehension mounted over what might come next in the religious war. Many hoped that Cárdenas would act immediately and with drastic measures. They knew that Garrido Canabal was the man who was really responsible, and not the president. The one thing to do, argued unprejudiced people, was to dismiss him from the cabinet.

Cárdenas, however, took his time. That he was out of sympathy with Garrido's tactics cannot be questioned, but his hands were tied. While the courts conducted an investigation he sent the son of the "Strong Man" by plane to consult his father, who was in the northern state of Sinaloa. Evidently orders were given to patch up the trouble with as little inconvenience as possible to Garrido and his Red-and-Blacks, for that is what happened. Public opinion, however, felt that justice had been over-ridden, and held it against the Administration. The Red Shirts went on fighting religion and scandalizing worshippers.

Another organization flaunting uniform-shirts emerged upon the scene. This group, called the Golden Shirts, was supposed to be fascist in character. Scenes of rivalry between the Red-and-Blacks and the Golden Shirts took place from time to time and often resulted in blows.

Anti-religious measures were made more severe in most of the Republic. Thirteen states, only one less than half the total number, closed the Roman Catholic churches and several of them prohibited all public services of a religious character. Devout Ambassador Josephus Daniels became alarmed and remonstrated, but could do little more than to try to influence President Cárdenas, a pressure which eventually bore fruit. The states of Tabasco, Vera Cruz, Campeche, Yucatán, Chihuahua, and Sonora were particularly severe in the suppression of religious gatherings. The governor of the large state of Chiapas boasted of having driven all vestiges of religion from his domain with the exception of one priest who had been allowed to remain because of his alleged participation in the public burning of icons, and his sympathy with the principles of the P. N. R.

State after state was left without a single priest unless he was in hiding. The one outstanding exception was that of San Luís Potosí, where the Indian warlord, General Saturnino Cedillo, held sway. Scores of priests are said to have taken refuge there, and

Cedillo came to be looked upon as the champion of religious liberty. With an armed organization of forty thousand *agraristas* (peasants who had shared in the distribution of lands), and with a reputation as a fighter, Cedillo was a foe to be respected, and the Calles machine left him alone.

In February Cárdenas signed a decree prohibiting the sending of religious literature through the mails. Large quantities of Bibles were frozen in transit at Vera Cruz. Religious periodicals were also held up for a time at all the ports of entry. The statue of the Virgin of Guadalupe, which had been erected over a hundred years before in the middle of the street at the entrance to Cuernavaca, was removed by iconoclasts, and a bust of the great patriot Morelos put in her place. Six years later Morelos was removed and the Virgin replaced. Other acts calculated to enrage devout Catholics took place in many parts of the country. There seemed to be no effort on the part of state or federal officials to put a stop to it.

Cárdenas tried to turn a deaf ear to the agitation about him, though the opposition nagged him with appeals like this one taken from the front page of *Hombre Libre:* "Cárdenas, be President! Rule the country yourself." People impatiently hoped that a break would come between the "Strong Man" and the "puppet". The latter, however, showed no inclination to hurry. Quietly, he went about strengthening his grip on the reins of government.

For one thing, he placed added emphasis upon the enforcement of the minimum wage law. There were places in Mexico where the people would labor for as little as fifty *centavos* a day (fourteen cents United States currency at that time). Such a situation brought no little reproach upon the Revolutionary cause, since no one can boast about its achievements when the people earn no more than they did under the old *hacienda* system. In spite of the law which had been passed calling for a minimum wage of one peso and a half per day (then forty-two cents U. S. currency), only rarely was that much actually paid. The situation of peasant labor was bad and something needed to be done. Cárdenas hoped to organize it on a more efficient and aggressive basis and thus secure help from its ranks in the battle for better wages and working conditions.

The old labor movement headed by Luís Morones was going to seed, but could be depended upon to side with Calles if a break came. A new labor movement was arising under the leadership of a clever and cultured lawyer, Lombardo Toledano, who was committed to a radical program. He had spent a month or two in Russia and had returned with many "Red" ideas which he expounded forcefully, among them, the hope of implanting a proletariat rule over Mexico. Today he professes no such ambitious objective, but during the early part of the Cárdenas administration his extreme radicalism was a nightmare to the more conservative sectors of society. A gifted agitator and organizer, it was not long until he had developed a much larger organization than that which gave allegiance to Morones. Strikes became more numerous, and labor learned that its demands were viewed with favor by the president. With its own ranks divided, however, it could not take proper advantage of official favor. Strife between one organization and the other resulted in bloodshed in various factory towns and added to the unsettled state of affairs.

In Congress trouble was also brewing, for efforts were being made very carefully to line up congressmen and senators behind Cárdenas, as opposed to Calles, the "Supreme Chief". Repeated warnings came from Calles, who had returned from Los Angeles, but sentiment could not help being divided. The way Calles had of duping labor with high-sounding phrases and of frightening industrialists with rabid socialistic talk, while at the same time discouraging strikes and other forceful measures that labor might take, was something which his supposedly loyal puppet simply would not follow indefinitely. Cárdenas had promised to help labor attain its just demands, and he was determined to fulfill his promise. To accomplish this he knew that he would have to break Calles' grip on Congress. From many angles the situation had become impossible, but the labor problem was the immediate cause of the final explosion.

I do not evade censure nor appraisals of the work of my administration. It shall go right ahead, however, in handling the agrarian problem. As it broke up the estates in La Laguna, Yucatán, Lower California, and along the Yaqui River instead of building up estates for a new bureaucracy that would constitute a threat to the tranquillity of the peasants, so also it will continue to turn centers of gambling and vice into schools for the laborers and hospitals for the sick. Instead of utilizing the deposits of the National Bank for private speculations on the part of functionaries of the Government, as happened in the case of the "El Mante" Sugar Mill that still owes the government seven million pesos, . . . mills like the one we built at Zacatepec will be founded for the collective benefit, and the funds of the people will be used in extending credit to aid enterprises owned by the laborers themselves.

— Lázaro Cárdenas — to the Nation
December 9, 1938

XII

THE CRISIS OF JUNE, 1935

PEOPLE WERE ELECTRIFIED when, on the morning of the twelfth of June, almost six and a half months after Cárdenas had taken office, the two largest dailies of Mexico City confronted their eyes. Blazoned across the front page was the seemingly harmless headline: *Patriotic Declarations of General Plutarco E. Calles.* The inhabitants were astounded when they read the terse statements which followed. Beyond a doubt the break had come. The "Strong Man", who had ruled the destinies of the nation for eleven years, the man whose word had brought obedience and at whose mailed fist opponents had trembled, had issued an ultimatum to his "puppet". As the puzzled populace read the accusations and warnings, Calles, incredible though it seemed, now appeared to be on the conservative side of the fence. His erstwhile enemies in the ranks of business who had longed for Cárdenas or anyone to eliminate him from power, hardly knew whether to cheer or not, though they were in hearty accord with his views.

His denouncement of labor was categorical. "For six months," he said, "the nation has been shaken with constant strikes, many of them entirely unjustified. The labor organizations are showing many examples of ingratitude . . . Nothing can check the selfishness of the organizations and their leaders," he continued after rehearsing a number of instances in which the labor movement and its leaders had been unfair. "They have no ethics, not even the most elemental respect for the rights of the collectivity."

He affirmed his close friendship with Cárdenas and referred to the "good intentions" with which the latter went about his "tireless labors", but he made it plain that the president would either have to change his tactics or else meet the fate of Ortiz Rubio. He decried the efforts which he professed to know were being made to divide Congress into two groups, his own fol-

109

lowers and those of Cárdenas—and warned that such divisions, if permitted, would extend successively "to congressmen, senators, governors, cabinet members, and finally, the army. As a result," he said, "there will be an armed struggle and disaster to the nation."

The Calles statement was given to the press by none other than Senator Ezequiel Padilla, and his part in the affair won him oblivion for the rest of the Cárdenas administration. It probably accounts in part at least for labor's coldness toward him also when he ran for president against Miguel Alemán in 1946, though it did not prevent Avila Camacho from utilizing his outstanding gifts as Minister of Foreign Affairs when Camacho succeeded Cárdenas in 1940.

The public was accustomed to having Calles pose as the embodiment of advanced thought in social matters and the champion of social righteousness as well as of the rights of the proletariat, but to have him complain about too much radicalism on the part of his "puppet" was novel. It was most amazing to have the very man who had for years been shocking them into hysterics by Russian phraseology and ultra-radical propaganda now posing as the defender of the status quo against too rapid advance.

Though the change seemed incredible, many people especially in the upper strata, heaved a sigh of relief to have the man whose influence had always been decisive call for a halt upon what they considered the irresponsible activities of labor unions. The Constitution of 1917 had gone far in legalizing the most advanced claims of the laboring classes, but for years employers who were clever enough to stand in with the government's Board of Conciliation and with labor inspectors had succeeded in carrying on their enterprises while at the same time maintaining low wages. With the arrival of Cárdenas on the scene, however, their troubles had increased.

Before the Revolution capital had carried on its exploitation so unhindered that it felt vexed over any and all concessions it was forced to make to the demands of the workingman. Labor, on the other hand, was feeling its oats, and went to excesses. A dissatisfied worker might cause so much annoyance that his employer would have to dismiss him, whereupon the law permitted him to claim three months' pay as a bonus to enable him to live while seeking other employment. Scheming lawyers might also get him to present further claims against the employer, so that the dismissal of an employee, no matter how low his category, was sure to be an expensive thing. Striking unions were not always discriminating either, in picking companies which were prospering sufficiently to be able to pay higher wages and meet their other demands. In such instances, a strike could be successful only in the sense that the company would ultimately be forced out of business.

However, Cárdenas had declared that he would not let factories stand idle while workmen and their families went hungry. The manufacturers wondered if that meant that the laborers would take over such factories. Everything depended on the attitude of the Labor Board. If it declared the strikers to be within their rights in making demands for higher pay, fewer hours of work, or better conditions under which to labor, the employer had no other recourse than to close shop until he could satisfy the workers, for the Constitution and labor laws required the government to prevent strike-breaking in such cases. On the other hand, if the Labor Board declared the strikers to be going beyond reason, the strike was as good as lost.

With Cárdenas so strong for labor, it was not easy for the Labor Commissions to arrange things for the industrial interests, so that the strikes were being declared legal in most instances. As regards most companies the movement was doubtless within the bounds of fairness, for wages were truly absurdly low. American concerns which paid from three to five dollars a day north of the Rio Grande would pay one-third that much or less for equivalent work to their employees in Mexico. No amount of explaining could convince the Mexicans of the justice of this procedure.

Living conditions among the laborers were naturally very poor. A vicious circle existed, for the purchasing power of the laborers was so small that commerce was greatly handicapped in its quest for markets and hence feared to raise wages. Capital did not see the point, however, and resisted when Cárdenas sought to bring labor to a place where it would want and could secure better things. In some industries, however, especially those related to the building trades, there had been considerable prosperity in recent months, and Cárdenas knew this. He knew that he did not need to fear that thriving concerns would close down even though he obliged them to share their prosperity with the workmen.

Cárdenas stuck to his guns. He had pledged to help labor, and capital was not to bluff him. A Portland cement company which owned two factories decided to close down the one nearest Mexico City and move the machinery to their other plant at Monterrey. The change would have left the community of laborers surrounding the factory without employment. The government intervened and told the company that the machinery could not be moved. When the concern refused to renew operatons, Cárdenas organized the laborers into a cooperative association, loaned them money with which to carry on, and put them back to making cement. Cries of "Communism!" rent the air.

As a matter of fact, communistic activities had been going on for a number of years. Employees of the Department of Education had organized many a communistic brotherhood. School teachers learned to sing communist hymns and taught them to their children at home. In labor unions, the agitators had not attained quite as much influence as among the teachers. The old labor organization, the C. R. O. M. was openly opposed to communism, though the new one, the C. T. M. under Lombardo Toledano, was more friendly. Among the peasants communism had made almost no headway, not even in the strictly agrarian communities. Fiery little papers edited here and there enjoyed, however, using communistic emblems and phraseology. They published speeches and lectures by politicians and educational officials who had picked up a large vocabulary of communistic terms. The importance of these little "red sheets" was not great, but they did contribute toward filling the public with apprehension.

All this had been going on under the Calles domination. It cannot be disputed that there was more communistic propaganda in Mexico just prior to the Cárdenas administration than there has been since. Many industrialists had learned that the propaganda was not to be feared as much as it would seem since wealthy "socialists" like General Calles were interested in protecting their own fortunes.

The new zealot Cárdenas, however, was quite evidently a different proposition. He had no wealth of his own to protect and preferred that his close followers should not amass it either. He was well aware of the fact that ardent revolutionists generally had dropped whatever socialistic customs they had practiced formerly, when they moved to the Capital to take over the reins of government. There they learned to live in the luxuries of the metropolis and were influenced by an atmosphere of commercialism. Cárdenas sought to counteract this influence by his own example and expected his colleagues to follow suit. For instance, I met an important employee in the president's own office who had been left landless by the agrarian zeal of his chief. He bore no resentment, though, for he knew that Cárdenas had practised what he preached, by first breaking up his own farm. One of the president's brothers told him one day of a large farm he had acquired. Soon the president visited the farm as his brother's guest, and when the peasants surrounded him and informed him of their needs for land, he obligingly told them that his brother would break up part of his farm and give them plots to meet their needs.

Such a man could not be enticed by money and his associates had to be wary of taking bribes. The time when capital could crassly buy its way out on a big scale had passed. Intimidation was the next resort, and the one person best calculated to attempt this was the "Supreme Chief".

Whether capital had a direct part in getting Calles to sound the alarm or not, I cannot say, but it was quick in making up its mind to applaud its new champion. The morning after Calles' startling declaration, the newspapers published telegrams and letters of congratulation sent to him by various business organizations. Editorially, the large independent dailies commented favorably on what they called "the patriotic stand" taken by him. The papers stated that the permanent commission of Congress had voted unanimously to "congratulate General Plutarco Elías Calles, 'Supreme Chief' of the Revolution for his patriotic declarations." They also reported that a majority of congressmen sided with Calles in his attack on the "left wing". Automobiles with officials and politicians wended their way to the Calles mansion in Cuernavaca throughout the day.

The country knew that the break had come at last and waited uneasily for the outcome. Some expected Cárdenas to resign.

Some thought he would be ousted forcibly. Some thought he would submit to Calles' commands and finish out his term as an obedient stooge. Few thought he would come out on top. All realized that armed strife could be expected at any time.

No word came from the National Palace, but the president had not been caught napping. Immediately personal emissaries of his were sent by air to the outlying state governors and military commanders. These emissaries, only captains in rank, humble in appearance, and courteous in bearing, were the embodiment of Cárdenas himself. They walked unannounced, past objecting sentinels, into the presence of the mighty generals. "The president has sent me to pay you his respects. He also inquires of you your attitude regarding the criticism which General Calles has made of his administration." If there was any hesitancy or uncertainty in the answer, the emissary noticed it, and reported it to the president, and that man found himself replaced by a faithful supporter of Cárdenas before he had time to entrench himself.

After two days of suspense the president gave his answer to the nation. The newspapers published without comment his calm and forceful reply to the charges of General Calles. First, he referred to the agitation of recent days as "grave and unjustified". Unhesitatingly he accepted full responsibility for the condition which Calles had criticized, though he denied having fostered divisions. He blamed former officials who had not been given jobs in his administration for opposing him unrelentingly.

Regarding the numerous strikes, he attributed them to an endeavor to find the proper adjustment between capital and labor, and said that in the end they would result in greater prosperity. He promised to defend the legal rights of capital and that it need not be alarmed at his efforts to carry out the Six Year Plan. It had only to adjust itself to the program outlined therein. Quite the opposite from General Calles, he declared,

"I have complete confidence in the labor and peasant organizations of the country, and I am confident that they will know how to behave themselves with the self-control and patriotism which are demanded by the legitimate interests which they represent."
"If I have committed errors these may be the result of different causes, but never of perversity or bad faith."

The same papers announced that a left wing had been definitely organized in the Senate with twenty-three members (a minority)

participating. Congratulations, however, continued to pour in from different sections to General Calles. A small last-minute news item said that the executive committee of the P. N. R. was about to resign. Things were coming to a head. Again the populace was submitted to a day of terrible suspense. That the president did not intend to submit was quite clear, but would he be able to resist the "Strong Man's" power?

The morning papers of June 15 reported a very unusual cabinet meeting held the evening before at eight o'clock. "For the first time in the history of Mexico", read the *Excélsior,* "occurred the case of a President of the Republic asking his cabinet members to present their resignations collectively in order to better orient the administrative action of the government." The notice terminated, "Approximately at ten o'clock last night we learned that several of the cabinet members had left the capital in the direction of Cuernavaca."

The cabinet meeting had lasted for half an hour during which the president asked each member his personal opinion as to whether he should compromise with Calles or settle once for all the issue of who was going to govern Mexico. Having made a mental note of each reaction, he then asked them all to present their resignations in order for him to assume full and sole responsibility for whatever might ensue.

That most unusual cabinet meeting had been attended by all members except Rodolfo Calles, who had been travelling in the north with the head of the Irrigation Commission, Vásquez Mercado. When the startling news of the twelfth reached them, they had parted immediately, each one knowing that trouble was brewing and which side to take. While the younger Calles returned by plane to the capital and Cuernavaca, Vásquez Mercado went over into Texas to open a bank account for the Commission so that the legitimate government would have that much cash available if it had to abandon the capital under pressure from rebel forces. He then made his way to General Cedillo's stronghold in San Luís Potosí where he figured that a stand would be made for Cárdenas even though Calles should gain control of the rest of the country.

By the morning of the sixteenth the papers reported that the left wing had grown by last minute conversions until it had attained a majority in the Senate. Ex-President Portes Gil had been made head of the P. N. R. An extra-special announcement told of Garrido Canabal's having left for Tabasco post-haste by plane, and that his Red Shirts would soon follow.

Calles, in Cuernavaca, was pacing the floor like a caged lion. Finally he stopped and blurted out, "I am an ass!"

"What do you mean?" asked a friend.

"I am a slave of my own device—institutional government," replied the leader.

He himself had taught discipline to his party and preached obedience to the duly constituted institutions of the Revolution. Now when his opponent by rapid march and determined drive had taken control of Congress, the P. N. R., and the Cabinet, he did not dare oppose his own teaching by raising the banner of rebellion.

Had the leaders of the party and Congress rallied as one man to his orders, Calles would have had the support necessary to oust even the president in accordance with party discipline, but he had acted too slowly for that. Now the only recourse left him, if he were to be consistent with his own doctrines, was to retire from the stage. He issued a brief statement that he had no intention of interfering with the government, and promised to leave for his plantation in Sinaloa.

The same paper which announced his retirement stated that 8,000 messages containing assurances of support had been sent to President Cárdenas. A promise of fidelity and help from General Cedillo was given prominent space. Eighteen state governors, it was announced, had also notified the president that he could count on them.

On the morning of the nineteenth General Calles left voluntarily for Sinaloa and shortly afterward continued northward to California. Born to command, feared for his relentless persecution of his enemies, admired for his firmness, force, and statesmanship by friends as well as by many who had suffered at his hands, the "Supreme Chief" had been maneuvered off a stage on which he had long been the leading actor. It was the first time in the history of Mexico that a powerful dictatorship of several years' duration had been overthrown without bloodshed. Mexicans of all political hues heralded the accomplishment with profound respect for the youthful president who had brought it about.

Dictators who have attained supremacy by the stern use of the

firing squad do not retire without a struggle. With all due credit
to General Calles' patriotic motives, there were other contributing
factors. One of these is said to have been a loss of vigor by the man
himself, possibly accounting for his not having rallied his forces
sooner and more energetically.

For three days Cárdenas had carried on without a cabinet, but
on the morning of the eighteenth the names of the new members
were announced. On the same day the president, as though oblivious to the national crisis, attended the opening of the twenty-sixth
international convention of Rotarians. As he extended them Mexico's cordial welcome he told them that they would only need to
keep their eyes open as they travelled about the country to see why
his government was endeavoring to help the common people. He
invited their moral support as he set forth his own attitude. "Many
of us", he said, "have taken for our banner and life work the
liberation and betterment of our underprivileged classes, both
Indians and *mestizos*. Their condition compared to that of other
sectors of society is truly distressing."

The new cabinet was made up in part of absolutely dependable
friends from the former cabinet, the men who had counseled firm
action, besides several capable politicians who had supported Cárdenas in Congress and in their respective states. In the eyes of the
public the outstanding pillar was General Saturnino Cedillo, who
had been called from his stronghold of San Luís Potosí to succeed
Garrido Canabal in the Ministry of Agriculture. By this wise move
Cárdenas had supplanted the arch-enemy of religion, "God's enemy
number one," with the one man who had been able to defend the
cause of religion against the Calles regime. The picture of Cedillo
was kept constantly before the public in newspapers and magazines.
This change served more to quiet the minds of the troubled followers of the Church than anything else.

Cárdenas, however, was quick to make further overtures and
repealed the law prohibiting the circulation of religious literature
through the mails. The bitter attacks upon religion which had been
appearing all but daily in the government newspaper *El Nacional*
ceased almost at once. Whereas the editorial staff had formerly
obliged columnists and reporters to abstain from using words such
as "spiritual" and "soul" in their articles, a change of policy was
made which continued until occasionally Christianity itself was

mentioned in a friendly way. However, contempt was still manifested toward ecclesiastical hypocrisy.

The choice of Portes Gil for president of the P. N. R. served to reasure the public, for in spite of the accusations of communism brought by Calles against the administration, the people were quite generally convinced that Portes Gil was opposed to the Red movement.

Some doubting Thomases suspected that the rupture between the president and the former dictator had been staged for effect, and they could not believe that the country was out from under the influence of the "Strong Man." The majority, however, took the change at its face value, and a flood of relief swept the land.

Cárdenas now had the nation behind him. His daring had appealed to the masses. He had been patient enough to wait until he had the government under control. Then when the time came he had acted rapidly and with decision. There was not a faltering moment, not even when the press acclaimed his antagonist and half his colleagues counseled caution. The equanimity and rectitude with which the president had faced the situation appealed to all. No one was thrown in jail. No one was executed. The man at the top kept calm and cool.

Ten days after the "Patriotic Declarations of General Calles" had shaken the nation, President Cárdenas was down in the region of Cuautla, Morelos, spending a day and night with the peasants. A farmer who was present attested to the president's calmness in solving their land and credit problems and then sitting down with them on the grass for a picnic dinner. The farmer carried a pistol, for he was an agrarian leader, and the politicians of the region had done likewise; but Cárdenas did not. Unguarded, he rubbed elbows with everyone.

We are not prejudiced against the higher culture; on the contrary, it is our duty as well as the duty of those who represent the higher culture to unite our efforts in order to make effective the program of economic betterment and to do away with the superstitions and vices that affect our people.

— Lázaro Cárdenas—to University Students
March 21, 1935

There must be no anti-religious propaganda in the classroom.

— Lázaro Cárdenas—to the Teachers
March, 1936

XIII

STRIVING FOR HARMONY

MEXICO HAS SIX LIVING EX-PRESIDENTS today, a fact which belies the reputed high mortality rate for chief executives in that nation. All six are now living in Mexico with the exception of Adolfo de la Huerta, who comes and goes. At the beginning of the Cárdenas administration de la Huerta was living in exile in Hollywood because he had led the big revolt against Obregón in 1923. Another, Ortiz Rubio, also was in exile because he had aroused the ire of Calles, the *Jefe Máximo*.

Cárdenas made it plain as soon as he had full control that all former presidents, whether they had a record of rebellion or not, were welcome to return. His opponents in the election were also made to understand that they could come back at any time. One was even given an official position. Every effort was made to conciliate political enemies without sacrificing the principles of the Revolution.

Bringing back the exile was a part of Cárdenas' striving for harmony. While campaigning for the presidency, he had stated:

The painful spectacle of exiled Mexicans will no longer be seen in foreign lands . . . . The opportunity of living together with us in our joys and sorrows shall be extended to the Mexican citizens who are now in exile. They can never again present a real danger to the Revolution, since it is on the march and shall continue to go forward, supported by organized laborers and peasants.

In order to further unite the Mexican nation he invited back nationals who had emigrated to the United States and other foreign lands.

It has been all too customary in Latin-American lands for new presidents to forget projects which have been initiated during former regimes. They prefer to begin and carry out their own plans and thus give the impression that they want to get all the credit for themselves. Cárdenas, however, was quite as in-

121

terested in completing a thing started by one of his predecessors as in beginning something new himself. In fact, he wanted everyone, ex-presidents included, to cooperate with him in carrying out constructive enterprises already begun as well as his own new undertakings.

Ortiz Rubio was quick to return and was soon put in charge of the government-backed petroleum company, the only truly Mexican concern then drilling for the black gold which is found in such abundance under the lowland jungles. All the rest of the industry was controlled by foreign capital until the expropriation of March, 1938.

The people at large were quick to recognize the admirable spirit which Cardenas displayed in welcoming back the political exiles and putting them to work. They also liked his plans for developing the country. They could not, however, associate much strength and statesmanship with his kindly features. They had been used to the square jaw and stern eyes of General Calles, which to them had stood for law and order. A kindly man was a pleasant change, but everyone speculated about his lasting very long.

There was still unrest in the country, but it was no longer nationwide. Many of the state governments had been imposed by the Calles machine and the people there were objecting to them. Cárdenas went about the necessary housecleaning determinedly. In some instances where the Senate declared the state government illegal, the president appointed a provisional governor of his own choosing. In other cases, the people took matters into their own hands. In the state of Tamaulipas five thousand peasants marched on Ciudad Victoria, the capital, and camped outside the city, refusing to leave until the governor had been changed.

In Tabasco, Garrido Canabal had fled to Costa Rica, but his henchmen who continued in power were also unpopular. A group of Tabascans living in Mexico City in virtual exile from their state banded together in a plan to overthrow the state government. They had hardly arrived in Tabascan territory when they were attacked and several of their number killed. Cárdenas ordered an investigation and appointed a substitute governor. For a while the state continued as Garrido had left it, with neither saloons nor churches, but political liberty was restored to a greater degree than for many years.

In other states disgruntled factions, seeing the changes that had been made around them, tried to overthow their governors. Cárdenas, convinced that the illegal governments had already been taken care of, was able to call a halt to the indiscriminate troublemakers.

The affairs of the country were just getting settled after the big turnover when the president began to cancel audiences and confine himself to his residence. The papers reported a very bad case of malaria, but when the weeks grew into months and he continued to be ill, reports were circulated that he had been poisoned on one of his journeys. One notice even claimed that an Indian medicine man had brought him under his spell by the use of some herb.

The president had had every opportunity to acquire any of the tropical diseases. In his many trips around the country he drank whatever water was at hand and ate whatever was set before him. Neither drenching rain nor scorching sun stopped him. Whether traveling by horseback or inspecting on foot, he kept going. His wife, concerned to see him start out on a long trip with a bad cold, learned to shrug her shoulders. He would come back well. He always did. His associates, knowing the chances he took without incurring harm, came to feel that there was something mystical about him.

But now he *was* sick. Often cabinet members got instructions from his bedside. Then again, they would meet him walking in the garden—his hand hot and feverish to their touch. (Mrs. Cárdenas found it almost impossible to keep him in bed). Sometimes his competent private secretary, with the aid of daily interviews, carried on.

As rumors grew that he had little chance for recovery the old unrest revived. At least three different factions began to carry on undercover campaigns for political ascendancy. One was composed of moderate socialists; another was admittedly radical and not afraid of even communistic tendencies; and in between was a group of men not so much concerned with political theory as with a chance to rule.

The Red Shirts had disappeared from the scene with the fall

of their leader, Garrido Canabal. The Gold Shirts continued to organize and stage demonstrations, and it was said that they were backed by the new Minister of Agriculture, General Cedillo. Checking them, and watching for their own chance, was the radical labor organization C. T. M., led by Lombardo Toledano and supported by, or at least enjoying the sympathy of, the Department of Education and the officials of the Department of Communications.

Even the National University became embroiled in the conflict of views that was going on. Students with extreme leftist affiliations decided to bring their dignified alma mater into the radical fold. It had been the last stronghold of moderate or conservative views. From his high position in the University's chair of philosophy, the late Dr. Antonio Caso, reputed to be Mexico's foremost thinker, delivered lectures and wrote learned articles defending the Christian philosophy and attacking Marxism. The radicals might have tolerated the first had it not been for the second. As it was, their feeling that the University was a privileged enemy of the Revolution was accentuated.

It had not been affected by the amendment to the Constitution calling for socialistic education. It had been granted complete independence from the government a few years previously and hence was not under official control. Although in outlying states there were other universities which were operating according to the program of socialistic education, the National University exercised the greatest influence upon the young people who were preparing for professional careers. Hoary with age, having been old when Harvard and Yale were born, it was slow to change. As long as it was permitted to defend the old philosophy against the new, the radicals felt that their position was not secure.

For some time liberal educators had looked upon the National University as a nest of opposition to their socialistic tendencies and Cárdenas shared in this sentiment. While campaigning for election he had observed:

The member of the laboring class who enters the halls of the university or of technical schools does not usually become the leader who returns to take culture and help to his fellows, but, rather, is the very one who turns his back upon them and goes over to the bourgeoisie. Under such conditions, each son of a workman who goes to schools of higher learning is lost as a potential leader to the syndicate or peasant organizations, and becomes another expert at the service of the wealthy classes. The cream of the proletariat come to be, by virtue of this phenomenon, rich spoil for the purposes of the bourgeoisie.[1]

Taking this theory literally, and giving practical vent to their feelings, some students who had organized themselves into a "left wing" took possession of the main university building and barred the doors, announcing that no conservative professors would be permitted to enter the classrooms in the future. The rebel faction and the university authorities were deadlocked for several days, and rumors were afloat that the University would be done away with entirely and that in its place the government would form a socialistic institution of higher learning.

The sympathies of the independent press and of practically all the upper circles of society were with Dr. Caso and his colleagues. The University could not function, however, without a subsidy from the National Treasury, and Cárdenas from his sick bed made it known that none would be forthcoming unless there were changes both in the teaching and policies of the school.

The tense situation was not relieved until the University agreed to require that all its students do a certain amount of social service in behalf of the peasants and other of Mexico's rural millions who were unable to pay for expensive professional services. A new rector was to be elected, and Dr. Caso and several other anti-Marxian professors were to be dismissed. In return, the government was to grant the University a subsidy of two million pesos for the year.

Even this arrangement was not satisfactory to the radical element. To placate them, a Laborers' University was set up for wage earners and their children, with teachers of radical ideology and fiery zeal. Also, a Polytechnic Institute under the Department of Education was inaugurated, its purpose being to provide courses more practical for daily living than those offered by the University. A publishing house for the poor was established as well.

In spite of excesses the outcome of the "Battle of the University" was helpful on the whole. Because of it, social service projects were planned by the school. The professional students, before graduating, had to spend a certain amount of time out among the peasants, placing their newly acquired knowledge at the service

[1] *La Jira General Lázaro Cárdenas*, p. 97.

of the masses. Even critical *Excélsior* applauded the new program, but pointed out that it called for self-sacrificing apostles and asked, "Where are they in this day and age?" Results have shown that Mexico did have more material from which such apostles could be made than *Excélsior* had supposed.

While the trouble at the University was still unsettled and Cárdenas remained ill, the populace was electrified one day in December by a persistent rumor which circulated that a plane had arrived from California with General Calles and Luís Morones on board. The following day, official confirmation of the event was given by the dismissal of high army and civilian officials who had gone to the airport to welcome back the former Chief. Evidently Calles had come to lead the opposition. The political teapot began to boil more furiously than ever.

A small newspaper was founded with the express purpose of propagating Calles' views. It began by publishing a series of articles in which the general undertook to defend himself. Other newspapers considered giving publicity to the former Chief's propaganda, but Cárdenas, who was now recovering, found subtle ways to discourage them. The goodwill of the government-controlled paper concern, *Pipsa,* was important enough to them financially to make them act with caution, though the director of the concern at that time told me that Cárdenas did not use this power. Cárdenas did not feel it necessary to muzzle the press in whose freedom he strongly believed, but he also felt that democratic principles were not meant to serve undemocratic purposes and persuasively presented this conviction to the right people.

The little Calles newspaper ceased publication and people wondered what its editor would do next. He had come back at an opportune time, for his opponent was still a sick man whose followers were uneasy. Then, to the amazement of everyone, the president got out of bed, sick as he was, motored to his own country home near Cuernavaca, mounted a horse, and with a handful of friends rode off into the mountains to be gone a week. The newspaper reporters were taken so by surprise that few of them went along. Perhaps they were unable, on such short notice, to secure horses on which to follow him over the mountain trails.

When reports did find their way out of the mountains between Cuernavaca and Toluca, they told of plantations being divided up among the peasants, new schools being planned, and grievances among laborers being settled. Calles had been ignored. The people were amused. No one could doubt that their young president was *muy macho,* a he-man.

By the time the president returned to the capital, the atmosphere definitely had been clarified. His disintegrating political family had drawn back to its headship as chickens frightened by a hawk scurry to the protecting wings of the mother hen. The ecclesiastical forces of the nation, too, manifested their preference for Cárdenas as against Calles, though neither of the men was to their liking. Telegrams poured into the president's office from all over the country asking that Calles be expelled. Cárdenas had said for months, however, that his old friend could return to the country whenever he so desired, and now he reaffirmed this attitude.

Nevertheless, on New Year's Day, when it appeared certain that Calles was instigating seditious acts, Cárdenas went before the microphone and delivered to the nation a message which, while urging the people to face the situation without alarm, denounced Calles and his tactics in forceful terms. Then he proceeded to render a long report of what had been accomplished during his first year in office and of what was being planned for the year just ahead.

There was no waver in the president's voice, and his vigorous manner showed that he had won the battle over what the doctors had found to be undulant fever. There was no wavering about his plans either, and that indicated a complete victory over Calles.

That is not a nation that does not guarantee to all its inhabitants the right to live; nor is it a Fatherland unless it is united in productive labor and inspired with the goal of social justice for the present and for the future.

— Lázaro Cárdenas—at Dolores Hidalgo
1934

As long as human contingents exist who have been dispossessed of the lands of their forefathers as well as of their rights as men and citizens, and as long as they are treated as beasts of burden or machines, it cannot be said that equality and justice reign in America.

— Lázaro Cárdenas—to the First Inter-
American Congress on Indian Affairs
April, 1940

XIV

FOURTEEN POINTS FOR CAPITAL AND LABOR

THE LABOR organization, C. R. O. M. *(Confederación Regional Obrera Mexicana)* had been organized in 1918. Its leader, Luís Morones, led labor in support of Obregón and later Calles, who made him a cabinet member and recognized C. R. O. M. officially. The organization with this encouragement grew in numbers, power, and prestige.

The C. T. M. *(Confederación de Trabajadores Mexicanos)* was organized in 1935 and led by the scholar, Vicente Lombardo Toledano. This group, favored by Cárdenas, grew at a tremendous rate until it had outstripped even the powerful C. R. O. M. The competition and strife which arose between the two groups added to the confusion caused by the wrangle between labor and capital in general.

On the heels of the president's New Year's speech came a purge from the government printing plant of all employees who belonged to Morones' C. R. O. M. In other ways as well, the C. R. O. M. began to suffer official reprisals for the fact that its leader had been directly responsible for the return of Calles to the country. Furthermore, when munitions were discovered in a building belonging to Morones, he was kept under close surveillance for a time.

Calles was also watched, but was permitted to go and come at will between his city residence and his large dairy farm on the outskirts of the city. Suggestions of bringing both men to trial on various charges were frowned upon by the president. He considered it unwise to pay that much attention to them.

A new epidemic of strikes, however, was calling for the president's attention. The focus of fresh trouble was in the largest industrial center of Mexico, Monterrey, only one hundred and fifty miles south of the Texan border. The workers at the glass factory had gone on strike, and agitators sent by Lombardo Toledano were causing no little trouble to other manufacturers.

The city of Monterrey was in a furor. It had not been very friendly to Cárdenas ever since he had permitted the P. N. R. to impose its candidate for governor upon the state in the face of greater popular favor and possibly votes for an idol of Monterrey. Furthermore, Monterrey as an industrial center represented quite a concentration of capital, and it offered a good place for reactionary sentiment to gain force.

On February 6, 1936, Genaro Vásquez, then Minister of Labor, received a sudden telephone call from the president instructing him to go almost immediately to a suburban station with important documents because the presidential train was about to leave on a journey. Not until he saw the president at the station did he learn that the destination was Monterrey. The minister himself was requested to follow secretly in a few hours for the same city.

The following afternoon the people of Monterrey were completely surprised by the news that President Cárdenas himself was in their metropolis. His private train was soon surrounded by officials, labor leaders, and representatives of capital. Without any public show the president went to work. "This difficulty must be ironed out, and the sooner the better" was the burden of his message to laborers and factory owners alike. They were all invited to confer with him, and after two days of conscientious investigations, the president presented a plan for settling not only that strike, but the labor question in general. It was quite famous during the first half of the Cárdenas administration and became known as the "Fourteen Points".

It was Cárdenas' own labor platform. Few people had come to realize that he was capable of writing such a fundamental charter, thinking that he was quite dependent on his private secretary and other advisers for anything that required thorough preparation. They attributed the "Fourteen Points" to the brilliant young man who was with him at the time, Dr. Ramón Beteta, but the first time the latter saw them was when the president pulled them from his own pocket before the committee of laborers and industrialists. Actually President Cárdenas was unusually particular about having all major documents as well as important personal letters couched in his own phraseology.

The fourteen points were as follows:

1.   The government will cooperate with labor and capital in the solution of its problems.

2.   In view of the fact that strife between rival labor organizations themselves is detrimental to the government as well as to workers and employers, a united labor front should be organized.

3.   The government is arbiter and regulator of social problems.

4.   The demands of labor will be taken into consideration only as they come within the limits of the ability of the various industries to pay.

5.   When labor's united front is organized, the government will deal with it to the exclusion of minority groups which might choose to continue.

6.   Employers shall have no right to intervene in the affairs of labor organizations.

7.   Employers shall have the same right as the workers have to associate themselves in a united front.

8.   The government desires the further development of industries within the nation, since it depends upon their prosperity for its income through taxation.

9.   Current labor agitation is not due to the existence of communistic groups since these are so small they have no real influence in the affairs of the nation. The real cause of labor agitation is the fact that the just needs of the laboring masses have not been met, and the labor laws have not been carried out faithfully.

10.   While it is true that small groups of communists do exist within the country, there is nothing exceptional about this fact, since they also exist in small minority groups in Europe, in the United States, and in all countries in general. Their activities in Mexico do not endanger the stability of our institutions nor do they alarm the government, and they need not alarm the industrialists.

11.   The fanatical religious factions who assassinate school teachers and oppose the carrying out of the laws and of the program of the Revolution cause more trouble to the nation than do the communists, and yet we are obliged to tolerate them.

12.   The attitude of the employers of Monterrey is not limited to this city, but is reduplicated in such important centers of the Republic as La Laguna, León, the Federal District, and Yucatán.

13.   Capital should be very careful not to continue provoking agitations because these would come to constitute a rallying point for political interests, and this would bring on civil warfare.

14.   The industrialists who do not wish to continue to operate because of the demands of the unions can turn over their industries to their laborers or to the government for it to operate. This would be a patriotic step, but simply to close down the factories would not be.

His logic was hard to controvert though his conclusions were sometimes startling. The last point sounded harsh, but later developments have proved that he was right and that the threats of the industrialists to close down were not much more than bluff. The exasperated employers would have been willing in some instances to close their factories in an effort to bring labor to terms, but quickly relinquished that thought with point 14 hanging like the famous old blade of Damocles over their heads. If the reader detects an apparent minimizing of communistic influence in points nine and ten, let him remember that the nefarious ambitions of the Reds to make their power globe-girdling were not as obvious then as they are now.

After the difficulty in Monterrey had been settled the president continued toward the Texas boundary, visiting frontier populations, from whence he turned south to Tampico where he had spent so much time prior to entering politics. There had been considerable discord within the ranks of labor in this important seaport, and this had been reflected in political affairs. After inspecting the harbor and authorizing the building of a new wharf and other projects, the president went into conference with the different factions, giving thorough consideration to all the points at issue and then delivering his decision. It was a lively meeting.

Mexican laborers no longer manifested the submissive bearing of pre-Revolution times, often expressing their minds with gross discourtesy when in the midst of a heated discussion. It was not to be wondered at, for they had learned that they were free men and the Revolution had taught them to defend that freedom jealously. Some day the politeness innate to Mexican culture will gain the upper hand even in heated discussions, but the laborers who were present that day in Tampico had not reached that point. They had a lesson to learn from the most poised and polite, though forceful and convincing debater I have ever known.

As soon as Cárdenas' decision was announced the faction which had lost out made insistent efforts to have another conference with him. One of the president's party, an experienced lawyer with unusual gifts as a calm and persuasive debater, was assigned the task of persuading them of the justness of the decision, but found himself helpless before the angered laborers. He finally appealed to the president who was busy attending to other urgent matters which needed attention before his train pulled out.

Reluctantly, Cárdenas once again met with the laborers, this time ushering them into his coach. They jammed it so full that the president and his aide found themselves crowded into one corner. As Cárdenas began to speak with carefully weighed words and serious mien, something he said evoked a sarcastic sneer from one of the men. He stopped short in his explanation and looked squarely at the mocker. The atmosphere became tensely subdued. When the president finally spoke again his words came slowly and with such gravity that everyone was awed into sobriety and listened in dead silence.

"You laugh," he said. "That is why you laborers are not getting farther with your problems. You do not take them seriously enough. Were you president of the nation you would realize the responsibility which rests upon your shoulders and would try, as I have done, to decide the issues soberly and with all fairness." With that brief reprimand he returned to the question under discussion and soon convinced the men that although the matter had not been decided in their favor, it was their duty to respect the decision and wait for another constitutional opportunity to express their wishes at the polls.

In the disputes between labor and management Cárdenas continued to look sympathetically upon strike after strike. But about that time the Railroad Worker's Union made demands which the president felt to be unreasonable. The railroads were virtually government property since it controlled over one half of the company stock. Cárdenas felt that, aside from the inconvenience to the public in general and the set back it would cause to the tourist trade, the strike would constitute too great a raid on the national treasury. The laborers accepted his decision, one of the few against labor, and the strike was called off.

The president had hardly returned to the capital when he decided to make a trip to the north-central region of the country in and around Jalisco. Again General Calles was left to stir the teapot alone. For some time Cárdenas had been anxious to attend personally to agrarian problems in the Bajío area, and this was his first opportunity.

While busily engaged thus, the alarming news reached him of another religious massacre in a town not far away. Immediately he hurried to the scene of trouble to make a personal investigation. It developed that a cultural mission (consisting of a group of government employees such as teachers, social workers, agriculturalists, etc.) had notified the town authorities that they would arrive on a Sunday and conduct a program, setting before the people the merits of "socialistic education".

Having learned of the plan the parish priest in consultation with followers had decided to hold a special service in the church at the same time the teachers would hold their session in the public square close by. The teachers came, accompanied by agrarian militiamen (peasants who had received not only lands but also arms with which to protect them). As the educational session got under way the mob in and around the church began to jeer. The commotion increased until there was an exchange of bullets. Some individuals were killed and others wounded.

From witnesses, the president found to his own satisfaction that the major part of the blame could be attributed to the priest. He went into the church building to speak to him personally. Unhesitatingly, and in the presence of the people, he served notice to the religious leader that as an undesirable agitator he would have to leave the town within forty-eight hours.

The conservative press criticized Cárdenas for his temerity at having entered a church building to administer justice in person and so summarily. He considered it necessary, however, to show the ecclesiastical authorities that though he had restored privileges to them, it did not entitle them to incite the people to violence.

From this tussle with the Church the president extended his trip to include a convention of peasants and a meeting of school teachers who had been encountering no little trouble in their efforts to implant socialistic education in the area which had been the scene of the *cristero* uprising eight years previous. Their experiences had not been different from those of instructors in many parts of the country. Here and there, in isolated towns from Jalisco to Yucatán, teachers had been tortured by having their ears cut off or otherwise maltreated. Some had even been killed. I myself visited a town in Yucatán where the teacher had been slain by fanatics.

The reasons generally given for these crimes by the devout worshippers who perpetrated them was that the teachers had been too zealous about implanting socialistic education, had argued too vehemently against idolatry or had pushed the distribution of lands too vigorously.

It must be admitted by all that the rural teachers took the risks involved in their mission in a heroic manner, but when the opportunity came to ask protection from the president they came in large numbers to the town in Jalisco where he had gone. There they told him of how their lives were imperiled due to the opposition of the peasants under the influence of the Church. On the other hand, some of the teachers had attached such importance to the combating of religious ideas that it had imperiled the whole program of social reform.

The president's reply to them was one of the most important pronouncements of recent Mexican history. By it he did more to eliminate the religious issue from Mexican politics than had any of his predecessors. In his statement he explained that his administration would not fall into the same error as had been committed by previous administrations in carrying on propaganda against religion.

"Hereafter", he said, "there must be no anti-religious propaganda in the classroom. All our attention must be concentrated upon the great Cause of social reform."

The declaration made there to the school teachers was published in all of the nation's dailies, and in the official organ of the Department of Education as well, which had previously taken delight in publishing anti-religious propaganda. Such articles, however, were faithfully excluded thereafter in compliance with the demand of the president.

April found Cárdenas back in the capital where Calles had been no little vexed that so little importance had been attached to him by the president. By then, however, Cárdenas did decide that the former strong man's presence was inadvisable. A number of train wrecks had occurred, and although it is possible that General Calles had nothing to do with them, yet the people were quick to attribute them to his machinations. Morones, too, continued to foster strife between the C. R. O. M. and the C. T. M.

On the tenth of April the president was expected at a celebration in the city of Cuautla, Morelos, in commemoration of the death of Zapata. Two members of the cabinet, one of them General Cedillo, led the parade. Manrique and Díaz Soto y Gama gave orations attacking communistic influences. They frankly said that they were for Cárdenas, their former opponent, as long as he continued to be for the people. Cárdenas' appearance was expected any time, but at the last moment word came not to wait for him. The celebration terminated without the president's having come.

He was busy in the capital, it was learned the next day, making arrangements for starting his old friend Calles off on a journey.

That night, shortly after ten o'clock, a high army officer marched into the residence of General Calles out at the dairy farm and informed him that he had come to spend the night there and help him pack for an airplane trip in the morning. The old general needed no further explanation, but proceeded to get ready. Morones had been similarly advised, and six o'clock the following morning found them both at the airport. They did not even have to buy tickets. Cárdenas had arranged this detail for them.

Everyone seemed anxious to help them get away. Even Ambassador Daniels seemed happy when a phone call came from the Ministry of Foreign Relations stating apologetically that Calles' plane was already nearing Brownsville and that he didn't have a visa. Would the ambassador kindly telephone instructions so that the general and Morones would not be left sitting on the border fence? The ambassador obligingly handled the visa problem and Calles and Morones were admitted at Brownsville.

In fact, a number of newspaper reporters met them. To them Calles stated, previous to continuing his trip to California, that Cárdenas was too weak to handle the situation very long and that inevitably his fatherland was going to fall into a chaotic condition in which it would become a ready prey for communism, a prediction that was even gloomier in the dim light of worldwide depression then prevailing.

But the "weakling" had once again gotten the better of the "strong man", and without resort to bloodshed.

Your chief executive does not seek applause, nor manifestations whether big or small, nor banquets that only lull to sleep the revolutionary spirit and place a burden on the budget . . . Rather may all sectors of society feel the benefits of the incumbent's services.

— *Lázaro Cárdenas—to Students in Jalisco*
July 18, 1935

Friends are all those whom you desire to serve even though they oppose you.

— *Lázaro Cárdenas—to Almada and Townsend*
July 7, 1939

XV

CARDENAS AS FRIEND

THE BIGGEST thing about Mexico is the heart of her people. Few foreigners understand this fact. They try to interpret the country in terms of dollars and cents and consequently fail to understand her. Mexico is a land of friendships. Friendship is the most valuable medium of exchange. It has no abiding substitute, though it is often found in such base alloy that it will not stand the acid test of political convenience or mercenary gain. Lázaro Cárdenas is a devout worshipper at the altar of friendship. This great friend of Mexicans is himself enshrined in thousands of hearts of forgotten men across the length and breadth of the land.

On a rocky trail in a remote region of the state of Oaxaca where Mixe aborigines still maintain their aloofness from civilization, a young American linguist met an Indian who could speak a little Spanish. In the ensuing conversation the Mixe manifested considerable interest over the fact that a foreigner had found his way into the mountain fastnesses of his tribe. Then his face brightened and he exclaimed, "Our president has traveled over this trail too. Other presidents have been afraid to come, for we have a bad reputation, but President Lázaro Cárdenas is not afraid. He goes every place. When he was here he did not even try to keep with his companions, but would get off his horse and walk out among our huts all by himself to talk with us."

In the Aztec village of Tetelcingo the mayor was a barefoot Indian who had spent eleven years in the army, first in the forces of Zapata and later in those of Carranza and Obregón. Through this contact with people who could not speak his own language he had learned to speak Spanish and hence was able to converse with the president without an interpreter on the occasion of his first visit to the village. Cárdenas conducted himself with the Indians

139

in such a sincere and earnest way and encouraged them to talk back with such frankness that he completely won their hearts.

After granting their requests for numerous improvements he rode off in his automobile waving a friendly farewell. The Indian mayor, seasoned soldier though he was, stood watching with tears in his eyes as the car drove away. Then he turned to me and said, "I would follow that man any place. Of course I would hate to leave my wife and children, but any day that man needs me I will go most gladly."

The following day I needed the assistance of the barefoot mayor and went to look for him. What was my surprise to find that the ignorant unschooled man who had learned to read and write beside the army campfires was in his hut bent over a soap box, straining to write in poetic form an expression of his devotion to the president. Cárdenas' love for the masses aroused the masses' love for him.

The concept Cárdenas holds of friendship is a far departure from the commonly accepted meaning of the term. One day after he had spoken to a large gathering I overheard a member of his official family say, "Mr. President, that's a large crowd and they are practically all your friends. A few among them are critics, but not many." The president replied, "The critics are my friends, too."

He did not mean merely that their criticisms were welcome. He went on to explain that a friend is anyone whom you desire to serve. Since he desired to help all, they were all his friends. He loves the common people and trusts them to a fault. His faith in humanity is so great that he seems to love and trust almost everyone.

This does not mean, dangerous as the trait would seem, that President Cárdenas closed his eyes to the failures of his friends to carry out the commissions he had entrusted into their hands. When he has given clear instructions to an associate who subsequently fails, he exhorts him patiently, but if this does not avail he proceeds to discipline him. One of his most trusted army officers failed to carry out his orders to keep the dens of vice closed in the territory over which he had been placed, and when the charges had been fully established the president discharged him without hesitation.

However, Cárdenas took pains to maintain the friendship of

his subordinates. Even though it meant a seeming loss of prestige to the president himself not to be able to secure immediate obedience upon the part of a cabinet member, politician, or labor leader, he waited to talk the man into doing his will and then let him take a certain amount of time complying, so as to give the public the impression that the man fell in line of his own volition. In the same way he frequently managed to maintain personal friendship with men who openly opposed his political measures.

In the fall of 1936 one cabinet member was caught using his position and part of his budget in an effort to build up a political machine of his own. His friends expected him to be fired, but Cárdenas hated to lose the services of an old and faithful friend. He talked to the overly ambitious member and pointed out how detrimental it was for the Revolutionary forces to divide their strength in a premature political struggle. The man acquiesced and continued in office.

I once went into Cárdenas' office with a book on Mexico in my hand. Cárdenas had seen it and knew that the American author, while absolving him completely of dishonest dealings, nevertheless had stated that through a tip concerning President Roosevelt's silver policy, Cárdenas had made an investment on the silver market in New York which had made him a millionaire.

It was nine o'clock at night, the president had had a very busy day, and during a visit to a public works project on the outskirts of the capital he had been drenched by rain so that he had caught cold and was quite hoarse. After we conversed awhile and he had noticed the book I carried, he called for a piece of paper and with his red pencil wrote out the following statement over his signature:

So-and-so writes in his book that I took part in a gamble on the stock exchange which made me a millionaire. It is a lie. Money does not interest me. My sole desire is to be able to fulfill my duty. — June 4, 1937.

His whole frame seemed to vibrate as he wrote out the statement. On his face was no expression of anger—just dynamic seriousness. The very way he drove the pencil across the page spoke of pent-up force. I wondered why he had made the statement in writing rather than verbally. Of course, his hoarseness offered one clue, and greater emphasis was another, but best of all, he gave a well-meditated declaration in permanent form regarding the falsity of the accusation.

During his six years in office Cárdenas was away from the capital approximately one-third of the time, or 673 work days. He traveled a total of 54,695 miles by train, automobile, horseback, steamship, bus, and on foot. In doing so he made 143 expeditions, and visited all 28 states, 3 territories, and 1,193 cities and towns of the Mexican Union. The mileage covered on his electoral campaign added to the figure already given makes a total of 71,950 miles traveled in a effort to establish close contact with the entire populace and to minister to their needs.

Wherever he went the crowds surrounded him from morning till night but rarely did his powerful shoulders seem to bend under the load. I watched him once in a desert town in Sonora on a bright tropical moonlight night after a two-months' traveling tour of the north. He had left the train and had been gone all day, motoring throughout the country district. Eighteen hours had been crammed full of activity, problems, and people, with some disappointing reverses in his own plans. At midnight he was returning for a little rest, but even at that late hour peasant women with babies on their backs, laborers, and aged infirm people were there waiting for him.

As he moved from the car to the train they crowded around, moving with him, jostling one another in their eagerness to touch the cuffs of his garments, all the while pouring into his ears one long stream of petitions. Cárdenas looked tired, worn, and somewhat discouraged. Then he mounted the steps of the rear platform and turned to say goodbye to a commission of laborers. Standing there on the train steps his visible weariness disappeared. As he took time to exchange a few words in neighborly fashion with the laborers, there was not one trace of discouragement on his face, though the silvery glow of the moon made his every feature discernible.

Cárdenas gained strength from the people—the common people—and with them to serve, he took in his stride the eighteen-hour days of problems and disappointments.

But the president did not pay attention to the common folk only when on trips. In the capital, too, audiences were granted to the public each evening until nine, ten, or later. Once I waited in the anteroom of his office at Los Pinos until after midnight in the hope of getting an interview. The vestibule was crowded with men more likely to get in than I—congressmen, generals, relatives, old friends, and labor leaders. At twelve-thirty, after a full hour with the president, a large commission of miners came out. Those of us in the anteroom waited, wondering which one would be next. To our amazement another commission composed of some thirty peasants was ushered from the street into the presence of the president. Realizing that they would be in for another hour, I for one went home.

I once asked President Cárdenas how he was able to work sixteen to eighteen hours a day consistently, and he replied: "While it is probably true that I have inherited an unusually strong constitution, I have found that even the weakest of bodies can accomplish a great deal of work when driven by the force of will."

I said nothing in reply, but inside I was thinking: "Quite true, Mr. President, but your stamina and driving power are not what surprise me the most in you. The world often produces leaders who have an inexplicable capacity for work, but what I cannot explain is the way you always keep patient under the load."

That problem still perplexes me. I have heard one of the general's hardest working associates, a man also of iron constitution who does not dissipate his energy in vices and who possesses unusual self-control and force of will, tell his secretary in exasspiration, "Don't let another person in to see me or I'll go crazy." He had been working excessively long hours for weeks on some of the president's most delicate problems, and yet was expected to meet job hunters, politicians, and the like up until ten o'clock at night. No wonder that his patience gave out!

President Cárdenas, however, would go right on receiving the multitudes, listening to their woes, trying to help, counseling and reproving, but never losing his patience. He is the world's champion listener. "Surely," he argues, "I can at least *listen* to what the people have to say when they have had to suffer so many centuries in silence."

The peasant's stock soared above par in Mexico for the first time in history. Even when shaking hands with a crowd President

Cárdenas would not make the slightest move to grasp the hand of an old friend or an influential politician in preference to that of an unknown peasant who was reaching for it.

People from every walk of life felt free to visit the president's anteroom: cabinet members or officials with scheduled interviews, teachers, professional men, barefoot Indians, city laborers. Almost anyone, even capitalists, seemed to get a hearing if they waited long enough.

Once admitted, the teacher, official, or humble peasant had the president's entire attention. No one was rushed. Each, according to Ignacio García Téllez, a close co-laborer of Cárdenas', was heard through; and when he finally finished speaking it was because he had exhausted his problem, never his listener.

In every interview the president revealed a remarkable absence of prejudice, basing his decision upon the merits of the case in question. This has resulted disadvantageously at times, for it would lead him to make promises whose fulfillment his more prejudiced colleagues might cleverly obstruct. However, this must not be taken to mean that he went into each interview with the weather-vane of his mind free to swing in any direction. On the contrary, he has certain predetermined principles which brought him to decisions rapidly in most cases.

Requests for favors were granted immediately if they were at all reasonable and possible. Labor and the poor were favored as over against capital if this could be done legally; suggestions for development projects were always welcomed and considered, even though they might have appeared to be just visionary schemes; and vindictiveness or favoritism among friends was squelched without delay. Opportunties to show kindness to antagonists have been utilized so consistently, some of his closest friends say that they would have gotten more favors from him had they been enemies.

The knowledge which the president had accumulated in his trips around the country made him quick to understand suggestions as they were made to him. I once heard a stranger propose to Cárdenas five different projects. The first two were concerning irrigation schemes in different sections of the country. It developed that the president had already studied both problems carefully and could give more figures concerning them than could the proponent himself. The third suggestion concerned the building of a breakwater at a forgotten port on the Pacific Coast. It so happened that the president had already visited the out-of-the-way place personally and knew just what a breakwater there would cost. The self-styled adviser tried again, this time suggesting the bringing up of wild grape vines from a region where they were found in abundance, setting them out in a valley not far from the capital where grapes were unknown, and grafting good varieties onto them. President Cárdenas accepted the idea with enthusiasm. The fifth suggestion involved the providing of drinking water and possible irrigation for a number of towns dependent during the dry season on waterholes for their supply. This fifth project was immediately taken up by Cárdenas, and he put into motion the machinery which was to carry it out.

Of course it was impossible for one man to listen to all the individual wants of a nation. To aid him in this task Cárdenas set up an office for complaints and placed General Pizá Martínez at the head of it. To Cárdenas, it was one of the most sacred tasks he allotted to anyone. Once a week Pizá Martínez dined with the president; frequently he rode with him to and from the office; and together, in these snatched moments, they went over the problems of the individuals. At times, when there seemed to be no other opportunity to hear a case to which the president wanted to give his personal attention, he invited the petitioner to eat with him or to come to the pool for a swim and a chat before breakfast.

Thus, even at the table or at recreation, he would listen to the heartaches and petitions of his people. It was the *sine qua non* of his day's duties, the mystical food of his spiritual being, the thing that kept his feet on the ground though it kept statesmen and diplomats up in the air. General Pizá and other presidential aides spent much time calling on government offices trying to put into effect the measures which the president had dictated to help the numerous petitioners. Even for personal emissaries of the president, however, the red tape involved in handling orders caused much delay and sometimes even thwarted the dispositions of the chief executive.

The president made himself one with the people in still other ways. In May, 1936, less than a month after Calles had been dispatched by plane for the States, the employees of the General Hospital in Mexico City were surprised to have President and Mrs. Cárdenas drive up to the entrance. Nor was it an inspection visit, nor even a friendly call to the patients. More serious business had brought them there.

The doctor had prescribed an appendectomy for the president and he had come to the General Hospital for it just as the common people did. He took an ordinary room such as a working man in the States could have afforded, and made public a request that no flowers be sent. On the third day after the operation, his doctor told him that since he had been doing so nicely he might get up a bit.

"Do you mean that I can go home?" inquired the president.

"Oh, no!" replied the physician, "I mean that you can get up for just a few minutes at a time when you want to."

"Is that what you mean?" answered the patient. "Why, doctor, I've been doing that since the first day."

On the next day he did return home. There had hardly been a break in his attention to matters of State. Again the common people applauded.

Cárdenas found that his tilt with the University had so prejudiced the intelligentsia against him that it was hard to make friends in that quarter, except of course, with radical elements. Nevertheless, those in learned circles gradually came to realize that the President was willing to cooperate whenever they could demonstrate the practical usefulness of their endeavors.

On a trip to the state of Oaxaca, the first time in over fifty years that a president of the Republic had visited there, Cárdenas went to the Monte Albán ruins where the eminent archeologist, Alfonso Caso, brother of the learned philosopher Antonio Caso, was carrying on excavations. He arrived in time to open a newly discovered tomb such as the one in which the famous Monte Albán jewels had been found. It was not hard to convince him of the practical value of the excavations in attracting tourists to the region. The demonstrations they gave of the greatness of pre-Columbian Mexico also appealed to him as an aid in stirring the Mexico of today to new efforts toward greatness. The result was a grant of one hundred thousand pesos for continuing the excavating and a subsequent reorganization of the Ministry of

Education in which the management of the archeological branch was entrusted to Alfonso Caso himself. Cárdenas went ahead to please the state of Oaxaca by ordering the return of the Monte Albán jewels from the National Museum in Mexico City to the local museum in Oaxaca City. A large expedition of archeologists, anthropologists, and linguists was dispatched later to spend a year and a half in research in Yucatán and Central America.

In the early part of 1936 a number of commercial interests had written to Cárdenas complaining against his policies and stating that because of them, business ruin was imminent. The president answered by saying that if all sectors of society would cooperate in helping the underprivileged, commerce itself would be benefited. He assured them that the government was interested in their prosperity, not only from a theoretical but also from a selfish standpoint, since it derived revenues from them. Then he offered to cooperate with them by setting aside time each month during which they might confer with him concerning their problems.

One of their chief complaints was against the government inspection. I was once conversing with a department head in the Ministry of Education concerning the opposition of an Indian *cacique*, or boss, to the presence of a scientific investigator in his town. The department head decided that the easiest thing to do was to give the *cacique* some money. "You know," he said, "everything is done in Mexico *a fuerza de mordidas.*[1]

An official once told me of how he had had to report to the president concerning a subordinate who had requested money in return for doing a job.

The president remained silent for a moment and then said, "Does it not seem as though ninety percent of our public servants expect to be bought?"

"Yes," replied the official, "only I would place the estimate at ninety-nine percent."

Even with the practice of bribery so common throughout Mexico I have never known of business or anyone else charging Cárdenas himself with dishonesty.

As president he earnestly desired that the people should be-

[1] by means of bribes

come acquainted with his true motives. He knew that if they did not believe in his honesty they would question all he did. To prove his sincerity he felt that he had to give away what little property he did have. He has given away his farm, his country home, and spent all of his salary that he could spare in educating children, helping widows and orphans and surprising needy *peons* with anonymous gifts.

In spite of all talk to the contrary, if he has any considerable capital left no one knows where it is. He is probably dependent on work for an income. From the time when, as a young army officer, he punished an American bartender on the Arizona border for offering him a bribe to permit his saloon to remain open in the face of a general closing order, up until the present, he has kept himself free from graft. He finds it hard to understand how anyone else can be swerved from doing his duty by the lure of money. Yet that very weakness on the part of many constitutes one of the greatest hindrances to advance in Mexico.

As 1936 drew to a close, even business began to appreciate President Cárdenas. They found that the government was helping more than its labor policy was hindering. Even when the strike movement had been at its peak, and people in Mexico City, especially the American Colony, were saying that it was going to ruin the country, it is interesting to note the statement made by the general manager of a large steel concern to a friend: "In spite of the unsettled labor conditions this has been our best year."

Various factors had cooperated in bringing about something of a boom in the building trades. I walked for twenty minutes in Mexico City one morning, and in the few blocks covered counted fifty-four new dwellings in the process of construction. These were of the better sort. Less costly homes in poorer sections of the city were even more numerous.

The boost Cárdenas had given to public works increased the buying power of those thus employed. Thousands of men were at work building roads: the International Highway crossing Mexico from the United States to Central America, the highway from the capital through the states of Michoacán and Jalisco and along the west coast to Arizona and California, the Transcontinental Highway from Matamoros and Brownsville to the Gulf of California, and another from ocean to ocean uniting the capital with Acapulco on the Pacific and Vera Cruz on the Gulf.

Other projects included four new railways, one of which for the first time in history was to connect by land the isthmus of Yucatán with the rest of Mexico. Dams — large and small — wharves, drainage canals, electric plants, water works, hospitals, and schools dotted the country. All gave work and all called for tools, machinery, and materials. Of course, everything that could be purchased in Mexico was bought there, but even so one-tenth of the federal budget for the year 1936 was spent in the United States purchasing machinery and supplies for the numerous projects. The factories in Mexico, too, were kept busy turning out supplies for the projects, and in spite of the fact that thousands of Mexican laborers who had been living in the United States returned at that time to Mexico and would normally have constituted a drag on the labor market, there was no unemployment to speak of.

The rise in the price of silver brought more money into the country. The law which placed a tax on all monies withdrawn from the land, together with the New York Stock Exchange's loss of attraction for the Mexican investor due to the depression, tended to keep money at home. Then, too, the lack of military revolutions gave confidence to investors.

Besides working in connection with the government's large building program, private capital found secure and profitable opportunities in the building of homes in the larger cities where, as industry developed, more housing quarters were needed; the erection of new factories, though capital was rather cautious along this line; and, particularly, the erection of office buildings, hotels, and apartment houses in the capital and other tourist centers.

Business was also helped by the encouragement of the tourist traffic. Cárdenas had demonstrated no little foresight in extending special facilities to tourists and students visiting Mexico. They were prompted not only by economic reasons—that is, in view of the money spent there—but also because the president felt that if the foreigners themselves saw the need, they too would be sympathetic toward the betterment of living conditions of the poor.

Formerly Mexico had prohibited tourists and other foreign travelers from taking pictures of beggars, peasants clothed in rags, or anything else considered derogatory to the nation. For many

years Mexico had felt that it was a disgrace for other countries
to know how pitiful was the condition of her laboring classes. It
is said that Porfirio Díaz tried to close his eyes to the plight of
the Indians by prohibiting their coming near the park that surrounded his home.

Revolutionary Mexico had followed Díaz's example to the
extent of trying to close the eyes of the world to the situation.
President Cárdenas, however, decided that each picture carried
abroad by a tourist constituted just so much propaganda in behalf of the Revoluntionary cause. The pictures would show foreigners the greatness of the need and the urgency of drastic
measures to meet it. It was for this reason that the ban on tell-
tale photos was lifted in July of 1937.

To aid the tourist, a special office was created in the immigration branch of government giving free aid to foreigners who
were traveling in the country. The president urged the railways,
consular offices, and other agencies to "sell" Mexico to the
American tourist. Students of Spanish, some of whom were diverted from Spain by the civil war there, were encouraged to
study in another Spanish-speaking country south of the border,
and take classes from instructors fluent in that tongue. The
tourists and students spent money not only on hotel bills and
traveling expenses, but also on the purchase of Mexican weaving,
basketry, pottery, silver work, etc., thereby increasing the purchasing power of native craftsmen.

The completion of each new highway augmented the tourist
travel. Cárdenas believed that mutual understanding and sympathetic interest would be increased by the traffic that would follow the completion of the Pan-American highway. Because of this
he desired, while he was still in office, the finishing of that section
of the span which traversed Mexico, but the financial difficulties
caused by the oil struggle prevented it.

He did have the satisfaction on July 1, 1936, of inaugurating
the portion of the highway which leads from Laredo, Texas, to
Mexico City. A monument was erected by the American Colony
in Mexico to commemorate the occasion and bears an inscription
which terminates with the desire that the highway may "serve
always as a path of mutual respect and as an indissoluble bond
of peace between the peoples of the two neighbor nations."

We are confident that the people and government of the United States will be able to grasp the fact that the breaking up of the large estates is the main point in our national program for improving the living conditions of the peasants of Mexico. The ideal of giving land to the masses was written into the Constitution at the cost of much bloodshed and my government is duty bound to comply with that mandate.

All holdings that are larger than what the Agrarian Code permits are subject to distribution if there are peasants nearby who do not have land to till. Each landowner, however, is permitted to retain 370 acres whether he is a foreigner or a Mexican. This is ample for him to earn a living from the soil . . . .

The government intends to grant indemnification for the affected lands, but it can do so only when the economic conditions of the country will permit. The granting of land to the villages cannot be delayed until the necessary funds are in hand for an immediate indemnification.

You well know that there are countries that are economically strong that have had to violate important property rights when the needs of the collectivity required it. They have conditioned their procedure upon the general condition of the country and in many cases did not pay indemnification. In the case of Mexico, however, the government, attentive to its obligations, will keep its contracts without repudiating a single one.

Lázaro Cárdenas
(Letter to Townsend — summer 1938)

XVI

LAND, THE PEASANTS' DIVINE RIGHT

As PRESIDENT, Lázaro Cárdenas inherited the accumulated aggravations of the problem of land for the peasants of Mexico. It was a problem which had begun four centuries before with the king of Spain, who granted large tracts to the *conquistadores* and other favorites of his, especially among the nobility. Those grants often took the land right out from under an entire community. Only by courtesy of, and at the mercy of, the king's favorite did the villagers continue to live on the land which had been theirs, for generations.

The arbitrary distribution of land persisted through to the days of Porfirio Díaz, who granted it not only to wealthy Mexican families but to foreigners as well. For the greedy, however, the grants and purchases of land were not enough. Often these holdings were enlarged by deceit and fraud. Dr. Ramón Beteta has stated in his *Economic and Social Program of Mexico* that "During the Díaz regime the process of concentration was accentuated and by both legal and foul means the rape of the *pueblos* continued until by the end of that dictatorship, 2% of the population owned 70% of the land, and in some states as much as 98% of the rural heads of families were landless". According to Dr. Frank Tannenbaum in *Peace by Revolution,* as late as 1923 fewer than 2,700 families held more than one-half of the property of the Republic and 114 owned approximately one-fourth. The Church also had for centuries been one of the big landowners which, in the interest of its wealth, systematically opposed any reform.

As their land was parcelled out to others, those Indians were fortunate who could push back and find a plot of ground in the mountains. But most of that hapless race were born, reared, and buried on the plantation of their landlord. And although he might loan them plots of ground to till as their own, his work always

came first, so that often there was no time left for the peasant to
farm his own crop. Some of the Indian and *mestizo* peasants gravi-
tated to the villages and cities, earning what they could as artisans
or going out to work on nearby plantations.

As a result of this systematic exploitation of labor beautiful
estates grew up, but the seeming prosperity was erected upon a
foundation of poverty and ignorance which no self-respecting country could endure indefinitely. Various leaders came to see that the
only way Mexico could attain a true greatness was through a redistribution of the resources of the country. Some men, such as Zapata,
paid little attention to the legal issues involved, merely saying that
what was right was right and should be put in force regardless of
cost.

However, extreme as Zapata seemed to be, his Plan de Ayala of
November 25, 1911, actually demanded the return of only one-
third of the monopolized lands and water rights to the peasants,
and that upon indemnification. Had his plan been followed at
the outset, without the devastating civil strife which took place, a
very different story could now be told. Landholders would have
gained greatly, for the peasants would have been able to have paid
not only fair value for the lands but also would have progressed
so much in their standards of living that they would have become
purchasers of hardware, implements, furniture, and commodities
of all kinds, so that the former landlords could have turned merchants and made large incomes in that way. However, the reasonable path is not always the easy path. Stubborn resistance resulted
in constant fighting for a decade or more and not only destroyed
the plantations but also forced many of the landlords to leave the
country while others lost their lives.

Peasants could not be allowed to starve to death while farms
lay abandoned by their fleeing owners. There was nothing to do
but distribute them to the people who depended on them for a
living. This was authorized by a law issued by Carranza on January
6, 1915, and was given the force of a constitutional mandate in
1917. All lands that had been taken from the villages by fraud
were to be restored; villages which had to have land in order to
exist were to receive it; and villages which had received insufficient
lands might receive more. Payment to the landholders was to be
made in agrarian bonds.

The lands which were turned over to the villages were broken up among the farmers on a basis of individual plots which could never be sold and which might revert at any time to the community for new distribution in case the peasant did not cultivate it, died without leaving an heir to farm it, or moved away. Actually, lands have been taken away at times by petty officials for political reasons.

Generally the plots were very small, without trees, barns or houses, and the majority without irrigation. The peasants often had no cattle, implements, oxen or mules with which to cultivate them. Until the administration of Avila Camacho they did not receive deeds to their parcels of ground, so that the incentive to improve them was slight. For that and other reasons the total production of farm produce showed a slump for a number of years.

However, in spite of any supposed slump in production as a whole, we find that, taking the importation statistics as a basis of comparison, more corn, flour, meats, and dairy products were imported during 1901-1907, years typical of the Díaz Regime, than during 1929-1934, years typical of the post-revolutionary period. Of note also is the fact that every year of the Díaz Regime, corn and beans, Mexico's first and second most important crops, both had to be imported, whereas in the year 1934-1935 Mexico exported corn and beans in comparatively large amounts.[1] And in 1950, according to *Pan American Magazine* for May of that year, the rise in exports in general had been so rapid that the Mexican government was thinking seriously of stimulating a national shipping industry to facilitate the carrying of Mexican goods abroad.

President Cárdenas believed that the agrarian problem had to be settled once and for all if stability in Mexico were to be attained. He believed it so thoroughly that problems which had seemed insurmountable to others did not stop him. He threw caution to the winds, and with the Constitution in one hand and a transit in the other he went about breaking up huge estates wherever he found them. One-fourth of all the land which had been distributed to the peasants since 1915 was given them during 1935, Cárdenas' first year in office. By the time he had been president

---

[1]from Ramón Beteta's *Economic Aspects of the Six-Year Plan*

twenty months, he had distributed over half as much land as had all his predecessors.

It might be supposed that the distribution of land at such a rapid pace was primarily to win the hearts of the peasants and that the personal visits from the Chief Executive to the rural communities were for the same purpose. What Indian or barefoot peasant would ever rise up in revolt against a man who had given him a parcel of land to till and then had sat down beside him in his hut and shared a bowl of beans? If viewed in this light it might be said that no lover ever courted his sweetheart more ardently than President Cárdenas courted the peasantry of Mexico. Certainly he was not oblivious to the whole-hearted support his policies won him from the masses, but those who are acquainted with him know that this was not the main motive behind them.

In some instances the land distribution took the form of the *ejido* system. It was a community ownership of the land, but individual farming of it. The *ejidos* had a certain historical precedent in that the Indians had had an age-old custom of joint ownership of their pasture and forest lands, and had managed them with quite a degree of fairness. Even then, however, they held tenaciously to whatever small plots of ground they preserved in private right and farmed them on a purely individual basis.

The Indian has never learned to cooperate with his fellows in the tilling of such farms unless this cooperation be with some friend at time of harvest, one man helping another in order to receive help in return. Centuries of suffering have inured the Indian not only to his own hardships but also to the pain and needs of his fellows. He can see his neighbors or even close relatives in dire want without lifting a hand to help them. While this is not true of all tribes or all regions, yet it is sufficiently widespread to constitute a serious obstacle for this type of farming.

The problem of training the peasants for handling their affairs in a democratic way is a very vital one. Where the community is one of a hundred farmers or more, it is quite difficult to get even one-half of them to give an active participation in the making of decisions for the community. Invariably a clever leader rises up, creates a faction through favoritism, and proceeds to manipulate matters to his own interest. The peasants who get the raw end of the deal become embittered and refuse even to attend town assemblies, so that the leader and his henchmen are left alone to dictate matters as they choose, while going through the formality of holding "democratic" assemblies from time to time. For lack of a smaller unit of organization, the *cacique* or leader has fastened his grip on the *ejido* system.

If then the peasant is not taught to be democratic—and the ambitious efforts made by the rural schools to teach cooperative methods to the peasant children have generally failed—the only way to overcome the evils of the *cacique* system would be to put full control into the hands of government technicians. This would place the government in a position similar to that of the old landlords, and even though we were to suppose that all the technicians were strictly honest, unselfish, and competent, the result would defeat the major objective of the Revolution, for the peasant would cease to be a free man.

President Cárdenas probably preferred a cooperative system somewhere between the *ejido* and the collective farms. He told me once how one had succeeded. A sugar plantation near his home town of Jiquilpan had been partially divided up among the workers, some three hundred in number, when he was Governor of Michoacán. One of these farmers had lived in the United States for fifteen years and had learned modern methods of farming. He had also observed cooperative enterprises and was able to convince the Mexican farmers that they should till their newly acquired land on that basis.

Each man was given a card upon which was marked the time he spent working for the group. The income from the crop was divided up according to the days each man had labored. The scheme prospered so decidedly that the peasants were able to purchase that part of the plantation which had not been expropriated, paying the owner 300,000 pesos. Their success was due not only to wise leadership but also to the fact that the group was large enough to be able to buy tractors, plows, and other implements for handling the sugar cane on a large scale.

The objections to collective farming in Mexico, where collective farms are so scarce as to make the charge of communism very far-fetched, are: 1) The peasant's preference for a farm of his own; 2) The development of *caciques* who tend to maltreat the peasants in much the same way as the plantation owners used to do; 3)

The lack of competent technical supervision for such farms; 4) The broken nature of the soil which in many regions makes it difficult to farm with tractors and other implements necessary for large scale production; and 5) The lack of both predilection and training calculated to fit the peasants for handling their interests in common.

While the basic justice of the agrarian movement cannot be disputed, the many defects which showed up were the chief causes of criticism. Even where lands were parceled out to individuals, political bosses succeeded in getting control of the area.

Let us take as an extreme case the Aztec village of Tetelcingo in Morelos where I lived for ten years. The Indians for thirteen generations had been accustomed to serving the four or five plantations of the surrounding area as peons. Men, women, and children would walk several miles daily during planting and harvest to go from their village to the nearby plantations to work from sunrise to sunset for a wage so small that they could barely eke out a miserable living of not much more than corn and chili with rags for garments. Little or no time was left for the children to play since they too worked from dawn till dusk. Study was not even considered, for any schooling might ruin them as laborers. The villagers themselves came to own less than one percent of the land that surrounded them. Theirs was the poorest soil and the farthest away from irrigation.

Then the Revolution came, and the plantations were destroyed, many of the Indians died either in battle or from starvation, and farming enterprises came to a standstill. The Indian no longer had a source of income from working for the landlords who had fled. For a number of years the peasants' life was most precarious. Some of them joined Zapata as soldiers to fight for land. Finally they were given small plots to farm, a quarter of an acre where irrigation was possible and ten or fifteen acres where it was not. However, even where the land could be irrigated it was no longer possible to raise sugar cane on a profitable basis, for the sugar mills had been burned. Nor did it pay to plant cane on a quarter acre of ground. Then again, the Indian needed corn and beans for his daily food, and so the rich cane-producing region was turned over to the cultivation of crops of less value from the commercial point of view.

Furthermore, even in this Indian village, politics played a big part in the distribution of lands. This is inevitable in a country were the system of *caciques* has prevailed. The *cacique* in Mexico was and is a man who through clever manipulation or through financial or political power keeps a community under his control for selfish interests. In former times he would have himself appointed judge and thus control the people. He would also run the village saloons where most of the earnings of the populace would be absorbed. As a less illicit activity he would buy up the peasants' crops of corn, coffee, and other commodities, as well as the basketry and other handcraft which they produced with their agile fingers. For these he would pay a very low price, and would ship them to the cities for resale at a great profit.

The Revolution has often subsituted that type of *cacique* with a political boss who endeavors to manipulate the votes of the peasants, and in turn is given special privileges and powers by congressmen and other officials who court his favor for the votes involved and a share in his profits. Most of the agrarian communities of Mexico are run by such men. Though no more unjust than the former *caciques,* they are nevertheless more demoralizing upon the peasantry since they do greater havoc to its simple code of right and wrong, lying, stealing, bribing, brow-beating, and even murdering to hold their power, and instructing their followers to do likewise. They exert a wretchedly corrupting influence.

In the town we have been describing, dishonesty is the expected thing in the management of community affairs. When lands were distributed the *cacique* was able to control the distribution to a large extent, giving the bigger plots to his friends and small plots or nothing at all to his enemies. When a large group of irate citizens would rise up against him with complaints to headquarters, he would send word quickly to his political protectors in Congress or in lower circles, and they would manipulate strings so effectively that though the federal government might attempt to rectify the situation, the *cacique* would always come out on top. The complaining peasants inevitably paid the piper. Thus they learned to fear the local boss more than the state or federal officials.

In Tetelcingo, the *cacique* openly sold rebates in taxes in return for personal favors. For a time he was able also to retain for his own use one hundred acres of irrigated soil on which rice could be raised, while many of the citizens were given only a quarter of an acre and some not any at all. In order to till the land which he had taken, he absorbed most of the federal land bank loans which he was supposed to administer for the town. Furthermore, he consistently took the irrigation water whenever he needed it even though others went without, for that too came under his jurisdiction. The lion's share of his profits went to his protectors higher up.

Finally, some of the Indians put in a complaint to President Cárdenas who had taken a personal interest in this as in many villages, and immediately an order was issued for an equitable redistribution of the village lands and a redress of grievances. No. less than a cabinet officer was sent by Cárdenas to supervise personally the administration of justice. The foxy *cacique* received warning ahead of time from his conniving superiors and conveniently contracted a bad cold, complete with a bedside physician and all the trimmings. When the cabinet member arrived the agrarian commissioner for the local district was on hand and pointed out the injustice of bringing trial when the accused man was sick in bed.

A long epistle from the indisposed one was then read to the assembled citizens. It was a letter which would have taken all of his energy for two days when in the best of health to write, for he had had very little schooling. It cleverly presented his defense although his accusers were not permitted to tell their side of the story since the accused was absent.

The cabinet member left, promising to come back later. In his busy life, however, there was no chance of his returning, and so the affair remained in the hands of regional officers who arranged the matter according to their own interests, and their friend the *cacique* remained in power. The peasants learned afresh from his reprisals the bitter lesson not to bring accusations against the local boss. Finally an angry peasant shot and killed him.

Fortunately there are more hopeful examples. In a town not far from the one described, the lands had likewise been distributed unfairly, but there a wise peasant with the qualities of a leader rose up and reminded the other peasants that it was not fair for one man to have ten *hectáreas* while another had only one, when each had approximately the same needs. He showed them that there was sufficient land to give each citizen two and a half *hectáreas* if an equitable distribution were made. As a result this town came to enjoy the distinction of having little or no unfairness in land distribution.

In between these two extremes lie most of the agrarian communities of Mexico. It will take years to iron out the injustices committed in connection with the distribution of lands to the peasants. Unless some definite effort is made to liquidate bossism and to raise the moral standards among the people, it is hard to see how the system will ever be freed from abuses. The fact, however, that the laws call for fair distribution, plus the efforts made by sincere leaders to eliminate fraud, should encourage the peasants to demand a righting of the wrongs, and if these demands become strong enough and reprisals from the *caciques* are not permitted, a measure of fairness of dealing may be attained.

Neither the government nor the peasants, and much less the opposition, can be satisfied with the situation. Most observers became convinced long ago that the peasant should be given land. It has also been generally recognized that he should be aided by technical supervision and government loans to make possible an adequate exploitation of the soil given him, but how to make the program effective is a question upon which opinion differs even within revolutionary circles.

Each administration has talked of satisfying agrarian demands, but always there have been extenuating circumstances. What president would break up holdings belonging to an army officer whose support was essential to the security of the administration? What agrarian commissioner could resist the offer of a bribe from a landholder? What politician could overlook a chance to gain vengeance on an enemy by singling out his plantation for distribution? How could administrations dependent on the good will of the United States feel strong enough to apply the mandate of the Constitution to lands held by American citizens of influence?

Such radical leaders as Lázaro Cárdenas, however, argued, "If eventually, why not now?"

Several months after he had retired to private life, I asked the general if his record of 45,330,000 acres distributed among 1,020,594 peasants had completed the task. He hesitated. I wondered if he was recalling his pledge of seven years before. I knew that he hated to admit failure, and yet I also knew that President Avila Camacho was continuing to distribute land. Perhaps he was thinking of how his engineers had bogged down, often taking a year to do a job that should have been finished in four months, or of how United States claims for agrarian indemnification had drained off funds that had been sorely needed elsewhere in the program, or of how his assistants had lacked efficiency.

Finally he said, "Yes, the task was almost completed though there are still some peasants who must be given land." In six short years he had almost undone the agrarian errors of the Conquest, the Reforma, and of Porfirio Díaz, though it shook the foundations of the nation to do it.

The Federal Government is desirous of offering to home and foreign capital interested in investing in the industrialization of Mexico such advantages and exemptions as are compatible with our laws and the social requirements of our government to insure a situation of equity and justice to capital soundly invested for industrial purposes. To help such capital and the laborers that it employs, I submitted to Congress a project calling for exemption from taxation for new industries that may be established.

— Lázaro Cárdenas—to Congress
September 1, 1939

XVII

MEXICO'S NEW DEAL WITHOUT BORROWING

A SURPLUS in the Treasury? Impossible! How could a president who knew nothing about finances, who was spending money on public works faster than any former chief executive in the history of Mexico, who had disrupted agriculture far and wide by breaking up the large *haciendas,* and who took labor's side against capital so consistently that business men talked of quitting, how could such a president do anything but put the country heavily in debt?

Nevertheless, revenues for 1936 exceeded all estimates and piled up a balance as the year drew to a close. Evidently the "foolish sentimentality" of the radical young president which caused him to spend, spend, spend in behalf of the lower sectors of society was not going to wreck the nation financially after all. People were surprised!

General Cárdenas' principles of public finance are simple: 1) Eliminate graft; 2) Spend money where it helps people most; 3) Do not increase taxation; 4) Pay as you go.

These were the rules that President Cardenas insisted upon, and his able Finance Minister, Eduardo Suárez, had to be a good swimmer to keep afloat the greatest development program in Mexican history with those last two millstones tied to his neck. Of course the upturn in business put the real floats under the financial burden, but even so the accomplishments of the Cárdenas-Suárez team merit study. Had not the struggle with the oil trusts come on, the miracle of 1936 and 1937 might have continued so that Cárdenas would have been applauded for his financial accomplishments rather than criticized by those who say that he left the coffers of the Treasury empty and ruined the country financially. The truth of the matter is that he gave Mexico New Deal developments without New Deal borrowing or New Deal taxation, and this in the face of bitter opposition from

165

such financial giants as Royal Dutch Shell and Standard Oil.
Let us examine his principles more closely. *Eliminate graft.*
How? As regards the top rank office holders, Cárdenas by his
own personal vigilance did this effectively enough to save the
country millions of pesos annually that had been going into the
pockets of politicians under Obregón and Calles. However, it
necessitated the firing of even some cabinet officers.

Spend money where it helps people most. As for the second
principle, this meant a careful planning of the budget and subsequent supervision of projects. Cárdenas may not be a skilled
economist, but he is watchful of details and a slave for work, so
that he would spend hours ferreting out foolish items from the
budget before it got past his desk. Then his constant supervision
of projects with his ceaseless inquiries, "What is that for?" "What
good will that do?" "Can't you get along without that frill?"
kept engineers on their toes and eliminated many a waste.

He not only kept his eye on the government spending, but
was also keenly observing of the personal habits of his companions.
One morning, when on an expedition to Oaxaca, the president
commented to a close companion, "It's a pity that some folks
don't have sense enough to put their money to good use."

"To what do you refer, Sir?" replied the companion.

"Didn't you notice that flashy ring on so-and-so's finger?"
answered Cárdenas, alluding to a member of his official family.
A merciful friend got word to the man in question, and the ring
was never again worn in the general's presence. He himself wears
no ring or pin. Mexico's officialdom did not constitute a good
market for jewelers during his administration.

Do not increase taxation. Cárdenas intended to do his job as
president with the money the people were accustomed to pay.
He was strongly opposed to burdening them with further taxa-
ation. I once heard him argue this point with Dr. Frank Tannenbaum of Columbia University who, like many a liberal economist had seen numerous overlooked sources of government
income.

Pay as you go was the last principle. As regards foreign loans,
Cárdenas' thumbs were down. Mexico had learned that foreign
debts meant foreign interference. That would wound Mexico's
national dignity irreparably. Furthermore, Mexico's credit in in-

ternational banking centers had not been good since Porfirio Díaz left Vera Cruz for Spain. Borrowing at home was possible, but Cárdenas made very little recourse to it. It was too easy to pile up debts for future generations to pay.

In this, Mexico's development program was more significant than that of Roosevelt's New Deal. The significance of course, is not revealed by a comparison of the sums involved. Figures in the States were astronomical whereas in Mexico they were ridiculously small. If you consider, however, the impact upon the community, an expenditure of a million dollars in any given locale in the United States meant improvement, whereas in a rural community in Mexico the spending of one-tenth that sum meant transformation.

The village where we lived had no electricity, only one water hydrant, no highway, no playground, little land to farm, and only a ramshackle schoolhouse. Cárdenas spent less than one hundred thousand dollars and gave the forgotten town an agricultural school with a good building, implements, some stock, a brick kiln, and a playground; he doubled the tillable soil, planted thousands of fruit trees, gave the town a eucalyptus grove for firewood and posts; provided a good water system with tanks, watering troughs, two native laundries and hydrants in four sections of town; established a hospital with a doctor and two nurses; introduced a paved highway, built homes for the homeless; and installed electric lights in most of the streets. Innumerable towns throughout Mexico felt to a greater or lesser degree the impact of Cárdenas' New Deal.

President Cárdenas wanted to spend money where it would make barren wastes produce, where it would improve transportation and thus increase trade and travel, and where it would expand productively by improving the health, skill, and morale of the people by stimulating their incentive to work through enlightenment as regards their privileges and responsibilities. Funds thus invested would bear greater dividends, though more slowly, than money spent where people were accustomed to have federal funds go, and where dividends tended to be more showy. Anything in line with this principle of broadening and strengthening the economic and cultural foundations of the nation received help from the president, even though it might mean a temporary loss of revenue. He granted free use of the mails to newspapers and magazines, even those that opposed him.

At one time Mr. H. T. Marroquín of the American Bible Society in Mexico presented a petition to the president requesting that the import duty on Bibles be cancelled. He told of what the Bible had meant to civilization and to Mexico in transforming the lives of many of its citizens, and of the high esteem in which Juárez, Madero, and other Mexican patriots had held the basic book of Christianity. (As Mr. Marroquín addressed the attentive chief executive, a lady in the large group listening in dropped her handkerchief. None of the rest of us who were present noticed, but the watchful president momentarily left Mr. Marroquín to pick up and return the handkerchief that not even its owner had missed, then quickly resumed the conversation in such a way that it was evident his thoughts had not been the least distracted from the subject at hand.) Soon after the interview a law was sponsored by the Executive and enacted by Congress permitting all books and music to enter Mexico duty free and exempting book stores from taxation. Books of an obscene nature were denied entrance to the country.

One big undertaking of 1936 was the construction of a railroad from the Isthmus of Tehuantepec to the Yucatán peninsula. By some it was considered a foolish enterprise which would cost too much money and too many lives because of the swampy nature of the terrain to be traversed. Cárdenas, however, looked upon the railroad as a means of uniting the long isolated states of Yucatán, Campeche, and Tabasco to the rest of the nation.

This populous region, rich in natural resources and historical interest, had been linked with the rest of the country only by ocean or air transportation. At one time in the last century Yucatán considered the possibility of seceding from Mexico and uniting with the United States.

Although Cárdenas is from Michoacán, as president he was just as concerned about Yucatán. This unusual freedom from provincialism of interests impelled him to view national unity as of prime importance. Even though the railroad to the southeast was a financial liability, it would be worthwhile to unite the Mayan states to the rest of the land. It was decided to borrow fifty million pesos to construct it rapidly. The loan, however, did not materialize, and the construction costs had to be taken from the surplus Treasury receipts of the closing months of 1936 and the spring of 1937.

When in September, 1936, the president declared in a message to a group of Indians that he desired to give the Indian problem the most emphasis during the remainder of his administration, the statement fell upon deaf ears as far as the press was concerned. Nor did it find much echo in public opinion. And not even the Indians themselves were well enough informed or aroused to be interested.

A few weeks later, however, when Cárdenas outlined over the radio an ambitious program calculated to develop the three Federal Territories on an unprecedented scale, the same press welcomed the plan with great applause.

The southernmost of the three territories is Quintana Roo, a region just north of British Honduras and south and east of the states of Yucatán and Campeche. The world is largely indebted to it for its chewing gum. Its lowland surface is covered by forests of chicle trees from which the inhabitants extract the sap of which gum is made. Other parts of the territory are dry, covered with a limestone formation, a section with few towns and little commerce.

The president's program for this territory included a road that would connect it with Yucatán. Wells would be drilled to provide that streamless region with wholesome drinking water. No one had dreamed that artesian water lay underneath the low limestone formation, but within a few months five flowing wells had been drilled. Colonies were to be established, and the fishing industry developed. The chicle industry benefited by the organization of cooperative associations to gather and market the product and by the intervention of the government in the control of prices. By June of 1937 chicle had gone up in value to seventy *centavos* a pound, whereas in 1935 a pound had been worth to the gatherer only twenty *centavos.*

The two other territories of Mexico are on the peninsula of Lower California. The Northern Territory includes fertile lands below Imperial Valley. The Southern Territory is quite isolated and sparsely populated. Both have played little part in the life of the nation though they have provided some prominent leaders.

Every so often someone in the United States has scandalized Mexico with the proposal that we purchase the peninsula of Lower California outright. In fact, on July 9, 1939, while President Cárdenas was paying it the first visit ever made by a chief executive of the nation, one of the Los Angeles dailies published an article in which the author referred to Lower California as the "forty-ninth state" of the American Union. Naturally such effrontery bothers our neighbor no little, and the good it accomplishes is limited to the added incentive it provides Mexico to do something to develop the region and strengthen its ties to the rest of the nation.

The program for Lower California included a railroad across the desert which lies between Sonora and the northern tip of the Gulf of California; colonies were to be opened; the fishing and shipping industries fostered and reforestation undertaken.

A commission composed of representatives from all the different branches of the government was formed to supervise the president's program and to advise concerning additions which might seem feasible later. The public looked on with enthusiasm. Unfortunately, most of the program had to stop when the oil conflict arose.

One of the developments of 1936 of greatest importance, and one around which a great deal of controversy has waged, was the president's handling of the Laguna problem. This region was a cotton and wheat producing section of considerable importance around Torreón. It was a sort of privileged inland empire where foreign interests and certain influential Mexican generals continued to own and maintain large farms in a manner which savored very much of the old colonial system. Wages were extremely low. The people lived in hovels, without schools, and with no chance of bettering their miserable state.

Whereas lands in most other parts of Mexico belonging to both nationals and foreigners had been affected by the agrarian program, the Laguna holdings had somehow escaped. Cárdenas determined that no favoritism should be shown anywhere. In spite of pressure from General Cedillo, Minister of Agriculture, and from politically minded colleagues, the president decided that the area should be broken up.

In view of the delicacy of the problem occasioned by the

foreign capital involved, and in an effort to avoid the abuses which had been attended upon much of the land distribution, he decided to handle the problem in person. His preliminary steps were taken during the summer of 1936, and then in the fall he met with the owners of the Laguna themselves, convincing at least some of them that he was doing the right thing, and proceeding to apply the agrarian law to the whole region. One of the triumphs of persuasion he attained was the voluntary deeding over, after a friendly interview, of land belonging to a general who had been Minister of War in a previous administration.

While the agrarian engineers were carrying out the subdividing of the large properties the president spent his time visiting surrounding farming communities small and large. He would ride for hours in a bus or on horseback to discuss with a group of farmers their problems, and to encourage them to plant the fields for their own benefit with greater care and diligence than they had exercised when laboring for the overlords. He granted them large loans from the agrarian bank and spent millions of pesos on purchasing implements and equipment either from the former landowners or importing it directly from the United States.

Within a period of six weeks the entire region passed from the control of large landowners to a regime of collective ownership and small individual holdings. Where it did not seem feasible to handle the large tracts on the regular *ejido* basis, a departure was made to permit experimentation with collective farming. This was done to facilitate the financing and technical supervision of the farming and also to permit a continuance of large scale farming methods.

Almost immediately, the charge of "communism" was brought against the regime. It did sound very much like a surrender on the part of the president's stand against a substitution of the state boss for the landowner boss, but he did not mean it that way. In this case it was intended that the workmen themselves run their farms as partners without excessive supervision from the government.

Less than ten percent of the *ejido* farmers of Mexico worked on this basis, and even then the danger of the state becoming a hard taskmaster was small as long as Cárdenas was in authority and came around to listen to the wishes and complaints of the laborers and keep watch on the technicians. Cárdenas realized that he was responsible for the daring departure and put forth special effort to keep a guardian eye on the collective projects, visiting them more frequently than he did the regular *ejidos*. He not only watched from an economic standpoint, but personally supervised the social and educational development of the section, founding schools, fostering athletics, and issuing a special call to the people of the Laguna against intemperance and gambling.

I did not visit the Laguna section, but had the opportunity to see a large wheat farm conducted on a similar basis in the Yaqui Valley in Sonora. I went, thoroughly preconvinced that I would find the system unsuccessful. To my great surprise, however, the workmen were happy about the results. They were better dressed than before and now had schools and hospital care. Their daily income had more than doubled over what they had formerly earned as farm hands. The farm, too, appeared to be in good condition. As I left I was forced to admit that at least there were some grounds for continuing the experiment in the few sections of the country where it had been established.

Cárdenas now had the whole-hearted support of the peasantry, but labor was still divided. The old leader of the C.R.O.M., Luís Morones, had been permitted to return to Mexico. Lombardo Toledano of C.T.M. objected strenuously to this fresh demonstration of the president's spirit of forgiveness. Some observers suggested that Cárdenas was glad to have Morones back to offset the growing power of Lombardo Toledano. Actually, Cárdenas was not averse to having the C. T. M. lead in labor's united front, but he wanted a *united front* and not just the ascendency of one group over the rest.

The president's labor program had bogged down during his absence for lack of team work between the two unions. The trouble between them came to a head in the mill town of Atlixco. The C.R.O.M. had held the supremacy there for a number of years, but agitators from the C.T.M. had been able to burrow in. The competition resulted in occasional killings on the part of both sides. It was not all the fault of the laborers, either, for judges were said to be accepting handsome bribes for letting the killers off easy.

Cárdenas decided to visit Atlixco in person and did so the

latter part of September. He called the leaders from both labor organizations together and made it plain to them that rivalry and bloodshed would have to cease, securing from them a promise to accept his personal arbitration. His decision stipulated that the two groups should work together for one year under the direction of a unification committee. At the end of the year the laborers were to be permitted to vote on whether to join permanently the C.T.M. or the C.R.O.M. Meanwhile, the ten most irreconcilable leaders of each group were to be ordered to leave the zone. If a laborer belonging to the C.T.M. were killed, the C.R.O.M. would have to pay indemnity to his family and vice versa.

The intervention of the president seemed to be rather dictatorial, but both the labor organizations and the factory owners submitted to it. Cárdenas also sent a judge of his own choice who could not be bought. He made it clear that any or all killers would be shipped by presidential order to Mexico's penal island within forty-eight hours of the time they were caught. The wisdom of the move has been attested by the fact that peace has reigned to a surprising degree in the turbulent town ever since.

Cárdenas seems to have had his program well planned from the very beginning of his administration and only awaited opportunities for developing it step by step. Some things took him more or less by surprise, such as the obstinacy of the oil companies that forced him to become more drastic with them than he had intended, but generally he had seen and planned the whole picture from the start, and his administration was just a systematic unfolding of that picture.

He wanted to be ready for any eventuality, however, and so took advantage at this time of the goodwill and prosperity that had resulted from his national conciliation and public works program, to sign a law which produced considerable alarm, but strengthened his hand tremendously. It was a Law of Expropriation which greatly amplified the right of the government to take over private property and have ten years in which to pay for it. It legalized the seizure of machinery and other equipment as well as of lands on the mere proof that the expropriation was for the general welfare of the community.

The immediate reason for the law had been the fact that in

Yucatán, lands had been given the peasants where the only crop harvested, sisal hemp, had to be sold to the old plantation owners at low prices because the planter retained the machinery for extracting the fiber. The government realized that single-crop land was of little use if the peasant was unable to sell the crop profitably, and accordingly sought legal means for taking over the hemp mills. The law was worded, however, so that under a broad interpretation of it a large proportion of private property was placed within reach of the government.

Cárdenas invoked the new law without a great deal of stir in the case of the fiber mills of Yucatán. At a later date, however, when he used it with such telling effect in his struggle with the oil companies, people awoke to the fact that the farsighted statesman had equipped himself with a weapon which he could use with telling effect in any case of need. At the time of its passage, however, there was much adverse criticism in business circles. Nevertheless, apprehension was more than overcome by the prosperity which prevailed and the unprecedented progress in the development of the nation.

To satisfy objections in our own minds, let us recall the words of Nathaniel and Sylvia Weyl in their book, *The Reconquest of Mexico,* concerning the subsequent taking over of oil properties: While this drastic remedy [expropriation] may be deemed a violation of property rights, it should be recalled that modern jurisprudence is abandoning the absolutist concept of "the right to use and abuse" in favor of a functional theory which correlates private right with the performance of social duty.[1]

The president's prestige had so grown by August of 1936 that he was no longer dependent on Portes Gil or General Cedillo to instil public confidence. In fact, trouble had resulted for the administration from the way Portes Gil, as head of the P.N.R., had managed the elections in various states. In the Senate and Chamber of Deputies he had been criticized severely for the decisions he had made in contested elections, and this opposition from the legislative branch of government finally forced him out. His fall caused little more than a ripple in public opinion.

At the time it happened Cárdenas was in a restaurant talking with a large group of school teachers. Excitement was high over the break between the head of the official political party and

---

[1] p. 184.

Congress, and note after note was sent in to Cárdenas urging him to leave the meeting and take care of the political situation. However, the man who can wait indefinitely wouldn't be hurried. For three hours he sat with the teachers, not budging until his job with them was finished. (The people of Jiquilpan say that his old uncle, the weaver, would often stand motionless for hours at a time silently watching the people go by, or the shadows grow. The nephew, in the midst of a political whirl, seemed to be just as impassive.)

A few weeks previous to this the Gold Shirts had been disbanded, a blow, it was said, to General Cedillo's influence. The organization had been endeavoring to stir up anti-Semitic sentiment, and since race prejudice was definitely opposed to the spirit of the Revolution, Cárdenas felt that he should wait no longer to dissolve it. He had waited, however, for over a year and this had given the public time to see that the organization had little of a constructive nature to offer. Its liquidation was consummated without a stir.

The administration, by this rebuff to Cedillo and by the fall of Portes Gil, had become very definitely a Cárdenas administration. He had demonstrated his ability to dominate the situation by virtually becoming a dictator, but it was he *and* the people. We shall see in a later chapter how the stability of government which had been attained was soon to permit him to step out of the place of dictator so as to install the people there alone as far as this could be done in a land like Mexico where the people have had little preparation for rule.

The transformation which had been brought about in the public frame of mind between January 1, 1936, and January 1, 1937, was almost incredible. Few periods of equal length in the history of Mexico have seen such a change for the better. At the beginning of the year people had feared that a revolution was due to break out because of the return of General Calles; industry had felt like closing shop due to the attitude of the government toward private property and labor; labor itself had been divided into warring camps; the president's long illness had brought considerable disintegration within the ranks of his own followers resulting in political scheming of all kinds; the Church had been passively rebellious at home and actively so abroad in stirring up adverse sentiment toward Cárdenas; and foreign countries had been doubtful of his ability to control the situation.

At the end of the year general tranquillity reigned throughout the nation; business was prospering; supremacy in the labor situation had been definitely won by the C. T. M., while its semi-communistic leader, satisfied by the progress of his quest for power, had eased up considerably in the stressing of his more radical ideas; the political and governmental machine was more completely under the president's control than ever before (Portes Gil, Cedillo, and many others who had lost out politically continued to be seen with him in friendly intercourse); the difficulty with the Church had been patched up; adverse criticism abroad was not only on the wane, but frankly commendatory articles were sometimes seen in the foreign press; and everyone realized that Cárdenas firmly seated in the saddle was guiding Mexico with a steady rein toward a definite goal.

As was his custom the president greeted the nation on New Year's Day, 1937, with a carefully worked out report. It was given by radio and went into considerable detail. As usual there was no sensationalism and very little oratory. Besides the important development projects in nearly every state and the extensive distribution of lands, he was able to report the introduction of drinking water into scores of towns, the opening of two thousand new schools, the virtual elimination of banditry, and a peace and prosperity which filled the nation with hope.

Dictatorships have been brought about [in Europe] that gravely disturb the international equilibrium. Their designs may bring a new conflagration upon the world. This would result in a serious loss to the triumphs of civilization and the advancement that humanity has attained through tedious struggles . . . . Mexico hopes that the American nations may form a bulwark of friendship and tolerance serving all of America so that it may not be dragged into the vortex engulfing other continents. Besides the weighty reasons of a moral nature that exist for such harmony, we also have the peculiar situation of the New Hemisphere. Her natural resources are abundant as also are opportunities of every kind. Her relatively sparse population, her geographical situation, and the absence of a multiplicity of creeds, languages, interests, and divergent cultures clearly indicate the possibility of settling whatever problems might arise by procedures in keeping with democratic institutions and in harmony with the majority opinion of our nations . . . .

Any tendency toward the implantation of a new dictatorship in our own land must be considered as not suitable for our social and political environment. Necessarily we desire that dictatorships be proscribed from all the nations of this hemisphere.

— *Lázaro Cárdenas* —
January 1, 1938

XVIII

CARDENAS AND FOREIGN AFFAIRS

THE TRIUMPHANT COURSE within the nation was crowned from without by a victory for Mexican diplomacy at the Pan-American Peace Conference in Buenos Aires. For many years Mexico had taken the stand that no government should interfere in the internal affairs of another country. The intrusion of American armed forces in Mexico during the administration of President Wilson, both at Vera Cruz and in the case of the punitive expedition against Villa, had filled her with rancor, and she viewed similar intrusions in other countries with the utmost animosity. When American marines intervened in Nicaragua she had raised her voice in condemnation and had given Sandino no little encouragement and material aid.

Armed intervention, however, as instanced by the Vera Cruz incident and the Villa expedition, had been resorted to, nominally at least, in defense of our national dignity. In *Shirt-Sleeve Diplomat,* Josephus Daniels gave another reason when he said: "It was to oust Huerta that Wilson adopted 'Watchful Waiting,' sent Pershing to Northern Mexico and John Lind as special Ambassador to Mexico City, and directed me to send the American Fleet to 'take the Custom House at Vera Cruz and prevent ammunition from falling into Huerta's hands.' " This is a frank statement of the dangerous type of "diplomacy" we resorted to before the Good Neighbor Policy of Franklin D. Roosevelt lined us up with the Estrada Doctrine of non-intervention. Daniels must be accurate in the main part of his statement, though he errs as regards the Pershing expedition which took place long after Huerta had fallen. Such expediencies proved to be too expensive in lives, money, and ill-will for the results obtained.

Today Mexico pays special honors to the men who fought the American marines at Vera Cruz and Pershing's soldiers when they violated the integrity of Mexican soil in pursuit of Villa, although she holds no brief for either Villa or for the regime that defended Vera Cruz.

Washington came to realize that other means were better. She found non-recognition or an embargo on arms to be more effective in making her wishes felt. With these weapons ambassadors of the United States played an important part in the course of the Revolutionary movement. They had not, however, won the goodwill of the Mexican people. On the contrary, very little love was lost between Mexicans and Americans.

Time and again at Pan-American diplomatic conferences Mexico had urged the policy of non-intervention, but had generally found herself isolated in her position. Her hopes were renewed, however, when President Roosevelt announced his Good Neighbor policy and later when he proposed the conference in Buenos Aires. In Ambassador Castillo Nájera and Under-secretary of Foreign Affairs Beteta, the Mexican delegation had two very able representatives in the conference who not only knew what Mexico wanted and were able to present the proposals in a convincing way, but who also knew American history and psychology in a way which enabled them to win the friendship and confidence of the representatives of the United States government.

As a result of various happy circumstances Mexico found herself closely aligned with the United States on a Pan-American diplomatic issue of major importance for the first time since the Revolutionary movement had triumphed.

With Uncle Sam willing to admit that perhaps his Latin-American brothers had outgrown the need of tutelage which had been read into the Monroe Doctrine by an imperialistic interpretation, the Mexican diplomats proposed a protocol which would definitely outlaw the intervention of one country in the internal affairs of another. It was adopted and the following morning Mexico hailed on the front pages of all her newspapers the great victory for non-intervention which had finally been won. Cárdenas had kept in close touch with his delegates in Buenos Aires and shared credit for their triumph.

"Whispers in Washington become shouts in Latin-American capitals" is a saying I first heard in Honduras thirty-three years ago. Mexicans readily admit that the foreign policies of the United States exert tremendous influence upon their own country.

For years most American diplomats had seemed to be haughty agents of the acquisitive interests of certain of their nationals on the cold basis of dollars and cents. It was a welcome change when Ambassador Dwight Morrow came to Mexico in 1927. Somehow he seemed to have learned that the first prerequisite in dealing with Latin Americans was to win their friendship. He went about this in unusual ways, such as inviting down popular Will Rogers to captivate Mexico with his smile and humor, and youthful Colonel Charles Lindbergh to inspire her with his long flights and his exemplary character.

Morrow had been alert for ways of making himself both friendly and useful, and in a short time wrought a miracle in changing Mexico's attitude toward the United States. I felt it as I made a trip to the southern part of the land. I was greeted with courtesy and the statement, "We Mexicans and you Americans are friends now!" On a previous journey I had encountered antipathy on every hand.

Perhaps the ambassador had learned from Mexico herself, for a few years before Cárdenas took office that nation had been using a strategy of friendliness in an effort to extend her influence to the south, especially in Central America. To Guatemala, for instance, Mexico had planned a spectacular presentation of an airplane manufactured in her own shops. The army aviator assigned to fly the machine to Guatemala City met with hard luck and wrecked the plane enroute, but this did not defeat the friendly gesture, for another plane was built and delivered in good condition. This was followed later on by the gift of a radio broadcasting station to the same Republic.

The relationships between Mexico and Guatemala had been none too good ever since their independence had been won simultaneously from Spain in 1821. This was due in part to the fact that territory formerly belonging to Guatemala had chosen to be part of Mexico when independence was won. This brought on interminable boundary disputes.

Of course Mexico realized that she had nothing to fear from her little neighbor, but for various reasons she desired to bring about better feeling between herself and Guatemala. Perhaps she envisioned the formation of an Indo-Latin group of nations to offset as far as possible the predominant influence of Anglo-Saxon America, a dream revived for a time by President Perón of Argentina. This attitude on Mexico's part had changed three or four years before Cárdenas took office. Events in El Salvador and elsewhere seemed to indicate that Mexico's influence was being directed toward an extension of her socialistic doctrines rather than toward counter balancing the influence of the United States as such.

In spite of the gifts, Mexico's many innovations of a radical nature in social and economic reforms had frightened Guatemala with her large plantations and extensive system of peonage. Soon after General Ubico became president of Guatemala, the little republic's suspicions of her big sister were accentuated, for Ubico felt that the government of Mexico was trying to propogate communism throughout Central America. With a hatred toward that doctrine quite as great as that of Mussolini's, General Ubico sounded the alarm and set about tightening the frontiers of his country against all possibility of propaganda coming in from Mexico. He was not averse to all reform; in fact, he showed some desire to alleviate the sufferings of the Indians. But he preferred to do it in his own way.

President Cárdenas decided that the situation should be rectified. Going out of his way to show courtesies to the Guatemalan ambassador and to citizens of that land, he was careful to refrain also from anything that could be considered meddling in the internal affairs of any of his southern neighbors. He was rewarded by a friendly response from Guatemala.

Fear of Mexico's reforms was not limited to Guatemala. I was told that for a time most of the countries of Latin America would not permit *El Nacional* (first, the official organ of the P. N. R., and then the government-supported newspaper) to enter their borders. It may be that Mexico had been trying to extend her socialistic doctrine southward, but Cárdenas determined not to participate in a struggle for influence over the rest of Latin America. In 1937 Peru and Mexico raised their diplomatic representations at the respective capitals to the rank of embassies, revealing the growing friendly feeling between Mexico and her southern neighbors.

The disappearance of ill-will beween the United States and

Mexico through the friendly diplomacy of Dwight Morrow, and the determination of Mexico's new ruler not to participate in a struggle for influence over the rest of Latin America presaged bright prospects for the Good Neighbor policy as far as our nearest neighbor southward was concerned.

Two other factors were of utmost importance: 1) President Roosevelt's appointment of friendly and liberal Josephus Daniels to the important diplomatic post of ambassador to Mexico; and 2) the fact that the Roosevelt administration had set out upon a program of social and economic reform in the U. S. A. that paralleled in many ways the objectives sought by Mexico herself. Ambassador Daniels did not hesitate to express orally and in the Mexican press his own liberal ideas on political economy and was hearty in his endorsement of the altruistic aims of his good friend General Cárdenas.

There had been, nevertheless, a cause for friction and uneasiness at the start of the Cárdenas administration. The Catholic press and congressmen in Washington had brought no little pressure to bear upon Congress and President Roosevelt to do something to stop the oppression of the Church in Mexico. The fall of General Calles, however, and the subsequent guaranteeing by Cárdenas of the Church's constitutional rights relieved this situation.

Then again, apprehension had been felt during the fall and winter of 1935-1936 that Cárdenas would not be able to preserve order, and efforts had been made from capitalistic quarters to accentuate this fear. In December of 1935 I learned that Ambassador Daniels had received so many complaints against the Cárdenas government that his brief case would be full of them when he went to Washington for his Christmas vacation. Knowing that he wanted to be fair, I prepared a report for him giving my own experiences and observations in having received considerable help in scientific and educational work from the Minister of Labor, Genaro Vásquez, and from officials in the Ministry of Education and the National University. Whether Daniels used the report or not, he himself had seen enough to have faith in the Mexican reformer, and Roosevelt and Hull seemed to share his sentiments. Their faith and patience were rewarded by improving conditions, and an era of good feeling, unparalleled till then, was built up between the two nations.

Mutual sympathy and understanding were to continue until the petroleum controversy poured oil on the peaceful waters with the reverse of the proverbial effect. The strain which the oil episode placed upon the relationships between our two nations would have been disastrous had we not had an ambassador in Mexico who not only had a lot of North Carolinian horse sense, but also enjoyed the confidence of President Roosevelt to such a degree that he could often do what he knew to be best whether the State Department concurred or not.

Daniels had much in common with Cárdenas, who appreciated the fact that the envoy of his most powerful neighbor was of such high personal ideals, agreed with him in his opposition to alcohol, gambling, and vice, and was a life-long friend of the poor and exploited. In spite of the language barrier and the big difference in their ages, a high personal esteem and mutual understanding came to exist between President and Mrs. Cárdenas and Ambassador and Mrs. Daniels, thus permitting the ambassador to influence the president as he could not have done otherwise. The handling of our affairs fitted in perfectly with the psychology of Cárdenas, though it did not satisfy the go-getting spirit of American capitalists in Mexico.

In a quiet, unobtrusive way Mexico under Cárdenas came to broaden her horizon to see and be seen beyond and apart from the overshadowing "Giant of the North" as the United States is called in the southern republics. Cárdenas did not hesitate to raise his voice in world affairs, for he felt that the twenty million people for whom he spoke had a right to be heard.

When Mussolini determined to take over Ethiopia as a colony of fascist Rome, Cárdenas spoke out in protest. Italy imagined, however, that his attitude would not be sustained in the face of financial loss. She had not reckoned aright, for as soon as the League of Nations placed an embargo on shipments of petroleum Cárdenas put the measure in force for Mexico. Tempting profits did not swerve him from his purpose to stand by the Ethiopian nation in trouble.

Mexico really came into the international limelight, however, through the trouble in Spain. From the start of the civil war there the sympathies of the Mexican government were strongly with the legally constituted regime. It is doubtful whether she would have shown much interest had the struggle not been between fascism and socialism, but since this was the case, and since a fascist victory in Spain would react against the tendencies toward semi-socialism in Mexico, the sympathies of the Cárdenas administration toward the Loyalist cause were expressed in many ways. In fact, Cárdenas' service to Republican Spain was generally considered to be his outstanding contribution to international affairs.

First and foremost was the shipping of arms and munitions to Madrid. Mexicans enrolled in the Republican army with Cárdenas' approval. Then, Mexico gave asylum to five hundred orphan children from Spain,—clothing, educating and providing for them as her own. Moral support was given at every opportunity.

When the Republic finally fell the Mexican ambassador, Colonel Tejeda, helped many refugees get to Mexico. Later, when the Republican refugees who had fled to France from Spain desired to find a safer haven, arrangements were made for Mexico to receive twenty thousand of them. Cárdenas, in reporting to Congress, said:

. . . This step was taken in compliance with the universal duty of hospitality in the face of the collective suffering that befell Spain, but we realized as well that it would bring us a contribution of man power from a race that is kindred to ours in spirit and blood . . . We have welcomed the Spanish refugees because by their ability and energy they make a valuable contribution to the development and progress of the nation, and are readily assimilated. Immigrants from other lands generally hold themselves aloof from our own people, supplant them in their economic activities, group together in the large centers, and manage their investments without identifying themselves with the destinies of our nation.

Republican Spain manifested her gratitude through the press, in public demonstrations, and by sending distinguished men as envoys of appreciation and to foster the sympathetic attitude of her former colony. It was decided to name a battalion in the Loyalist army in honor of President Cárdenas. When the request for his consent reached him he replied characteristically: "While I appreciate profoundly the honor which has been offered me, I beg of the commander of the division that he permit me to decline it, since I am convinced that final judgment cannot be made concerning men who are still exercising responsibilities of a public character until their work has been finished and history has thoroughly judged it." Even within Mexico Cárdenas tolerated for only a year or so the tendency on the part of school teachers, appreciative laborers, and politicians to name new schools, hospitals, social centers, and even towns in his honor. Then he made public a request that the practice stop while he was still in office.

Cárdenas' help to the socialistic forces of the Iberian peninsula was not appreciated by Italy and Germany. Cárdenas realized this would be the case. In December, he called his Under-secretary of Foreign Affairs, Dr. Ramón Beteta, to the state of Michoacán where he happened to be on a trip, to give him instructions concerning the peace conference in Argentina, and in the course of the interview asked Beteta's opinion about the advisability of sending a note to the League of Nations as well as to all countries with whom Mexico maintained diplomatic relations, carefully defining Mexico's position toward Spain. The under-secretary was not favorably inclined, and the matter was dropped.

After Beteta's return from the Argentine Conference, however, he was again called to the side of the president, who this time was on a tour in Oaxaca. Together they discussed the Spanish situation once more. When they separated late that night no decision had been reached, but early the next morning as Dr. Beteta said farewell to catch a plane back to the capital, the president took from 'his pocket a slip of paper on which he had drafted a note. Beteta suggested only a few slight modifications. Then the president said, "Dispatch this to the various powers as soon as possible, for I have a feeling that our stand concerning Spain is going to be called into question." Back in the capital the under-secretary labored feverishly with his aides to put the message into code and get it off.

True enough, Italy and Germany did present charges against Mexico, but they had been answered a few hours previously by the logic of the Cárdenas note. Presentiment had synchronized them most advantageously for Mexico.

Leon Trotsky also brought world attention to Cárdenas when he appealed to Mexico for refuge and was granted it. The big labor organization, C. T. M., and the Communist Party of Mexico immediately raised their voices in protest, saying that Trotsky would carry on propaganda against the government of Russia. Other sectors of society manifested concern for fear that Trotsky would scheme to bring about a dictatorship of the proletariat in Mexico. Cárdenas calmly replied that his government did not entertain either fear and would welcome Trotsky as it would any other political refugee.

Trotsky came and was received at the port of Tampico by Mexico's world-renowned painter, Diego Rivera, who offered him the hospitality of his home. For several months some space in the newspapers was dedicated to the Russian political refugee, and in December of 1936 this publicity was extended to the United States through the intervention of a committee which came to Mexico professedly to conduct an investigation of Trotsky's alleged interventions in the affairs of Russia subsequent to his having been exiled. The committee included in its membership the educator and philosopher, John Dewey.

People in the States feared that Mexico with Trotsky there would surely suffer from communistic intrigues, but Cárdenas knew better. On the contrary, his presence really divided the communistic forces and weakened their influence. After Trotsky's murder, General and Mrs. Cárdenas showed Mrs. Trotsky no little friendship in her widowhood.

Cárdenas opened the doors of Mexico to other political refugees early in his regime. When Venezuela expelled twenty-two men as communists, they too found a cordial welcome in Mexico. This was a foretaste of what was to come in 1939 when Cárdenas made Mexico a haven of hope to thousands of refugees from Spain and the Jewish persecutions in Germany and Poland. He felt that Mexico would gain by the influx of men of such firm convictions that they were willing to suffer for them even though these convictions were often more radical than his own. He was convinced that they could not affect the stability of the Mexican government since they had no official support from foreign governments. Paid propagandists from other lands were viewed in an entirely different light and were under surveillance.

When Russia invaded Finland without provocation, Cárdenas further irritated Mexican communists by sending a message of sympathy to the Finnish people. After extolling their virtues, he said:

Finland is worthy of the esteem of civilized nations that, like her, live in the embrace of democratic institutions. It is illogical and contrary to human dignity that countries of such superior quality should not be permitted to peacefully enjoy the benefits of their progress and love for liberty. In view of the aggression of which the Finnish people are now the victims, the people and government of Mexico extend to them their cordial sympathy.

This attitude was consistent with his policy of keeping Mexico on the side of democratic countries against totalitarian and militaristic aggression. We once discussed together the possibility of selling oil to Japan who was at that time trampling upon the sovereignty of China. Cárdenas pointed out that American companies, though they had refused to sell teraethyl to Mexico (following expropriation), were selling all their products, including airplane gasoline, to Japan, thus helping her whip China. I suggested that the Mexican government should have more scruples in such matters and asked him to wait until further attempts were made to reach a settlement that would obviate the necessity of selling to Japan. He consented, but the attempts failed and the deal with Japan went through.

This was followed up by a visit from a special trade envoy from Tokyo who invited a group of distinguished Mexican leaders to visit Japan in April of 1940 where they were entertained lavishly, visiting her factories and listening to her arguments for a trade agreement. After Pearl Harbor, however, no country handled the Japanese settlers within her borders more effectively and decisively than Mexico.

The problem of identification with the people of Mexico had made the Revolution a bit reticent about immigration from certain lands. Germans would take a generation, and English and Americans two or three, before they really became a part of their adopted fatherland. But Spanish immigrants were absorbed almost immediately as is witnessed by the number of professors in the National University and other institutions of higher learning. Chemists, doctors, manufacturers, and people representing almost every occupation except farming, who came over from Spain after the advent of Franco, are looked upon as Mexicans.

The matter of Jewish immigration is a mooted question. In one way they identify themselves with the people of the country and some, it is said, become better *tamale* merchants than the Mexicans themselves. On the other hand, there is an aloofness about them socially that bothers many Mexicans. Cárdenas, however, received many Jewish refugees and defended them against an anti-Semitic movement that was quite strong in Mexico in 1937, but proved to be more political than nationalistic. In gratitude, he was elected Honorary President of the Friends of Israel Society.

As regards financial responsibilities towards other nations Cárdenas followed the policy of recognizing just debts and claims while endeavoring not to pay more than the unavoidable minimum in cold cash. He needed every available *peso* for the reconstruction of his country and sought to convince foreign governments that this policy was not altogether opposed to their own interests, since a reconstructed Mexico would be in a far better position to pay. It was the same reasoning that made banks in the U. S. A. reticent about foreclosing on the properties of defaulters during the depression if they were found to be making every effort to get back on their feet.

President Cárdenas applied to foreign affairs his customary method of trying to acquaint the other party of the exact situation in order to reach a harmonious and fair understanding. With the politicians who opposed his policies, with the estate owner who balked at the idea of his land being distributed among the peasants, with the labor leaders who wanted to have some rival organization disbanded, and with peasants who would go too far in their demands for soil, he would patiently talk over each point involved. He endeavored to use the same procedure with foreign citizens and diplomats.

To acquaint the diplomatic corps of the true situation which prevailed, he organized three extensive tours for the representatives of foreign governments to observe conditions among the peasants, city laborers, and all. It was the most effective way for him to convince them, too, that the nation was free from disorders and that the people were friendly to foreigners. Ambassador Daniels, an inveterate traveler during his stay in Mexico, went on all three tours (plus many others), although they were too strenuous for some younger diplomats.

Cárdenas willingly took time and pains to familiarize foreign representatives with the country and its program, but he was reticent to spend time on mere diplomatic formalities. Occasionally a diplomat had to wait to present his credentials until another had arrived. Then the ceremonies were hurried through, two at a time, like a double wedding. The president never wore anything more formal than a dark business suit, so the envoy too had to dress accordingly. Some of the representatives of monarchies found it rather hard to give up their plumes, medals, and other regalia, for too often there wasn't much distinction left. The president did very little official entertaining and only rarely did he attend state balls. This attitude of his at times embarrassed his associates in the Ministry of Foreign Affairs, but they learned to make the best of it.

In April of 1937 President Manuel Quezón of the Philippine Islands visited Mexico to investigate personally the Revolutionary movement.When he reached Mexico City he found that President Cárdenas was far away from the capital, visiting rural communities. The Minister of Foreign Affairs, Eduardo Hay, had been called home from a trip to the States to act as host to the distinguished visitor.

He informed President Quezón that while President Cárdenas would like very much to know him and welcome him to Mexico personally, yet there were numerous towns which had been waiting many months for the president to come and help them with their problems, and they would be greatly disappointed if he failed to keep his promise to visit them. Quezón replied that he would really prefer to meet him away from the capital among the peasants anyway. Though he was told that to do this would necessitate a tiresome journey by auto and possibly horseback riding, President Quezón was enthusiastic about the trip. Cárdenas then wired that he would facilitate matters by going himself to the quaint old town of Taxco where Quezón would be able to reach him by auto.

At one o'clock in the morning, while President Quezón was being entertained at a diplomatic ball in the capital, a telegram was received announcing that President Cárdenas would reach Taxco at ten o'clock that same morning. Those who were to make the trip excused themselves, and after snatching just a few hours of sleep started out by automobile for the picturesque old colonial city where intermingling barefoot peasants and tourists alike breathe the atmosphere of the seventeenth century, and wander together over the narrow hilly streets. There, two modern transformers of important parts of Spain's old empire met, embraced, and discussed their hopes and plans.

When President Quezón returned to the United States, he issued a statement concerning Mexico and the Cárdenas Administration which appeared in *El Nacional* of April 17, 1937.

"General Cárdenas, in my opinion," said the Philippine ruler, "is one of the greatest Presidents that Mexico has had. Under his efficient and honest administration, his wise and strong direction, and thanks to his great heart of human kindness, opportunities are being given to the Mexican people such as they have never had before to better their economic, cultural, and political condition. It was my good fortune to meet President Cárdenas, not in Mexico City, but in the town of Taxco. The General is austere in bearing, soldierly through and through. At first sight no one would ever think that beneath a bearing so tranquil and stern could be a heart so utterly kind, and the affability and courtesy of a polished gentleman . . .

"He has given to Mexico a truly honest administration. He not only sees to it that the officials of the Mexican government work hard, but he himself sets the example, working harder than anyone. He is determined to raise the standard of living of the people of Mexico. For the first time in the history of that country the laborers in the factories and in the fields are to receive that which justly belongs to them due principally to the efforts which he is making in their behalf. President Cárdenas is today the strongest man in Mexico, but his power does not rest in any fear which he inspires in the Mexican people, nor does it depend upon the bayonets which he has at his command. He rose to power without shedding a single drop of blood, and no blood has been shed during his regime due to political motives. His power rests solely upon the support and confidence of his people.

"During my short stay in Mexico I also noticed the great change which has taken place in the attitude of the Mexican people toward the United States. The distrust and aversion which Mexicans formerly felt toward North Americans has disappeared, and a feeling of trust and friendship has taken its place."

Cárdenas won the esteem of all democratic elements in his handling of international affairs. He sought to have Mexico respected by her sister nations not because of her heavy armaments, but because of the sincerity of her endeavors and by a strict adherence to the principles of friendship and justice. He was fearless in his insistence that Mexico be treated and in turn treat others as truly sovereign nations.

To the insinuations that I should run for reelection . . . I have replied that I consider such a suggestion to be contrary to popular sentiment. The cause of social reform in Mexico has always gone hand in hand with the doctrine that opposes more than one term in office. I consider this doctrine to be one of our important triumphs and believe that the progressive march of our Revolution would be affected if it were to be abandoned. Men and groups would reappear who would be called indispensable. Political bosses would become entrenched. The present regime might become a closed oligarchy, a reincarnation of the old systems that have been an obstacle to all progress.

In view of this, it is the firm purpose of my government to be faithful to the Revolutionary program and not lend itself to personal ambitions. Furthermore, I believe that those of us who have reached the post of chief executive of the Republic should, when our term of office has expired, abstain completely from further participation in politics. This we should do if we wish to serve with loyalty the democratic principles upon which our nation is founded.

— Lázaro Cárdenas —
February 21, 1940

XIX

THE SIX YEAR PLAN IN ACTION

THE COMING STORM did not break all at once. Indeed the skies continued rosy until the fall of 1937. A cloud would appear now and again at home, but beyond her borders there was little indication of trouble ahead. Mexico was buying heavily from her northern neighbor and it seems that big orders of goods are among the most effective aids in holding Uncle Sam's friendship. Friendship in turn brings trade. It is a virtuous circle.

American exporters shipped over one hundred million dollars worth of goods to Mexico during 1937. This reflected well upon the Good Neighbor policy and also upon Mexico's internal policies, and it required powerful influences to overturn the situation. We shall see how these were not lacking, and how seriously they were to threaten tranquillity in Mexico and friendship abroad. They were to be, however, almost wholly foreign in origin.

Cárdenas did not allow the thought of popularity with foreign lands to deflect him one moment in his drive for a greater Mexico. He urged his own people to better themselves, and not look to foreign interests to bring prosperity to the land. He realized that upon him rested the responsibility of organizing and leading the march toward the internal greatness that would have to be attained if from outside her borders Mexico were to be treated with the esteem and respect that would permit her to be the mistress of her own destinies and the beneficiary of the resources with which God had endowed her. He realized too that the time he had at his disposal was desperately short and that his six years in the presidency constituted one intensely busy campaign to attain pre-planned goals of reconstruction and development. It was more relentless than hurried.

Still, in the midst of it all his heart pulled him aside on a sentimental yet practical errand. Mexico owed something to the mountain hamlet that had given birth to her great hero, Benito Juárez. Cárdenas wanted to visit the Zapotec village far back in the mountains of Oaxaca not only as a patriotic pilgrimage, but also to give it a good school and to see how he could help the neglected kinsmen of Juárez in other ways. Perhaps other great leaders would be discovered among its rustic inhabitants if pains were taken to seek them out.

The trip to the out-of-the-way village was made by automobile and on horseback with occasional stretches covered on foot. When nightfall came the president and his party would enter a village schoolhouse, roll themselves up in blankets, and stretch out on benches for a few hours' sleep. There was no thought of insecurity. Yet the people of that mountainous region had been at each other's throats over the outcome of the local state elections, feeling that their favorite candidate had lost through fraud. For some time they had been clamoring for the president to come and administer justice.

When he did arrive the people thronged into the towns from all the outlying regions and presented to him their complaints. Somehow their troubles seemed to dwindle before the president's serene, sympathetic and confident bearing. Then petitions for schools, waterworks, mills for grinding the hominy into dough for *tortillas,* hydroelectric plants, roads, bridges, etc. were granted, and everyone was happy. The Zapotec town of Ixtlán de Juárez was given a hospital in honor of the great patriot it had cradled.

On his trip through the region Cárdenas found two children, descendents of Juárez, who were neglected and living in poverty and ignorance. The president took them to his own home in the capital and brought them up with his own son, Cuauhtémoc.

Just before leaving Oaxaca he issued a message to the people urging them to unite their energies with those of the federal government in a comprehensive campaign for the development of the whole state. The program he outlined included the improvement of the existing railway lines and the construction of a new one which would open up a route from Oaxaca City to the west coast; extensive explorations for iron and coal deposits; the completion of the Oaxaca section of the Pan-American Highway to connect the state not only with Mexico City on the one side but also with the Isthmus of Tehuantepec on the other; the conservation of the timber resources; the development of electrical power; and a call to womanhood to rally to the support of the schools and the cause of temperance and civic righteousness.

Leaving Oaxaca City, the president followed the route by which the Pan-American Highway was to cross the states of Puebla and Morelos. It had not yet been opened to motor vehicles so that his party was treated to the thrills of pathfinders.

At one point a mayor of a town asked him to have the highway diverted so that it would go through his village.

"What for?" asked the president. "Do you want the tourists to see how many weeds there are in your streets and how few of your houses are painted?"

Quickly the abashed mayor replied, "I'll compel the citizens to paint their homes."

The president's answer voiced one of the basic principles of his life, "Persuade rather than compel."

Some towns, seeking praise, were rebuked. A conservative old village near the boundary of Oaxaca and Puebla strove hard for his approval. The local politicians of the P. N. R. had endeavored to make a showing by giving liquor to a number of laborers and peasants and then hauling them out in trucks to meet the president. Rather than being pleased at the crowd that came to honor him, the president was disgusted at the drunkenness of his alleged partisans. In that same town, he found that due to clerical influences the children were not attending school. That night when a reception was held in his honor he refused to attend.

If that town was reproved a less proud community a little farther on was honored by being the stage for one of Cárdenas' most important declarations. The immediate provocation was the suggestion to him by a local official in Chila, Puebla, that he be returned to the presidency for another term in order to carry out all his projects. Though the presidential election was more than three years in the offing, Cárdenas took pains to kill the suggestion at once. He did not want anyone to think that the tireless efforts he was putting forth were motivated in the least by the desire to build up such popularity that he could secure a re-election.

Neither the workers nor the peasants should speak of re-election nor of a prolongation of my term as president. We are endeavoring to establish firmly the public's peace of mind by satisfying the needs of the people of Mexico by giving lands and credit to the peasants, and by providing the laborers with better means of making a livelihood . . . Our country does not desire re-election but rather renovation. It desires that each official should excel his predecessor, and one regime excel another.

"No re-election" was one of the chief tenets of the Revolution. The Constitution of 1917 definitely prohibited a president from succeeding himself. It also provided that the election take place five months before the president take office. The P. N. R., in turn, was accustomed to naming its candidate seven months before the election so that early political maneuvering was hard to avoid.

In spite of the Constitution, however, it was not surprising that many people discounted the Chila Declaration. There have been numerous Mexican leaders who have taken a stand against re-election only to succumb later to the advice of friends or to their own personal desires to continue in power. Díaz, in 1877, led a rebellion under the slogan of "constitutional government and no re-election". But once in power he had himself re-elected seven times. Obregón, President from 1920 to 1924, had had the Constitution amended to permit his re-election in 1928. Many believed that Cárdenas was strong enough so that he, too, could have secured the passage of such an amendment for himself.

When the matter was brought up again in a public way some months later through a suggestion on the part of a labor organization that he be re-elected, Cárdenas again answered publicly that he would not consider it for a moment. In addition to hampering his work of reconstruction, ruinous jealousies on the part of other aspirants to the office would have developed, state governors, city mayors, and other minor officials would also have begun scheming on how to hold their jobs, and finally the whole country would have become a political hotbed instead of a beehive of progress as he desired. It should be added here that in this respect the impressive example Cárdenas had set both of his successors have followed.

From Chila, the president continued his journey across Puebla and Morelos to the state of Guerrero. The expedition there was interrupted by the visit of President Quezón, but only briefly, for Cárdenas continued that very day with the problems of the *pueblos*. Ways and means were sought to develop that large mountainous state which had remained isolated for years in spite of its proximity to the capital.

Labor problems awaited the president's return to Mexico City. There had been serious trouble in the important weaving mills near Orizaba in Vera Cruz between members of the C.R.O.M. and those of the C.T.M. Lives had been lost, feeling ran high, and the industry was suffering. Cárdenas' pet idea, that of a united front for the working classes, seemed to be receiving a decided set-back, and he determined to handle the situation in person. Finding that justice lay on the side of the C.R.O.M. in a number of mills he handed down his decision accordingly. It was the first major rebuff for the C.T.M. in over a year

In May of 1937 an exhibition was held in the Palace of Fine Arts in Mexico City graphically portraying what had been accomplished by the different branches of government toward carrying out the Six Year Plan. The president desired that the people of the capital who even then constituted over five percent of the total population of the nation (today the proportion is much greater) should be convinced of the worthwhileness of the government's many-phased program in outlying sections of the country. It was gratifying indeed to observe how the people thronged to the exhibition day after day, and how, as they caught a vision of a Mexico of which they had been ignorant being made great by definite planning and united effort, differences of political philosophies seemed to dwindle in importance.

Then, a general meeting of the cabinet was held, something which did not take place very often, and at this gathering each member was requested to present a report on what his department had done in carrying out the Six Year Plan and what it expected to do during the remainder of the year. The president told them emphatically that he considered it of utmost importance that the Plan be carried out and even exceeded if possible. The people were pleased over this inventory, for many had felt that the president's high desires were being defeated by lack of cooperation from his own political family. Seeing the harness being tightened up on the leaders made the people themselves more enthusiastic about cooperating.

Cárdenas had been issuing messages to the people with increasing frequency. He felt that they were his co-partners, and to inspire further cooperation from them he informed them of what was going on in government circles. Roosevelt could use the radio for his fireside chats, but although Cárdenas used that medium also for his messages to the people he realized that such a small proportion of the twenty million Mexicans had radios, it was necessary to reach them by pamphlets and through the press. But here too he was confronted with a big problem. Half of the people could not read.

He decided to appeal to the twenty-eight governors to assist him in fighting illiteracy. Some of them had not been cooperating too well. A state governor could plead states' right when he was not in accord with some part of the federal program, or if he wanted to hide some inefficiency or misuse of funds. The president realized, however, that their help to a greater extent was necessary if illiteracy were to be wiped out as he hoped.

A complete centralization of the school system under the federal government was being carried forward rapidly, but the advantages gained were partially offset by the loss of interest on the part of the governors that too often accompanied the loss of direction. That meant diminishing financial support. Dr. Tannenbaum once urged Cárdenas to give the municipalities greater participation in the school system so as to get more school taxes from them, but the Six Year Plan called for a federal school system and so Cárdenas rejected the idea.

In his appeal to the governors he pointed out that the federal government would not be able to cope with the situation alone. With 3,100,946 absolutely illiterate males out of a total of 5,681,-300 male inhabitants above ten years of age, and with 3,861,571 absolutely illiterate women and girls out of a total of 6,067,636 female inhabitants above ten years of age, it was evident that every agency possible would have to cooperate in a crusade against illiteracy and for the improvement of the schools. The call brought heartening response.

The latter part of May saw a major strike in the petroleum industry. For two weeks all the petroleum companies except the government-owned Petromex had to close their doors, and gasoline was so hard to get that few automobiles were seen on the street. Finally the shortage became so great that even the bus lines were partially paralyzed.

The petroleum companies claimed that the demands of the strikers were unreasonable and beyond their financial ability to meet. Cárdenas tried to convince the laborers in long midnight conferences that they should either accept the concessions which the companies did offer them, or else agree to go back to work pending a thorough study by the government of the financial status of the oil concerns.

The laborers insisted upon fighting the issue through by continuing the strike, but the president reasoned with them that this would cause the nation to suffer. They positively refused to pare down their demands to the extent that the oil companies requested, but they also hesitated about accepting the other alternative, for they knew how often government agents had been influenced in the past to accept the employers' viewpoint. The president replied that he would be personally responsible for a just decision.

Three times the announcement was made officially that the strike was over, but each time it proved to be that the president had been overly optimistic—the laborers did not go back to work. Cárdenas made no demonstration of power to coerce them, but simply waited, willing to let the laborers save face if possible. Within a few days the workers were back on the job, having accepted the president's personal guarantee, and had turned their cause over to the Federal Board of Conciliation and Arbitration for a thorough investigation and decision. The happy citizens took to the roads once again.

Soon after this temporary settlement of a problem which was to become the most serious of the administration, President Cárdenas used the new Law of Expropriation in a way which should have served as a warning to the oil companies. The railway, *Ferrocarriles Nacionales de México,* National Railways of Mexico, was virtually bankrupt. The rolling stock and other equipment had not been kept up and the railroad workers were unhappy. In spite of the fact that fifty-five percent of the gross receipts were spent for salaries and wages, the average workman earned a lower wage than laborers in other important industries. The government feared that at any time the commerce of the nation might be seriously hampered by the inadequacy of the principal means of transportation. Also Cárdenas desired to place the railway network more at the service of school teachers, welfare workers, medical relief workers, and of projects of general public interest. Due to those considerations, and the fact that the government already owned fifty-one percent of the stock, the lines were expropriated in June 1937, and taken over by the government. The measure was welcomed by the public.

Cárdenas, however, was well aware of the dangers of permanent government ownership, with its politics, sectional favoritism, and bureacratic inefficiency. When the laborers made demands that the government could not meet, he told them that they could have the whole industry on the condition that they make stipulated payments on the debt, keep up the equipment, make improvements, and give the country a proper type of service. It was simply invoking the same principle, he reasoned, that had guided the Revolution's solution to the agrarian problem: "The land belongs to those who work it."

The unions were canvassed by labor leaders appointed to the task and a vote was taken. Some of the men felt that their own organization would not be equal to the task of management, and they preferred to work for the government or a private concern. The majority, however, voted for acceptance, and early in May of 1938 the railway workers of Mexico became the owners and administrators of the largest railway system in the land.

They started off fairly well, but it was not long until President Cárdenas had to step into the picture with the voice of authority after several railway wrecks, one of them of major proportions, had shaken the confidence of the public in the management. The labor organization recognized its responsibility, accepted the resignations of the directors, elected new ones, and proceeded to work for a higher morale among all the workmen.

The income from the lines in 1939 exceeded by 16,000,000 *pesos* the income of previous years. Nevertheless, there was a grave lack of discipline, and union ownership of the lines turned out to be a failure. It was one of the most serious errors of the Cárdenas administration, and his successor, Avila Camacho restored government ownership as soon as he took over the presidency.

When President Cárdenas was in the capital he would take time at least once each week to inspect some of the projects that were under way in and around the great city. One of his favorites was the reclamation project of Lake Texcoco.

When the Spanish conquerors under dauntless Cortez came to the Valley of Tenochtitlán they found most of it covered by lakes. The capital city of the Aztecs stood on an island in the midst of the largest of the lakes. The water was brackish and drinking water was brought to the city by means of an aqueduct. On this same island and the surrounding shores the Spaniards built their capital, the City of Mexico. For three centuries traffic was carried on between the capital and neighboring Indian towns in canoes over the lakes and along picturesque canals. It is said that even as late as the time of Emperor Maximilian it was possible to go by boat to the center of the city and almost to the National Palace.

Efforts had been made at different times to drain the region and reclaim land upon which the growing city might expand. The first of these attempts came during the rule of the viceroys. Then, in the administration of Porfirio Díaz, the Grand Canal was built. It carried much of the excess water of the Valley to the mountain rim which girded the plateau and there a tunnel was dug to give the waters an outlet toward the Gulf of Mexico. This canal did not eliminate the swamps, however, which came up to the suburbs of the city, nor did it drain Lake Texcoco a few miles distant.

During the administration of Ortiz Rubio (1930-1932), a project had been started which was to reclaim for agriculture the area covered by the lake and swamps amounting to about one hundred square miles. Cárdenas was as alert to carry on a constructive project started by a predecessor as he was to initiate one of his own. He ordered the work continued and gave it his personal interest.

As things progressed the alkaline dust from the bottom of the lake lay exposed. The winds of the dry season picked it up and blew it across the valley and into the eyes of the citizens of the metropolis. Many of the people wanted Cárdenas to discontinue the project. One of the large dailies published an editorial urging that the work cease and the land be flooded again, but Cárdenas was sure that the soil could eventually be made fruitful and a source of wealth to the nation.

He hated to stop any functioning worthwhile activity, so he looked around for a solution to the dust and other problems, visiting the area frequently and discussing the matter with the engineer in charge. According to this engineer the president was able to listen to suggestions or plans and "catch them on the wing". Pipes were laid and pumps installed to flood the reclaimed land with the sewage of the city. Grass was planted, and thousands of trees set out. As quickly as land became useable it was made available to the poor people in and around Mexico City. The project went almost unnoticed except when dust storms resulted, but it compared favorably in size with Mussolini's reclamation of the Pontine marshes.

No satisfactory solution has been found for the dust storms, however, and many of the citizens of Mexico City wish that the Lake had never been drained. The planting part of the project has been neglected since Cárdenas left office, and in the winds of the dry season the dust can be bad enough to hinder visability at the big central airport nearby.

The reclamation project was not the only enterprise undertaken for the Federal District. In spite of Cárdenas' interest in rural communities the main center of population was not neglected, although there were many who contended that it was. Tunnels and a canal were built to prevent flood waters from inundating the city's suburbs.

In order to bring a much needed additional supply of drinking water from the Lake of Lerma, plans were formulated and work started on a tunnel through the mountain which separates Mexico City from the Plateau of Toluca. President Alemán finished the system and inaugurated it in September, 1951 bringing more water to the city than the drainage system could handle. Projects were started to develop more electricity as the increase in industrialization overtaxed the limited supply. There was still a shortage when Cárdenas left office however.

The president did much to beautify an already beautiful capital. New avenues were opened and others broadened. The Monument to the Revolution was completed, parks were improved and extended, play grounds and schools were built, large public edifices such as the Supreme Court and the Military Hospital were either started or completed. Cárdenas was responsible for this to a great degree since the capital city is governed by a cabinet member who is named by the president. Nevertheless he was anxious not to fall into the mistake made by some administrations of trying to make a good impression on the upper classes and foreign visitors by spending too much of the nation's revenue on beautifying the capital and other large cities to the neglect of smaller communities.

For his central concern, always, was for the peasants in rural Mexico. "To solve the rural problem intergrally," he said, "would be the best justification of our social revolution." He also believed that in doing justice to the rural sections he was indirectly benefiting the great urban centers, which would profit from the resultant increase in trade.

The Government of Mexico has not socialized the means of production. It has not taken over our export trade. The State has not assumed the ownership of our factories, homes, lands, or warehouses. The instances have been isolated and exceptional where machinery has been expropriated for purposes of public welfare as in the case of La Laguna, the petroleum industry, the railroads, the Mante sugar mill and hemp mills in Yucatán. These were fully justified by the special conditions which existed in each instance, and were forced upon us by the attitude of the owners.

The Government of Mexico, then, is not communistic. Our Constitution is democratic and liberal with a few features of moderate socialism such as the articles that regulate the tenure of land and the relationships between capital and labor. These latter cannot be considered by any stretch of the imagination to be more radical than those that prevail in some other democratic countries and even monarchies. In line with the dictates of the Constitution and without infringing upon our democratic traditions, we have carried out the necessary reforms. We have sought only to organize and intensify production so that our poverty-stricken land may be able to take care of its most urgent needs. In doing so, we have been careful to respect the personal rights of laborers, the freedom of the press, the sanctity of human life, and the development of individual initiative and gifts.

— Lázaro Cárdenas —
February 21, 1940

XX

MEASURES IN YUCATAN AND ELSEWHERE

THE PENINSULA of Yucatán is low and flat. Its surface is composed largely of limestone rock, so much so that when a farmer desires to make lime he merely piles together some stones out of his field, covers them with firewood, and lights a match to the heap. In order to get a crop of corn the inhabitants follow the procedure of letting the land grow up to brush and trees for a few years and then they burn it off and plant. After two or three crops the land must be surrendered to the jungle again to regain some fertility. Sometimes only one small crop of corn is produced after a burning.

The whole peninsula has no rivers. Brainerd Legters, a missionary, tells of the time he took a Yucatán Mayan with him to Tabasco. The Indian was fascinated by the river he saw there. For hours he watched it. Then he turned to Legters and asked, "Does it flow like this at night, too?"

The only possibility of irrigation in Yucatán would be to install large pumps to lift water from subterranean streams where the earth's crust has fallen through and natural wells have been formed. This has not been attempted on a large scale, and the scanty soil hardly warrants the expense of installing machinery for extensive irrigation.

In view of these handicaps agriculture has followed the line of least resistance and has resorted to henequen, a crop that needs little soil and no irrigation. Henequen, or sisal hemp, for export is the one commercial crop of the region, corn, beans, and fruit being produced only in small quantities. The prosperity of Yucatán depends upon the market price of henequen. The large plantations have been cultivated by Indian *peons* who have lived in poverty while the profits went to the plantation owner and commission men who did the marketing.

The peninsula is populated by some 300,000 Mayan Indians whose beautiful language predominates in that region, for the *mestizos* and, in some instances, foreigners who live among them also speak it even in their own homes. The Indians preserve no traditions of the greatness of their forefathers who built Chichen Itzá, Uxmal, and other cities whose monumental remains still tower above the encroaching undergrowth here and there throughout the jungle, and whose archeological attractions entice scientists both Mexican and foreign.

The Revolutionary movement, prior to the arrival of President Cárdenas, had given the Indians of Yucatán some lands and had attempted much for them along educational and political lines, but for the most part the large plantations continued as ever, and little effort was made to improve the living conditions of the *peons*. Cárdenas had visited the area when on his electoral campaign and had resolved to bring it in line with the rest of the country in economic and agrarian reforms.

Accordingly, when his presidential party landed at the port of El Progreso in July of 1937, the death knell sounded for the old plantation system in Yucatán. One reason for the failure to distribute lands previously on a large scale had been the fact that the Indians had had no machinery with which to extract the henequen fibre, and hence were forced to sell their crops to the planters for whatever these were willing to pay. Cárdenas therefore not only distributed more lands but also expropriated the machinery and entrusted it to the peasants under technical supervision.

This policy was possible only because in Yucatán the mills had not been destroyed during the military phase of the Revolution, unlike Morelos where the sugar mills, the chief industry of that state, were completely ruined. In Yucatán, however, the hemp mills had been functioning in good order, so that it was merely necessary to take over the ones which the peasants really needed. Each owner was permitted to keep three hundred and seventy acres of henequen for himself, and the mills were to be paid for on the installment plan over a period of ten years. The peasants were to operate their new grants of land and the mills cooperatively, the only way it could be done efficiently in view of the nature of the crop.

Cárdenas stayed on the peninsula almost six weeks. During that time he traveled extensively, encouraging, helping, urging the peasants on. While there he decided to drive to Peto, and at one point along the route the town authorities came to General Pizá Martínez and insisted that the road beyond was impassable.

The general went to the president and said, "Sir, the people say that you cannot get your car through."

"So the road is bad, is it?" asked the president.

"Yes, sir," answered the general.

The president's eyes twinkled and a slight smile played around his lips. "So the cars will get stuck, will they? Well, that's fine. We'll have a change of work while we get them out again." On such occasions he seemed to become *El Chamaco* (The Kid) again, in a way that is pleasant to write about though not always so funny to his companions at the time unless they are able to enter into the spirit of the thing.

The economic reforms as carried on in Yucatán did not prove to be an immediate success. The *peons* had been subjugated for so many centuries that when given their chance to be free they could not shake off the habit of submission. *Caciques* arose, and politics entered in, hampering the cooperative method as applied to the henequen industry.

Yet the Cárdenas program had one undebatable advantage over the old regime. After four hundred years of trial the old system gave no opportunity for the peasants en masse ever to progress, whereas Cárdenas broke the shell and gave them a chance to go forward if the economy of the region could stand the shock. The initial shock has been withstood, though not without help from the federal treasury.

The next and crucial step in the process involves a long period of training and development, but success is possible and certainly worth working for. The solution lies in the prescription for success that President Cárdenas gave the laborers of Mexico just five days before he left office. He said, "We must demonstrate for the prestige of our cause that the Mexican Revolution means disciplined, efficient, and honest work." In Yucatán, it also must mean honest, efficient, and truly patriotic supervision of the work that the Mayan Indians have always been willing to give. With right leadership Yucatán may become once more the pride of Mexico as it was eight hundred years ago.

Cárdenas revisited the area in November and December of 1939. Both his calls to that state were in marked contrast to one which the old dictator, Porfirio Díaz, had made years before. It is said that on that occasion the inhabitants had been obliged to raise a million and a half *pesos* to pay for the pompous celebrations. Cárdenas, on the other hand, came with no display whatever, and caused the people no expense. His sole purpose was to enact measures which would gradually take much of the misery out of life for the poor.

On the second trip the president and his party circumnavigated the peninsula to the isolated territory of Quintana Roo. When their gunboat, the Durango, reached Tulum, the tide was low, making it impossible for the ship to anchor close in. Rowboats were scarce, the presidential party was large, and the big crowd on shore was anxious to welcome the first president they had ever seen. The most expedient thing to do (and probably the most comfortable with the thermometer hovering around 100°) seemed to be to swim ashore. Mrs. Cárdenas, who had remained in Mérida, says that she has not been able to figure out yet how her husband could have preserved his customary dignity while marching with the throng from the beach to the grandstand clad in his bathing suit.

In the summer of 1937, while on his first expedition to Yucatán, word came to the president from the capital that a plot had been discovered against the regime, and that the leading conspirators, some of whom were prominent lawyers, had been put in jail. The instructions which Cárdenas wired back were typical of the man. They read, "Suspend all action against group of accused plotters at once. Refrain even from citing them for testimony because the government feels that its institutions cannot be endangered by any acts of seditions."

Such an attitude was new in Latin America and diametrically opposed to what was going on at the time in Germany and Russia. Somehow, though, Cárdenas made this policy of disregarding danger work, or at least he was uncanny about knowing when and how far to let it govern his actions.

The attitude of General Cedillo was also cause for concern to many, and had been for a number of months. Early in 1937 the president's close adviser, Dr. Beteta, indicated that the presence of Cedillo on the cabinet had come to be a disturbing factor. The radical element in the government mistrusted him and felt that he constituted a danger to the cause of reform due to his popularity among the more conservative sectors of the nation. They feared him, too, because he continued to keep up a private army in his home state of San Luís Potosí.

Efforts were made to influence the president to ask for Cedillo's resignation. Cárdenas, however, did not view his old friend with much misgiving, especially since he had lost his political influence to a great extent. He had sought rather to show confidence in him by letting him continue as Minister of Agriculture and even by going to his home for breakfast one day in March, 1937. The latter courtesy was an attention which was not often shown by Cárdenas to anyone in the capital while he was so engrossed in the duties of his office. The press made quite a bit of it.

The president was not willing, however, to let Cedillo continue his dictatorial control over political developments in San Luís Potosí. Opponents of the Cedillo machine in that state were dreaming of wresting his power from him. Professor Manrique, who had once been governor of the state and who had opposed Cárdenas in the presidential campaign, went to the City of San Luís Potosí to launch an opposition campaign, but henchmen of General Cedillo caught him as he was making a speech in the public square and sheared off his long, black beard. Officials of the P. N. R. in the capital smiled, but there were threats beneath the smiles. They refused to endorse the candidates of the Cedillo machine. The war lord was deeply offended and appealed to the president, but evidently his demands were not granted, for in July he presented his resignation and returned to his state to strengthen his militia.

This move eighteen months earlier would have constituted a serious problem to the Cárdenas regime, but coming when it did there was little repercussion. Some magazines in the United States, however, published General Cedillo's picture and suggested that his resignation from the cabinet presaged trouble. President Cárdenas attached little importance to the resignation and went on with his plans for the trip to Yucatán.

Congress was to convene on the first day of September, so that the president returned to the capital in time to give an account to the legislative branch of government. He was able to report a marked increase in the harvest of grains. There had been an increase also in the production of minerals, the figures for the year being twenty three tons of gold, 2400 tons of silver, and 424,000 tons of other metals.

In contrast to the old Díaz regime under which Mexico had likewise experienced a period of material development, the program of increasing production along every line had as its objective not only the enhancement of the nation's capacity to produce but also to increase the workers' share of the profits so as to make possible a higher standard of living and higher cultural development. There was an increase of nearly 35,000,000 *pesos* in the amount of money in circulation. An expenditure of nearly 31,000,000 *pesos* was reported for irrigation projects which included thirty-one kilometers of canals and tunnels and fourteen dams under construction.

Over three hundred properties of the clergy had been confiscated in compliance with the law which prohibited clergymen from owning real estate. These buildings had been turned over to the Department of Education and were serving as schools.

Some years later during the administration of Avila Camacho the Supreme Court investigated the expropriation of these buildings and ordered that many of them be returned to their previous owners. The basis of the decision was that, according to the court, the buildings had not all been controlled by ecclesiastical organizations, although it was well known that some actually had been. The government found it to be impossible to return as many of the buildings as the court had ordered released, for the Treasury Department could not pay for them, nor could hundreds of school children have been turned out on the streets. The buildings were getting double use as it was. One group of pupils came to school in the morning, and still another in the afternoon.

The most outstanding thing about the president's report was the independent spirit manifested toward foreign interests which were operating in Mexico. Cárdenas made it apparent that he intended to put forth every effort to secure for the Mexican people a participation in the natural wealth of the land. His determination presaged a struggle with foreign monopolies which refused to relinquish their hold on the country without putting up a powerful opposition.

But before involving ourselves in Mexico's Battle of the Century, it is well to notice several items of special interest in the president's 1938 New Year's message. Ten percent of the federal government's income had been spent in the United States buying machinery and other equipment for the development projects. Over fifteen per cent of the budget had been spent on education. Work had been started on the large Military Hospital in Mexico City and the Supreme Court Building across from the Presidential Palace. A Federal Commission of Electrification had been established. Five governmental credit agencies had been founded. Over two hundred towns had received a water system, hospital, drainage, or some other benefit from the federal government. Highways had been opened in many directions.

The beautiful capital of Mexico at the close of 1937 was no longer the isolated city it had been when Cárdenas was inaugurated three years before. Then it had been linked with paved highways to only four or five nearby cities—Puebla, Cuernavaca, Toluca, and Pachuca. Now its citizens could drive their cars north through Ciudad Victoria and Monterrey all the way to Texas; west, through Morelia and Pátzcuaro to queenly Guadalajara; south all the way to the Pacific Ocean; and east or north-east to the Gulf of Mexico. Cárdenas' vigorous policy of highway construction had set the stage for a great influx into the capital of tourists, commerce, industry, and workmen, and made it possible for Mexico City to about double its population in the next ten years.

The New Year's message also contained a reference to a step of extreme importance that the president had taken toward democratic government. He had refused to accept extraordinary powers any more from Congress. This reveals a turning point in Cárdenas' program, a turning point he had carefully planned—and one so important that it will be discussed at length in the next chapter.

We reject communisim because the adoption of a system which would deprive our people of the full enjoyment of the fruit of their labors is not in keeping with their temperament, nor do we desire that the old system of capitalistic overlords be substitiuted by an overlordship of the State.

— Lázaro Cárdenas

The foundations of democracy rest upon a better distribution of wealth, the general raising of living standards, an equality of opportunity as regards culture, and an equal chance for the working people, who constitute the majority, to attain power.

— Lázaro Cárdenas—to the Nation
December 9, 1938

XXI

TUTOR IN DEMOCRACY

CÁRDENAS' LIFE has been one constant effort to break the shackles of the past and give the people of Mexico a chance. This, in one sentence, presents his political philosophy and accounts for his governmental procedure. It explains his daring departures from custom and epitomizes his faith in humanity. By the fall of 1937 he had become strong enough to break many of those shackles. Now the people had to become strong enough to prevent their being re-formed. He himself would step out of the picture and turn everything over to the people, but first they would have to be prepared to use and protect their liberties or else they would fall prey to ambitious leaders. If the people failed, he would fail. He would stake all on his faith in the masses, the everyday run of Mexicans, people whom not only foreigners, but Mexicans themselves, felt were incapable of self-government. This was the essense of democracy, but to leave the people unprepared would be presumption.

Up until 1911 when Porfirio Díaz, the dean of Latin-American dictators, retired from the scene, a benign or paternal dictatorship had been considered quite universally to be the ideal system of government for Latin-American countries. Many still claim that it is the most desirable system for lands south of the Rio Grande.

The Revolution that ousted Díaz decried the system and promised Mexico a taste of democracy. As Díaz sailed away from the land he had ruled for thirty years he prophesied failure for the new venture. "No one," said he, "will ever be able to govern Mexico except by the stern methods I have used."

Could Díaz have been right? Certainly the history of Latin America—and of Mexico in particular with its many bloody dictatorships—seemed to bear him out. The system seemed to be native to the soil. Capital found it safer; the Church liked it (if

213

the dictator would grant her special privileges in exchange for her support, and this was quite generally arranged); foreign countries, even democracies, were not averse to it since it facilitated the granting of concessions for the expansion of their economic empires; and the people—well, they were used to taking orders, and it would require a long time to teach them to rule their own destinies. Even democratic reformers did not have the patience to do it, and hence were content to sow their seeds in the plateaus of the upper crust of society without even attempting to fallow and seed the broad lowland plains.

When Cárdenas came upon the scene he was soon able to overthrow the virtual dictatorship of his old friend Calles, and within two years had made his own grip so firm upon the affairs of the nation that no one could block him. He had done so without using any repressive measures or intimidating anyone. Instead of trying to impress the people with power he had rubbed elbows with the masses day after day as their equal. His only protection had been the people themselves and his own sincerity of purpose. Old, experienced observers had inquired, "Is the man presumptuous? How long can he keep control in that careless fashion? Surely he should know that Mexico can only be governed by the timely use of firing squads."

No, he had proceeded to let all former rebels return to the country, yet guerilla warfare had died down. His political enemies (he had no personal ones) had been permitted to come and go at will, yet he had firmly withstood a return to political power on the part of the clergy. He had left the capital for weeks at a time to mingle with the peasants here, there, and everywhere, but there had been no decentralization of rule. He had been very considerate about giving orders and had seldom coerced, but civil officials, military commanders, and politicians had learned to comply with his quietly expressed wishes.

People had at first mistaken Cárdenas' kindly features for weakness and had said that he could not last long. True enough, serious difficulties had arisen, but both enemies and friends, capitalists and labor leaders, politicians with jobs as well as those without, had been invited to the Presidential Palace on Constitution Square to talk things over with the serene man there and somehow had been persuaded to fall in line. He had demonstrated unquestionably an uncanny ability to ride without spurs the bucking bronco which had thrown presidents over a one hundred year stretch at the rate of one every eight months.

The people had been won by his amazingly new methods, actually far more significant and unusual than his radical political doctrines. The latter had not been his innovations at all, but merely the mandates of the revoluntionary movement as enunciated by the Constitution of 1917. Gradually a wave of popularity had billowed up from the peasant stratum below until it had carried with it the strata above. With rising popularity he had come to wield a dictatorship over the land, but a unique one— a dictatorship without parallel in the history of Latin America.

The Weyls in *The Reconquest of Mexico* evaluated Cárdenas in this way:

> . . . He has displayed profound originality in evolving a new pattern for the hard journey from one social system to the other. His instinct has been to make this transition peacefully, to undermine the power of a recalcitrant class without killing its members . . . In its emphasis on the intrinsic values of democracy, cultural multiformity, and the right of the individual to dissent, the Cárdenas viewpoint differs markedly from that of contemporary Russia.[1]

Many Mexicans began to wonder if the power and popularity resulting from this policy would turn Cárdenas' head. An answer was soon forthcoming from the president himself. In his New Year's Day message to the nation for 1938 he strongly decried the prevailing tendency throughout the world toward one-man rule, and declared that it was time for democratic countries to return to normalcy in government. He was able to speak because he himself had just demonstrated his sincerity by curtailing his own powers.

Of his own volition he had submitted the budget for 1938 to Congress for its consideration and revision. This had been the first time in years that a Mexican president had requested a docile Congress to take this liberty. Furthermore, he told Congress that he would not only refuse to again accept extraordinary powers from it, but also persuaded it in the fall of 1937 to submit to the states an amendment to the Constitution which would absolutely prohibit the delegation of extraordinary powers to the chief executive except in cases of grave national emergency.

---

[1] p. 381

After thus voluntarily relinquishing the extensive powers Congress had been giving the chief executive without a murmur year after year and after making it impossible to rule by executive decree the remaining three years of his term, he proceeded to plan a complete reorganization of the ruling political party.

Ever since Cárdenas had taken complete control of the P. N. R. in June 1935, he had managed to get the party to do just about what he had wanted it to do, seemingly dictating its principal officers, its policies, and at times the winners in its primary contests. Now he hoped to dismantle it and build up a new machine free from the old abuses and as democratic as Mexico's undemocratic background would permit.

At the time he was about to launch out undauntedly on the marathon of democracy which he desired the remaining three years of his Administration to be, he told me:

There are few people in Mexico who really want democracy. Each man wants to impose his will upon someone else. One politician wants to boss another; capital wants to lord it over labor; labor wants to run capital; companies strive to establish monopolies; and leaders want to control as many followers as possible for their own aggrandizement. It is a selfish picture, but we are going to do our best to curb the tendency.

His faith in humanity had not wavered. He was hopeful that even the ambitious leaders would fall in line if they could be harnessed together in a way that would necessitate their cooperating with one another. He cast about for a harness that would make it difficult for one man or one faction to impose his or its will upon the rest.

The solution he hit upon was to organize a federated party composed of four equal sectors—military, labor, peasant, and popular. Although the army was made up at the time of not more than sixty thousand citizens, he felt that a good way to keep it from running the whole country, as happens in militarist nations and had often occurred in the history of Mexico, was frankly to concede it only one voice in four. This brought him the criticism that he had put the army into politics. I asked him later about the accusation, and he replied: "We did not put the army in politics. It was already there. In fact it had been dominating the situation, and we did well to reduce its influence to one vote out of four." Organized labor was far more vociferous and progressive than its burly country cousin, the peasantry, but the two were placed on an equal footing in the new party. The popular sector was to include everyone who aligned himself with the party but could not be classified with the other three groups. Its task was to bring the voice of the middle class to the party parleys, and Cárdenas hoped that there it would be weaned from its friendship toward capitalism. The new party was to be as all-inclusive as possible, but would not admit either communists or the clergy. All the four sectors were to learn to talk their problems over together and to respect the rights and interests of the others as well as to abide by the decisions reached in conference.

Thus the National Revolutionary Party, *Partido Nacional Revolucionario,* the P. N. R., went out of existence, and the Party of the Mexican Revolution, *Partido de la Revolución Mexicana,* the P. R. M., was born on December 19, 1937. It was dedicated to the cause of making Mexico safe for democracy.

The first test to which the new party was submitted was a financial one. The old P. N. R. was supported by compulsory contributions. To get a government position it was necessary to belong to the party and to pay seven days wages as annual dues according to the size of one's salary. The grand new fellowship of army, labor, peasantry, and middle class was to be maintained on the basis of voluntary contributions with no more obligatory assessments.

The second test was whether or not the party could function as a truly representative team. As regards the labor front, Cárdenas had said prior to his election:

. . . I constantly persist in recommending a united front to the men and women of all the country. Let them overlook all their enmities. Let them liquidate the divisions that hinder the people from attaining better things. Let them study and experiment with the cooperative system which offers us effective formulas for endeavor and attainment, so that they may convince themselves of the great advantages which will result from the union of the workers who, in their double role of producers and consumers, constitute the marrow of national economy.

And in his inaugural address he had repeated those sentiments:

The struggles which the laboring classes carry on between unions when they contend between themselves in the heat of passion and selfishness, have only served to weaken their ranks and to retard the attainment of their aspirations . . . inasmuch as the needs of the workmen are identical, they themselves should well be able to form a united front with a general program which would contain their just demands.

If unity had been highly desirable then, it was indispensable now in order to give labor a strong voice in the new party. It was not attained fully, but by the end of the Cárdenas administration had reached a point that did credit not only to the faith, patience, and persuasive powers of the president but also to the labor leaders themselves, especially to Vicente Lombardo Toledano, erratic though he often seemed. Unity on the part of the military sector was not hard to attain, for it was natural in a body accustomed to discipline. The peasantry, however, proved to be an unwieldy and difficult problem. The ground work was laid, but it will take a long time for this sector to be able to give suitable expression to its desires. The big labor leaders would have liked to have mobilized the peasants in their ranks, but Cárdenas wanted them to retain a separate identity. The popular sector was harder to define and hence to reckon with, but it was a problem which did not call for as urgent attention.

Cárdenas' dream of one big political party composed of a united peasantry, proletariat, and middle class, backed by an army free from selfish interests and working only for the welfare of the nation, and of politicians who would forget politics as soon as they became high public officials, was foredoomed to failure. It was to be one of the first things that his successor would revamp. He could have read the warning of history that all such dreams have failed, but he kept on dreaming. Mexico will forgive you if you do not realize your dreams, but she will never forgive you— no, she cannot even understand you—if you do not dream.

President Cárdenas had been dictatorial in the imposition of such an idealistic mold on the body politic, but he believed that it would make one-man leadership impossible in the future and would guarantee a voice to all revolutionary minded people in the management of their political affairs. His disappointment was great when the new structure proved to be an air castle instead of an abiding temple of liberty, and President Avila Camacho first modified it and then tore it down. Its main weakness was its underpinning. Though Cárdenas had been strong enough to take the reins of government out of the grasping hands of politicians and war lords, he did not have time to train the rank and file of Mexico's poorer classes to throw off the bonds of local *caciquismo* and to rule democratically.

The vision of a united Mexico dreaming together was Cárdenas' goal, but he failed to get the press, the writers, and even the students sufficiently fired to propagate the vision far and wide. He could catch the imagination of the peasants, but they were unable to carry on the vision after their hero quit the stage. The seeds of propagation were not sown effectively enough in the proper strata.

Just about the time he was working out his idealistic plan for the four-sector party, he expressed himself to me very soberly though not with despair on the basic difficulty. "The greatest problem of Mexico," he said, "and I believe of thé whole world, is the human heart." He knows its perfidy, yet he continues to trust it.

I do not now refer to the trust that causes him to go everywhere unarmed and unguarded. That is another matter. Regarding his personal safety he simply believes that no one will seek to harm him when he has been so careful not to harm others. That is the way he has put it when he has seen one of his non-military aides carrying a revolver. "What have we done," he would ask, "to cause anyone to want to kill us?"

His trust in humanity is much more far-reaching. Strong leaders are often suspicious of others. Dictators confide in no one indefinitely. Cárdenas, to the contrary, makes all about him feel that he trusts them completely. He gives the impression of being the most unsuspecting individual in Mexico.

It is hard to reconcile this characteristic with the keen political insight which everyone recognizes and which often kept him from making serious political blunders. Perhaps he did not really trust the politicians he had to use, but made them feel that he did. All the integrity which they could muster was brought to the top by the very confidence which Cárdenas bestowed. Of course, a reckoning day would come sooner or later, and future confidences depended on the outcome. In fact, many a change in his official family was due to his having become convinced that a trusted helper had been dishonest or faithless to a trust.

Cárdenas tried to make the common people realize that they had big tasks to perform, responsibilities formerly carried by their leaders. At first he would point out their personal or class interests, but invariably, as they followed on, he would lead them to think of their duty to the nation. The emphasis in the latter part of his administration was not upon stirring the masses to a realization of their rights as it was during the first part. Rather, in tones of increasing volume during 1938 and 1939, he emphasized the call of duty. Labor was willing to listen about duty when it was its best friend who spoke, a friend who had gone the whole way with it in securing its just demands. Cárdenas knew that it was necessary to awaken a sense of responsibility and fairness in the laborers and peasants which would go a long way toward stopping the abuses that abounded and always will abound when oppressed people come into power for the first time.

If he found it necessary first to stir laborers and peasants to rebel against injustice and then guide their ardor toward paths of duty and self-respect, he also found that the same procedure was called for with government employees. The bureaucracy in Mexico as elsewhere in Latin America had known little of democracy. Every office chief had been a dictator over his subordinates but a "yes man" to his superiors. The sentiment of the Revolution in Mexico had been strongly against this situation, but up to December, 1934, when Cárdenas became president, a department chief might literally kick a government employee of lower rank out of his office without getting in trouble. While Cárdenas himself demands implicit obedience from his subordinates, he is very careful not to humiliate them in any way. He listens to their opinions with utmost respect though he rarely solicits advice. He always listens to their grievances.

Government employees were quick to see that their opportunity had come, and asked for a civil service law. Until that time they had been subject to wholesale dismissals whenever a new chief came into office. They now demanded security and the right to strike, some threatening the latter without waiting for Congress to concede that right. Cárdenas persuaded them not to try this, but gladly engineered through Congress in the fall of 1937 a civil service law designed to free them of the risks and humiliations of the past.

Thereupon the workers organized syndicates and began to use their new liberties to excess. Gross inefficiencies became more numerous in the transaction of government business. Clerks began to arrive late at their desks and to take time out for a smoke, a chat, or a flirtation whenever they wished. The president was

not surprised nor discouraged, but once again sounded the call
of duty tactfully but forcefully. Though it took a while for the
government employees to learn not to abuse their new rights, the
law is considered by such an experienced and fair-minded man as
Dr. Manuel Gamio, Director of the Inter-American Indian Institute, to be one of the big contributions of the Cárdenas Administration. Others concur in this opinion.

Democracy cannot exist without liberty and individual dignity. Cárdenas and other leaders of the Revolution were right
when they went to alarming lengths to get all that had been subservient in Mexico to be independent. Liberty, however, must
know one master if she is to survive and that is duty.

Cárdenas, personally, is a devoted worshipper at that shrine.
Each advancement in responsibility has been accepted by him
not as an honor, but rather as a call to greater service. He also
sought to steer along conscientious paths the forces he had prodded into a feeling of independence that had often resulted temporarily, at least, in irresponsible action. This might have been expected by those who heard a speech he made back in 1933 in
which he said:

Fundamentally, I consider that the failures of the people in their struggles
toward a clearly defined goal . . . have not consisted in the lack of a more
or less brilliant expression of doctrines. They have been due, rather, in
great part to the folly or bad faith of the men who sought to carry them
out. Therefore, the errors of an institution can be corrected by the wholesome influence of the members who are regenerated.

Fellow Mexicans, during the year that terminates today, the world has seen the immense majority of us united in the task of repelling by the moral force that comes from a close solidarity, the attacks that have been made on the Fatherland. May this harmony, born in hours of struggle in a common cause, be the permanent symbol of our nationality. Mexico needs the help of each one of her sons if she is to unfetter herself by her own efforts. For that reason we should dedicate ourselves more and more to disciplined effort to raise our cultural level, augment our production, and attain better living conditions for all our homes.

If, as we hope, all our activities are carried out by all sectors of our society in the spirit of brotherhood and discipline, and if we take unitedly as our goal the well-being of our Nation we shall give a lofty example of what a people can accomplish when it sets itself to make the Fatherland great.

May peace and happiness ever abide in all the homes of Mexico!

— Lázaro Cárdenas —
December 31, 1938

XXII

CARDENAS IN CLOSE-UP

THE CÁRDENAS FAMILY consists of the general himself, Mrs. Amalia Cárdenas his wife, a married daughter Alicia, and their teen-age son Cuauhtémoc, who is a picture of his father. During the general's term in the presidency, however, you could see eight or nine boys and a girl playing around the rooms and grounds of Los Pinos, the presidential home.

Who are these youngsters?" you would ask Mrs. Cárdenas.

"Oh, they are children of poor parents whom the general has brought back with him from different trips," would be the reply.

For fear that Cuauhtémoc might come to feel that he was more important than other children, and in order to allay the mother's anxiety that too much indulgence from a solicitous father might contribute to the same result, both parents agreed that their son should have older playmates. Hence, the greatly expanded presidential family.

The young and beautiful Mrs. Cárdenas has fitted into the strenuous life of her husband with grace, charm, and a spiritual partnership that understands and goes along where other women might balk or be unsympathetic. Doña Amalia, except on special occasions, dressed as simply as a business woman though with extremely good taste. The general likewise is plain in his attire, except for fine neckties for which he seems to have a special liking. Their home was kept as a shrine for the family, special friends, and relatives, and was seldom without guests, although very little official entertaining was done.

When Cárdenas became president many customs were thrown to the winds. He did not entertain the diplomatic corps or other functionaries either at his home or in Chapultepec Castle, except as he might choose to invite some individual diplomat whose companionship he particularly enjoyed.

223

During the six years that Cárdenas was president, proud Mexico City was a capital without its chief executive nearly a third of the time. Even when there, he was generally at his desk or inspecting public works and seldom appeared at public functions. You might have noticed by the papers that the day before he had entertained at dinner a group of Spanish orphans, and if you had happened along at the right time, you could have seen him dancing with the wives of humble soldiers at a military picnic in the park. I once saw him riding down Reforma Drive in Mexico City in an open car with a number of boys on bicycles hanging on to his auto, merrily getting a tow. The president was enjoying it immensely. But you would never see him at balls, theatricals, or even bull fights, Mexico's best-beloved sport. He hated to lose time from work and despised ostentation.

When he became president, Cárdenas cut his own salary in two and eliminated the usual grant in the budget for the First Lady, explaining to his Chief of Staff that he would be able to support his wife without drawing on the national budget. He used to own a large farm in the State of Michoacán, but deeded part of it to the laborers who tilled it, and part to a nearby hospital which he himself had founded previously. His son Cuauhtémoc participated in the distribution, share and share alike with the laborers.

Cárdenas believed that the peasants had been last long enough, and decided that it was time for the last to be first. The proud hilltop castle, Chapultepec, was seldom used by this commoner-president, but when these rare occasions did roll around, aristocratic Emperor Maximilian and pompous old General Diaz must have stirred fitfully in their graves because of the motley assortment of guests. I myself have eaten there with a group of unknown students, just because the president wished to encourage us in helping the Indians whose languages we were studying. Seminole Indians from Oklahoma were feasted there while the president, with delight, joined them in breaking bread over the rich table cloth. Surely, in dismay, the costly crystal chandeliers must have looked down upon the scene. Yes, Cárdenas has even taken some of these humble aborigines to his own plunge and gone swimming with them.

Naturally, those who used to be first didn't like this reversal in accepted procedure and derided him for it, but he moved right ahead anyway, jealously cultivating contacts with the poor to protect himself and his socialistic tenets against the sophisticating influences of Mexico City, and encouraging his wife along the same lines. Many were the orphanages, schools, and poor homes which received calls and gifts from the First Lady.

Cárdenas' pockets are merely sieves when he sees others in need. I once introduced to him an old Zapatista colonel whom I knew to be living with his family on an *ejido* in Morelos in abject poverty, though he was a worthy man with a patriotic record. The president spoke kindly to him, but I saw no money change hands. A week later, however, the old soldier came to see me again and told me: "Last week when I left home to come here, my wife was desperate, for we were completely out of money, and our children needed food and clothing. I told her that God would provide, and came away. Here, much to my surprise, I met the president and he gave me twenty-five *pesos*. When I got home my wife could hardly believe her eyes when she saw the money."

Books could be filled with such examples of liberality and sharing on the part of General Cárdenas, but he is careful to keep them out of print. His friends are expected to respect his wishes, a fact which leaves me but one consolation in breaking the rule. This is the knowledge that the general has never executed anyone in all his long career, something of a record for a commander of troops throughout the Mexican Revolution.

Cárdenas' relatives remonstrated with him about his liberality, saying, "Lázaro, when you are out of office, you will no longer be surrounded by so many friends, and you are going to need a good big bank account."

The general replied quietly, though in an undercurrent of disgust, "I am not afraid of being unable to earn a living for my family. I shall still have two hands with which to work."

This same industrious spirit has dominated everything he has ever done. Six-thirty each morning found President Cárdenas up and under a shower or in the open air pool, swimming (his favorite and almost only diversion). Intimate friends or cabinet officers used to come to his home early in the morning for "emergency" interviews. The president began to show them a hospitality not altogether guileless, for he would, with playful delight, send an aide to invite the would-be interviewers to join him in a cold plunge. It was not long until the only person he could find around to swim with him at that chilly hour was the caretaker of the stable.

Some mornings a canter or gallop through the park would follow or be substituted for the swim. He is a good rider, having previously engaged in equestrian sports considerably. In 1924, however, while matching his skill at lassoing with other army officers, his mount became unmanageable and carried him with tremendous force against a stone wall. His left arm was almost torn from its socket, and his left eye so seriously injured that the doctor feared he would lose it. Today, however, there is just a stiffness in the arm which prevents his bending it freely, and only after excessive exertion and long hours without sleep does the eye develop a slight misalignment. As a young man he would ride alone a great deal at night just for the fun of it. Over thirty years ago when he was in command of a post among the Yaquis in Sonora, he would gallop fifty kilometers to town to see a girl friend after Saturday's work was over.

Cárdenas frequently took a walk before breakfast, and at first Mrs. Cárdenas, seeing him go out alone at 6:00 A.M., was somewhat concerned. She ordered her chauffeur to follow at a discreet distance as protector. The president soon noticed his shadow and told the would-be guard to go back to work. He had gone everywhere else unarmed and virtually unprotected, and he was not going to be trailed on an innocent little matutinal amble.

Now Mrs. Cárdenas has lost all visible concern over her husband as he continues to go everywhere unarmed. So have all his intimate friends. It is inconceivable that a man who walks the common road and seeks the common good as he does, and who is ready to share his very home with the children of the poor, should ever be the target of base injury.

The general not only enjoyed the exercise of those morning walks, but he considered it unpardonable for any man not to be thoroughly acquainted with the country for a radius of six miles of his home. When he would see a man milking cows he would stop and ask how they were doing. If he was favorably impressed with his dairyman neighbor he might offer him a position with the Department of Agriculture. On one occasion he

took a young man home with him, an utter stranger, and gave
him an opportunity to learn typing and shorthand in his own
offices at "Los Pinos".

After this early morning ritual the president might talk over
some problem with a colleague. At breakfast, which was over by
eight-thirty, he would confer with others. Later, more interviews
might be held in his private office at home or while walking in
the garden. At nine, however, the big sedan (an ordinary stock
model) would roll out of the gate and on through beautiful
Chapultepec Park and across town to the Presidential offices on
the central plaza. Someone would generally be invited to ride
along to discuss his assignment.

After his arrival at the Palace, matters which called for immediate attention were taken up, and then men of special confidence who had been detailed for some undertaking particularly
dear to the president's heart, might be received in quick though
never hurried succession.

Daily correspondence was attended to with the aid of several
male stenographers. Cárdenas has never employed women in his
own office though he has been an outstanding defender of
women's rights. After the desk had been cleared of correspondence and routine business the president would be ready for
scheduled interviews with cabinet members and officials, plus
anyone else there was time to see.

At three, or soon after, he would descend to the patio, enter
his car with an official or two or possibly some other intimate
who wanted to talk over a problem, and off they would go for
dinner (the seven-hour interlude between breakfast and dinner
was never broken by a lunch). If dinner were to be at home,
the other occupants of the car would ride only as far as the door,
and then the president would find himself alone with his family
and possibly some household guests.

After the brief time with his family at afternoon dinner he
would go back to work in his private office in one wing of "Los
Pinos" or perhaps to the National Palace. There audiences were
granted until nine or ten, and not infrequently until midnight.
After a very late supper, if one were indulged in at all, and another
brief time with his family, the president would dedicate two hours
to reading and study, no matter how advanced the hour might be.

Then, in the small morning hours he liked to review the work of the day and settle upon his program. Cabinet officers might hear their telephones ring any time from one to three o'clock in the morning and find that the president wanted them to go on a trip with him, or to send some special engineer or professor to his office the first thing, or perhaps it was an invitation to an eight o'clock breakfast to talk over a pending problem.

He managed to keep his colleagues very busy. One morning an official in the Ministry of Education found his desk piled high with orders from the President's office.

"How strange!" he remarked to a clerk. "I thought that the president was off on a trip."

"He is," replied the clerk, "but these orders came by mail."

While he did not hesitate to delegate ample work to others he was no sluggard in the pursuit of his private objectives. Let us watch him at work on one of these many trips by following him for a day in Morelos.

No collective action is complete from its beginning. It is the work of successive generations to carry it through to perfection. The big thing is to make the start.

— Lázaro Cárdenas — to Military Commanders
September 5, 1939

Does it seem dangerous? Well, it's better to lose one's life doing good than to do evil in order to live.

— Lázaro Cárdenas—to Frank Tannenbaum

XXIII

A DAY IN MORELOS WITH CARDENAS

No ONE can properly understand Lázaro Cárdenas as a man without observing him closely on one of his trips among the people. Before we become engrossed in his struggle with the powers of petroleum, let us visit with him the Zacatepec Sugar Mill in Morelos.

To get to the president's home we drive down El Paseo de la Reforma, one of the most stately avenues in America. When we come to a broad entrance guarded by two crouching lions, we pass between them and enter beautiful Chapultepec Park, so named for the hill around which it lies and which was called by the Aztecs *Chapultépetl,* or "Hill of the Locusts". We do not follow the winding drive which leads to the majestic *Castillo* on its crest, for the new White House of Mexico is a modest structure hidden away among friendly pines at the rear of the hill. It does not get its name, *Los Pinos* from those pines, but because President Cárdenas, when he had remodeled it from an old telegraph school, chose to name it after the place near Tacámbaro where he had first met Amalia.

There we find an anteroom to the president's office already crowded with people hoping to see him, although it is but a quarter past eight in the morning. Among the number we see many day laborers, for they have come to find that they are always welcome. Indeed, the rugless floors, simple furnishings, and bare walls indicate that the president wants to make them feel at home.

Four members of the cabinet, two bankers, two army officers, a few other officials, and ourselves are admitted into the inner court to await the start of the one-day tour. Soon the president's Chief of Staff, dressed in civilian clothes, opens an inner door and we are all ushered onto a veranda where President Cárdenas stands waiting. A cordial handshake for each guest takes but a moment and then we enter automobiles and are whisked away.

We ride with the minister of Labor, Genaro Vásquez, an Indian from Juárez' tribe who has had a long career in public affairs. He is accompanied by Professor Javier Uranga, a scion of an old aristocratic family from Chihuahua who dedicated years of service taking education to Indian hamlets scattered over the mountains of many states, especially Oaxaca, when Vásquez was governor there.

Vásquez tells us that the president had called him over the telephone at three o'clock that morning, requesting that he locate Uranga and bring him along. Another tells us of an occasion when he had ridden horseback with the president until one A. M. and then being called at five to start again. The president himself had been the alarm clock. A general who had been on Cárdenas' staff in the campaign against Escobar tells us that it was no uncommon thing to see General Cárdenas at his typewriter at two o'clock in the morning, and then to be awakened at five hearing him take a shower if their campaign quarters were equipped with such a luxury.

We follow beautiful avenues across a residential section of Mexico City and then on through Coyoacán, the suburb where Cortez and Alvarado had had their homes. Some of the residences are four centuries old and cast a spell of history over us as we traverse the narrow street. Soon we begin to climb up over the ridge across which, at a point farther east, fearless Cortez, followed by a handful of Spanish daredevils thirsting for gold and fame, had swept down into the broad Valley of Tenochititlán to bring to an end the great Aztec civilization. It is for the ragged descendants of those magnificent Aztecs that our expedition has sallied forth.

Soon we reach an altitude of nine thousand feet above sea level and the cool, snappy atmosphere causes us to close the car windows. At one side of the road among the pines we notice a cluster of crosses and ask what they mean. There are no houses nearby, and there is no indication of a shrine. They mark the execution site, we are told, of General Francisco Serrano and about a dozen friends who were disposed of without trial. (The story is that, in 1928, General Serrano, a candidate for the presidency in opposition to Obregón's second term, was dining in Cuernavaca with friends. Federal soldiers were sent to take them into custody and escort them to Mexico City. At this point along the road they were shot as they tried to "escape"). The crosses are silent reminders of the price which Mexico has paid for the liberties she has won through years of bloodshed. They also increase our appreciation for the mild methods by which the present government holds control.

We soon enter the state of Morelos and arrive at the mountain village of Tres Cumbres (Three Summits). It was formerly called Las Tres Marías (The Three Marys), but the Revolution has changed the names of many towns which had a religious significance and substituted either non-religious descriptive names or the names of humble peasants who gave their lives in the Revolutionary cause. Especially is this true in Tabasco.

Suddenly our cars come to an abrupt halt, for the highway ahead is blocked with a large crowd. The president has alighted and stands attentively in the midst of the crowd listening with a grave but noncommittal expression to a man in peasant attire who stands before him, reading at the top of his voice, a long list of complaints against some of the local authorities. Cárdenas promises to order an investigation, and then presses forward through the milling mass to the schoolhouse which stands at one side of the road.

Children shower the chief executive with confetti. The authorities express the gratitude of the town for the new water system which had been inaugurated that very morning. The teachers present to him the needs of the school. Then delegations from other towns of the region flood him with petitions for aid as well as expressions of gratitude for help already rendered. Some ask for roads to connect their villages with the outside world. Others ask for schools or water systems. The president explains that while his administration plans to do all within its power to provide drinking water for all the towns, yet it would be impossible at the moment to do more along this line for the state of Morelos, inasmuch as twenty-six of its communities had already been given water during 1937. It was only fair to attend to the needs of other states also.

The evening before, the president had given me in rapid fire succession the names of all twenty-six towns including such impossible ones as Tlaquitenango and Amimilzingo. I had not had time to write them down, however, and so now I take the first opportunity of asking for the list from an official of the Department of Public Health which had directed the work. He is nonplussed and says that he would have to ask someone more familiar with the zone. The informant he secures is also unable to give many of the names.

I then tell them that the president had named all twenty-six without difficulty. They laugh and explain that Cárdenas has an amazing memory which enables him to recall the names of places and people all over the nation, as well as minute details concerning all the projects he had on foot. It is this memory which enables him to keep a check on all his subordinates, for he never forgets something which he has requested them to do.

When the president has heard all that the people have to say, he speaks to them briefly and informally concerning the government's program on their behalf and concerning the need of harmony in their ranks. Then he makes his way to the door, the peasants pressing about him. There are no soldiers or plain clothes men to guard him. There never are.

We are reminded of the incident told us by a fellow linguist, Maxwell D. Lathrop. The president had visited his Indian town on the shores of Lake Pátzcuaro where about eighty-five percent of the inhabitants had asked that the local church building be turned into a school house since there was no building for educational purposes. Fifteen percent, however, were opposed to the move. So much bitterness had resulted that the president had felt it would be wise for him to go in person to handle the problem.

When he reached the town in his launch, Mr. Lathrop and a throng of Indians met him on the beach. Mr. Lathrop observed that a number of angry women were carrying daggers under their shawls. The president walked among them without hesitation. After listening to their objections he patiently explained the reasons why the eighty-five percent wanted to use the church building as a schoolhouse. As the women listened anger gradually disappeared from their faces, and some of them even said, "*Tata Lacho* has a right to use the temple any way he wants to."

Soon after leaving Tres Cumbres the presidential caravan begins to descend rapidly and we see the picturesque city of Cuernavaca spread before us. It is the capital of Morelos and also a popular tourist resort. Formerly, one of the wealthiest states in the Republic, Morelos had presented a scene of apparent prosperity. Appearances, however, were deceiving, for the large plantations had belonged to a few families who lived like feudal lords while the masses, hungry, poorly clothed, and sick, eked out a meager living of beans and *tortillas* and found a miserable shelter under roofs of thatch. Today the grandees have departed and the rabble have taken over.

Before entering Cuernavaca we stop at an old plantation whose extensive buildings stand in semi-ruin. They testify to us that we are in the state where Zapata was born and where he did much of his fighting as the champion of the landless classes. We are told that this particular *hacienda* had included a large distillery where tons of sugar cane had been converted into firewater to drown the peasants' sorrows and ferment their woes—also to keep them in debt to the landlords so that the labor laws might hold them in virtual slavery until the debt was paid. The debt did not die with the death of the debtor, but was passed to his heirs. Thus for generations people were tied to the same plantation or *hacienda*.

The president leads our party on an inspection of the walls and grounds, not so much for his own information, for this project has already been well thought out, but to acquaint the rest of us with the possibilities offered by the old ruins for a school for soldiers' children.

Newspaper photographers who accompany our expedition hustle about taking pictures, a regular feature on the less rigorous presidential tours. The trips not only make great news, but also teach geography through the accounts of the travels. The publicity is good propaganda for his projects and a means of keeping the welfare of the country in the hearts and minds of the populace.

As we pass through the historic old city of Cuernavaca our cars do not even slow down. To the left we see the tower of the Municipal Palace built four centuries ago by Hernán Cortez. Only half a block from the highway stands the Morrow home where Lindbergh courted Anne in its romantic gardens. On the side of the city toward Acapulco we see modern mansions and one of them is pointed out as belonging to General Calles. As the road descends the temperature becomes hotter and hotter. Vegetation is scant, for we are in the dry season when months of rainless heat scorch everything.

About twenty miles below Cuernavaca we leave the highway and approach the squalid Indian town of Xoxocotla. The president prefers not to enter in his car, but rather alights on the outskirts and, with peasants pressing about him on every side, proceeds down the street to the schoolhouse, radiating a paternal joy from his close contact with the masses.

Xoxocotla is decorated in festive fashion with bunting and tissue paper in national colors of green, white, and red in honor of its special visitor, and also because of the new water system which is to be inaugurated this day. The precious liquid has been piped in over a distance of sixty kilometers (thirty-seven miles) so that for the first time in history the people can go to a spigot and fill their jars with nice clear water instead of having to carry it two miles from a dirty waterhole.

The Director of Rural Education, Professor Flores Zamora, has told us of a certain occasion when he had accompanied this peasant-loving president on a busy, tiresome, day-long visit by launch to various towns on Lake Pátzcuaro. (Politicians and legislators, the professor says, swell up with pride the first time they are invited to accompany the president on a trip; but after an early morning start and after miles of travel over mountain trails on foot or horseback with nothing to eat until three o'clock in the afternoon, and then many more miles to cover and hundreds of people to meet until well after nightfall, their pride is humbled by aches and pains.)

On this particular trip dusk was settling down upon the weary, inexperienced travelers when their launch put in at an island town. The party disembarked and walked to the town's square where the president dismissed them saying, "I want to be alone for two hours, after which we shall gather again at the launch and return to Pátzcuaro."

All withdrew, but the professor found a place from which he could watch the president unobserved. The latter made his way "alone" among the Indians in the village square, greeting one, asking questions of another, and sitting down beside a third for a quiet chat. Then, for over an hour he just sat on a stone in a pensive mood and somehow took rest from simply being among the humble Indian folk.

Here in Xoxocotla, however, there is no opportunity for quiet contacts. The village band blasts forth its patriotic airs deafeningly. We follow the milling townfolk right to the schoolhouse, one of the best to be seen in rural Mexico. The president had made a special grant of a large sum of money to this Indian community to give it an up-to-date school. Even water-closets are in evidence, a *very* unusual thing in rural Mexico.

The schoolyard is crowded, and as soon as the president enters and the band stops playing an Aztec Indian orator who has learned Spanish mounts a balustrade and in a powerful voice addresses the president, telling how his town has suffered, and describing vividly its poverty, ignorance, superstitions, and hopelessness. Then he tells of how Zapata had led them to battle in the hope of securing land to till and of how, when this leader had fallen before a traitor's gun, they had followed an uncertain pathway between hopes and disappointments until President Cárdenas had come to fulfill their dreams. His voice becomes husky, as with Indian sincerity he thanks the president for the schoolhouse and water supply and the credit the land bank has given them to enable them to farm their newly acquired lands. Then he bursts into a flight of Indian oratory and cries, "You are the first President of the Indians! We have not erected triumphal arches to greet you, nor have we strewn flowers upon your pathway, but we welcome you with gratitude and spread before you in utmost confidence our petitions."

The orator stops. The people applaud, not in the animated American fashion but with simple cries of *"Viva Cárdenas!"* *"Viva Zapata!" "Viva la Revolución!"* The band strikes up a stirring tune to indicate its approval.

As the strains of music cease a crippled colonel of Zapata's old army who has climbed on top of the base of a pillar begins a speech of welcome in the name of his comrades-at-arms. His old companions surround him, dressed as the country farmers they really are. Zapata had utilized the peasants almost exclusively to fight his battles. One day his soldiers would be determinedly using the rifle, the next innocently hoeing corn. The president listens to the old soldier with unusual feeling, and after the speech is finished the rural farmers, proud possessors of commissions signed by Zapata declaring them to be colonels and generals, press forward to clasp Cárdenas' hand. He assures them of his support in their agricultural battles.

Representatives from neighboring towns press around him and put written petitions in his hands. Some bring complaints and to these he listens with particular attention. When one peasant brings charges against a representative of the land bank, the Attorney General, in order to catch every detail, pushes his way through the crowd to a position near the president, saying ominously, "This may interest me."

The president requests one of his colleagues to make known to the crowd his desire to have their complaints thoroughly aired and thereupon one after another of the peasants steps forward to testify—certainly a unique method of administering justice.

From Xoxocotla our party takes the dusty road through the ruined plantation of Galeana to another shell of former wealth called Zacatepec. Our companions tell of numerous battles having taken place in the region. The Revolution is now faced with the problem of reconstruction. The peasants have learned that they are to be utilized in the project not as beasts of burden as under the old regime but as partners or rather proprietors, while the government merely plays the role of helper.

The soil and climate are admirably fitted for the growing of sugar cane, but due to the destruction of the mills and also to the difficulty of growing that commodity on a small scale, the lands had been turned over to the cultivation of corn and rice. Here at Zacatepec, however, we find that twelve and a half square miles in a cooperative pool are being set out to sugar cane to supply the large government-constructed mill whose capacity, when finished, will be 300,000 tons annually.

As we arrive at the site we find that construction is far along. Nearby are squalid hovels, temporary homes, where several hundred laborers are camped while working on the mill. They hope to share with the peasants of the region in the operation of the plant, and one of the problems which is brought to the president is whether the laborers from other areas can share with the local peasants in its ownership.

We learn that the project is to cost over twelve million *pesos* and that an American firm has received the contract to supply the machinery. The plant is to belong to the laborers, but the government will provide technical direction and financial oversight. Profits are to be distributed among the laborers. Nine months of the year they are to till the soil, and the three months of harvest they will man the mill.

The president walks from point to point inspecting the construction work. While he leads the way on foot a hundred horsemen who have ridden in from nearby farms follow him about, kicking up such a dust that we can hardly breathe as we hurry to keep up with the crowd.

Cárdenas, in explaining the project to the peasants, tells them, "Since there is not enough land to meet your needs, we are creating other means of gaining a livelihood. That is why we are building this mill. It is yours. Accept it as a provision made by the government for the solution of your economic problems."

The president listens stoically to two tiresome speeches by men who are not peasants, listens even when one of the youthful agitators tells him that he has dangerous enemies within his official family. Then Cárdenas goes into conference with the engineers. One by one blueprints are presented to him, and as he examines them he asks questions and offers suggestions. He insists particularly that every effort be made to make the homes of the employees as comfortable as possible. He suggests the construction of an athletic field and of an up-to-date school. Then he indicates where a bridge should be built and a hospital erected, and expresses his opinion concerning the laying of tracks for transporting the cane.

The clock has struck three before we hear the call to dinner. Most of us are hungry, for we have eaten nothing since an early breakfast. A bountiful meal prepared in country fashion is spread out before us on three large tables. The president eats heartily as is his custom, particularly relishing the corn on the cob. He converses some, but spends more time listening. Occasionally he steers the conversation by the injection of a word or sentence. He is serious but cordial throughout the meal. Only once do we see him break loose and laugh. This is when General Gonzáles tells us about a trip he had taken with the president.

"The man is barbarous!" he exclaims, pointing to Cárdenas with an expression of despair. "He will make you ride horse-back all day long without giving you time to even eat breakfast. On one occasion we did not reach a village until two o'clock in the afternoon, and I was starved, for we had been in the saddle for eight hours without taking time to eat. When we finally reached the town, the president found that the local women had arranged a dance in his honor, and he insisted that we should not disappoint them. Accordingly, we danced for two hours before he was willing to quit and eat!"

Not once during the day have we seen the president manifest anger or impatience, nor have we heard his voice raised in discussion above the pitch of ordinary conversation. We notice that his eyes are as kind as they are serious and as considerate as they are penetrating. In fact, when he is dealing with peasants they become unmistakably tender. "He has the eyes of an Apostle", a photographer from the United States has said.

Something about his bearing does not permit loud joking or jesting, and yet there is a spirit of conviviality not fostered by wines nor liquors of any kind, for the only drinks on the table are orangeade and mineral water. The president's old friend, Ambassador Castillo Nájera, does pull out a bottle of wine from somewhere and pours out a few drinks, but when he offers one to the president, suggesting a toast, the latter replies, "I shall drink mine with water."

From Zacatepec we drive to an irrigation project which is to put twenty-five square miles under cultivation. The president inspects the dam and then drives on to the office of the engineer in charge. There he retires behind a closed door and is left alone for the first time that day. Evidently he is going over the impressions of the day and thinking out the instructions he must give to the different members of the party. When the door is finally opened and we see two members of the expedition ushered in, we notice that the president looks refreshed. His physical endurance is a puzzle to everyone. They say that no one can become president of Mexico unless he has a dynamic personality and great endurance, and is *muy macho* (a he-man).

We have the privilege of listening while the president gives instructions to Professor Uranga concerning a project which had been presented to him the evening before for transforming a sterile valley, inhabited by poverty-stricken Indians, into a garden of orange groves and model peasant homes. We hear Cárdenas repeat each of the details as they had been given him without making a single reference to notes. As he goes over different matters with several of his colleagues one by one, we notice his broad grasp of facts and figures concerning not only his country but also of markets and problems abroad which have a bearing on Mexico.

Each of us who has been invited on the expedition is given an opportunity to chat with him, and then the caravan starts on the return trip.

As we ride back to the capital the Minister of Labor explains to us that besides immediate results, such trips serve as training schools for his colleagues. "In all the cars of our party", he continues, "discussions are going on concerning ways and means for building up our nation. All on the expedition are catching the spirit of the president and are bent on discovering ways to help. They observe how the president meets the people and realize that they should do the same."

A beautiful moon lights a mellow tropical sky as we climb the pine-clad slopes of the ridge separating us from Mexico City. By ten-thirty we arrive at the president's home. He alights from his car without a sign of weariness and takes his stand on the steps leading to the porch where he shakes hands with us one by one in the same friendly, humble way in which he has borne himself all day long.

As we ride home with the Attorney General, Ignacio García Téllez, he observes to us: "Mexico has never had such a president before. He has started so many projects and has established such intimate links with the common people that the man who follows him will have to be a superman to be able to continue his example."

The oil companies have had money, arms, and munitions to support rebel bands, money for an unpatriotic press that defends their interests, money to enrich their unconditional defenders, but for the progress of the country, for establishing a true balance by means of fair remuneration for work done, for sanitation of the districts in which they operate—for none of these has money ever been forthcoming.

Investors have lacked sufficient moral character to induce them to give something in exchange for the wealth they drew from the land.

— Lázaro Cárdenas — Expropriation Speech
March 18, 1938

XXIV

THE OIL STRUGGLE: TACTICS AND CONTESTANTS

IF THE RECORD of the oil trusts has been far from lily white in the United States where they have had to cope with enlightened public opinion and restrictive laws, any thinking person can readily understand what has happened in lands where the companies had a free hand and where the light of justice was slow to break through the dense tropical jungles to resist unscrupulous exploitation.

And yet there has been resistance. The Motilón Indians of Venezuela have fought the oil men with gruesome success. Over a period of six months it is said that a man died every day. Sometimes they were Indians, but often they were employees of the oil companies, Venezuelans or foreigners. Geologists, in their advance into Indian territory, would suddenly find their trail blocked by a row of ominous arrows driven into the ground. They knew that it was a warning from the Indians to proceed no farther. However, the thirst for oil—not their own thirst altogether, for their share in the spoils would be meager—but that of company managers in lands far away, impelled them to risk their lives and cross that line. Those who returned often brought an arrow or several piercing their bodies. The jagged darts could seldom be removed without tearing the flesh so much that the sufferer bled to death. One doctor developed a procedure by which a sharp glass tube was pushed down over the arrow so as to leave a cleaner wound, but even this would not always work. Finally, an Indian woman was captured and taken to the city to learn Spanish and then to return to her people to talk them into submission, but the day after she was sent back to her jungle haunts, she was found dead. Her tribe had looked upon her as a traitor, for they had made up their minds to resist to the finish all outside encroachment.

The Indians of the oil-bearing lowlands of Mexico could make no such spectacular defense against foreign intrusion. They had been conquered long before, and when oil was discovered on a large scale in 1901 the president of the country, General Porfirio Díaz, was carrying out a policy of unprecedented give-away to enterprising foreigners. British and American capital which preferred to work under the Anglo-American system which gave the man who owned the land on the surface of the earth, possession of the earth beneath the surface as well, persuaded Díaz to give up the nation's rights to her subsoil wealth.

The oil-seeking pathfinders of civilization could see no point in paying royalties on oil leases to uncouth Indians or peasants, and so they went about buying up the land and its precious liquid gold beneath at the ridiculously low prices of timber or pasture lands. It is said that Edward L. Doheny bought nearly three hundred thousand acres at a little over a dollar an acre. Both Americans and Mexicans familiar with the development of the oil fields have attested to the fact that when the Indians refused to sell their lands, chicanery was resorted to or else the recalcitrant property holders might even be put out of the way by a gunman. Possibly free lance promoters were responsible for most of these atrocities and later sold out to our large and respectable firms. At all events, the titles acquired by many of the large as well as smaller concerns affected years later by the expropriation could not always bear close scrutiny.

For many years the exploitation of Mexican oil proceeded rapidly. There was little to hamper in the way of governmental regulations, for subsoil rights was not the only privilege which Díaz had granted the oil companies. Machinery imported for the development of the fields was exempt from import taxes. There was no tax on the capital invested in oil, and while Díaz was president, no export tax. There was no tax on the by-products of oil. The fields themselves were taxed, but as cheap agricultural lands without regard to their fabulous subsoil wealth.

As far as the laborers were concerned they were at the mercy of the companies. Just how much mercy there was can be imagined if we recall that as late as the fall of 1939, petroleum companies operating in Venezuela permitted waste oil to collect on the surface of a lake over which their Venezuelan employees lived in homes on stilts. When the scum had become thick enough it caught on fire, the homes were burned down, and hundreds of lives lost.

The thing was outrageous enough in itself, but since it happened to be the second such catastrophe within a decade, it was doubly criminal. If the men, women, and children who were burned to death had been English, Dutch, or American, a furor of protest would have been raised against the carelessness of the companies; but they were "just Venezuelans", the people who were allowing their foreign guests to make great inroads upon the natural resources of their country, and had been promised good jobs in return for the concession.

Things are different in Venezuela today, for the oil trusts have learned their lesson. But it took a "tough" Mexican by the name of Lázaro Cárdenas to pound it into their heads.

In Mexico the adoption of the Constitution of 1917 was the first real rebuff to be given the inordinate draining of the nation's oil deposits for foreign benefits. The new Constitution, in addition to establishing protective laws for the workers, returned the ownership of subsoil wealth to the nation as it had been under Spanish law. According to that law all underground wealth was the property of the Spanish crown. This was reiterated in 1783 when the Royal Orders for New Spain were issued. When private concessions to the subsoil resources were made, all unexplored wealth remained in the possession of the crown, and the individual to whom that concession was made became owner of the "metals, semi-metallic ores, bitumens and juices of the earth" only after it had been extracted and brought to the surface.

A payment, in proportion to the amount extracted from the earth, was to be made to the Royal Treasury. If the individual or private concern failed to comply with the royal regulations, that party forfeited his concession. When Mexico achieved her independence in 1821 the rights of the Spanish Crown were transferred to the Mexican government. This of course included her possession of all subsoil materials.

Following the Constitution of 1917, however, successive governments were too weak to insist that the nation receive a royalty on its extracted oil. In 1917 also, a tax was levied on crude petroleum, casing-head gas, and by-products of oil. But the companies were *unwilling* to be taxed. Doggedly and persistently they fought all forms of government regulation, getting diplomatic support from London and Washington for their contention that the new Constitution could not affect them since they had secured their holdings prior to its adoption. It was as though a foreign slave owner had argued that the Emancipation Proclamation could not free his slaves, since he had bought them before the Proclamation had been issued.

They overlooked the fact that the Revolution itself had been fought not only to obtain land for the landless, but as a protest against Díaz and his near-donations to foreign landholders, mine owners, and oil companies. He had sold Mexico's subsoil heritage for a mess of pottage. When she had come of age and had sought to reclaim her birthright, she had found that the foreigners who had already made fortunes from it were unwilling to relinquish their grasp.

Not only was the treasure beneath her soil being drained without much benefit left in return, but also the foreign interests which had been attracted by it showed little respect for her sovereignty and used their financial power for meddling in her political affairs. Mexico could do little, however, to remedy the situation. An export tax was levied, and the oil fields were taxed, though not without objections from Washington. These objectionable taxes, totaled together, came to only one-fourth the tax imposed by the United States on similar oil fields.

Labor unions were organized to defend to some degree the rights of the workmen, and the companies were obliged to reorganize as Mexican concerns, thus ostensibly renouncing all rights of appeal to foreign governments. In actual practice, however, they ignored the local courts and appealed to their own governments, thus turning what should have been Mexico's private affair into an international matter. All this in spite of the fact that the Constitution of 1917 stated that aliens might be granted concessions to the subsoil only provided that

they agree before the Department of Foreign Affairs, to be considered Mexicans in respect to such property, and accordingly not to invoke the protection of their governments in respect to the same, under penalty, in case of breach of this agreement, of forfeiture to the nation of property so acquired.

The basic issue of the ownership of the oil deposits was left pending. Mexico did not renounce her constitutional right, but she did not dare to try to collect royalties from the powerful companies so strongly protected by diplomatic influence.

Josephus Daniels, after telling of the ridiculously small sums paid for oil leases, summarizes the story as follows in his *Shirt Sleeve Diplomat:*

The bald fact stood out that foreign oil men had come into the possession of Mexico's greatest wealth without paying anything like its value, that they had been given largesses in the shape of tax concessions and other favors, that the wages paid to workers in the oil fields were scandalously low although in keeping with the Mexican standard, and that the laborers in the oil section lived under wretched conditions as to housing and health protection.[1]

This was the situation when Lázaro Cárdenas came to the presidency. He himself summarized it in his speech of March 18, 1938:

It has been stated *ad nauseam* that the petroleum industry has brought into this country enormous capital for its development. This assertion is an exaggeration. The oil companies have enjoyed for many years, during most of their existence, in fact, great privileges for their development and expansion; they have been granted customs rebates, fiscal exemptions, and numberless other prerogatives, and their privileges, joined to the gigantic potentialities of the oil fields granted to them by the nation oftentimes against the will of the latter and in violation of the country's laws, make up almost the whole of the actual capital so often talked about. The potential wealth of the nation, wretchedly underpaid native labor, exemptions from taxation, economic privilege and government tolerance: these are the factors that built up the boom in the Mexican petroleum industry.

From 1901 to 1933 the records show that the average production was 53,089,412 barrels a year and the records may not tell the whole story, for it has been suspected that quantities of oil were shipped out in tankers without a full record being kept, especially after taxes were imposed on each barrel. Among the wells brought into production was one that has never been equalled in daily output anywhere.

It is almost inevitable in a world inhabited by grasping, competitive human beings, that many eyes would lust after the spoils of such a rich prize. In order to exact the maxium profits from such booty the oil companies had had trouble being fair with their laborers. In 1935 President Cárdenas, inheriting the accumulated grievances, had tried to mediate a satisfactory settlement, but in

---
[1] p. 214

July of 1936 representatives of the 18,000 members of the Union of Petroleum Workers had met in Mexico City and formulated a proposal for a collective labor contract. The companies had rejected the proposal so that the oil workers had decided to strike in November, but Cárdenas had succeeded in getting the men to stay on the job while a commission representing their unions and the companies tried to work out a settlement. The laborers had grown impatient of waiting and left their jobs in May, 1937—and stayed away until the consequent shortage of petroleum products had grown serious, and the president had almost forced them to go back to work.

When Cárdenas had returned from Yucatán he had found another strike pending, but this time only in the Poza Rica field. In spite of warnings from the government, Poza Rica Union struck, and President Cárdenas issued a message to the entire Union of Petroleum Workers on September 12, politely branding the strike as treason to the cause of labor in general. He urged the Poza Rica men to get back to work before there was another shortage of petroleum which would cripple operations of the National Railways and delay the completion of important irrigation projects that were in need of cement which could be supplied by the factories only if they had fuel to keep the machinery going. He also complained that the Poza Rica men were playing into the hands of the obstinate companies and of certain reactionary groups by maintaining their disregard of authority. It was like a quarrel between lovers, for the president could truthfully say that he had invariably been on the alert to defend the just demands of labor. The rebellious union finally fell in line and the investigations of the ability of the companies to pay continued.

The companies, in the meantime, were holding back on new drilling and improvements of all kinds. Their refineries and other equipment were permitted to get into poor condition. Rumors were circulated that the oil companies might even pull out and leave Mexico until labor had learned its lesson.

The deposits that the companies maintained in Mexican banks were also permitted to get low. Cárdenas began to show some evidence of alarm in the face of all this and on the sixteenth of October issued a statement on the economic status of the nation. He took up the rumors one by one and then stated the true situation, showing that each month of 1937 the federal income had exceeded the original estimate by many millions of *pesos*. He admitted that the expenditures on the numerous development projects had also been boosted, but promised to curtail them if there should be a decrease in income.

To the rumor that he had borrowed so heavily from the Bank of Mexico that its reserves had been reduced to the point that the rate of exchange was apt to drop, he answered in his usual frank way that it was true that something over thirteen million dollars was owed the Bank on account of the road building program. He was certain, however, that this small amount would not affect the situation of the Bank. Later, when the oil struggle did bring about a drop in the rate of exchange, Cárdenas not only kept his promise to curtail development projects, but also consented to a ruling that made it impossible in the future for the government to overdraw its account with the Bank of Mexico.

On November 11, 1937, Cárdenas demonstrated his desire to get along with the oil companies by entering into an important agreement with the Shell subsidiary, *Compañía Mexicana de Petroleo-El Aguila,* which strengthened the company's position through a recognition of its claims to certain disputed fields. The company, in turn, according to the president's interpretation of the agreement, recognized the government's constitutional right to the subsoil wealth by agreeing to drill wells for it and otherwise to contribute to the development of the government's own oil business. This was looked upon by the Government as a royalty. The president defended the seeming lapse in his determination not to extend further concessions to the foreign oil interests by pointing out that the agreement with Shell was not a matter of new concessions, but rather a compromise in the dispute over concessions that former administrations had given.

The Shell interests probably thought that their contract which seemed to open for them a new era of development was indicative of weakening on the part of President Cárdenas, and that he would exert pressure on the Labor Board to render a decision that would be favorable to them. If so, they had a rude awakening when the Labor Board handed down a decision that gave the laborers about 40% of their demands or about one million dollars more than the seventeen companies involved were willing to pay. The companies replied on the twenty-eighth of December—which

it may be noted is Mexico's equivalent of our All Fool's Day—
by appealing to the Supreme Court for an injunction against the
Labor Board's decision.

Cárdenas, even after this "April Fool" rebuff, manifested a
conciliatory attitude in his message to the nation three days later
when he declared categorically that his government would be glad
to celebrate more contracts with private concerns for developing
of the industry on the condition that they would pay a royalty to
the government, the constitutional owner of subsoil wealth. He
was definitely proferring the peace pipe, but the oil companies
took it as a sign of weakness and prepared to fight rather than
concede the difference of a million dollars a year.

It does not seem that Cárdenas contemplated forcing the companies out of Mexico. In fact, he stated in his expropriation speech
that the decision was one "which we would neither have wished
nor sought had it depended on ourselves alone."

His plan had been merely to increase Mexico's participation in
the wealth nature had stored under her soil by promoting a
government oil business. This had been started during a former
administration as a private corporation with the government as
principal stockholder, but was reorganized by President Cárdenas
as a strictly governmental enterprise. Valuable experience was
gained by the government in this way, but little dent was made
in the oil industry. The year before expropriation, it produced
less than 3% of the oil, though the agreement with the British-
Dutch interests in the fall of 1937 would have substantially increased this figure within a few years.

However, the companies precipitated trouble in their appeal
to the Supreme Court, arguing that it was impossible for them to
meet the demands of the laborers because the government itself
had prohibited their raising the price of gasoline for domestic
consumption. Attorneys for the workers, however, had found
from an examination of the books that actual profits were much
greater than was admitted. Profits, they found, had been con-
cealed by the selling of the oil to sister or parent organizations
in foreign lands at a price far below that of the world market.
The investigation also found that the oil companies had been
discriminating against Mexico in that they had sold their products at from 171.75% to 350.76% higher on the home mar-

ket than in other countries. This, the investigating commission
had maintained, constituted an obstacle for the economic development of the nation.

It had discovered that the cost of living in the oil fields had
gone up, though the wages in many instances were less than in
1934. The oil companies argued that the wages they paid were
as high or higher than those of any other industry in the country,
but the laborers answered that they were less than half what the
same companies paid their employees in the United States for
the same work. On the other hand, a comparison of figures showed
that it took a capital investment five times greater in the United
States than in Mexico to produce a barrel of oil.

Furthermore, the risks taken by the Mexican oil worker due
to malaria, dysentery, and other tropical diseases were much
greater, for the oil companies had not cleaned up the areas nor
protected the homes of the workmen. Profits, it was found, during
1934, 1935, and 1936 had been ample to warrant an increase
in wages, and indications were said to be favorable for the business in the immediate future.

The companies, we have said, had appealed to the Supreme
Court because the Labor Board's decision had provided for an
expenditure in wages and social benefits of about $91,000 a
month more than they had been willing to pay. This small sum,
remember, would have been distributed among seventeen companies, one of which had a larger yearly income than that of
the Mexican government itself. (Gulf Oil had paid its employees
in Mexico at the same rate as its workers in the United States.
Gulf laborers had not unionized, and hence this company was
not involved in the controversy. It held and operated its properties until 1951 when it sold out to the Mexican Government.)

On March 1, 1938, the highest tribunal in the land rejected
their appeal and ratified the findings of the Board. The only
choice left the companies was either to abide by the Supreme
Court's decision until time had shown if there had been a mis-
carriage of justice or not, or else refuse to obey the Court and
see what the government would do about it. They chose the
latter course. They had begun with a bluff, namely, the contention that the business was not profitable enough to make it interesting to them if they had to pay the increase demanded, and

when their bluff had been called they decided upon defiance as their next resort.

Subsequently, their tactics included retaliation through boycotts and embargoes, insults to the chief executive whose honesty they openly questioned, complaints to London and Washington, renewed appeals to Mexican courts, the holding out of tempting plums to the Mexican government in one serious effort at conciliation, more rebellion against the Supreme Court, and finally a last and desperate appeal to Washington. It is a record that reveals very little of shrewd business ability and much bullheadedness.

This writer had the opportunity of going to the offices of some of the oil executives in this country and suggesting to them conciliatory measures that would have won for them not only the goodwill of the Mexican government, laborers, and people, but also the privilege of staying on in Mexico and probably making more money than ever. They bluntly told me that they preferred to "fight it out on the same old basis." Had they not clung to the false hope of getting help from Washington, they might have used their common sense as they are now doing in countries where they still have large holdings.

On the side of the oil companies there was one outstanding example of common sense and ability, but unfortunately he represented only the Sinclair interests which were relatively small. It was General Pat Hurley of whom Daniels wrote in *Shirt-Sleeve Diplomat*:

I found he had not come bristling with demands or in the hope that the Marines would be sent down to compel the return of the properties. He was a realist and knew that the interest of his company depended upon the policy of give and take. President Cárdenas and his Cabinet members liked him and his desire to reach an understanding. Cárdenas, who is an Indian, was pleased to learn that Hurley likewise had Indian blood. They both talked directly, brusquely, . . . disagreed, agreed, exchanged an *abrazo,* and parted as fast friends. The result was that Hurley received a fair price for the Sinclair Company and did not join in the campaign of vilification of all things Mexican. His willingness to confer and accept payment was not relished by the big oil companies that had not learned that the days of the Big Stick were over.[1]

At any rate, through the whole contest, which we have yet to discuss in its entirety, one man stood out above all other partici-

---

[1]p. 214

pants. Neither Dutch, English, nor North American, he was a Mexican who demonstrated courage, integrity, self-control, business ability, patience, and dignity. Lázaro Cárdenas showed more character than genius, but by simply following up the errors of his opponents in an energetic, logical way, he was able to make a contribution to the economic future of his nation which will bring him the undying gratitude of posterity, not only Mexican but American. He has shown us how to clear the ground of economic injusties in order to build an abiding foundation for inter-American unity.

Even when the conflict was at its height in the summer of 1938, a prominent oil executive in New York City paid Cárdenas a grudging compliment by telling me that although he was fighting the chief executive with everything he had, he still considered him to be the best president in Mexico's history.

When a monopoly becomes so strong that it can dictate to a government, it is time the people of that country should either buy out such a giant business or elect to starve rather than to become smothered by the great power which endangers the country's sovereignty. The Mexican government did everything possible to reach an amicable agreement before expropriation, but the companies, sure of their power, sat back and defied the Labor Arbitration Board and even the Mexican Supreme Court's decision. Not satisfied with our promise to pay for the oil properties, they have circulated calumnies through books, the press, and radio, poisoning the minds of the American public against a government that is doing its very best to improve the living conditions of the Mexican people. Their stories have made us appear like a band of arrant thieves, and now they are pressing the State Department in Washington for help.

— Lázaro Cárdenas—
to José Navarro, Los Angeles Examiner, August 26, 1939..

XXV

THE DECLARATION OF MEXICO'S
ECONOMIC INDEPENDENCE

ONE DAY EARLY in February, 1938, when it had become quite evident what the attitude of the oil companies was to be, I was surprised to see one of the president's aides enter our yard in the Aztec village. His message was brief and delivered with dignified courtesy: "The president asks", said the polite captain, "if you would do him the favor of inviting Mrs. Cárdenas and himself to dine with you tomorrow."

Naturally our little household was delighted, and on the following day a big black Buick drove into our yard bringing the President and Mrs. Cárdenas and some guests of theirs. Two aides drove off in another car to Cuautla, five miles away, leaving the little group alone with us in the Indian village. Crowded into the tiny room that served us as parlor, dining room, and kitchen, we enjoyed a congenial carefree time over the simple meal which Mrs. Townsend had prepared. Then the president and I excused ourselves, carried our folding camp chairs to the shade at the rear of our trailer, and talked.

The president was obviously burdened. He spoke of the attitude of the oil companies, of how confident he was that there would be no trouble if he could only talk the problem over with the stockholders personally instead of having to deal with their high-salaried agents in Mexico who wished to appear indispensable to their employers but who actually were working against their best interests. It was his old confidence in the people reasserting itself, only the people he trusted now were scattered far and wide in England, Holland, and the United States, linguistically dissimilar from him, but anxious, he was sure, to do the right thing if he could only get the facts to them. Of their agents

255

he had little hope, for some letters they had written to company directors in England had fallen into the hands of the government and from them it had been learned how unfairly Mexico's case has been presented.

Firm resolution settled down over the president's serious though serene features as he said, "Former administrations did not feel strong enough to confront the petroleum problem energetically. I believe, however, that my government enjoys sufficient popular support to be able to meet the issue squarely. This I intend to do should the companies persist in their attitude of defiance."

A month later their rebellion against the highest court in the land was complete. Everywhere people were speculating as to how Cárdenas would answer the question the oil companies had asked with insolent assurance of their own security, "What are you going to do about it?"

Labor answered first by requesting the government to free them from their contracts with the companies since the latter refused to make valid the concessions granted them by the Labor Board. This was a legal request, but the strike that would have followed would have tied up business and travel all over the land.

The companies expected the government to place their properties in a receivership which would have given them time to work. The government, hampered by the economic problems that the companies could have created had they been permitted to keep their fingers in the pie, would have found it impossible to have run the business successfully. The companies were in a better position to withstand a long drawn-out struggle than Mexico was. They thought, too, that by prolonging the conflict they would be able to profit from divided opinion among the Mexicans themselves and would be able to build up anti-Mexican opinion in the United States.

President Cárdenas, however, realized that every moment of delay made the companies more powerful in their position and placed the government more at their mercy. He determined to take from them their power to cripple the nation from within. Without serving notice to anyone, not even to solicitous Ambassador Daniels who might have been able to bring the companies to their senses had he been able to warn them how serious their situation had become, he went before the microphone on March

18, 1938, and announced his decree of expropriation against the seventeen oil companies. Speaking to the nation, he said:

A total halt or even a limited production of petroleum would cause in a short time a crisis which would endanger not only our progress but also the peace of the nation. Banks and commerce would be paralyzed, public works of general interest would find their completion impossible, and the very existence of the government would be gravely imperiled because when the State loses its economic power it loses also its political power, producing chaos.

It is evident that the problem which the oil companies have placed before the executive power of the nation by their refusal to obey the decree of the highest judicial tribunal is not the simple one of executing the judgment of a court, but rather it is an acute situation which drastically demands a solution. The social interests of the laboring classes of all the industries of the country demand it. It is to the public interest of Mexicans and even of those aliens who live in the Republic and who need peace first and afterwards petroleum with which to continue their productive activities. It is the sovereignty of the nation which is thwarted through the maneuvers of foreign capitalists who, forgetting that they have formed themselves into Mexican compaines, now attempt to elude the mandates and avoid the obligations placed upon them by the authorities of this country.

The attitude of the oil companies is premeditated and their decision has been too deliberately thought out to permit the government to resort to any means less final, or adopt a stand less severe (than expropriation) . . . I call upon the whole nation to furnish such moral and physical support as may be needed to face the consequences that may result from a decision which we would neither have wished nor sought had it depended on ourselves alone.

The people did respond with their full support. The president's bold stroke appealed to their patriotism and they became united as I have never seen them before or since. A great manifestation of confidence and support took place in the capital five days later, and it was my privilege to observe from a point of vantage that spontaneous mobilization of feeling on the part of the Mexican people.

The notes I made right on the spot will describe it:

I sit writing in a large room on the second floor of the National Palace which forms one side of the *Plaza de la Constitución (El Zócalo)*. Here at crucial times throughout many centuries events of utmost importance in the history of Mexico have taken place. On a balcony nearby stands President Lázaro Cárdenas accompanied by members of his cabinet and scores of other officials watching the greatest popular demonstration which has taken place in this land during recent years.

The broad plaza, flanked on our right by the anciently solemn but stately Cathedral, and on the left by the more modern Municipal Palace, is thronged with thousands of people, while thousands more march by beneath the president's balcony in a steady stream which will continue for hours and then flow on out into history as Mexico's second Declaration of Independence.

Just above where President Cárdenas stands waving a frequent recognition to the acclaims of the laborers and students as they march before him, there hangs the very bell which Hidalgo the priest rang one hundred and twenty eight years ago in the far-off town of Dolores, announcing the intention of a handful of patriots to fight for the political independence of Mexico from Spain

Last Friday, March 18th, President Cárdenas figuratively rang the bell for economic independence by declaring that his government would not bow before the oil interests, principally British and Dutch, in their defiance of the Supreme Court which had found the demands of their employees for better wages and working conditions to be just. The impasse which resulted when the companies balked left the president no other alternative than to take over most of the oil industry.

Consternation has resulted in financial circles. The foreign colony here in Mexico City is decidedly partisan to the oil interests, fearing that what has been done will serve as a precedent for the confiscation of their own investments. Some declare their intention of selling out while they can and returning to their respective countries, though others say that they are making such large profits they will remain as long as they can buy more trinkets and can go more places with the same number of dollars.

President Cárdenas, in an effort to calm industry in its very reasonable fear of further confiscation, published a statement yesterday calling the attention of the public to the emergency conditions under which the expropriation law was resorted to in the case of the oil industry, and promising that it will not be applied to other enterprises. On the contrary, he promised that they will be given every encouragement possible.

The Bank of Mexico has had to redeem ten million *pesos'* worth of its bills with silver coin during the past two days, but the run seems to be over and plans have been formulated to mint fifty million more silver *pesos* so that there will be ample coin in circulation if the lack of confidence in bank bills should continue.

I stop writing long enough to step out onto a balcony and watch the communist section march by. It consists of just a handful of demonstrators sandwiched in the multitude. They carry a large red banner which reads, "The Communist Party of Mexico", and a white and red one which says something about "On with the International Revolution". It is noteworthy today that the red and black emblems, which had almost supplanted the Mexican flag in parades here a few years ago, are less in evidence, while the national colors of green, white, and red are seen everywhere.

Labor unions, peasant leagues, and syndicates of school teachers and other federal employees have called a halt, temporarily at least, in their almost incessant petitioning for rights. The majority of the people have forgotten for the moment to complain against the rising cost of living, injustices, and this, that, and everything, in order to join in the nationwide rally to the support of their daring leader.

Perhaps the Mexican Revolution has passed into a new phase as regards the psychological basis of its program. For a number of years past it has endeavored to teach the masses, long trained to subserviency, to rebel against all imposition and to demand their rights at every step. Very little was said about duty. The pendulum swung so far in that direction, especially during the first two years of the administration of General Cárdenas, who democratically insists that the only citizenry which can be properly and enduringly developed is one which is free and realizes that it is free, that at times chaos threatened not only laborers but also in the ranks of the school teachers and other government employees. Many observers wondered how a sense of duty would ever be instilled into them. The emergency of today, however, may perform the necessary miracle.

Two hundred thousand people are parading, carrying banners which express their approbation in terms such as these: "Down with imperialism", "The laborers desire the economic independence of Mexico", "General Cárdenas, you are the only one who has had the courage to defend our rights", and "President Cárdenas, we are with you in the enthusiasm of today and we will be with you in the struggle of tomorrow" (the economic struggle which will be necessary for Mexico to pay for the expropriated property).

The president, of course, must realize that he has bitten off a chunk which will require all his exceptional energy and that of his colleagues to chew to a point of semi-digestion during the remaining three years of his administration. Everyone knows the government has been spending every *centavo* it could lay its hands on to promote development projects among the peasants where returns will be very slow to materialize. They know that for three months it has been hard put to meet its minimum obligations, due largely, it claims, to deliberate efforts on the part of the oil companies to embarrass it financially. How, then, can it hope to pay the large sum required to reimburse the companies even over the ten-year period which the expropriation law permits and at the same time meet the demands of the laborers?

Perhaps the rebirth of patriotism which is in evidence today will prove to be the solution of the situation. Not only the laborers, but the thinking citizenry in general realize that the honor of the nation is now at stake, and a do-or-die attitude seems to have been aroused. Both labor unions and government employees have declared in printed statements a willingness to tighten up their belts ten notches if necessary and sacrifice until Mexico has met the obligation with which she has saddled herself.

A united and duty-conscious Mexico *can* refund the oil companies. The industry which has been 90% foreign-controlled, something which we would never permit in the United States, will then be placed at the service of the nation. The living conditions of the laborers will be improved, and further exploitation will be directed by the consideration of national expediency rather than by the whims of foreign interests.

On the other hand, Mexico has been slack about the meeting of obligations accruing from the confiscation of farm lands and railroad lines. Furthermore, will the government be able to manage the oil industry efficiently? For many years its management of the Post Office and Telegraph Department was decidedly inefficient, but recently this has improved so much that last year the Department showed a profit of over a million dollars.

The government-controlled Bank of Mexico, it must be admitted, can show a creditable business record. The many irrigation projects, including four major dams and thirty-six smaller undertakings, are being constructed by the government itself, and though results have not been entirely satisfactory, they are nevertheless impressive when the observer stops to realize that three years ago Mexico was dependent upon foreign contractors for most of such engineering projects and has had to develop her own engineers in a very short time.

One of the most promising factors is President Cárdenas' universally recognized personal integrity, a factor which has played no small part in the unprecedented material development of the country during the past three years. An administration which has to its credit the greatest physical advances in Mexico's history should be able to handle 42,000,000 barrels of oil a year successfully. Certainly the problem would not puzzle Texas oil men, and both the president and labor leaders have stated their intention of bringing in independent oil men from north of the border to help them.

Other problems, of course, are involved such as the willingness of Washington to continue to purchase Mexican silver at the present figure. If she does, Mexico is certain to continue to purchase large quantities of machinery and other equipment for public works from United States manufacturers. If Washington ceases to buy her silver, her financial difficulties will be increased and her development program will be crippled considerably.

While this demonstration of apparent national unity goes on, some of the American oil companies are appealing right now to Washington to defend their rights, diplomats are conferring, government employees are taking over the oil fields, refineries, distribution systems, and other holdings of the foreign concerns, and Mexican citizens are commenting with no little appreciation upon the fact that the "Good Neighbor" north of the Rio Grande has not yet sent any gunboats to their ports.

The bands are still playing, the Cathedral bells continue to peal, the president radiates confidence, the crowds have been surging past for five hours and the end of the long parade is not yet in sight nor is the end of this day's doings. Mexico has truly declared her economic independence!

The enthusiasm of those hours might have intoxicated the mind of a less sober ruler, but Lázaro Cárdenas kept his feet on the ground and his hands to the plow. Carefully avoiding anything that would have fed the fires of anti-foreign feeling which excitable minds had kindled, he faced the crowds and spoke to them of Mexico's responsibility before the world:

We place ourselves on a high legal and moral plane that our country may be great and respected . . . It is timely to declare in these solemn moments and to make it known to all the countries of the world, that Mexicans will honor their foreign debts.

Upon leaving Mexico, the expropriated oil companies did not leave behind them, after years of exploitation, a single thing whereby the Mexican people could remember them with gratitude.

— *Lázaro Cárdenas—to Congress*
September 1, 1939

XXVI

RIDING IT OUT

IN SPITE of their enthusiasm and determination the Mexican people were anxious. "Would England send warships to demand the return of the British-owned properties?" "Would the Monroe Doctrine stop her?" "If so, would she request Washington to take up the issue energetically?" "Regardless of what England might do, would Washington herself send gunboats to Mexican ports?" These and similar questions were asked time and again in stores, restaurants, clubs, and wherever the middle and upper classes congregated.

Up to this time the United States had been buying Mexican silver, in accordance with the Roosevelt Administration's silver policy, at the same preferential price we had been paying Canada. This had been a big help not only to the Americans who owned 85 or 90% of Mexico's mines, but also to the Mexican government which received 10% of its income from taxation of the mining industry. When the agreement had expired at the close of 1937 Washington had notified Mexico that it would renew the arrangement for only a month at a time, though nothing like that was said to Canada.

The oil trouble was already extremely acute. The companies, in pursuance of their policy to put the screws on Mexico financially, had withdrawn their funds so rapidly from the country that the value of the *peso* had dropped and the government was forced to make desperate efforts to avert the crash which seemed imminent. For the United States to have discontinued the silver purchases at that juncture would have been calamitous.

The provision for only a month to month renewal was a threat that certainly looked like a master stroke to keep Mexico from going too far in compelling the companies to submit to her laws.

263

Thus encouraged, they had refused to abide by the decision of the Labor Board. Had they not been so confident that the ruse would have deterred Cárdenas, they might have come to terms before he expropriated their properties.

When the maneuver had proved insufficient, however, and on March 18 the company managers learned that the president, risking financial ruin, had announced the decree of expropriation over the radio, it is said that they scurried to his office and indicated that they would give in on most of the points at issue and would submit the other points to fresh discussion. Cárdenas naturally had answered that it was too late for more discussion. It would have placed Mexico in a ridiculous position to have signed the decree one day and repealed it the next.

The first word from Washington after expropriation was an announcement by Secretary of the Treasury Morgenthau that the silver purchases from Mexico would be discontinued on the first of April. This news, coming before Washington's later admission that Mexico had acted within her rights, and being followed immediately by a tough note from Cordell Hull on March 26, must have given Cárdenas a good many anxious moments. His first concern, however, was to prevent resentment on the part of his people. He knew how bitter anti-gringoism had often been in the past and he was determined to keep the atmosphere friendly and confident as long as possible. Accordingly, with assurance and no indication of resentment, he spoke on March 26, 1938:

It must further be taken into account that the government of the United States of America has announced that purchases by it of a part of Mexico's silver production, as heretofore made, are going to be cancelled as of April first next. We are keenly desirous, now that this fact is known to the nation, that the people judge said action calmly and properly . . . We are ready to prevent the effect of that decision from injuring our economy. To accomplish this, it will be required that silver producers, on their part, lend all necessary cooperation to the government so that our production may find an outlet on the world market.

Four days later he told me in private conversation, "We do not expect a continuance of the silver purchases if these are no longer a part of the financial program of the United States, but we cannot understand why the cancellation was made just when the step bore all the earmarks of retaliation." I could detect no evidence, however, of exasperation or vindictiveness in his attitude.

Fortunately, Ambassador Daniels wrote to Washington immediately urging that the matter of silver purchases be handled separately from the petroleum question. The silver bloc in Congress wanted us to continue purchasing silver, and since there was no good reason for paying Mexico less than Canada, an arrangement was soon announced which provided for the purchase of Mexican silver on the New York market, though at a somewhat lower price than before the expropriation. This kept silver out of the petroleum fight for the time being.

Not only Mexicans but aliens as well were speculating as to what would happen next. British residents thought that their government might do something drastic, for it was in partnership with the oil interests affected. Americans argued, however, that the British Lion had been letting Japan twist its tail much more painfully in China without evincing any ferociousness and they doubted if it would get any tougher with Mexico. They doubted, too, if our own government would use the Army or Navy to support the American companies in their demands.

Nevertheless, most American residents in Mexico were certain that Mexico's doughty leader had gone too far. He would never be able to run his country without foreign aid. The oil companies would whip him if they could get just a little cooperation from Washington. They would starve him into submission. They would make it impossible for him to continue his reconstruction projects. They would tug so hard at the purse strings of the nation that there would be no money to pay government employees, and then Cárdenas, in spite of all his patriotic appeals, would have trouble in his own household. Dissatisfaction in the ranks of his supporters could be fanned into a flame by clever propaganda. Eventually, Cárdenas could be overthrown and people would return to a sane realization of the necessity of running Mexico in harmony with foreign interests.

A great many Mexicans were truly alarmed over the daring of their leader, fearing that he had underestimated the power of the enemy, and dreading the consequences. Rumors got out that all federal employees were to undergo a drastic cut in salaries that were far too low already.

The campaign of the alarmists did not perturb President Cár-

denas. He calmly met it with a call to optimism. In his message of
March 18, he had said:

The government has already adopted suitable measures to prevent constructive activities all over the Republic from declining. All I ask of the people
is their absolute confidence and ample backing for enforcing any provisions
the government may have to enact . . .

Again, on the occasion of the great manifestation of popular support a few days later, he reminded them:

Is our task dangerous? Must some sacrifice be demanded of the country?
There is no doubt about this. But faced by a danger which certainly is not
that of armed intervention, the people are responding by the offer not only
of financial assistance but even of their lives if necessary . . . The Revolution,
having come into power will, with the fullest support of all the patriots of
the country, save the honor of Mexico.

With a united Mexico behind him, Cárdenas felt that nothing
short of armed intervention could defeat him. "The conflict was
won," I heard him say, "when several days went by and no gunboats appeared off our shores." He believed strongly in the American sense of justice and in the sincerity of our stand for liberty
and peace and hence did not expect armed intervention. Nevertheless, he had taken it into consideration. He knew how a lot of
blustering on the part of the American press, coupled with a little
blundering at Washington, might easily precipitate trouble.

Cárdenas stated privately what would have been done if Washington had sent down an army to take back the oil fields. The
Mexicans would have seen to it that there was nothing left worth
taking. Every derrick would have been burned down, every well
dynamited, and all the tanks and refineries blown to bits. Mexico
would have sacrificed her oil before her self-respect.

Secretary of State Cordell Hull was incensed, however, when
Mexicans acted first and talked about pay later. After a week of
breathless suspense he sent a message on March 26 in which he
asked for an immediate reply as to when Mexico was going to
pay for the oil properties and also for the agrarian lands it had
been taking. In the note he insisted "that under every rule of
generally recognized law as well as equity the rightful owners are
entitled to the payment of just compensation, having a present
effective value."

Ambassador Daniels had already called on President Cárdenas
and received assurances that Mexico would pay for the properties
it had taken. Cárdenas had also asked him to notify the oil com-

panies that they would be welcome to confer with him regarding the valuation of the property and the terms of payment.

In view of such assurances Daniels felt that Hull's stiff note would only be a hindrance to successful negotiations inasmuch as it asked Mexico to do something that she had already promised to do. He obeyed instructions, nevertheless, and delivered the note, only to meet with the anticipated objections. The Foreign Minister, General Eduardo Hay, was surprised that Secretary Hull would ask a question that had already been answered by President Cárdenas himself. Daniels wisely told the Minister to regard the note "as not received."

Cárdenas, however, felt that it was only fair that the American Ambassador should receive his promise in writing to allay Washington's fears, and sent the following message:

That the Mexican government is fully able to pay the affected petroleum companies the indemnities which may be due them for the irrevocable expropriation of their properties.

That the Ministry of Finance will receive and give consideration to the representatives of the companies as soon as they present themselves to that department for the purpose of entering into discussions.

The Mexican Government, in order to effect these payments, will not await the final appraisal of the amount of indemnity legally due the companies.

It seems likely that Ambassador Daniels was able to get his arguments to President Roosevelt directly and to convince him that the expropriation was an accomplished fact and that the best thing to do was to get the companies to negotiate a valuation and payment, for Hull declared at Washington on March 30 that Mexico was perfectly within her rights when she expropriated the oil companies, and that the only condition the United States would insist upon was that proper indemnity be given for the properties taken.

I breakfasted with President Cárdenas on the morning the unconfirmed report of our government's attitude reached him. We walked for a few minutes afterwards in the *patio* before he left for the Palace. He had been profoundly touched. With great feeling he said, "If this report is true, I have only words of admiration and gratitude for the men at Washington who have known how to understand and defend the justice of our position."

Adherence by the United States government to principles of national sovereignty had filled the heart of Mexico's leader with unbounded gratitude which was expressed in a letter to Ambassador Daniels delivered the following day. It manifests depth of feeling on the president's part which is quite foreign to stilted diplomacy but which is inherent in Mexican friendship. As a frank expression of sentiment it reveals not only the heart of the man who wrote it but also the vast possibilities of the Good Neighbor Policy. It was published in the newspapers of Mexico City March 31, 1938:

His Excellency, Mr. Josephus Daniels, Ambassador of the United States of North America:

My government considers the attitude assumed by the government of the United States of North America in the case of the expropriation of the petroleum companies to be a reaffirmation of the sovereignty of the nations of this continent which the statesman of the most powerful country of America, his Excellency President Roosevelt, has with such care been defending.

By this attitude, Mr. Ambassador, your president and your people have won the esteem of the people of Mexico.

The Mexican nation during the past few days has lived moments of testing. We did not know if we would have to give expansion to our patriotic sentiments or to applaud an act of justice on the part of the neighboring nation which your excellency represents.

Today my country is rejoicing. It quietly celebrates the proof of friendship which it has received from your country, the which it will treasure up in the heart of its people.

Mexico has always desired to maintain her prestige by fulfilling her obligations, but elements which did not understand her hindered these high and noble purposes. Today a new dawn breaks on her future as the doors of opportunity swing open before her. Kindly rest assured, Mr. Ambassador, that Mexico will be careful to honor her engagements, both those made today and those of yesterday.

"Mr. Ambassador, it provides satisfaction to the Mexican people to enjoy the friendship of a people whose president continues to maintain a policy of friendship and respect for each nation, a policy which is winning for your country the affection of many people throughout the world."

(Signed) Lázaro Cárdenas,
President of the Republic."

That Mexico had acted within her rights was a recognized fact after our Secretary of State's declaration. Commenting on Mexican-American relations and the expropriation, F. S. C. Northrop in *The Meeting of East and West* had this to say in his chapter, "The Rich Culture of Mexico":

. . . The wonder is not that Mexican policy has come at points into conflict with the legal and political doctrines of the United States, but that in her internal and international behaviour she (Mexico) has been as restrained and conventional as has been the case.

Two factors have contributed to the state of affairs. One is the unequivocal democracy of the Cárdenas Government between 1934 and 1940 . . . Clearly something had to be done to bring the natural resources of Mexico under Mexican ownership and control . . .

The other fact is that, thanks to the foundations for understanding between Mexico and the United States constructed by Dwight Morrow and to the Good Neighbor Policy initiated by President Roosevelt and Secretary Hull, the latter—very wisely, in the final stages of the negotiations—did not insist upon the letter of the minimum standard law as he had previously interpreted it, but instead accepted a compromise . . . It is to the great credit of Secretary of State Hull and the Foreign Ministers of the government of Cárdenas and Camacho that they have gone so far and so amicably toward such a settlement, especially when the people of the United States, at least, have not appreciated the conflict of economic ideas and cultural values which lies behind the negotiations.

The biggest question to be settled was how much indemnity Mexico would have to give. Would she have to refund only the amount of money that the companies had actually invested and had not yet earned back? Or would she have to pay the fantastic sum (four hundred and fifty million dollars) at which the companies valued the concessions on the basis of estimated future productivity?

This question was settled the day after President Cárdenas' letter had been delivered to Ambassador Daniels. Curiously, the answer was given on our All Fool's Day, just as the oil companies' rejection of the Labor Board's decision had come on Mexico's All Fool's Day. In a sensible effort to pave the way to an early settlement, President Roosevelt stated on April 1, 1938, that the actual investments minus profits would be the basis for arriving at a fair indemnity. The companies refused to admit that the joke was on them and continued to give the American public the impression that their stake in Mexico was four hundred million dollars or more. In addition, they spread the idea that Mexico would not be able to pay at all.

Technically, the companies had forfeited a right to indemnity. Printed on each share of stock was an agreement (based on Article 27 of the Constitution) which stated that any appeal to their own government from the decisions of Mexican courts would automatically result in the loss of ownership. The companies, then, were in error, but Mexico did not quibble over that bit of legality. The whole nation as one man rose up and said, "We will pay!"

Catholics and Protestants, revolutionists and reactionary elements, rich and poor, government employees and government critics, *all* responded with contributions. Committees were formed to collect funds. I heard only one old lady complain about having to pay for something that had already yielded fabulous returns to the foreign owners. Such unanimity of spirit is seldom seen in any country. Checks written in four figures were received from people who were not wealthy. The poor came forward with their *pesos*. School children brought *centavos*. Peasants brought chickens, pigs, or vegetables.

Mrs. Cárdenas herself took the lead in the women's committee that was formed. On April 12 women by the thousands came to the Palace of Fine Arts and dropped their offerings into the big receptacles provided for that purpose. The sacrificial gifts included earrings, bracelets, brooches, wedding rings, and other valuables. All day long and far into the night the people came. It was their response to a man who believed in them, and in whom they believed. It was a people coming to the aid of the country they loved.

It would have been good had executives of the petroleum companies been on hand to see barefoot Indians dropping a mite or two into the fund of economic redemption. Also, American editors who shed pitiful tears of ink over the "theft" which was being perpetrated against the oil trusts might have benefited by that sight.

When, however, Mexico was draining her pockets to the last pittance in an effort to pay for that which she had been forced to take, and President Roosevelt had paved the way for a quick and amicable settlement, the companies that had balked at the Labor Commission and balked at the Supreme Court now refused to evaluate the properties.

That Mexico did not become more exasperated than she did was due to the patience and prudence of Lázaro Cárdenas in controlling affairs. There were inevitably some manifestations against Americans on the part of student groups and irresponsible individuals, but they were utterly insignificant in comparsion with antipathies which Mexico has been capable of revealing in the past. Cárdenas used all his influence to discourage such an attitude. He consistently endeavored to attach no responsibility to the people and government of the United States for the misdeeds of the oil companies, and preferred to consider Washington's acts of an offensive nature as innocent errors into which the oil trusts had forced her. Negotiations between the State Department and the Mexican Ambassador, Francisco Castillo Nájera, were carried on for many months. Ambassador Daniels continued his contacts with Cárdenas on a friendly basis which ultimately saved the day when it was clear to all that Hull's emphasis on immediate payment would get nowhere with Cárdenas.

England, however, had no Daniels to teach her to respect Mexico's sovereignty and she had no Good Neighbor Policy at stake. Accordingly, she took the side of the oil companies and demanded the return of properties belonging to her subjects. The expropriation was "tantamount to confiscation carried out under a veil of legality", she said in a note dated April 8. "The only remedy for the expropriation", she continued, "is the return of the expropriated properties to the companies."

Mexico replied that the British oil investors involved had been operating through a duly organized Mexican company and hence the treatment accorded them was an internal affair subject to review by Mexican courts, but entirely outside of English jurisdiction. On April 21, England sent a second note in which she argued that although it was true that the particular company in question was organized under the laws of Mexico, the majority of the stockholders were English and therefore subject to English protection. Whereas the United States only asked for compensation for her subjects, England continued to demand that the properties be returned.

When Mexico replied refuting all the British arguments, the foreign office in London changed its tactics. Instead of insisting any further on the return of English oil properties, her third note, May 11, reminded Mexico that the annual payment she had consented to make to British subjects as indemnity for damages they had suffered during the armed strife of the Revolution was four months overdue. In the note, the British government took occasion to point out that Mexico was so deeply in debt that her credit was virtually worthless.

The Mexican Foreign Office could not resist using a little irony in its reply two days later reminding Great Britain "that many of the powerful nations which possess abundant resources could not pride themselves on having taken care of their financial obligations up to date." Powerful England, in arrears to the United States thousands of times more than Mexico was to her, haughtily demanded that Mexico pay at once a comparatively paltry sum— $361,737.

But Mexico paid. Right in the midst of a life-and-death struggle she raised the money and paid. Furthermore she kept on paying. Each year the United States, England, France, and Italy received checks to reimburse their citizens for what they lost during the turbulent years that followed 1910 when Mexico was scarcely responsible for what went on.

The same day, however, that she presented the check, she recalled her envoy from London and diplomatic relations with Great Britain were broken off. Cárdenas felt that England had not acted as a friend.

Our country needs a phalanx of new men, men in whom there is a blend of cultural and technical preparation together with a dynamic drive and a clear sense of duty in the face of the needs of the destitute classes.

> — *Lázaro Cárdenas—to University Students*
> *March 21, 1935*

Mr. President, during my early business career I had a heart of stone. The welfare of my employees and my fellowmen in general was of little importance to me. Then through the Bible God gave me a new heart. The welfare of others became more important to me than money. I had no more problems with my laborers. I myself felt happier and incidentally my business prospered more than ever.

> — *Wm. G. Nyman at International Picnic*
> *held in honor of President Cárdenas*
> *at Tijuana, Lower California*
> *July 7, 1939*

XXVII

IN THE WAKE OF EXPROPRIATION

AN OLD friend in Mexico had also ceased to be friendly. To him Cárdenas devoted his attention next. General Saturnino Cedillo, who had been skulking in the mountains of his home state of San Luís Potosí since resigning from the cabinet was opposed to the expropriation. He was also ambitious. Otherwise, all Mexico appeared to be united behind the president. Even the archbishops and bishops of the Catholic Church issued a circular calling upon Catholics to contribute toward the fund to pay for the expropriated properties.

At that moment of high patriotism the only possibility the oil companies had of support in Mexico was Cedillo and his private army of peasants. Cárdenas realized this and decided to give his old friend a chance to get back on the national band wagon by appointing him commander of the military zone that included the president's own state of Michoacán. He also dispatched two prominent generals who were on friendy terms with Cedillo to try to persuade him to come to the defence of the Fatherland. It was all to no avail, however, and Cedillo hastened preparations to rebel. A German was in charge of his army, and it is said that he had planes of German and Italian make. One of his pilots, however, was an American and there was reason to believe that he received not only encouragement but also material help from the oil companies.

Cárdenas was reluctant to force his old friend out into the open where he would be branded by all as a traitor, but finally the safety of the nation demanded that he act. On the afternoon of the seventeenth of May, one month after Cedillo had rejected the overtures of friendship and two months after the expropriation, Minister of the Interior, García Téllez received a telephone call from the president.

"Pack your grip for a trip and join me immediately at Los Pinos" was the extent of the conversation. García Téllez had learned during his three and a half years as a member of the official family to keep a suitcase in his office ready for traveling upon a moment's notice from the circuit-riding president. Accordingly, he simply telephoned to his wife that he was leaving town with the president, told his secretary to cancel all engagements, and drove to the president's home.

Then Cárdenas, García Téllez, and a handful of aides left Mexico City on the presidential train well-named "The Olive Branch". No hint of destination was made at first, but finally the president confided to his companion that he was going to San Luís Potosí to make one last attempt to bring Cedillo back to his senses.

"To San Luís Potosí?" gasped the startled minister.

"Yes," the president replied. "If Cedillo sees that I have enough confidence in him to go right to his doorstep, he will surely be willing to talk to me and I shall be able to convince him of his duty."

In vain García Téllez remonstrated with the president, pointing out that he was going into the lair of an irresponsible madman, that for the sake of the nation he could not afford to take such a chance, and that Cedillo did not merit so much consideration. Cárdenas could not forget, however, that Cedillo had made a big contribution to the revolutionary cause and had also stood by him in the crisis of June, 1935.

Cárdenas argued that Cedillo should be dissuaded from his folly before it was too late. He would show Cedillo he could not possibly win and then give him a grand opportunity to save face. After all, he was up in his sixties, almost illiterate, in poor health, and with no backing whatever apart from his own peasant army, a few henchmen in positions of authority in his state, and the sympathy and possibly money of unpopular foreign interests.

A few miles outside of the city of San Luís Potosí the president and minister left the train and made their entrance by automobile. They found that although Cedillo had received the president's invitation he had been unwilling to leave his headquarters at Palomas to come to the state capital for a conference. He had granted permission, however, to his cohorts, including the governor of the state, to show the proper courtesy to the president, and they gave him an official reception.

Cárdenas got out of his car and walked among armed henchmen of the disgruntled chieftan. Many armed peasants lining the streets were ready to do the bidding of Cedillo, the only overlord they had known for twenty some years. García Téllez later explained that as he looked around on the crowd of rebels surrounding them, it seemed to him that they had walked right into the mouth of the wolf and that the only reason why the fierce teeth did not clamp down was that Cedillo's men thought the president had come to honor their chief and grant him what he wanted. They were not left in doubt very long.

The president mounted the balcony of the Governor's Palace and called upon the citizens of the state to rally to the support of the federal government in its struggle with foreign interests. Far from paying Cedillo any compliments, he was referred to as one who had been won over by the enemies of the Revolution, one who did not want the government to encourage the organization of the laboring classes.

"When from every part of our nation," he said, " the people are rallying to defend the interests of the Fatherland which have been menaced by the arrogant attitude of the petroleum trusts, it is painful to have to admit that in San Luís Potosí there is talk of rebellion. . . . The one who is to blame for all this is General Saturnino Cedillo."

Then the president told of how he had tried to disregard Cedillo's errors and had conferred a commission of trust upon him, but that the old general had refused, pleading illness. When the Ministry of War had insisted, Cedillo had resigned his commission saying that he was going to give his time to farming. Then acts of violence had occurred in several towns, and newspaper reporters had come to him asking if Cedillo were going to rebel.

"To this question I replied categorically," the president continued, "that there would not be a rebellion because I was confident that even the groups that have served one man [Cedillo] unreservedly, would come to realize that our country comes first."

Referring to the federal troops that had been detailed to various parts of the state, he said they had "come to live among their brethren and to give them protection as they went about their daily activities." He offered the support of the federal authorities in bringing about a solution of the problems that had resulted from the fact that Cedillo and his clique had enthroned themselves as permanent arbiters of the political and social activities of the state.

"As regards General Cedillo," the president continued, "the authorities will extend him every security to which he has a right as a citizen, but it must be understood that he will have to quit organizing armed forces and will have to turn over to the military commander of this zone the arms and munitions that he has in his possession." To the peasants he gave the assurance that they could continue to serve in the militia, but under the command of the duly appointed military authority.

When the president's speech began the governor of the state had stood confident and proud as a cock, for he had expected to hear compliments for Cedillo; but as the address of frank and well-measured indictment progressed his shoulders slumped more and more until he resembled a drooping rooster wilting in the heat.

Nevertheless, he went ahead with plans for a big dinner and sat next to the president at the table. As they were eating a plane roared overhead. An aide went outside to see what was happening and found the air filled with pamphlets. He caught one and took it to the president who stopped eating long enough to read it and then calmly hand it to the Governor whose signature as well as that of Cedillo appeared on it. It was the call to rebellion planned by the two of them. His face turned crimson and without a word, he got up from the table and left to join his chief in the mountains.

Cárdenas remained in the city for three weeks inspecting schools and hospitals and talking with committees of citizens. He too had pamphlets printed and sent airplanes to distribute them throughout the state. They were calls to loyalty and promises of pardon to the peasants under arms if they would come to the federal outposts and surrender. They could keep their guns and would be given plows and mules for farming.

Day after day more and more accepted the offer until only Cedillo and a mere handful of followers were left at bay in the mountains. A little shooting was done and Cedillo's troops dynamited the railroad at a place or two, but the federal troops adhered so closely to the peaceful methods learned under Cárdenas that there was little chance for a real fight.

The little there was, however, together with the fact that at the beginning a Cedillo plane had bombed the home in San Luís Potosí where Cárdenas had his headquarters, was sufficient to cause papers north of the Rio Grande to play up the affair as a real threat to the Cárdenas regime. Mexicans, however, looked upon it as a lost cause as soon as their *muy macho* president had bearded the lion in his den.

Some weeks after Cárdenas had returned to Mexico City he was visited by Cedillo's sisters who said their brother was in poor health. The president reportedly assured them that the national troops would not bother their brother if he would leave the country. Months went by and Cedillo failed to take advantage of the offer. Meanwhile, small detachments of federal troops were constantly coming and going through Cedillo's old haunts to take him prisoner if they could, and to be sure that the oil companies did not get to him. One morning before the fog that often caps the mountains had lifted, a pre-dawn patrol came upon the hideout of the rebel chieftain. The two bands could distinguish little of each other in the mists, but shots were exchanged and when Cedillo's group left the field their leader was found dead, having been shot just as he was going to mount his steed.

Cárdenas was in Mexico City when the news reached him. Nothing had provoked him so much in his entire administration. For days he refused to smile. That the life of anyone, and especially his old friend, had been lost, to him meant defeat in victory. He had hoped that the affair might have been quelled in his customary manner, without bloodshed.

While he had been in San Luís Potosí, Cárdenas had had to give much attention also to the ever-present oil problem. After expropriation, the government might have let Gulf handle all its export oil. But an official of that company stated that it had to live with Standard and Shell all over the world and it did not dare aid Mexico against such formidable opposition.

With the big trusts fighting them, the Mexicans found it difficult to get tankers. Some captains of independent ships took a chance of making a big profit by hauling oil to Europe, but when their cargoes were attached in European ports as property of the expropriated companies and their ships were tied up for weeks during the court hearings, they lost interest. Invariably the courts upheld Mexico's right to the oil, but the delay and resulting loss of profits had the effect of closing that outlet.

Suggestions had been made that Mexico sell its oil to the totalitarian powers, but Cárdenas had replied, "Our petroleum operations will not swerve in the slightest from the moral solidarity that binds our land to other nations of democratic tendencies." This resolve not to sell oil to the totalitarian countries coupled with the refusals of American and English buyers to touch Mexican oil, with the exception of a few independents, left Latin America as the only possible outlet. Cárdenas therefore set about wooing her. For several months, however, such sales were insignificant.

On one occasion I asked the president if he did not find the numerous problems which constantly confronted him a wearisome load. With a quick smile he replied, "Problems simply serve, like water in a mill race, to make the wheels go around." Probably the wheels had never gone so fast as they did in that year of 1938.

The bitter reality is that the weaker nations find themselves necessarily taking extreme precautions regarding foreign investors. While these investors do increase the resources of the nation, often in exchange for fabulous profits, they sometimes become an obstacle to the carrying out of the government's program. Latin America has found it so, and if it has been possible to give a positive value to Pan-Americanism, it can be attributed to the fact that the principle has come to be established that foreigners cannot hope for privileges that will be detrimental to the country's own citizens.

— Ramón Beteta — to American Consuls
February 20, 1940

Let us hope that if foreign capital seeks investments in Mexico in the future it will come with a different attitude—seeking not exploitation of the Mexican people, but the development of the country's resources with the cooperation of Mexican labor; capital that will not attempt to operate contrary to law, capital that will improve the standard of living of the Mexican people, enabling them to buy the products of American industry and to become good neighbors and good consumers.

— Lázaro Cárdenas — to Congress
September 1, 1938

XXVIII

NEW FRIENDS AND OLD ENEMIES

AFTER THE PAN-AMERICAN PEACE CONFERENCE in Argentina in 1937 Cárdenas had become so convinced of the sincerity of the good neighbor intentions of the United States and so satisfied over Washington's promise not to intervene in the internal affairs of her sister American nations that he had decided that Mexico should withdraw from competition for influence in Latin America. Accordingly, Mexican ambassadors had been recalled from all Central and South American countries save one. The economies thus attained were to be used in carrying forward the welfare projects at home.

Following the expropriation, however, when Cárdenas realized that the majority of petroleum sales must be made to Latin American countries, the embassies were revived and missions of good-will were sent to Cuba, Central America, Brazil, Chile, and elsewhere.

On the fifth of June, 1938, while Cárdenas was still in San Luís Potosí handling the Cedillo matter, Alfredo Sanjines, Minister of the Republic of Bolivia, arrived to decorate him with the Great Cross of the Order of the Condor of the Andes. Cárdenas, in his brief speech of acceptance, referred first to the efforts Bolivia and Mexico were mutually making in behalf of their Indian tribes, "who are habitually forgotten except for economic exploitation and who live so isolated within the borders of the nation that they are like foreigners within their own Fatherland." Then he continued:

It is the Indian aspect that has molded the physiognomy of the Latin-American peoples. These young nations of America are neither Spanish nor pure Indian, but are an amalgamation . . .
The slogan on this medal with which I am honored today, *Union is Strength,* could well be made the slogan of this continent: *Union* within each country representing internal peace and the cooperation of its inhabitants and in-

suring its political independence and economic autonomy; *Union* of all the nations of America in the face of whatever common danger the future may hold in store; *Union* that is free, spontaneous, and strong on behalf of peace and democracy in the world.

Mexico returned this display of friendship by sending two missions to Bolivia. One was composed of civil engineers led by the government's builder of dams and irrigation systems, Francisco Vásquez del Mercado. The mission went in January of 1939 and did not return until it had made an extensive report on Bolivia's engineering problems, particularly those connected with irrigation. Two months later an educational mission was sent, led by a former head of Indian education in Mexico, the ethnologist Carlos Basauri. This group spent a number of months studying Bolivia's problem of rural education and making suggestions concerning it. Its contribution was one that Bolivia knew how to appreciate, and she responded by sending teachers to study Mexican methods of reaching the masses with the rudiments of culture.

Colonel Ignacio Beteta, one of the president's most trusted colleagues, led a highly successful mission by plane to Cuba. Arrangements had been made for Cárdenas, who was in Tampico, to direct a radio message to the people of that island domain on the twelfth of June. The speech which he gave on that occasion was one of his best pieces of oratory. In it he did not follow the classroom style he customarily used with the Mexican peasants, nor the cold logic of his political pronouncements, nor the factual heaviness of his reports to Congress. Rather, he gave way to a mystical longing for a united hemisphere. He saw the world conflagration ahead, and wanted the American nations to unite beforehand as a bulwark for democracy and peace. With spiritual fervor he proceeded to lay down some pratical principles to be followed in order to attain a strong union.

The two spurs Cárdenas used to urge action were 1) Unnamed selfish exploiters and 2) The danger of war. The president addressed his Cuban friends in part as follows:

. . . It is essential that all the peoples of America unite and that all our citizens who love true liberty join together, basing their unity upon a better distribution of the public wealth.

Let us banish internal strife as well as insignificant quarrels between neighbors. They are always unproductive, weaken our unity, and increase the possibility of armed intervention or diplomatic pressure. Let us be careful to carry out our international agreements as regards nonintervention, inviolability of territory, and peaceful cooperation. Let us lose no time in strengthening the cultural, economic, and political ties that unite us. Let us do away with tariff wars, though not neglecting the industrialization of regional products. Let us seek to develop lines of communication that shall be of mutual benefit.

Let us encourage investors who identify themselves with the progress of our people. Let us uproot prejudices fomented by selfish interests against the social reforms that have been instituted by our several nations . . . Let us endeavor to bring back to our peoples a confidence in their own destinies and their sacred right to govern themselves without foreign interference.

Let us instil in the conscience of our laborers the need for self-discipline, of greater efficiency in their work, and of a stronger sense of responsibility in their service to the collectivity. Thus, in a union of all the peoples of this continent, let us insure for our democracies true peace and progress.

We should not wait for the morrow with its armed violence that shall bring suffering to innocent generations. Let us endeavor now to draw our peoples close together. Instead of boundaries of hate, let us have a strong and free union based upon the solidarity of our laborers. Now and unreservedly let us condemn the crime of expansion by enemies of liberty and of the sovereignty of our nations.

Colonel Ignacio Beteta's courtesy call was returned by a man well-known in Cuban politics, Colonel Fulgencio Batista, who was enthusiastically acclaimed in Mexico and spent considerable time as personal guest of President Cárdenas. He went home satisfied with Mexico's friendly spirit.

After that speech in Tampico President Cárdenas visited various camps in the oil fields, operating now under Mexican direction, rallying the workmen and also the new managers to a realization of the important part they were playing in the reconstruction of their country.

On this trip he was accompanied by a highly esteemed friend of Mexico and of Cárdenas personally, Professor Frank Tannenbaum of Columbia University, who had joined him in San Luís Potosí early in June. Tannenbaum informed me that on the trip through the hot lowlands the president actually took time out for a vacation—the only one of which I have found any record during his entire administration.

For a week the two of them, together with Dr. Ramón Beteta who was then Under-Secretary of Foreign Affairs, lived in a cabin near the seashore. Not that the president quit working, but at least he took time out for a swim each day. He had worked every week day since he took office except when unable to do so on account of illness. Even when he has been free from official duties he has preferred work to fun. He knows how I enjoy a game of tennis or baseball, but in 1949 he told me when I mentioned the subject of recreation to him: "It would be almost a crime for me to spend time playing *frontón* or tennis when I get so much pleasure from constructive effort. It is true that as a young man I rode horseback a lot for pure sport, especially at night after the day's work was over. Now, however, I get more fun out of planting, cultivating, and pruning trees. I love trees. When people come to call on me, however, I can hardly invite them to work with me in the orchard. I am obliged to sit down and talk with them. The hardest thing for me to do is to remain seated."

The only relaxation this hyper-industrious individual took was on Sundays. When in the capital, both as president and since, he has tried to reserve that day to take his family on simple outings to some quiet place of beauty such as the snow-covered peak of Toluca or their country home near Cuernavaca.

In spite of incessant activity always surrounded by people, Cárdenas has somehow managed to get sufficient relaxation to keep from breaking down. He did not age unduly nor grow weary under the heavy load of his six years as president. His spirit seems to abide at such a depth of repose that surface winds never ruffle it. Yet in the midst of weighty discussions he is so much on the surface that he will be the first to notice that a lady has dropped her handkerchief, a cripple is in need of assistance, or courtesy demands his thanking a peasant hostess for refreshments. He has been known to sit in discussion with quarreling laborers for three straight hours and then emerge as cool and calm as though he had just gotten up from the breakfast table.

When Cárdenas returned from his protracted visit to the oil fields, Washington was saying little about the expropriation of March 18, but a great deal about payment for lands which had been taken over from American citizens in the process of carrying out the agrarian reform. According to a list which the Department of State presented to the Mexican Ambassador in Washington late in June, 1938, the land-indemnity claims which had accumulated since 1927 amounted to $10,132,388. Our State Department manifested great concern over the debt. Notes were sent on July 21 and August 22 demanding a settlement at the earliest possible moment or else that the matter be submitted to arbitration. The notes were logical in their reasoning. Mexico owed the money and she should pay. They were almost as logical as though they had been addressed to England, France, Germany, Italy, and other European powers demanding immediate settlement for what these powers owed us.

The State Department found it easier to try to collect from Mexico than from Europe. The regretable part of it was that we exerted pressure on Mexico at a moment when by doing so we abetted the oil companies in their economic war on that country. Furthermore, we were quibbling over ten million dollars while Italy and Germany were putting on full steam to capture Latin American friendship and trade. By estranging Mexico to get our pound of flesh we were imperilling our position of vantage in all of Latin America.

It is hard to understand why fair-minded Hull was willing to take the role of debt collector from a close neighbor just at that time. It placed him definitely on the side of the oil companies. Otherwise, what was ten million dollars to a nation that had spent many times that figure in a program of plowing under crops and slaughtering livestock because she had too much? On the basis of Mexico's promise to pay we could have advanced the money to the Americans who had lost land, and our neighbor would have reimbursed our Treasury at the first opportunity. It would merely have been putting a wise banking principle in operation.

Within six months after Hull's misjudgment, Washington awoke to the need of beating out Italy and Germany in the race for Latin-American commerce, and gave Inter-American unity an important place in our program. By providing millions of dollars of credit for Latin America we gave financial assistance not only for their own domestic needs but also enabled them to help us in the big war program.

The situation between Washington and Mexico grew more and more tense through August and on into September, 1938. Cárdenas had already promised Ambassador Daniels to write indemnity for American agrarian claims into the federal budget at the earliest possible moment. It was the fight with the oil companies that had brought a postponement. Now Cárdenas refused to embarrass his country financially by trying to pay the debt all at once.

At last the Department of State realized that it would not do to send more harsh notes unless they were to be followed up with force. With the change in attitude an agreement was reached on the agrarian problem early in November. By it, Mexico agreed to pay the United States one million dollars each year toward the total indemnity which was to be fixed by a joint commission. This group was to have reached a decision in six months, but at the end of that period most of the claims that had been received were from wealthy land companies and totalled only about one-third of the ten million dollars which our State Department had claimed. Both governments were convinced that the claims had not been padded that much and that some Americans who had lost land must have just been slow about getting their claims presented. Hence the time limit was extended. The commission's final report was accepted in the over-all settlement signed November 19, 1941.

In view of the preferential treatment which President Cárdenas had found necessary to concede to American land owners, he called upon Mexican citizens who had lost lands to demonstrate their national loyalty by surrendering their rights to remuneration. Many responded favorably, undergoing the loss imposed on them by the Revolution in a spirit of patriotism. The self-sacrifice of the people in behalf of their country touched the heart of the president, who wrote many a letter of appreciation, and also gave their names honorable mention in his message of December 31, 1938.

Mexico's responsibleness in meeting her foreign obligations was demonstrated by the fact that before Cárdenas left office she was paying to the United States alone about one and a half percent of her entire federal budget for old claims occasioned by the destruction and reforms of the Revolution.

The impasse on the oil question which caused our Department of State to shift to a discussion of the agrarian claims would have been almost humorous had it not been so serious. Washington had told Mexico that it had to pay the companies for their properties. Mexico had replied that it would be glad to pay if the oil companies would present themselves to help work out a valuation. This they had refused to do.

Rather than accept payment on President Roosevelt's basis the companies, with all the obstructionist ingenuity they could muster, sought to make payment impossible. They sought to drown her in her own oil by boycotting her oil exports and by curtailing her sales at home through frightening automobile tourists away from Mexico. They sought to discourage manufacturers from selling replacement parts for the expropriated refineries, tools for drilling and tetraethyl to give the Mexican-made gasoline proper performance. With gasoline-driven vehicles all over the country knocking from bad gas, Cárdenas would be cursed from Yucatán to Sonora for the expropriation and popular demand would bring about the return of the companies to Mexico.

If Cárdenas found ways and means to circumvent the embargo and the boycott, other ways of stopping him were not overlooked. Pressure was brought on Washington to discontinue the purchase of Mexican silver at the old preferential price and also to insist on immediate payment of our agrarian claims. They would also discourage American capital from investing in Mexico. They would bring about a big drop in the value of the *peso* that would make it difficult for Mexico to continue buying from our manufacturers, who in turn would become unhappy and add their voices to those of the oil companies in urging Washington to use force. They would halt Cárdenas' constructive programs by getting American manufacturers and finance corporations to make it difficult for him to get trucks, graders, and other necessary equipment. A halt in the projects would further cripple the economy of the nation and add to the discontent. Internal discord would result in rebellion, Cárdenas would be overthrown, and the oil companies would be given back their properties.

The oil companies did receive cooperation from Washington in the matter of exerting pressure for the payment of claims. Later, Washington made a further bow to Standard and Shell in that an agreement was worked out whereby big quantities of Venezuelan and Dutch oil could be shipped into the United States at an advantage over Mexican oil. This was a slap in the face to Mexico that further reduced her sales of oil.

Thus, while Mexico sought to cultivate new friends in Latin America and, she hoped, new customers for her dwindling petroleum trade, the oil companies showed themselves to be formidable enemies. In the six months that followed expropriation, exports of petroleum dropped 45%.

My government has decreed measures that not only provide for full liberty of the press, but also the free circulation through the mails of 13,200,000 pounds of newspapers, magazines, and other printed matter each year . . . . These facilities are extended without regard to political tendencies or even untruthful and scandalous attacks.

— *Lázaro Cárdenas* —
September 1, 1937

XXIX

PROBLEMS OF PROPAGANDA

S<small>INCE</small> W<small>ASHINGTON</small> <small>REFUSED</small> even to think of armed intervention thanks to Roosevelt's Good Neighbor Policy, the oil companies set out on a plan of propaganda to turn the American people against Mexico so that they in turn would put pressure on Congress.

Cárdenas had foreseen this danger, and within a week after expropriation he had sent twenty men to the United States to present Mexico's position before colleges, labor unions, churches, clubs, and the press. Among them was Professor Moisés Sáenz, one of Mexico's foremost educators, an expert in Indian affairs, and a man highly esteemed in the United States. Such men were able to inform editors and other leaders in intellectual circles of the history of the expropriation and to prepare them to withstand the tidal wave of anti-Mexican propaganda that soon began to inundate the country. Many of our labor leaders were also primed by Mexican labor leaders. And United States Congressmen were paid courtesy calls by congressional leaders from Mexico.

The oil companies, however, feeling that the only way of saving their huge stake in Latin America was to have the American people commit themselves to a policy of protecting investments abroad at all costs, spent money freely on propaganda. They set up a publicity office in Rockefeller Center, New York, from which notices were sent out weekly to newspapers far and wide throughout the country.

The editor of a little daily published in the Arkansan Ozarks showed me the bulletins he received as well as a propaganda sheet called *The Lamp*. Ambassador Daniels, himself a newspaper man, was contemptuous of the flagrant nature of their pronouncements and cartoons, saying what many of us thought after perusing them:

It did not confine itself to oil discussion but sought to inflame sentiment in the United States against Mexico by parading every crime or incident that

291

would injure the standing of Mexico in the United States and to broadcast every item to injure the Cárdenas government clipped from subsidized and other papers in Mexico and the United States. Also it sought by scare heads to frighten possible investors in Mexico. It demanded a discontinuance of silver purchases in the hope of bankrupting the Mexican treasury.

The cartoons were, if possible, more insulting. They represented Mexicans as of a lesser breed, whose chief business was brigandage and lawlessness and theft. No reader of *The Lamp* could have any conception of Mexico other than as a country occupied by uncivilized and degraded people who were happy only when robbing American investors. . . .[1]

Besides the deluge of direct propaganda a great number of articles and news items began to appear in magazines and newspapers that had not showed much interest in Mexico before. No less a trusted peer in the literary world than the *Atlantic Monthly* published a special edition in July, 1938, dedicated to what it called "Trouble Below the Border". It had a decidedly oily flavor and offended any one who knew the facts. Other periodicals also filled complete editions with material calculated to arouse mistrust and even hatred toward Mexico. One publication distributed bore the imprint *New York Daily News,* a freak edition of reprints from that newspaper. The cover page carried the following titles: "Mexico Seen Ripe for Rightist Revolt", "Fifth Column in Mexico Turns Its Face North", "Mexico Finds Oil Grab Gigantic Flop", "Capital Flees Iron Squeeze of Mexican Labor", and "Peons Find Cárdenas Is No Santa Claus".

The New York Times was much more careful, but its correspondent in Mexico, Frank Kluckhohn, gave such a bias to his articles and news items in the opinion of Mexican officials that they became highly incensed. They called his attention to what they considered gross inaccuracies and finally submitted his reports to a certain amount of censorship, but this brought no improvement. Finally, in January, 1939, the Minister of the Interior gave him twenty-four hours to leave Mexico or be arrested. If Ambassador Daniels had been in the country at the time, Kluckhohn believes that he could have secured a cancellation of the order, due to Daniels' influence with President Cárdenas and his strong stand for the liberty of the press.

In Kluckhohn's account of the affair in his book, *The Mexican Challenge,* he criticizes the Department of Press and Publicity, but of President Cárdenas writes that he "has always been glad to

[1]*Shirt-Sleeve Diplomat,* pp. 255, 256

receive correspondents, give them views frankly, and tell them that the thing he had to say was 'off the record'. His statements have always been run, without comment, in newspapers abroad. Once again his ideal attitude has been sabotaged by his own order."

Ambassador Daniels, upon his return from Washington, presented strong objections both to President Cárdenas and to Under-Secretary of Foreign Affairs Beteta. There were no more expulsions and no more attempts at censorship.

If Cárdenas himself were to blame for the expulsion (Kluckhohn raised a doubt about this in his correspondence with Daniels), it was due to his deep concern that the people of the United States should get the truth about Mexico. He knew that they were getting a great deal of false propaganda and he hoped that a newspaper of the standing of *The New York Times* would have corrected this as far as it could.

In 1938 and 1939, however, it was hard to find a major newspaper in the United States that had gone to the trouble of getting and publishing Mexico's side of the story. Finally on August 26, 1939, the *Los Angeles Examiner* published a statement Cárdenas had given to its reporter, José Navarro. It read in part as follows:

I am definitely interested in having the American public know the truth about the oil expropriation. No doubt the American public does not know that the oil companies were for many years the real dictators of Mexico. They could finance uprisings if the men in power refused to comply with the wishes of company officials. . . .

I am ready at all times to receive their new proposals. I have many times repeated that we want foreign capital to come into this country and work and make fair returns on its investment; but we have laws that are clear and defined—laws that must be obeyed. This is true in all civilized countries of the world. Mining companies operating in Mexico are abiding by the Constitution of this country. They are fully protected and their returns on investments are justified. This is also true of large American cattle and agricultural companies.

If the oil companies continue to assume their present challenging attitude, then there is small hope for them to return to Mexico. Please make clear that this country will not place any obstacle to the attainment of a fair agreement, but the dignity of our people cannot tolerate intransigent policies and methods such as the oil companies have employed.

In spite of the one attempt at censorship of foreign reporters the Mexican press, both supporting and opposition, was always given full liberty under Cárdenas. He continued to give newspapers and magazines whether friendly or otherwise free use of mails and had Saldaña Galván, a strong believer in the freedom of the press and at that time head of the official paper supply house PIPSA, provide both sides with paper at the same favorable rate.

One of the leading weeklies of Mexico, *Hoy*, published an editorial on Cárdenas the day before he left office in which it admitted its numerous criticisms of him, but simultaneously wanted to honor him for having granted full liberty to the Mexican press:

General Cárdenas refused to be a tyrant. . . . When he broke the yoke of Calles, he broke it not only for himself but also for the enslaved people . . . . During the past five years newspapers and magazines have said all they cared to. . . . Lázaro Cárdenas made the experiment of governing in an atmosphere of adverse criticism, and has had the glory of crowning his experiment with complete success. . . .

Naturally, this tribute does not mean that we applaud with the same fervor his administrative work. Our readers know how much we have criticized the economic policies of his government. His fundamental error consisted in believing that the injustices and mistakes of centuries could disappear miraculously in one presidential period.

Grieved over the wretched conditions of poverty in which our lower layers of society were submerged, he despoiled plantation owners to redeem the peasants without realizing that the redemption of humanity cannot come from sacrificing justice. The result has been the ruin of our agriculture. . . .

The fact, however, that he respected his critics establishes a noble precedent in the history of Mexican journalism. No one has been muzzled during the past five years and this constitutes an advance, a formidable advance toward the future.

However, the life of the reporter who was assigned to cover President Cárdenas was a difficult one, especially when presidential tours were on the docket. A newsman had to be able to put in long hours on horseback and often on foot without getting more than a few hours' rest each night. Nor was he able to secure food at regular hours, and when obtained it was often of poor quality. Cárdenas himself seems to be immune to hardship and he lives a life on his long trips that not everyone can take. Perhaps this is one reason for the feud that eventually developed between Cárdenas and a large sector of the press.

It is to be deeply regretted that large American dailies did not send correspondents with some of the physical stamina and spiritual aggressiveness with which Stanley tracked Livingstone. They could have followed President Cárdenas on his journeys and awakened America to their importance. As it was, most correspondents either ignored them or else made hearsay reports. Naturally the latter were inaccurate and frequently of such a

biased view that the president lost what little love he ever did
have for newspaper men.

In 1939 I asked an Associated Press reporter for an explanation
and he defended his guild by saying that when other rulers make
trips, comfortable accommodations are provided for the press. The
visit of the King of England to America was cited as an example.
I could not resist asking him if American newspaper men were
unwilling to go after the news but wanted it to be handed them
on silver platters. He was finally convinced that he himself should
go to the border where President Cárdenas was travelling at the
time and get some news of the unusual occurrence—the first time
a Mexican president had visited Lower California.

I then wired the president who was still in Sonora and secured
an assurance of an audience for my friend the newspaper man,
and also sent Professor Eugene Nida of our Institute to serve the
reporter as guide and interpreter. At the border they found other
correspondents waiting, but Professor Nida knew the folly of waiting and so pushed on into the desert south of Mexicali where the
president was to enter Lower California territory.

The next morning the first audience the courteous chief executive conceded was to Dr. Nida, whom he knew, and the reporter.
He explained to the newsman why he was giving him a personal
interview instead of referring him to his publicity secretary. He
said, simply: "I pay you this special attention because of my
sincere appreciation for the work being done by the young American linguists who labor among the Indian tribes of my country,
seeking to help them. You have been recommended to me by
their leader, and for that reason I am glad to give you my time."

The reporter got his interview, had his photographer take pictures of the president surrounded by happy peasants, and then
ran off from the scorching heat so fast that when Cárdenas' aide
came to invite him and Professor Nida to the president's table
for dinner, the AP man had gone.

When Cárdenas promised that Mexico's oil would be kept at
the disposal of democratic nations one of the large conservative
newspapers in the capital called him to task for this attitude, telling him not "to try to mix the principles of the four Gospels and
the oil business." He was forced to abandon this high resolve when
he found that there were almost no buyers in the democratic

nations sufficiently free from the control of the oil trusts to be able to bid for Mexican oil. He also found that the oil companies themselves were selling to the totalitarian powers. The result was that Germany and Italy began to receive most of Mexico's export oil. Since the Germans insisted on barter—merchandise in exchange for oil—much of Mexico's trade was taken from our manufacturers and diverted to Germany.

In spite of this Cárdenas still tried to place orders for machinery with American firms. In May of 1939 he told me of twenty-eight fourteen-ton trucks which had been contracted for in the United States. Delivery had not been made, however, because certain financial powers in New York had heard about the deal and secured its cancellation even after the contract had been signed and the cash placed on the barrel head.

Even after the sales agreement with Germany had been reached, however, President Cárdenas proposed to President Roosevelt in the fall of 1938 that all the American nations be invited to unite in an agreement not to sell anything to the European nations that might persist in provoking war. He said that Mexico would gladly join in such a boycott even though she would lose heavily by cancelling her oil contract. President Roosevelt replied that the situation in Europe was looking better and that such a drastic step would not be necessary at that moment. And about the Cárdenas proposal, Ambassador Daniels wrote home, "I am afraid the United States would not agree to that."

We went ahead selling to Franco, Hitler, Mussolini, and Hirohito with the consequent grief it brought us, and Mexico under idealistic President Cárdenas was obliged to follow suit. Italy agreed to build three tankers to transport her oil. Germany sent machinery, bridges, railroad equipment, etc., for Mexico's development projects.

One thing that kept Standard and Shell hopeful was a dissatisfaction toward Cárdenas that began to grow a few months after expropriation and increased little by little until the presidential election got under way, when it became formidable. As early as the fall of 1938 some people began to talk about what they called the "Cárdenas dictatorship". This grieved the president, for he had just turned back to Congress all the prerogatives it had been granting him and had taken other important steps to strengthen

Mexico's democracy. On the ninth of December he delivered a special address to the nation in which he said:

I welcome criticism no matter how malevolent it may be, for criticism helps to improve the program of the Revolution. . . . It is audacious nonsense to affirm that the present regime is dictatorial when under this regime political assassinations have been proscribed, exiles who had suffered bitterly have returned to the Fatherland with full protection from the authorities, the opposition press can engage in the most aggressive criticism without any restriction whatever, when the jails hold only non-political delinquents, when thinkers can freely diffuse their creeds and opinions, when outstanding contenders of other lands enjoy our hospitality, and the victims of political persecution abroad take refuge within our doors, and when the government with only moral force accruing from popular support has been able to overthrow without the shedding of blood the recent futile conspiracy of conservative elements in San Luís Potosí.

The president's statement that the Cedillo rebellion had been put down without bloodshed was accurate at the time. It was not until a few weeks later that Cedillo himself was killed. Cárdenas could be justly proud of having put down a rebellion with only one or two deaths and those virtually accidental six months after peace had been restored.

The collective farming which Cárdenas had introduced in La Laguna and two or three other places had also been the brunt of frequent attacks. To this criticism he replied:

Ignoring in good faith or maliciously the fact that the capitalistic system itself has had to concentrate great economic resources and use machinery on a vast scale in order to reduce costs and increase profits, the critics desire that the peasant cultivate his plot of ground single handed in a non-cooperative form, pulverizing as it were, the ownership of the soil and bringing anarchy to the cultivation of the community lands.

They do not take into consideration the fact that to intensify crops it is necessary to make a careful selection of seeds and to have machinery, irrigation systems, credit, and technical advice, all of which one peasant by himself cannot hope to secure. Nor can he free himself of profiteers and middle men.

After making his strong defence in that speech of December ninth, he went on to promise that he would not try to pick his successor and that there would be full liberty for all political viewpoints to participate in the oncoming presidential campaign. He concluded by stating that his government "would go right ahead carrying out till the last day of his term, the program that is bound up with the redemption of the masses and that is born of the letter and essence of our republican institutions."

Mexico cannot be indifferent to anything that befalls the American nations in their legitimate aspirations for collective betterment. We have always felt that our Revolution had more than a local significance, that it would bring about the solution of the economic problems that affect in common our peoples on both continents. We realize that each nation has its own special needs and that the routes which the respective nations take to fulfill their destinies may be different, but we also know that the love of justice unites us and that together we should defend ourselves against everything that might result in economic, political, or moral imperialism or that might hinder or delay our advance as sovereign nations when we seek to carry out programs that will insure the liberation of our peoples.

— *Lázaro Cárdenas* — *To Cuba*
June 12, 1938

Sister nations have seen in our struggle their own defense against the attitude of a handful of rich men who believe that we are still countries open to conquest and attempt to deny us our economic freedom.

— *Lázaro Cárdenas* —
To Federation of Laborers, November 25, 1940

XXX

NEGOTIATIONS COLLAPSE

WE HAVE SEEN that, following the expropriation of the oil companies, Mexico had to face an economic war with all the propaganda and diplomatic pressure that went with it. How did she make out? President Cárdenas in his report to Congress September 1, 1938, was able to present an encouraging account of his country's resistance.

The public income had been reduced but little; imports had decreased, but the value of exports increased; taxes on silver had produced less but on other metals more; exports of petroleum had gone down 45%, but internal consumption had been greater; the value of the *peso* in foreign exchange had dropped, but this had resulted in huge profits to certain enterprises and these had been duly taxed; economies had been necessary in development projects, but the ones already started were continuing. Citizens and friends of Mexico had contributed 2,016,263 *pesos* toward the fund to pay the oil companies for their properties, and to this was being added regularly 20% of the income from all petroleum that was exported.

England had been eliminated on the diplomatic front, and although the Department of State at Washington was insisting in note after note that Mexico's agrarian legislation and her way of carrying it out were "opposed to the fundamental principles of human rights, morals, and justice", the discussion was being conducted in a friendly and respectful way and Mexico was amply supported by Latin-American jurisprudence in her conviction that collective rights have the preeminence over individual rights. (To clinch the last argument, Cárdenas told Congress how important nations had forcibly taken away gold and gold certificates not only from their own citizens but also from foreigners, and had given no indemnity for the loss entailed.)

Mexico was more than holding her own, but Cárdenas confessed that he was anxious to reach an early agreement so as to put an end to the "costly, violent, and insidious campaign which was being carried on against Mexico in the United States" and which was at variance with the Inter-American pacts of solidarity, cooperation, and harmony between the Republics of this continent. He also mentioned with gratitude the fact that labor groups in England had expressed their sympathy with Mexico in the conflict and that in other countries manifestations of sympathy had also been made. Mexican laborers, too, living in foreign lands, and even foreigners themselves, had sent contributions to help pay the oil companies.

The oil companies eventually consented to do something constructive toward a settlement of the problem, and in March, 1939, sent Donald Richberg to Mexico City to negotiate personally with President Cárdenas. The conversations were conducted in such a cordial atmosphere that a successful outcome seemed likely, though Mr. Richberg had received very limited authority from his clients.

President Cárdenas tentatively offered to permit the seventeen expropriated companies to renew the utilization of their old properties on the condition they be merged into one big concern with control in Mexican hands. Furthermore, the companies were to promise to withdraw and turn the business over to the nation upon the expiration of a long-term contract. The fact that Cárdenas was willing to consider the return of the companies to Mexico even though they had been fighting his government so bitterly also shows how anxious he was to eliminate friction and get on with his program of helping the masses by putting Mexico in a position where she could produce enough to raise her standard of living.

Mr. Richberg made a second trip a few weeks later and conferred further with the president, who was in Saltillo at the time on an extended tour of the northern states. The results were not made public, but it was understood that an earnest effort was being made to find a workable basis on which the government and the companies could cooperate in the petroleum industry without endangering Mexico's economic independence. Cárdenas felt that this meant that Mexicans would have to control activities.

Shell interests, however, were reported to have said that their company would never consent to placing the technical direction of its activities in Mexico in the hands of Mexicans.

Then in August, 1939, after special trips between Washington and Mexico by both Ambassador Castillo Nájera and Under-Secretary of Foreign Affairs Beteta, there came a complete collapse of negotiations. The oil companies attributed the failure to a reversal of attitude on the part of the president, due they claimed to opposition from labor leaders and others who wished to retain the positions and influence which had resulted for them from the governmental operation of the industry.

The real difficulty, however, was more likely the problem of who would have the final voice in the proposed partnership, the government or the companies. President Cárdenas knew that Mexico's struggle for economic self-sufficiency would have been largely in vain had the companies returned with power to command. The companies, in turn, realized that it would be risky for them not to be able to direct operations. They might have been willing to let the Mexicans hold the reins as long as a man like Cárdenas was in authority, for his powers of persuasion were sufficient to hold both managers and laborers fairly well in line, but they refused to take a chance with the future. In fact, they made the astounding proposal that the government guarantee that taxes and wages would not be increased during the fifty years the contract would last. Mexico also wondered what it would get back at the end of the half-century.

My personal opinion from the beginning was that the plan for cooperation was impracticable. President Cárdenas failed to realize how great the differences are which exist both racially and in objectives between the two elements he wanted to link together in harmonious partnership. The merger of the English and American interests into one organization also constituted a big problem. A solution that would not work would have been worse than no solution at all. Probably it would have been better all around for the government to have purchased a 51% interest in all the companies with an understanding that until it had completed paying for its share, it would have direction only of internal trade while the companies took charge of export trade and of production.

Another workable arrangement might have been a division of the oil fields, the government getting a little over 50% and a monopoly of internal trade. If the companies under this arrangement had succeeded in making their production grow faster than the government, the latter would have had no one to blame but itself. Being occupied with its own business, the government would not have meddled unduly in that of the companies.

It was hard to understand why the president had been so optimistic. He was keenly disappointed when his prophecy of an agreement before he left office proved inaccurate. The basis for his confidence was never revealed, but he must have analyzed his enemy's situation as he is accustomed to do and, finding it to be untenable, made his calculations accordingly. His references in speeches and conversations during 1938, 1939, and 1940 to war clouds showed that he expected much of what actually happened and he knew that Mexico's help and Mexico's oil would be valuable to the democracies where his sympathies lay.

This strong conviction was shared by other Mexican leaders. On March 19, 1939, Vicente Lombardo Toledano gave a stirring address in which he called upon Mexico to link arms closely with the people and government of the United States as equals and work together with the remaining countries of the continent under Uncle Sam's leadership to make the Western Hemisphere safe for democracy.

The absolute confidence that Cárdenas had in Roosevelt's fidelity to the causes of labor and Inter-American harmony was another reason for his optimism. His trust in and affection toward Ambassador Daniels further strengthened his assurance that the oil conflict would be settled soon.

In his report to Congress in September, 1939, after the Richberg negotiations had failed, he stated his appreciative attitude toward the United States government:

Important financial groups in the United States petitioned the government of Washington to intervene by means of diplomatic pressure in decisions that pertain to our sovereign courts. It gives satisfaction to my government and to all our people to mention here that Washington has been perfectly proper in its attitude. It did not care to meddle in that way. After a time it limited its actions to customary and friendly efforts to get the companies to deal directly with the Mexican government.

A third reason why he anticipated a happy end to the conflict for Mexico was that the Sinclair interests saw the writing on the wall, and after Richberg had failed sent the previously mentioned Patrick Hurley to negotiate separately for them. Sinclair settled for eight million dollars and took part payment in oil. With the opposition front broken Cárdenas was sure of success. It is strange and lamentable that the other companies failed even then to open their eyes to the new world in which they were living.

President Cárdenas reported to the nation in his final New Year's message that during 1939 the oil industry under inexperienced government management had brought in twenty-three new wells with a potential production of about fifty-five thousand barrels; had contracted for new drilling equipment to the amount of 3,600,000 *pesos;* had repaired pipe lines and refineries; had built a plant to produce a substitute for tetraethyl so as to break the effect of the companies' embargo on that article; had secured or contracted for seven tankers with a total capacity of 91,500 tons with which to break the boycott; had increased its sales within the country from 153,000,000 *pesos* in 1938 to 172,000,-000 in 1939; had exported 110,000,000 *pesos* of oil to other lands, 75,000,000 *pesos* of the amount in cash and 35,000,000 in trade; and had spent many millions of *pesos* in improving the status of the laborers. All this for beginners.

By 1951 the government-owned industry had far outstripped all previous records. Crude production was nearly twice as much as it had been the last year that the foreign companies had been in control. On March 18th of 1951, thirteen years after expropriation, the keen business man whom President Alemán placed at the helm of the industry, Senator Antonio Bermudez, was able to report progress all along the line. During the year 133 new wells had been brought into production, several new pipe lines had been installed, eighteen tankers were hauling products over ocean lanes, more schools and medical services had been instituted for the oil workers, sales had mounted to $1,619,660,510.00 *pesos,* and the government had profited to the amount of $429,-915,000.00.

With the failure of negotiations, the companies left themselves only the recourse of appealing for an injunction against the decree of expropriation. This was denied them by the Supreme

Court late in 1939. President Cárdenas declared in his message of January first, 1940, "The definite termination of the petroleum matter will have to be found in the payment of indemnification." A commission was named to evaluate the properties, but the companies refused to name their own representatives as the law required them to do. And so the Mexican government and the expropriated oil companies were locked in a prolonged stalemate with settlement deferred for some time to come.

It is detrimental to the United States for her neighbors to be weak and poor. It would be to her advantage to help them bring their standard of living up to a par with what is considered decent in the United States. To attain this goal Mexico will have to be industrialized. It cannot get very far promoting small arts and crafts such as some of my American friends have suggested.

Machinery is sorely needed for factories, and the United States could help us this way. An agreement should be made, for instance, that for every thousand braceros Mexico sends to the United States to help in the harvest there, a certain number of tractors will be shipped to Mexico to make up for the loss of man power.

Lázaro Cárdenas — to Townsend   April, 1946

XXXI

RURAL PROBLEMS

PRESIDENT CÁRDENAS had his own plans for the practical development of neglected or barren areas of Mexico. Accordingly, he announced in Chilpancingo early in 1937:

The natural increase of population makes the problem of over-population more and more critical and urgent to solve. We have, however, rich areas, especially along the coasts, that have not been developed as much as could be desired. In fact, some of them remain isolated from the general economic life of the nation. . . . It is necessary to take groups of peasants from over-populated areas where there is insufficient land for cultivation, and move them to new zones.

To make this colonization possible the Federal Government will continue to spend large sums in the construction of roads and railroads to these areas for economic and social purposes as well as in sanitation projects to improve the factors that make for health so that the population may be more wisely distributed and new sources of production be developed.

On November 20, 1938, Cárdenas spoke to the crowds who were celebrating the twenty-eighth anniversary of the beginning of the Revolution, saying in part:

It is our obligation to extend help to our fellow citizens who have been living in the United States and now find themselves in need. We should bring them back and reinstate them . . . for they will come to give greater impulse to our constructive enterprises, and to help us solve our problems. To make their return practical we are creating various large irrigation systems where fertilized lands put in proper condition for cultivation will be a decisive factor in the betterment of the people. We are opening lines of communication to isolated though favorable regions. . . . Modern mills have been installed where the peasants can process their products and thus secure more returns from their labor and lands. . . . Flour mills for various grains are being installed for the same purpose. Electric plants are being provided where the consumers become the owners.

And finally, institutions of credit are being organized to promote other lines of productive labor on a cooperative basis. All these developments will doubtless bring better living conditions. . . . They should be shared not only by those of us who have had the good fortune to live within our borders during the progress of the social movement, but also by those who emigrated for a while but preserved within their hearts and consciences an abiding love for their Fatherland.

He came to attach so much importance to this project that in 1939 he sent two of his most gifted colleagues, Dr. Ramón Beteta and Dr. Manuel Gamio, to tour Texas and extend to Mexicans there a cordial invitation to return. Many more responded than the government could handle. A settlement was established near Matamoros, and land was reclaimed from the mesquite brush. The fertile farms north of the border similarly reclaimed served as patterns. The settlers were assisted with government funds. Other returned emigrants scattered to towns where they had relatives or some other attraction, and possibly made a more effective contribution to the country than those who were grouped together in settlements.

In his Tepecuacuilco speech back in 1937 Cárdenas had dealt with the problem of having foreign immigrants settle among Indian farmers, a desirable situation to those who argued that the Indians learn rapidly from example. But he warned against the tendency for the foreigner gradually to secure control of the land and for the Indians to become his servants.

Under Cárdenas' successor, General Manuel Avila Camacho, many thousands of Mexican farmers went to the United States as *braceros* to help in the harvests and in other rural jobs left vacant by our soldiers. A few who later returned made a valuable contribution to Mexico by putting their new ideas and money to good use. They were enough to show that the farmers of the United States could be a great help to their neighbors below the border if a practical way were found and if we as a nation were awakened to the need of assisting them for our own sake as well as theirs.

When we discussed this subject, however, Cárdenas took a rather pessimistic attitude. He could see little help accruing to Mexico from the returning *braceros,* for they came back speaking a little English, which they soon forgot, with a little money, which they soon drank up, and with ideas, but no implements to develop them. They were left with only a desire to go back again to the land of plenty and abandon their fatherland that needed their boost in an all too weak farming program.

It seemed to me that if our manufacturers of agricultural equipment were to adopt a long-range policy and help the Mexican government to train and finance agricultural missions of young men with know-how, patience, and a selfless spirit from lands where agriculture and cooperative methods are more advanced (such as the United States, Sweden, or Canada), they would get their money back with interest through future sales of machinery and would render a great service to Mexico.

Mexico had been losing in her battle for tillable land until Cárdenas. In a personal letter to General Oviedo Mota he stated one aspect of the problem:

The seriousness of the problem which results from the ruthless destruction of our forests in many parts of our country is evidenced by the aridness of the treeless soil. The task of replacing the trees is difficult. In fact, the total work of reforestation on the part of the government, and in a few cases of private individuals in the Federal District, in some of the states, and along the highways, doesn't amount to 12,000 acres.

When we compare this scant reforestation—the work of various administrations—with the great acreage that is constantly being stripped of trees, we realize that within a few generations our forests can be totally destroyed. For that reason it is urgent that every Mexican citizen become interested in this serious problem that every day is getting worse.

Near the close of his term Cárdenas summarized for the delegates to the first Inter-American Indian Congress in Patzcuaro in 1940, the program that should be carried out for the Indians of Latin America. It is so pertinent to the problem of helping the rural communities in general that we shall quote it here rather than in our discussion of the Indian problem:

Mexico counts among its most pressing obligations the handling of the Indian problem. In effect, a plan has been developed which includes the following measures: 1) Greater emphasis upon the restoration or granting of lands, forests, and water; 2) Credit and implements for cultivating their crops; 3) Irrigation projects; 4) The combating of endemic diseases and insanitary conditions; 5) The combating of vices, principally drunkenness; 6) Greater impetus to sports; 7) The development of native industries; 8) The extension of educational efforts to include the adults both in a literacy crusade and the impartation of basic information for the improvement of antiquated systems of production; 9) Efforts on the part of the teachers in rural schools, boarding schools, and cultural missions to improve the Indians' living conditions, winning his confidence, pointing out to him the way to secure the commodities necessary to satisfy his newly acquired wants, and teaching him likewise his rights and responsibilities. Thus equipped he can enter into the life of the nation with all the factors that contribute to his economic progress and democratic development.

President Cárdenas had expressed concern for the health of the country in his first New Year's message: "We should send the greatest number possible of doctors and nurses to the outlying areas of the country, especially to the more unhealthy regions." And to help facilitate this program the National University had decreed that every medical student should practice medicine in a rural community for two years before he could receive his diploma. Results have been gratifying though most rural communities are still without doctors, and indeed few cities under five thousand inhabitants have them.

In the reference Cárdenas made to combating the waste of means and energies on liquor, he touched upon one of the basic problems. The development projects would rest on a foundation of sand unless drunkenness decreased.

A story is told of the great liberal of Guatemala, General Justo Rufino Barrios. He was a circuit-riding ruler like General Cárdenas. Back in the eighties, on one of his trips to the hinterland, he was met at some distance from town by two hundred men on horseback. As they rode along together, Rufino Barrios inquired about the school that had been established on the occasion of a previous visit. The men replied that they had not been able to support it, and so they had closed it down.

Barrios thought a while and then asked them how many saloons there were in their town. They replied that there were six, and all of them were prospering. He then said he would like to make a note about the situation and asked if someone would lend him a pencil. No one had a pencil inasmuch as no one knew how to write. This brought a stiff rebuke from the general, who felt that it was a pity that they could support six saloons but not a single school when their need for one was so apparent.

Then, seeing how crestfallen the party had become, Barrios stopped his tirade and suggested that a little drink of wine would not be amiss to cheer up their spirits. He took a bottle from his saddle bag and asked if someone would lend him a corkscrew. Immediately, two hundred corkscrews were flashed into the air.

The above story could just as easily have taken place in parts of Mexico at that time. The drunkenness caused by excessive drinking was not only a problem in itself, but a mother of problems. Most of the frequent murders in rural communities are committed either during religious festivals when everyone is "piously" drunk, or during political campaigns when they get "patriotically" drunk.

Cárdenas knew that if half the money that the working people spent for liquor went into improving their standard of living, Mexico would be a different country. Laborers in city and country had always taken drunkenness for granted. It was part of their social and religious life.

I once asked an Aztec youth twenty years of age if he ever got drunk.

"Oh, no," he replied. "I'm not married yet."

I asked him what that had to do with getting drunk, and he explained: "Well, it's this way. Custom in our town dictates that a man has to be married before he can take active part in our religious activities. Most boys in our town marry by the time they are fourteen, but I'm taking my time. When I get married I'll be admitted to our religious functions and I will have to take an offering of rum to the images of the saints. Since they can't drink it I'll drink it for them. Soon after that I'll get the habit and become a drunkard like my father."

While conservative groups in Latin America have done little about solving this basic problem many revolutionary leaders have taken it seriously. They may not be greatly interested in temperance for themselves (though many are), but they can see that there is little hope for the peasant until he quits spending his increased income on an increased supply of liquor.

At the beginning of his administration Cárdenas promised eventual prohibition to solve the situation, but when he realized that nothing short of a dictatorship could accomplish this he gave it up. Instead, he sponsored a law that prohibited the sale of liquor in centers where laborers were concentrated. As far as I know the law was enforced only on development projects and a few other places where considerable local sentiment was in favor of it.

An educational campaign was organized, however, that resulted in the organization of 400,000 school children into temperance societies where they were taught the evils of drunkenness. The problem continues, however, and though some advance against it has been made through education and the expansion of the sports program, it seems that only a moral and spiritual crusade can solve it.

From April 18 to July 25, 1939, Cárdenas was away from the capital on one of the longest of the many tours that he made.

He traveled from one end of the northern states to the other. Again he made the tedious horseback trip through the Pulpit Canyon of Chihuahua where as a young lieutenant colonel he had led his troops in campaigns against Pancho Villa.

Much time was spent in Sonora where the local regime had not been pushing the program of the Revolution fast enough to suit him. In that state he found a bad shortage of gasoline, typical of other shortages that occurred during the worst part of the struggle with the oil companies.

While in Sonora some outstanding leaders of the Spanish Republic, recently from Europe, arrived to pay their respects to the man who had helped them when most of the world had either refused help or had turned against them. An official banquet was held in their honor, but much to the disappointment of all Cárdenas was too busy to come. Only a little over a year remained for him to accomplish a great many tasks for the people and he had to drive on, especially since the electoral agitation and the oil conflict were interfering greatly with constructive effort.

Also in Sonora Cárdenas had an opportunity to put his theory of pacification-by-justice rather then subjugation-by-force into practice with the Yaqui Indians. It was my privilege to be with him as an observing guest when he visited the tribe.

The scene was a big spreading mesquite tree before the town hall at Torim. The rulers from the eight Yaqui towns had gathered with great dignity earlier in the morning to the beating of drums. A formal welcome came from the authorities of Torim. Each leader was accompanied by his assistant who had also been elected by the people and who was held responsible in Yaqui democracy for the good behavior of his chief.

The rulers and their assistants now sat facing President Cárdenas and his party. The president matched the grave dignity of the Yaquis with his own serious though gracious bearing. In fact, all of us were serious as the rulers of the two nations began the discussion of a treaty of peace.

An introductory speech made in Yaqui and interpreted into Spanish went somewhat as follows:

Fellow Yaquis, former presidents of Mexico have never left their thrones to come to see us. This is the first who has come. We have never been able to present our complaints to the president because he was far off.

Now that the president has come, we want him to know what is going on in the Yaqui nation—the harm that is being done by the Mexican settlers who have taken our lands.

The secretary of the head man of Potam had drawn up a document wherein the Yaquis demanded the restitution of all the land that had belonged to the tribe back in 1740. This would have forced the evacuation of thousands of Mexicans and some foreigners from the settlements they had made on the fertile plains that line the Yaqui River.

As the Yaqui rulers pressed their claims and denounced the settlers their official interpreter became so agitated he waved his arms excitedly, which, according to Yaqui etiquette, was a discourtesy toward their distinguished guest. Proceedings were halted while the rulers rebuked their interpreter and ordered his assistant to stand beside him and keep him from making gestures.

President Cárdenas listened patiently until they had told their story. Then he presented the document that he had drawn up and left them while they studied it over. When he returned late in the afternoon the Yaquis had agreed to the terms of settlement. The treaty was signed under the big mesquite.

In his report to Congress on September first Cárdenas told the results of that memorable meeting:

880,000 acres of land have been restored to the Yaqui Indians, who, as all Mexico well knows, had maintained an age-long struggle in defense of their legitimate rights. They now have tillable soil sufficient to take care of all the Yaqui tribe living in Mexico and also all of the same tribe who have been residing in the United States but who are disposed to return to their country as soon as the irrigation system that will provide water for their lands has been completed. They have been given title to 50% of the water that will be stored up by the Angostura Dam on the upper Yaqui River.

Restored to the legitimate possession of their lands, and aided by the government to improve their living conditions, these Indians have shown their ability and desire to work as well as a real interest in the education of their children. In view of their vigor and strong character and the justice of their cause, these Indians represent an important asset for the Mexican nation.

The Yaquis showed their appreciation. According to a report by Gontrán Noble, head of the Department of Agrarian Organizations, production of wheat jumped in four years from forty tons to five thousand tons annually. It is probable that the Yaquis will never again rise up in armed revolt.

However, even among them, the people feared their local bosses and were reluctant to talk before them. Whenever possible Cárdenas arranged to speak to the peasants or Indians alone. With these Yaquis he took a group off a hundred yards away from the officials, both local and those who had come from Mexico City, and standing under a tree out of the hearing of the leaders he conversed with the Indians for two hours.

It was also in Yaqui-land that a group of disgruntled Indians refused to attend the general meeting due to differences among the chiefs. Cárdenas drove over a deserted country road by night to confer with them. There, with no officials or enemy *caciques* to overhear their camplaints, the reticency of the Indians was overcome and they told their story to the man whom they felt was their friend.

But Cárdenas never catered to his own friends. They had to be ready to compete with unknown peasants for his attentions. Once while the presidential train was stopped in a little village on that same trip through Sonora, Professor Tannenbaum and I found ourselves within hailing distance of the building where Cárdenas had been working. As he came out and entered a car to go off to lunch he evidently instructed an official to call us to join him. The aide looked in our direction and called out the professor's name. He also glanced at me in a way which I might have interpreted as a call to come, had not the car appeared to be full. Since he did not mention my name I did not move, and since Professor Tannenbaum had not heard his name called he did not budge either.

I noticed the president say something to the official, whereupon the latter went over to a peasant who stood watching the scene and invited him to join the presidential party. The president, of course, did not know of the indefiniteness which his aide had exercised in calling us, but it did not bother him in the slightest that his American friends had to go off and eat beans and *tortillas* wherever they could find them. On the other hand he enjoyed having the startled peasant substitute for us at the bounty of the presidential dining car.

In those three weeks in which I was with the party I noticed that officials who were designated by the president to address the people on his behalf did not receive a second invitation if they extolled Cárdenas personally. The officials who were invited to

speak time and again were the ones who spoke of the program
of the government and of the Revolution and the people's share in
it. They referred to the president himself only when conveying
his gratitude to the throngs for the welcome they had accorded
him.

Cárdenas had no patience for praise, especially for himself. He
talked, and wanted his colleagues to talk, of the Revolution and
its program. In Hermosillo, Sonora, the speaker from that city
extolled the state government for its desire to help the Indians. I
thought the president looked a bit bored. Sometime later I learned
the reason why. We were talking about the Seri tribe of Tiburón
Island in the Gulf of California.

"Why doesn't the state government do something for the Seris,
if they love the Indians as much as that orator said they do?"
was the president's comment. Then he proceeded to give me
interesting information about one of the smallest and most backward Indian tribes of Mexico.

Action! Deeds instead of words, or at least deeds to vindicate
words. That was one of the reasons that Cárdenas constantly made
inspection tours. He knew the human tendency to procrastinate.
His trips were not only to see what needed to be done, but also
to check to see that his orders were being carried out.

From Sonora to Lower California Cárdenas took the hot, dusty
desert road where four engineers had lost their lives while surveying
the railroad that Cárdenas had initiated to connect the territory
of Lower California with the rest of the nation by land. His party
came out at the delta of the Colorado River where a number of
agrarian problems were calling for his attention. Lands that had
belonged to Harry Chandler of the *Los Angeles Times* had been
distributed among the laborers. The president was anxious that
they should be handled as efficiently as possible in view of the
attention that had been attracted to the affair. The wise utilization
of Mexico's share of the Colorado River was also given consideration.

While in Lower California the president consented to eat a
picnic dinner with friends of our Summer Institute of Linguistics
from Southern California. After a late session in Mexicali the night
of July 6, 1939, the president and his party got up at three o'clock
in the morning for the rough tiresome ride to Tijuana.

A little before noon the dusty travelers arrived at the beautiful old gambling casino which had been closed four years before by presidential decree in spite of political pull. Since it had stood idle all that time Cárdenas had decided to take it over for a school. It made a beautiful site for an international picnic.

Two hundred Americans from some thirty Southern California cities and towns soon arrived with baskets full of delicious food —delicious to the American taste though too poorly seasoned to appeal much to Mexican palates. Long tables were spread along the verandas of a beautiful patio. The president's party, twenty strong, scattered out among the Americans to get acquainted and then all sat down to a bountiful repast. The pastor of the Mexican Baptist Church in San Diego said grace, a custom that the president had become familiar with both at our home in Tetelcingo and at the American Embassy where the staunch old Methodist, Josephus Daniels, was as he said "priest in his own household."

A lively time ensued with Mexicans and Americans exchanging English for Spanish while they ate. Before introducing the after-dinner speakers I expressed the gratitude of the Institute to the president for the help he had extended us so generously from the very founding of our organization. Then I asked the parents who had sons or daughters working with the Institute among Mexico's Indian tribes to stand that the president might know who they were. All did so except my own father, who was then eighty-four years of age and completely deaf. My sisters motioned to him and he arose.

Immediately the president got to his feet as a tribute to an American peasant whose son was leader of a group that was serving Mexican peasants. With the president on his feet, everyone had to stand up. Every heart was touched by this sincere courtesy.

Six or seven Americans from different walks of life then spoke and the president commissioned Dr. Beteta to reply for him to their cordial messages. Dr. Beteta explained what the Mexican Revolution was endeavoring to do, and his eloquent address delivered in perfect English was interrupted time and again by applause as the Americans learned of how Mexico was trying to give her people privileges that they themselves had long enjoyed.

Little four-year-old Shirley Lucas, my father's great-granddaughter, presented the president with a bouquet and he promptly took her up in his arms and placed her beside him.

When the program was over President Cárdenas invited all present to come forward and shake hands with him. As the long line marched by, the fact that he could not speak their language seemed to handicap friendly relations but little, even when the interpreter lagged, for he and his greeters seemed to understand each other through the warmth of handshake and frankness of smile. Then requests for autographs kept him busy for about half an hour with no sign of impatience on his part. Even the request of a little girl that he eat one of her fudgecicles while she took his picture was smilingly granted.

The hearts of the Americans were completely won. As a distinguished American physician watched the scene he said to those around him, "Another Lincoln!" It had been a meeting of good neighbors. Catholics, Protestants, and agnostics had spent nearly three hours together and had enjoyed the democratic spirit that had prevailed. No one had guarded the president. Not a soldier, policeman, or plain clothes man was in sight.

It is not true that the Indian is recalcitrant toward improvement, or indifferent to progress. If frequently he fails to reveal his joy or sorrow, hiding sphinx-like the secret of his emotions, it is because he is accustomed to the oblivion in which he has been held. He cultivates fields that do not recompense his efforts; he operates looms that do not clothe him; he labors on constructions that do not improve his living conditions; he overthrows dictatorships only to see new exploiters succeed them; he assumes an attitude of apparent indifference and justifiable distrust.

When, however, a persevering governmental program has been able to bridge the abyss of misunderstanding and has succeeded in inspiring his confidence, and when he has become convinced that government authorities exercise their power as a means for his liberation, then he responds with unfailing enthusiasm, tenacity, and loyalty.

— Lázaro Cárdenas — To the Inter-American Indian Congress held at Pátzcuaro.
April 14, 1940

XXXII

"FIRST PRESIDENT OF THE INDIANS"

In the Aztec Cuauhtémoc, the Indians gave Mexico a hero but found for themselves defeat; in the Zapotec Juárez, the Indians gave a liberator but remained in slavery themselves; in the Spanish-Tarascan Cárdenas, the Indians gave a blend and found a champion who discovered them to their fatherland as potential factors of national greatness.

Cárdenas became more painfully aware than ever of the condition of the Indians while on his long campaign tour in 1934. (It was comparable to Lincoln's experience on his trip down the Mississippi and his visit to the slave market in New Orleans). On April 17 of that year Cárdenas had referred to the Indian problem in a speech delivered in Oaxaca:

In towns far away from the highways we encounter the greatest need both of an educational and economic order. Large numbers of Indians are found there who do not speak our language, who are dominated by the vice of drunkenness, and who are almost in their entirety stupefied by fanaticism and poverty resulting from their failure to receive a legal wage and in some cases from unjust taxation.

On the eve of his inauguration he repeated the vision that haunted him:

. . . Nothing can justify with more eloquence the long struggle and sacrifices of the Revolution than the existence of whole regions in which men of Mexico live outside the pale of material and spiritual civilization. They are submerged in the most complete ignorance and poverty and are subjected to a system of living as regards food, clothing and shelter which is so inferior that it is outrageous in a country such as ours which has sufficient material resources to warrant a more just situation.

At first Cárdenas worked through a bureau in the Ministry of Education where the ethnologist, Carlos Basauri, tackled the Indian program enthusiastically. Then Cárdenas seemed to incline toward the views of his Indian Minister of Labor, Genaro Vásquez, who wanted to give strong powers to an independent Department

319

of Indian Affairs. (Vásquez was author of the famous phrase: *Hay que dar al indio la razón, aunque no la tenga!—The Indian is right even though he appears to be wrong!*)

Finally, however, Cárdenas followed the dictates of more cautious advisers who suggested that a strong department with authority to act would most certainly step on the toes of other departments and also give too much attention to the line of demarcation between Indian and non-Indian.

A department was created with just enough money to do a little investigating and advocating, and Professor Graciano Sánchez, a sincere but politically-minded man who had never specialized on distinctively Indian affairs, was placed at its head. It turned out to be a weak office, with only enough power to advise and promote.

One profitable sphere of activity was to organize regional Indian conferences, and for this endeavor Graciano Sánchez was gifted. Ixmiquilpan in the heart of the needy Otomí tribe was the site of the first conference held in 1936. The president himself attended and in his opening speech declared categorically that he would give first place to the Indian problem during the remaining four years of his term. It caused him no little grief that the struggle with the oil companies prevented his carrying out this promise.

His heart was and is with the Indians. When Genaro Vásquez saw him shed tears in silence over the condition of the race, he told me what Ignacio García Téllez and others had said: "The man is a mystic."

Our own John Colliers, at that time United States Commissioner of Indian Affairs, in reviewing Cárdenas' accomplishments for the original Americans said in a speech to the Inter-American Indian Congress in April, 1940:

No individual, public or private, in these current years has more massively or more significantly served the Indian—and therefore—more has served all the nations of the West, and—therefore—more has served human justice and the spirit of mankind, than President Cárdenas has done in the six years behind. Among living men he is the greatest protagonist of the Indian.

Cárdenas not only associated closely with the Indians, but took delight in placing his companions in situations where they too had to reckon with the Indian as a vital factor in Mexican life. On one occasion in Michoacán he decided suddenly to leave his train and go on an expedition to surrounding villages. It was almost time for the main meal of the day (midafternoon), and the intendant of the train came to ask him to dine before leaving.

"No," replied the president, "we will pick up a bite to eat in one of the villages."

"But sir," remonstrated the steward, "what will I do with all the delicious food that is prepared?"

A group of hungry officials standing around rapidly decided in their minds to stay by the food and not accompany their chief on the afternoon's trip. What was their dismay when the president pointed to a large group of curious peasants and told the intendant, "Those people will enjoy it. Give it to them."

Officials who did not have to go on the trip scampered elsewhere for food, while the few who could not escape tightened their belts and went along with their chuckling leader.

Though he never indulges them, in the vital things Cárdenas is considerate of his friends. When he sees that someone, whether an intimate or not, understands what he is after and endeavors to help in an unselfish way, he is exceedingly thoughtful about manifesting appreciation either in a letter or in personal conversation.

Even when his ordinary duties were so augmented by the petroleum problem in the summer of 1938, he took time to write a long letter of appreciation to Professor Angel Corzo, who had written a treatise on the problem of Indian education. The pleased president, having gone over the work carefully, went into detail discussing its merits.

About the same time he invited Professor Rafael Ramírez, an educator who played a very important part in the development of the rural school system of Mexico, to take breakfast with him on various occasions so that they might discuss the contents of textbooks which the professor was preparing for the elementary schools. Cárdenas' mind was occupied more by items such as these than by the petroleum issue and other problems concerning which he could do just so much and no more.

About the time that Hitler was promulgating the theory of superiority of the Teutonic peoples, Cárdenas countered with the statement that the Mexican Indian was potentially the equal of any race. In a speech given in the town of Tepecuacuilco, Guerrero, in April, 1937, he pointed out that the modern descendants of the old Aztecs, Mayans, and other civilized tribes possessed valuable innate qualities.

According to this view the Indian masses ceased to be objects of pity, or even subjects for justice, and were pictured rather as mines of untold wealth. He pointed out that they had already demonstrated an ability for full participation in the modern scheme of living by having contributed to the nation outstanding leaders in the realms of literature, science, and statesmanship. He maintained that by their handicrafts and dogged pursuit of the solution of life's problems, the Indians of Mexico had given ample evidence of their capacity for constructive and artistic endeavor. He also referred to their high sense of human dignity as revealed by the respect and courtesy which are customary among them within their own habitat. "The Indian is a hard worker," he declared. "He has never refused to do the hardest type of labor. The reason why he has been called lazy is that he refused to perform willingly the tasks which were assigned to him without pay on plantations belonging to government officials under the old regime."

He called attention to the Indians' industry as shown in their willingness to perform, frequently without pay, tasks undertaken as a group in the interests of the community. Allowances should be made also for under-nourishment, disease (hookworm, malaria, etc.), the effects of wholesale drunkenness, and the lack of incentive. If these handicaps are taken into consideration, however, most of the Indians of Mexico and Guatemala can be said to be exceedingly industrious.

An American aviator who worked for Francisco Sarabio in the state of Chiapas once told me, "These people are not lazy. It is nothing uncommon for me to start a flight at four o'clock in the morning, and invariably I see the winding trails below me lined with barefoot Indian farmers hurrying along to work their meagre mountain-side plot."

The main burden of the president's Tepecuacuilco discussion was how to raise the Indian's standard of living. He mentioned that manufacturers complained of the fact that the Indians are not consumers, and then asked, "How could they be expected to be either producers or consumers when they have been kept in such a plight as has been theirs?"

When Cárdenas was Minister of Defense after Mexico had declared war on the Axis powers in 1942, a reporter asked him if Mexico would send a contingent of soldiers to fight.

Cárdenas asked, "With what? Bows and arrows?"

How can you expect a watch to keep good time if you use it as a hammer? Or an Indian to function as a modern man if you use him as a beast of burden?

These are questions which should be asked of the ruling classes in all the countries whose Indian population suffers from exploitation. How can they expect commerce and prosperity from a populace that, aside from what they raise in their fields, know no other essential commodities than candles, alcoholic drinks, and fireworks, all used mainly in connection with religious festivals?

I have seen Indian communities with only one or two shabby stores for ten thousand inhabitants. In the average Indian town there are no hardware stores, no furniture stores, no establishments selling shoes, books, radios, implements, or drugs. The "grocery store" of that area would contain for the most part salt, sugar, matches, rice, cigarettes, soap, canned salmon, chiles, and candy. The "clothing store" might have straw hats, cloth, *rebozos* (shawls), thread, buttons, ribbon, and earrings.

The president did not profess to find the solution to the Indian problem in charity, though his government was spending quite a bit of money in caring for hungry children among the Otomí tribe where starvation was prevalent. Economic opportunities, rather, and education were what the president insisted the Indians needed. And he promised highways which would bring the Indian regions in contact with the outside world and give them markets for their products. Cooperative Indian organizations for the purpose of exploiting their mineral resources, community lands and forests, as well as new community enterprises were to be established. Later, a law was enacted giving these societies the privilege of importing equipment and supplies duty-free.

The thirty-three Indian boarding schools were to be doubled and their designation changed to rural boarding schools so as to minimize the tendency to regard them as inferior. For this same purpose a certain number of students from the mixed or *mestizo* racial group would also be admitted. Teachers of these schools were to be better prepared and were even to receive some instruction in law so as to be able to counsel their communities in elementary legal matters.

For the health of the isolated doctor-less communities where witchcraft dominates and where (in central and southern Mexico) the percentage of Indians who attain the age of fifty is very low, Cárdenas proposed to create the career of Rural Doctor. Much opposition developed to this plan to take humanitarian-minded men and women and give them some practical training in the basic principles of health and sanitation, the objection being raised that they would be just quack doctors. Considerable good, however, has resulted, for a "quack" with some modern medicines is better than a witch doctor who tells you to make an offering before an ant hill or to sacrifice a chicken to a tree in order to recover from malaria or some other malady.

Much of the Plan of Tepecuacuilco had to remain in abeyance during 1938 owing to the economic struggle with the oil companies, but in the spring of 1939 it was taken up afresh. The cultural aspect of the problem was attacked with energy by a new chief of Indian Affairs, Professor Chávez Orozco. He assigned to the new National Polytechnic Institute the highly technical problem of preparing Indian-language primers and linguistically-trained instructors. The Department of Anthropology of this institution, with the consent of President Cárdenas, called in Dr. Morris Swadesh, an authority in the field of American linguistics, and entrusted the technical supervision of the project to him.

Prior to Cárdenas, the rural teachers had instructed their pupils as our teachers in Alaska and on Indian reservations in Oklahoma and elsewhere had done. "Leave your own language outside the schoolhouse door. Learn in my language or not at all."

Too often is was not at all. As a result the educational movement was greatly retarded. There are over a million people today in Mexico who can speak no Spanish and another million more who prefer their own Indian languages to Spanish.

It had been quite a task to convince the teachers that the old inhibitions regarding the Indian languages were unscientific. As far back as May 19, 1911, Dr. Jesus Díaz de León who, I believe, was head of the Mexican Society of Specialists in Indian Affairs, stated to a reporter of the big capital daily, *El Imparcial:*

Let us suppose that there are five million Indians in Mexico who do not speak Spanish. Then we must prepare teachers to instruct this great number of illiterates. It will be necessary either to prepare special teachers, or else secure people from the tribes who are able to teach and also know the languages that their pupils speak.

One of the experts on whose eminent labors Cárdenas built was Dr. Mariano Silva y Aceves who had founded a department in the National University called the *Instituto Mexicano de Investigaciones Lingüísticas* (Mexican Institute of Linguistic Investigation). Patiently and tactfully he had gone about persuading teachers and ethnologists inside the Ministry of Education and out that the most effective way to approach the Indian was in his own language.

During September 1937, an international convention of school teachers was held in Mexico City. At that time a recommendation was made to all the countries of Indo-America that the tribes within their borders be taught by means of the bilingual system. Later a convention of Mexican teachers considered the problem again. After much heated discussion it was decided that wherever it was possible to secure bilingual teachers and proper textbooks, the Indian languages should be used in reaching monolingual Indians.

Still, some educators could not see the wisdom of using the Indian languages for the initial step. Some also felt that it would endanger the supremacy of Spanish as the national tongue. But others fell in line immediately. Professor Moisés Sáenz suggested that the government should call in hundreds of rural school teachers and give them linguistic training immediately in order that they themselves could master the languages of the areas in which they worked.

Experiments had shown that Indians could learn to read in their own tongues within a very few weeks, whereas in Spanish it required a long time. The boost to their morale that came from learning how to understand "paper that talks", and the new world it opened up to them, made the Indians tackle the study of Spanish with much more confidence. Instead of supplanting Spanish, it put them in a far better position to learn it. There was no adequate reason for delaying the entrance of the Indians into the realm of literacy even though it was through a gate other than Spanish.

In May, 1939, Professor Chávez Orozco, following instructions from Cárdenas, invited linguists from the *Universidad Nacional, Instituto Politécnico,* the Ministry of Education, and other institutions to participate in what was called the First Assembly of Philologists. Dr. Swadesh led the discussions which resulted in elaborate plans for literacy campaigns in several Indian languages.

The principal one was held among Cárdenas' own Tarascans in Michoacán. A phonetic alphabet was used to write the sweet Tarascan language which appears to be unrelated to the other interesting and widely divergent tongues of the "genuine Mexicans." A primer was prepared and thirty young men were trained to use it in teaching others. A printing plant was also installed. The project was to have had many other ramifications, but it had been operating only a little over a year when Cárdenas went out of office and it temporarily folded up. Later it was revived and today continues with very worthwhile results.

After doing all he could during his term as president, Cárdenas stated:

To better the situation of the Indian groups plans should be drawn up for a campaign which will take generations to carry out and will call for the combined efforts of many successive governments inspired by a common purpose.

Years later he told me,

Naturally, the Indian problem could not be solved in six years, but that is no excuse for neglecting it. The Indians should receive their just dues even though it takes fifty years.

Naturally he was pleased when, in 1946, during President Avila Camacho's Administration, the project of teaching the Indians to read by means of lessons in their own languages was revived through the Indian Literacy Institute of the Ministry of Education. Many other tribal projects were initiated at that time also. Now, under President Alemán, the movement is receiving fresh impulse. The Indian literacy movement is a great undertaking and if successful, will be an outstanding achievement that can be credited to Silva y Aceves, Cárdenas, and many many others who have followed their leading. Already the approach through the Indian language is being used in Peru, Bolivia, and elsewhere with promising results.

However, work with the Indians has its discouraging aspect as well, and sometimes patience is even more necessary than good planning. For example, to the Aztec village of Tetelcingo, Cárdenas sent some blooded livestock. His representative raffled them off. A winner of a sow became frightened, the sow was so big, and refused to accept it. Another winner took the second sow home, but a few days later it died (no one knew just why), and the neighbors were invited to a feast. The school teachers took possession of the rejected sow, but when they went on a vacation the Indian caretakers forgot to give her water and she died. A fancy boar survived, however, and today you see better pigs in the village than formerly.

To the same village he gave five thousand budded orange trees. He told me that they would have to be producing enough fruit by the time he went out of office to make the Indians themselves want to care for them, for his successor would be busy about other matters. With that in mind he ordered that three-year-old nursery stock should be imported for the grove. When he went to see the new orchard he found that the trees away from the highway were only two years old. He ordered them all uprooted and replaced with the trees he had requested. Finally, he relented, after his Minister of Agriculture had been thoroughly frightened, but he knew that the grove was doomed. After he went out of office the Indians quarreled over the fruit and no one took care of the trees. Eventually they died. The eucalyptus trees he sent the same village, however, are doing well without much care.

About the same time, when the Indians were failing to co-operate adequately in carrying forward many other projects he had initiated in the village, a professor who had been sent to coordinate the activities recommended that the supervisor be a military man whom the Indians would respect or at least obey through fear. To this suggestion the president replied, "I am fearful of placing military men in such posts." The work of democracy might have prospered, but the principles of democracy would have suffered. The immediate loss to the village was great, for the professor could neither persuade nor compel them to co-operate.

Cárdenas sought to interest organized labor in the plight of their less fortunate brothers. In his speech to the Confederation of Mexican Laborers on February 24, 1939, he said:

. . . We have seen that the laboring class does not limit its objectives to its own problems, but feels rather that it is intimately related to the solution of all the serious problems of the nation, among them that of freeing from prostration the groups of Indians that live in various sections of our territory still in conditions of misery.

Response to Cárdenas' visions concerning the Indians was slight. Unfortunately, he has not been able to impart his own dreams on a greater scale to others. This is not for lack of a dynamic personality. On the contrary, ever since he joined the Revolution as a lad he has demonstrated such a forceful bearing that wherever he goes he immediately commands respect. But his convictions are strong that movements should be based on ideas rather than personalities; he refuses to give the "follow me" call that would rally a crusade. He has expounded the ideas; he has set the example; other capable men have declared their adherence; they should carry on. That attitude is due, I believe, to his extremely sincere belief that democracy suffers whenever too much depends on one man. As president he could lead, but now he should not. Hence, he had to get all his plans started while president and inspire men who would continue them.

In order to further the pro-Indian movement throughout the hemisphere, all the American nations were invited to send delegates to the First Inter-American Congress on Indian Affairs. It was opened in April, 1940, by Cárdenas himself at the picturesque town of Pátzcuaro in the Tarascan Indian country so dear to the president.

Experts had come from many nations. Many projects were endorsed, the most permanent of which was the establishment of an Inter-American Indian Institute to promote sentiment and endeavors on behalf of the many million Indians of the Western Hemisphere. Mexico City was to be the headquarters and many of the principles of the Mexican Revolution the pattern.

Cárdenas summed up in his speech the goals of the program that was ultimately adopted, when he said:

Any regime that aspires to a true democracy should consider as essential factors in its program the utilization of the virtues of the Indian peoples, and the elimination of the vices and wrongful practices imposed upon them by their oppressors.

As long as human contingents exist who have been dispossessed of the lands of their forefathers as well as of their rights as men and citizens, and as long as they are treated as beasts of burden or machines, it cannot be said that equality and justice reign in America.

Two or three years after he left the presidency, Cárdenas visited an Indian village in Michoacán where the people gathered around him as soon as they saw his car. Cárdenas got out to shake hands and then sat down on a log for a friendly visit.

One of the Indians came up to make a petition, addressing him "Mr. President."

The General stopped him saying, "I am not president any more. General Manuel Avila Camacho is president now."

The unperturbed Indian answered, "To us Indians you will always be president."

This is one reason why Cárdenas has rarely appeared in public with either of his successors. The peasants embarrass him by showing him affection that detracts from the pre-eminence that he feels should always go to the chief ruler alone.

The people of Mexico are anxious to give their undistracted attention to the tilling of their fields, to working in their shops, to promoting industry and commerce, and to cultural progress, so that they may become a strong, prosperous and respected nation . . .

— Lázaro Cárdenas
May 24, 1938

Every laborer with an opportunity to produce who does not throw all his effort and capacity into his work or who gives himself over to vice or parasitic practises, is evading his responsibility. He is a traitor to his class and an enemy of Mexico's revindicating movement.

— Cárdenas to laborers—
November 25, 1940

XXXIII

THE ELECTION OF 1940

"IF YOU want to stay in office, stay out of politics", was the sub-
stance of President Cárdenas' message to his cabinet members and
other high ranking officials who had received their appointments
from him. Accordingly, Generals Mugica, Almazán, Avila Camacho, and Sánchez Tapia presented their resignations early in
1939 because thay all wanted to run for president in 1940. General
Magaña, Governor of Michoacán, also aspired to the presidency,
but his gubernatorial position was elective. Other officials who
wanted to participate actively in support of one of the candidates
also resigned.

All who remained in Cárdenas' immediate official family were
pledged to refrain from taking sides. Cárdenas could see no other
way of preventing the old trouble of directed elections. Futher-
more, he desired that the members of his government pay strict
attention to the work that had to be done before he left office.
He himself set the example and refused to give an inkling of his
own attitude toward the candidates but simply forged ahead with
the development projects as though it made no difference to him
who was elected.

Cárdenas has had uncanny success in keeping close friends and
relatives from running for office. There is little doubt that his
brother Dámaso could have been elected governor of Michoacán
and that others of his four brothers could have been elected to
Congress had the president been willing. He was not. He had seen
the evils of family rule too often and brought all his powers of
persuasion into play with such telling effect that at the close of
his term in office, none of his brothers was high in government
circles. Under President Avila Camacho, Cárdenas' youngest
brother José was chief clerk in the Treasury Department, but

otherwise the family was out because of their oldest brother's attitude. Not until 1951 did Dámaso feel free to accept the post of Governor.

In April, 1946, the general went to his wife's home town, Tacámbaro, for a day's outing. I was invited to go along. Just as our station wagon was about to leave, one of Mrs. Cárdenas' brothers-in-law arrived, and he accompanied us, for politeness demanded that the general invite him. Under ordinary circumstances he would have been happy to do so, for he delights to be with old friends and relatives—provided they do not try to talk politics. But in this instance the general was obviously not at ease.

We drove through Tacámbaro so fast that few noticed who was in the station wagon. We spent the day on the farm of a friend, food being brought to us from town when lunch time came. In the afternoon, Cárdenas talked at length with the young brother-in-law who was planning to run for senator from Michoacán. Both of them looked extremely serious, and later the would-be candidate told me that the general had discouraged him from running. The general also explained to me privately that the young man's going with us had kept him from visiting friends in Tacámbaro, for he had not wanted to be seen in public with a candidate for office. In this case, however, the dissuasion was not permanent; the young man finally decided to run in spite of the general's expressed preference and was elected.

Many questions have been repeatedly asked concerning the campaign of 1939 and 1940: Did Cárdenas pick the candidate of the official party? Did Cárdenas manipulate that candidate's election? Did Cárdenas steer his successor from behind the scenes? His critics answer a categorial "yes" to all three questions. But keen impartial observers, both Mexican and Foreign, are perplexed, thinking of course he must have, yet being unable to find proofs.

The facts about the election and subsequent events as they are known are these: prior to January, 1939, General Mugica was the candidate for nomination by the Revolutionary Party who seemed to have the inside track. He was a close personal friend of the president, with a clean revolutionary record dating back to his prominent role in framing the Constitution of 1917, and as Minister of Public Works he had made a valuable contribution to Cárdenas' administration. He was popular with the radical wing, had frequently been invited to speak to leftist school teachers, and had even been known to give the communist salute.

In 1938, however, the rumor was abroad that the governor of Puebla, General Maximino Avila Camacho, was quietly working for the candidacy of his brother Manuel, the Minister of War, although no one knew whether Cárdenas was favorable to him or not. For months he had been merely Acting Minister of War and had not been promoted to *General de División* as would have been expected had Cárdenas been grooming him for the presidency. Soon after the various candidates had resigned from Cárdenas' official family, however, the Confederation of Mexican Laborers announced that it would support Avila Camacho for nomination by the Revolutionary Party. This declaration, which became the official attitude of the labor sector of the party, was soon followed by similar pronouncements from the peasants' sector, and then from the other two branches, thus assuring Avila Camacho of the nomination.

Mugica then withdrew. Magaña died. Sánchez Tapia continued to work for votes, but with only a small following. Almazán withdrew from the Revolutionary Party and ran independently. Two other candidates, one a communist and the other an independent, tried to attract voters, but without much success.

The contest settled down to a struggle between the party in power—whose candidate, Manuel Avila Camacho, was considered colorless—and all the opposition groups led by a more striking figure, General Almazán. Cárdenas wanted to make the campaign strictly a matter of issues rather than personalities, and to this end arranged for General Jara, an elderly man with a mild disposition, to be head of the Revolutionary Party.

In his address to Congress of September 1, 1938, Cárdenas had expressed his reasons for such procedure by saying:

If the on-coming presidential and congressional campaign is initiated and carried out around the big problems that confront us rather than around candidates, we can rest assured that personalities will have been relegated to a place of secondary importance. A brief investigation of antecedents, ability, qualities, and integrity will be sufficient to select candidates who will fill the bill. This procedure would fundamentally solve the most troublesome problem of the political life of Mexico.

If personalities could be kept in the background there would be no more dictatorships. That was more important, Cárdenas felt, than to have strong, efficient government. He hoped, though, that it would be possible to have both.

No one doubted the president's sincerity in promising a free and open election. His statements had been definite. On November 20, 1938, he had said:

It was the iron hand of dictatorship suppressing the civic aspirations of public opinion . . . that was the immediate cause of the initiation of the revolutionary movement that we commemorate today. It is therefore our basic duty to remain serene when faced by groups that are opposed to our party. We should permit them to organize fully and freely. . . . Even reactionary groups organized under the protection of our civil liberties should be able to enter into the contest and have the same protection throughout the electoral campaign as that which is given to the revolutionary groups.

Then on September 1, 1939, he stated:

It is essential to take care that the future election be democratic, free, and with complete guarantees that the result of the balloting shall be the authentic expression of the popular will. Whether the outcome is wise or unwise, the responsibility will be directly that of the citizens of the land. It is our most fervent desire to promote the free development of opinion and the demonstration of the will of the citizens in order that they themselves shall be the best support and the strongest mainstay of the new national government that will result from the next election.

Cárdenas did his best to make his promises good, but his control over state officials was indirect and Almazán and his fellow campaigners did meet with some rough play.

The president wanted a full and free discussion of the issues and candidates. This policy was quite different from that of his successor, who preferred to arrange things whenever possible so that there would only be one candidate for governor, congressman, or senator. If two men aspired to the same office he would call in one and give him some gratifying news about himself such as a promotion in rank—if he were an army officer—and then explain to him that for the sake of public harmony it would be wise for him to withdraw his candidacy. As a result Mexico was much more quiet politically under Avila Camacho than under Cárdenas.

In the heat of the primary campaign the president went before Congress on September first, 1939, and prodded them to act upon important pieces of legislation, one of which was an amendment to the Constitution that would grant women the right to vote, saying:

From the very beginning of my term I have been urging that the grave injustice be rectified that cheats Mexican women of substantial rights while, on the other hand, it imposes upon them all the obligations of citizenship.

Suffrage in Mexico should be made complete by giving women the right to vote. Otherwise, the electoral function remains incomplete. . . . Although the idea commonly prevails that women's suffrage, if enacted, will be accompanied by problems of a reactionary nature, this should not prevent the enactment of the measure, for it is one of our basic duties to organize and guide along channels that are favorable to the nation, the fundamental functions of the sovereign prerogatives of the people.

And just a year before, he had told Congress:

An estimable proportion of Mexican women has taken part for years in the social struggle of our nation. They have been of high quality and numerous. Frequently, when our pride permitted it, they have taken part in the most dangerous activities in behalf of the most advanced ideas.

Another law that the president asked Congress to pass was one that would require officials to state in an affidavit the amount of their personal fortune when they took office, and then again when their term expired. Theoretically, the difference between the low and high marks of this thermometer was to indicate the degree of honesty the official had maintained. Cárdenas had said early in his administration: "Any man who goes into public office poor and comes out rich advertises his venality." The venality thermometer was adopted, but one of President Avila Camacho's associates is said to have blown the top off it with one of the worst records of graft in Mexican history, and little attention has been paid to the thermometer since.

The Party of the Mexican Revolution held its convention in November, 1939, and even though the political pot had been boiling furiously for a year, it was not till then that its official candidate was named. The political purge for high office holders was repeated at the close of 1939 so as to remove all semblance of official favoritism on the side of the P. R. M. as against its opponents.

In that same fall of 1939 Cárdenas pushed two laws through Congress that cost him a great deal of popularity and embittered and increased the opposition that had been growing against his government because of the economic sacrifices that had resulted from the oil struggle, the attacks of political aspirants, the failure of the laborers to manage the railroads efficiently, and the unsatisfactory conditions prevailing in the community farms.

The first and less important law was one that imposed a high tax on excess profits. Commercial circles howled and wished that Porfirio Díaz might rise from the dead in the person of General Almazán and restore their privileges. The second law established procedures for enforcing the Constitutional amendment that provided for socialistic education. As a matter of fact, under Cárdenas himself his pet provision for attaining and perpetuating a truly socialistic society in Mexico had become a dead letter.

To stand in well with Cárdenas, officials would swear their loyalty to socialistic education and then do nothing about it. What could they do? The people were opposed to it. The teachers needed to learn and love practical socialism before they could properly teach the theory.

Cárdenas had hoped to indoctrinate the teachers thoroughly so they would have known what was expected of them. But only a dictatorship could impose, and Cárdenas refused to dictate. Instead he tried persuasion once more. He began his effort to enact this law by asking the military commanders in September, 1939, not to stop short in the path they had taken at the beginning of the Revolution. Some of its initiators had been socialistically inclined, and many of the framers of the Constitutoin of 1917 were socialists.

The goal before Obregón, Calles, and the men who had drawn up the Six Year Plan had been a Mexico free from capitalistic abuses and at least moderately socialistic in its distribution of wealth and the means of production. True, many had betrayed the ideal and had become capitalists themselves through dishonesty. But, said Cárdenas:

It is not the accidental that determines the loftiness of a cause. Alongside the impostors, there are sectors . . . of the masses that are sincere and unselfish in their unwavering support of the ideals of the Revolution. . . . To modify an ideal that the nation has aspired to and labored toward for thirty years would be to betray it. To go only half way would be cowardice.

Congress complied, and enacted the law, though it is likely that they would have preferred something less visionary and more acceptable to the people for whose votes their party was appealing. Cárdenas, however, accepted the responsibility of explaining to the people, and in his speech in Chiapas commemorating the expropriation of the petroleum companies, he said:

The socialistic school is an institution of social service. It strives for a well-rounded preparation of all indivduals for the benefit of the collectivity. It desires true liberty inasmuch as it desires that the light of reason should regulate conduct instead of blind obedience to dogma. In that light it seeks to explain life by understanding natural phenomena rather than being guided by superstitious fear. It teaches that work is the source of wealth and well-being, and not the curse of servitude, that productive effort ennobles, and

that castes and races predestined to the privilege of happiness at the expense
of enslaved groups simply do not exist.

The Revolution cannot be indifferent concerning the development of the
national conscience, but on the contrary, must prepare children and youth
to understand and continue its work.

Cárdenas got his law, but in winning he lost. He lost much
popularity and he lost his point, for a modified program that will
succeed is better than a radical one that is dead. It was inevitable
that socialistic education would be repealed though it lived on
the books until President Alemán's administration. It represents in
one way the high water mark of the Revolution. As such Cárdenas
tried to make it a symbol, a rallying point for liberals and a point
of attack for opponents. The latter grouped around Almazán for
the electoral contest.

Almazán was a good campaigner. To the average observer it
looked as though his forces would win. It was rumored that he
received financial assistance from the oil companies. His mobilizing
of the groups that wanted a change looked to them like their golden
opportunity. Catholic groups such as the *Sinarquistas* and *Acción
Nacional* were for Almazán. An American Catholic writer, Bishop
Kelly, was strong for him and said that he would do for Mexico
what Franco did for Spain. Business men preferred Almazán, and
even many government employees supported him.

Avila Camacho's main strength came from organized labor,
except for the C. R. O. M. He was too mild to create much of
a stir, but the chairman of his campaign committee, Miguel
Alemán, was something of a spell binder by his manners if not
his oratory, and fiery labor leaders such as Lombardo Toledano
put plenty of fight into the resistance that the P. R. M. presented
to the aggressive attacks of discontented elements. The peasants
also backed Avila Camacho in large numbers. After all, the party
that had nominated him had given them lands, schools, and
credit, and they did not want to take a chance on losing their
gains. Peasants are not very vocal, however, in national politics,
and the humorist, Roberto Soto, drew more attention when he
referred to their candidate as "the unknown soldier".

Avila Camacho had not been well known. He had been an
efficient Minister of Defense, but had never done anything spectacular since his polo playing days unless it was to import the first
50,000 steel helmets and the first tanks for the army which he

and President Cárdenas were trying to modernize. He was just a very serene, level-headed, and gracious administrator with a clean though limited political record, and an exceptional ability to get people of antagonistic views to cooperate. He had never occupied a prominent post until Cárdenas made him Under-Secretary of Defense and later promoted him to top-man after that post had been made vacant by death.

Almazán, on the other hand, had had an outstanding though somewhat checkered carrer. At one time, while commanding a brigade under Zapata, he decided to lead his troops through the jungles of Chiapas and Tabasco to take British Honduras away from the English. He lacked money and munitions, though, for such an undertaking, and it fizzled out before the march had proceeded very far. Since that time he had made considerable money in building roads and in other business ventures, and was in a better position financially for his march on the presidency.

Almazán made the big mistake of his campaign four days before the balloting, which took place on July 7, 1940. He issued a statement that was sold by newsboys on the streets of Mexico City saying that if he were robbed of the election he would start a revolt that would place him in power. The ultimatum sounded too much like the way Mussolini and Hitler had talked preceding their rise to power to please the man who was trying his best to hold a truly democratic election. After that, it is doubtful if Cárdenas was much concerned about the counting of the votes.

Most of the country seemed to feel the same way six months after it was over. Almazán had offered to lead a revolt, but did nothing more than let some of his followers make an abortive pass at power in Monterrey. It was a complete fiasco. This disappointed his ranks, and they accepted Avila Camacho with surprising resignation and almost satisfaction, especially after he had declared himself a Catholic and attended mass with his brother Maximino.

Unprejudiced American observers are inclined to believe that there was gross unfairness about the counting of the votes, but almost all agree that President Cárdenas had done all that he could to give everyone the privilege of voting, as well as to permit and protect free campaigning. He himself, rode unprotected from poll to poll on election day in Mexico City to quiet opposing factions, though when he arrived at his own polling place he found that it had been taken over and closed by labor groups who supported Avila Camacho. Thus, the president himself could not vote. There were probably many like him.

The election laws in Mexico were very inadequate in this regard. The first faction that arrived at the polls would take charge while the other faction would try to rout their opponents and take over. This resulted in rioting and bloodshed when the opposing groups were evenly matched, not in numbers but in fighting strength. Five angered union laborers could out-match ten clerks, bankers, etc. That possibly explains why Avila Camacho carried Mexico City and other cities where Almazán appeared to have an overwhelming majority. Even had Almazán carried these places, however, the strong peasant vote would likely have offset his advantage in the cities. As it was, Congress reported that the ballots when counted had shown a huge majority for the candidate of the Party of the Mexican Revolution, Manuel Avila Camacho.

I go out of office with a tranquil mind and with the inward peace that comes from having put forth the maximum effort to fulfill our highest duties.

— Lázaro Cárdenas—to the Laborers,
November 25, 1940

XXXIV

POPULAR UNREST

IF THERE HAD BEEN a great swing of popular favor toward Cárdenas in 1936 and 1937 after he had thrown off the yoke of Calles and had given the Church her constitutional rights, there was just as great a swing away from him during and after the election in 1940. Many were the charges brought against him of communist, dictator, thwarter of the public will, impoverisher of the nation, enemy of the Church, fanatical supporter of labor, and wild dreamer. There was much talk of revolt. Many Americans thought that he would be unable to finish the final months of his term. Indeed, there was a rumor at one time that he himself would resign.

Nothing was farther from his mind than to quit, especially when so much of the opposition bore the mark of "Made in the United States" and savored of oil. On the contrary, he continued his trips and projects at the same furious pace he had maintained throughout his term. The year 1940 found him visiting in the states of Guerrero, Chiapas, Morelos, Oaxaca, México, Michoacán, Guanajuato, Puebla, Coahuila, Durango, Nuevo León, Querétaro, Tamaulipas, Vera Cruz, Zacatecas, Hidalgo, Aguas Calientes, Chihuahua, and Jalisco — nineteen states out of Mexico's twenty-eight, and many of them were visited on two or three different occasions. Fifteen weeks out of a possible forty-eight were spent on the road. Only January and November found him in the capital the entire month.

He went to Guerrero because it was Almazán's home state, and it was reported there was much opposition to the government. In his main speech given there in February, 1940, he did not mention the candidates, but he did try to clear his own administration since its alleged failures were the main basis of attack. The

341

obstacles and attainments were summed up forcefully in the following terse statements:

The passionate condemnation that the critics make of the work of our revolutionary government evidences very superficial thinking. When they insist upon immediate success they maliciously forget the powerful resistance that we have encountered. Selfish interests at home that have been entrenched for centuries in a regime that has consistently opposed the aspirations of the people for social justice have allied themselves with foreign interests that only seek the control of our natural resources and the exploitation of our man power. This united opposition combined with the dead weight of ignorance, abject poverty, and insecurity of the laboring masses as well as their biological and moral debilitation has constituted a formidable barrier. As a result it has been difficult to consolidate our constructive efforts and make them effectual in satisfying the growing needs of our population . . .

It cannot be denied, however, that my administration has made definite gains in the fight for the welfare of the rural districts. Land has been distributed, farm credit provided, irrigation projects developed, and sanitation undertaken. Electrification and reforestation have been pushed forward, cattle-raising promoted, hospitals, asylums, water works, rural schools, technical institutes, and cooperative sugar mills have been built, and associations of producers have been formed to steer our economy.

Monopolies, unemployment, and the high cost of living have been combated by encouraging cooperatives and establishing commissions to regulate the sale of commodities. For the Army we have provided new equipment and modern barracks, as well as special schools and boarding schools for the soldiers' children. Ships have been acquired for our merchant marine. New railroads and highways have been built. Cultural and commercial interchange has been encouraged among our inhabitants and also tourist travel. The economy of the nation has been maintained in the midst of world crisis and our monetary exchange protected. Our national income has increased and far sighted financial policies have been established on a sound basis.

The trip to Chiapas did not have even an indirect connection with the campaign. It was the one state of the nation that he had not visited during his first five years in office, and he had long desired to attend in person to the needs of the "Chamulas" and other Indian tribes that had profited little from the Revolution. He visited the big coffee plantations, impressive feudal institutions that were the pride of Chiapas. They belonged mostly to industrious Germans who worked themselves and their Indian help like slaves. There is something grand about a big manor house surrounded at a short distance by huts of thatch and flanked by drying yards where the coffee berries are dumped after going through the pulping machine moved by cool, clear streams of water that have tumbled down from the mountains through big pipes or picturesque aqueducts. The extensive sloping hills, covered with huge shade trees spaced so as to function as umbrellas for the coffee shrubs underneath, are beautiful. When the shrubs are covered with their red cranberry-like fruit and the chattering Indian pickers—men, women, and children—go from bush to bush bending down the branches and pulling off the berries into their baskets, it is a sight that cheers. That is, it would cheer if the Indians were not dressed in tatters and if their looks did not betray the ravages of malaria, drunkenness, and under-nourishment.

The latter is what Cárdenas saw, and he sometimes went to extremes to help. He not only broke up large portions of the plantations and provided credit for the new peasant owners, but once he had all the politicians and officials who had accompanied him take off their wrist watches and fountain pens and place them in a heap. Then he called the tattered Indians to come and help themselves. It was an unfair, arbitrary thing to do, but those politicians had spent days with him eating food the Indians had prepared and observing their poverty without doing a thing to help them. After all, the despoiled ones could hunt up the Indian who had his watch or pen and buy it back.

If a friend of means is with Cárdenas when a worthy case of charity appears, Cárdenas will all but put his hand in the friend's pocket to get him to loosen up after he himself has contributed liberally. Those who often travel with him have learned not to carry much cash or else to hide it, for after Cárdenas has given away all that he has he despoils his friends on behalf of the needy.

The trip to Chiapas took the president right to the border of Guatemala where Mexico had built a bridge over the Suchiate River to make automobile travel possible between Mexico and her interesting neighbor to the south. It was an important link in the Pan-American highway, and was so significant to the sister republic that its president should have been there to meet the man who had ordered it constructed.

President Ubico of Guatemala, however, had never felt sympathetic toward the Mexican Revolution and he merely sent an army officer of low rank to be at the bridge when President Cárdenas arrived. Unperturbed by this slight, and perhaps relieved inasmuch as Ubico was a dictator, Cárdenas proceeded to assure Guatemala that Mexico sympathized with her in her demand that England restore British Honduras to her dominion. This claim was pressed even more insistently by Ubico's successor, Professor Arévalo.

The president that Cárdenas would have enjoyed meeting very much was our own Franklin D. Roosevelt. But though invited by the latter to meet him at sea on one of his fishing trips on the Gulf of Mexico, Cárdenas declined because, as he explained to me several years later, he could not understand English. He did not want to depend on an interpreter to convey his views. This is probably one big reason why he has not visited the United States since leaving office.

Two weeks prior to the election President Cárdenas travelled through the states where there was most talk of disorder. As president, it was his responsibility to keep order, and one of the best ways of doing it, he felt, was to go in person—and unprotected—right to the focus of the trouble. When nothing happened people would say, "There must be nothing to it. The president was there himself and they did not touch him." He continued these tactics after the election. There were no arrests. The jails held no political prisoners.

For the traditional celebration of Mexico's Independence Day on the sixteenth of September, instead of remaining in the capital to ring the independence bell at midnight as usual, he went right to the town of Dolores Hidalgo in Guanajuato where Hidalgo the priest had rallied the peasants and a few well-to-do patriots around him, and had rung the bell that now hangs in a niche above the president's balcony overlooking the central square in Mexico City. It was a fitting pilgrimage to the shrine of independence.

Back in the capital by the eleventh of October, and with only a month and a half left to complete his term, the president dedicated all his abundant energy to clearing off his desk. The oil question had not been settled and there was little prospect of an agreement being reached under his leadership. The labor management of the railroads had functioned so poorly that he had been obliged to have the government intervene through a special representative.

Some of the projects had not been terminated for lack of money, though even so Cárdenas was being called upon incessantly to attend inauguration programs for other completed works. The

Agrarian Department had bogged down under the tremendous load of distributing over forty million acres and he had to sign land grants to peasants almost up to the hour of leaving Los Pinos to go to turn over the red, white, and green ribbon and an in-completed task to General Avila Camacho.

During those days of high pressure I made a call at Los Pinos to say "good bye" to the president. Finding one of his confidential clerks—a trusted cousin—in tears, I asked what was wrong. He replied that he had just performed the hardest task of his lifetime. He had been obliged to destroy the files that he had been working on for years.

It had been his task to keep a record of the people who had received some personal assistance from General Cárdenas. He had put love and admiration into the toil of each day as he wrote down the name of the orphan who had been placed in school, the inventor who had been given money to make his model, the old soldier who had been set up with a small shop, the widow who had received a sewing machine on which to make a living as Felícitas de Cárdenas had done in Jiquilpan, the cripple who had been given crutches, the wayward lad who had received a ticket to return home, the sick man just out of the hospital for whom medicines and clothing had been purchased—22,000 individual cases of aid that Cárdenas first as governor and then as president had extended to the needy and had been recorded, not to mention the innumerable instances in which people had been helped di-rectly from his pocket when not even his aides knew about it.

The cousin was proud of the file and longed for the day when it would be made public. Never before had such a record been amassed by one man, he was sure. It would win for his distin-guished relative a permanent place in the world's hall of fame. What then was his amazement and grief when the president had come into his office and spoken to this effect: "Miguel, your task is complete. You have done a good job. There is no more need of your files, for all the obligations have been met to date, and now that my salary stops I shall not be able to do much more charity. I do not want history to judge me for personal deeds of mercy that I have done, but rather for my acts of state. These other matters were things that needed to be done and I was able to do them. It was my duty to help and I received a great deal of pleasure from it. It is my personal affair, however, and so I request you to burn those files. Everything else, of course, must be packed and preserved."

The general's real farewell message was given on the twenty-fifth of November when he spoke to the movement that in many ways had been his sweetheart—organized labor. He reminded them that friendship gives the right to exhort:

Now that my term of office is drawing to a close, and with the authority derived from my being a friend of you laborers, I wish to beg you to spare no effort toward the elimination of personal animosities. Terminate your quarrels no matter how deep-seated they may be. Do not let your efforts cease until you have attained the complete unification of the proletariat of Mexico. Until this unification is attained, the cause of nationalism cannot advance; our revolutionary institutions, as well as the public peace, will not be stable; nor will our complete cultural and political autonomy be secured. As the Revolution desires the maximum of happiness for all Mexicans, it is logical and just that as fast as laborers attain for themselves greater economic, cultural, and political power, their responsibility to themselves and to the nation is likewise increased. The turning over to them of sources and means of production should carry with it in like degree the obligation to do their part to increase production so that all the inhabitants of Mexico may live better and do away with the wretched conditions that as a mill stone have hindered the forward surge of our land. Every laborer with an opportunity to produce who does not throw all his effort and capacity into his work or who gives himself over to vice or parasitic practices, is evading his responsibility. He is a traitor to his class and an enemy of Mexico's re-vindicating movement.

The president then referred to Mexico's great need of pressing the battle for progress. He reminded the men whom he had befriended so diligently that Mexico was still backward in its industry and that where there had been advances, they were in the hands of foreigners.

All that is Mexican about the big industry that is developing in our land is the fact that our resources and man power are utilized, and that a revolution-ary government watches over it, seeking to eliminate unfair practices.

He recognized that reaction had revived, but he used this fact to stimulate the laborers into uniting their ranks and disciplining themselves:

Confronted by restored conservative ranks, it is urgent not to abandon the field of battle, but to correct with rigor the deficiencies and errors that serve as a pretext for retarding groups. These groups, whether they bear the name of National Action, Sinarquism, or so-called anti-communism, use for their arguments any lack of concord among peasants, laborers, women, and students to make these the unconscious victims of a work that tends to weaken the revolutionary ranks. This work, they should realize, would mean the sacrificing of new generations in lamentable fratricidal strife.

His great concern was that the struggle of thirty years that had cost so many lives and so much effort might have been in vain and that the price so dearly paid might have to be paid again. Unless the laborers responded to the call of duty their enemies would win. But why be concerned? They would respond. His faith in the masses did not waver.

Cárdenas had announced on his visit to far-off Quintana Roo late in 1939 that he would take up farming upon leaving the presidency. Early in 1940 while on his visit to Chiapas he told friends that he would make the provincial town of Las Casas in that state his home. It was picturesque, his beloved Indians were more primitive and more numerous there than almost anywhere else, and best of all he would be far from politics.

Mrs. Cárdenas, however, had something to say about Chiapas when her husband returned from the trip. It would be too much like being buried to go to Las Casas. She loved Mexico City and wanted their son Cuauhtèmoc to have the advantages of the good schools there. But she would be willing to be a farmerette at least part of the time in her own home state of Michoacán. That was that. And so Michoacán was chosen for the experimental farming enterprise.

Lázaro Cárdenas fulfilled his term. Loved more ardently and denounced more bitterly than any president since Juárez, he had done his best as he understood it. As he left office the rich heaved a sigh of relief, but the peasants moaned. One told me, "If he positively will not consent to serve another term we ought to insist at least that he become Minister of Education. He would accomplish much good for us at that post." Another peasant said to me, "We'll never have another president like him, one that will do so much to help us."

Such pessimism bothers Lázaro Cárdenas. He looks for constant improvement. And as he told a group of students just three months after he took office:

We welcome the assuming by youth of its responsibility before history. May it rectify the lines and processes of our administration. May that rectification, however, always be a movement of renovation, of purifying transformation, that will keep as its lodestar the strengthening of our concept of social justice ever improving in purity and virtue.

This from the man who placed a ban on gambling, prohibited the manufacture and sale of dice and gambling cards, closed the infamous red light districts of Mexico City, fought graft, combated drunkenness, outlawed obscene literature, and permitted the American Bible Society to distribute portions of the Bible among his troops.

The mission of this congress of distinguished scientists will not be complete nor its findings important unless it directs its principal activities toward orienting the peoples of this hemisphere in the path of peace and genuine understanding. Appeals to force, far from being a legitimate means to settle differences between nations, should be looked upon as a shameful reminder of a primitive social state and as a means unworthy of cultured peoples.

— Lázaro Cárdenas —
To the Seventh American Scientific Congress, September, 1935

We believe that all tendency toward conquest contributes greatly toward the corruption and spiritual slavery of the conquerors themselves. May strong nations follow a more humane path and may they seek their future satisfaction through showing respect and doing good to young nations instead of destroying their personality.

— Lázaro Cárdenas —
to President Quezón of the Philippine Islands,
April 12, 1937

XXXV

FARMING INTERRUPTED BY WORLD WAR II

ON THE FIRST DAY of December, 1940, Lázaro Cárdenas began the hardest task of his career. He had always carried responsibility from the time of his father's death when he had taken the burden of the home upon his shoulders, although not yet in his teens. Since 1913 he had always been in command. Now at the age of forty-five and full of vigor and vision, he was out. His only public responsibilitly was to keep out of the way of his successor. No strong ruler in Mexico had ever done this before without going abroad, and Cárdenas did not plan to travel. He was going to remain in Mexico and serve without dictating.

People of course would not believe it. Both critics and friends said it didn't make sense. His critics argued that his personality was so strong, he would impose his opinions upon his successor who would not dare go against him. His friends reasoned that naturally he wanted to have his policies carried out, therefore he would guide them and keep them united in an effort to steer things properly.

Both critics and friends were surprised at developments. Almost immediately after assuming the presidency, Avila Camacho took the railroads out from under the management of the laborers. Radical elements in the Ministry of Education and elsewhere had their wings clipped. Peasants began to receive certificates of title for the village lands that formerly had been controlled by the community and given to individuals only for as long as they used them. Some of the development projects were dropped. Textbooks that were considered to be somewhat communistic were discarded.

Some army officers began to attend Mass as the new president had done. At the shrine of Guadalupe on the twelfth of October —when Bishop Cantwell came down with letters of introduction

351

from President Roosevelt—army officers dared to appear wearing their uniforms, a thing that had not been done since the inception of the struggle between the Church and the revolutionary forces.

There was talk, too, of making the Virgin of Guadalupe the patron Saint of the Western Hemisphere newly united through the Good Neighbor Policy. In fact, adoration of the Virgin of Guadalupe was boldly proclaimed to be the test of patriotism of a Mexican. Some even suggested that all non-worshippers of Guadalupe should be persecuted. Here and there Protestants were driven from their homes or their homes burned. The newspapers that belonged to organized labor and to the Revolutionary Party published accounts of some of the persecutions, but the other dailies ignored them. Before many months the radical Minister of Education was replaced by a man who immediately pacified the Church on the issue of socialistic education, and permitted it to reopen its day schools.

Where was Cárdenas? Where were his followers? The latter were, in large numbers, out in the cold. A few key men had been carried over by the new administration—Suárez, Beteta, Foglio, Buenrostro, García Téllez, Castillo Nájera, and others—but the majority had disappeared from prominence. Cárdenas was down in the lowlands acquiring a bad case of malaria, but saying nothing.

Then people began to talk about an estrangement between Avila Camacho and his predecessor, for they knew that the changes being made would necessarily hurt Cárdenas, especially the virtual surrender of socialistic education to the Church. While it was true that he himself had restored to the Church all the privileges that the Constitution granted her, yet he had stood like a stone wall against what he considered to be ecclesiastical encroachments upon the prerogatives of the State. In 1936 Cárdenas had told Ambassador Daniels:

We are neither pro nor anti-clergy. While realizing fully the necessity for religion, and believing that morality and education are necessary corrolaries thereto, we have always insisted that the clergy must confine its activities to its religious sphere and not attempt to use influence in the domain of politics or government. You should realize that there is a difference between the clergy and its actions in the United States and in Mexico. The Church here has often been politically-minded, and when it directed education, comparatively few of the people were educated.

Years later, in referring to the Church's new influence, he said to me, "It would not be so bad if the Church had learned its lesson and was returning to influence without such things as the same old unsanitary practice of letting thousands of people kiss the image on the same spot, and crawl for blocks on their hands and knees, etc." He had not a word to say about the political implications.

The talk of estrangement would probably have gone on but for the fact that Cárdenas was taken seriously ill at his ranch in the lowlands where he had been living with the peasants without either comforts or proper protection from insects. He had thought that his rugged constitution would stand anything, but that year Apatzingán was unusually bad for malaria, and in October Cárdenas became so desperately ill that he made a dash for Jiquilpan and the home of his birth. A note came out in the newspapers about his illness, but no one realized how serious it was until President Avila Camacho left the capital suddenly and went to the bedside of his old friend. That visit to Jiquilpan did much to squelch the rumors of estrangement, especially when Cárdenas repaid it in the capital as soon as he was able to travel.

That practice of returning the sick-calls of friends with social visits was faithfully followed even by the ex-president. I happened to be in Jiquilpan when General Cárdenas was just beginning to get around once more, and was impressed to see how he took his wife with him walking from house to house throughout the town calling on all the neighbors who had come to inquire about his health during his illness.

He was the first president of Mexico, I have been told, who returned to his home town after his term in office. The home in Jiquilpan is built on the old colonial style with pretty patios. There is a restfulness as well as a simple stateliness that both doña Amalia and the general enjoy. The furniture, plants, and general arrangement are all in good taste, and one is not surprised that its owners come to spend a while in it as frequently as possible.

If reactionary forces thought that President Avila Camacho was going to make many more concessions to them, they were mistaken. Organized labor called a number of strikes, and while business men thought that the new president would take their side, they found him just as careful as Cárdenas had been to defend the striking privilege. Spanish Republicans also found Avila Camacho to be a staunch friend. The oil companies likewise saw that he was determined to continue the policies of his predecessor regarding them.

The oil impasse continued, in fact, until Ambassador Daniels went to President Roosevelt personally and explained that it was useless to wait longer for the companies to participate in valuating the properties and that, with war clouds growing more threatening every day, it was essential to reach an agreement with Mexico before the trouble had affected Inter-American unity. Roosevelt saw the point and gave both Daniels and Hull the go signal. Hull may have needed a little more persuading, but if so this was facilitated by the perfect cooperation that Avila Camacho and his Minister of Foreign Affairs Padilla had been giving the United States in its foreign policies.

On the nineteenth of November, 1941, just a few days before Pearl Harbor, the agreement was reached for which Daniels had labored so long and tactfully. It included not only the oil problem but most of the problems that had been causing trouble. There was great rejoicing in Mexico, and all of Latin America was convinced that we meant business when we said that we wanted to be a good neighbor. It prepared the way for the remarkable harmony with which our southern sisters rallied to our support when they saw us attacked by the Japanese.

Under the terms of the agreement of November 19, 1941, American and Mexican experts were appointed to "determine the just compensation to be paid to the nationals of the United States of America whose property rights, or interests, in the petroleum industry were affected to their detriment by acts of the Government of Mexico subsequent to March 17, 1938". The mixed commission made a careful valuation, and reported within five months that the American companies should be paid nearly thirty-two million dollars. This amount added to the eight million paid the Sinclair interests made a total sum of forty million dollars. That was the comparative pittance for which intrenched interests wanted us to forfeit our right to a peaceful and united neighborhood of nations in the Western Hemisphere. Cárdenas and Avila Camacho had triumphed; Roosevelt and Daniels had triumphed; best of all, our ideal of One America had triumphed.

Upon his retirement to Jiquilpan in December, 1940, Cárdenas had stationery printed that bore his name without a title. "In reality," he explained to me, "I am not a professional soldier. I never studied in a military school. My title of general is an accident of the Revolution." When he was not in active service he refused to accept the salary to which he had a right as the highest ranking general in the Mexican Army. With very few savings and constant expenditures to develop his farm, he had to sell a house in Uruapan and some cattle to keep solvent. He could have sold his summer home at Palmira to advantage, but instead he chose to give it to the government for a school.

He had recovered fully and was farming once more when the news of Pearl Harbor reached him. Stirred with indignation against Japan, he was at the point of offering his serivces as a soldier to President Roosevelt, when the old language difficulty checked him and directed his defense of democracy along other lines. He sat down and wrote the following telegram to President Avila Camacho: "As a result of the painful event of the declaration of war between the United States and Japan, I am honored to place myself immediately at the disposition of your government."

General Rodríguez and civilian ex-president Ortiz Rubio wired Avila Camacho in the same tenor. After conferring together with the president, it was arrounced that two special defense zones would be set up, one on the Pacific coast with Cárdenas in command, and the other on the Gulf of Mexico under General Rodríguez. The spirit of harmony among all the ex-presidents was fine to see.

At a later date, all of them, even including old and ailing General Calles who had returned to Mexico for his last days, stood with the president in the balcony of the presidential palace under the liberty bell as Mexico's declaration of war on the Axis powers was made known to the world.

Cárdenas' attitude toward war had been expressed in his message of April 12, 1937, to President Quezón of the Philippine Islands:

Mexico does not aspire to be a military nation and much less to conquer more territory. We realize that triumphs over weaker nations, regardless of the motive for attacking them, prove to be blots that time cannot erase.

Furthermore, we believe that all tendency toward conquest contributes greatly toward the corruption and spiritual slavery of the conquerors themselves. May strong nations follow a more humane path and may they seek their future satisfaction through showing respect and doing good to young nations instead of destroying their personality.

In an effort to establish the nation's preparedness upon a safer psychological basis he had changed the name of the Ministry of War and Marine Affairs to that of Ministry of National Defense.

Back in February of 1938 when war clouds had already been gathering in Europe, President Cárdenas had gone before a convention of laborers in Mexico City and asked them to call an assembly of labor representatives from all over the world to discuss ways and means of preventing war:

We should go directly to the conscience of the masses, inasmuch as it has been impossible for an international tribunal to prevent the savagery that is being perpetrated and the aggressions that have been consummated in quest of territory, markets, and zones of influence wherein to exploit raw materials and cheap labor. The masses are capable of understanding and fixing responsibilities. . . .

Above all, let us appeal to the conscience of the proletariat of the world, for the elimination of imperialistic wars depends upon the solidarity of the laborers of the world for pacificism. . . . .

It falls to the lot of organized labor, then, to make it evident that their social struggle is governed by higher ethics, calling for respect toward human life, and that science and skill should be dedicated to purposes of common welfare and be applied to the task of transforming regimes of violence and hate into systems where social brotherhood and the dignity of work shall be the accurate index of the culture of a people.

The Peace Congress of World Laborers was held and gave Mexico's brainy labor leader, Vicente Lombardo Toledano, a golden opportunity which he did not muff to broaden his contacts; but the results for the cause of peace were about what could be expected from such a visionary program projected into the world of Hitler, Mussolini, and Stalin.

Although the call of Cárdenas for world peace seemed like nothing more than the voice of one crying in the wilderness, he was able to crown his efforts at home with a novel blending of the sentimental and the practical. It was almost a literal turning of swords into plow shares and spears into pruning hooks when an old munitions factory was turned over to its workers organized on the cooperative basis, and plows were manufactured from old, junked war materials. The laborers made money and the peasants got implements at lower prices. Everyone was happy—especially General Cárdenas.

Cárdenas took his new post in dead earnest. He traveled the full length of the peninsula of Lower California by airplane, jeep, and on foot, getting every possible point of invasion studied for defense. After weeks in the bush he would come back to his headquarters at Ensenada with dusty and torn uniforms.

As president he had taken an excursion by ship from Ensenada to Mazatlán, Sinaloa, where there had been opportunity to take note of the great potential source of wealth the Pacific Ocean presented, as well as of Mexico's vulnerability to invasion. Now, as commander of defenses in this area, Cárdenas was gratified to find that several fish canneries had been established, but again it was impressed upon him how much Mexico needed a navy and a merchant marine.

Indeed, there was little of anything to work with and appeals to Mexico City brought but poor response. He decided to go personally to try to speed things up. The Japanese were advancing steadily in the Orient, and there seemed to be no time to lose in getting defenses ready in America. Lower California with its Magdalena Bay and other favorable points for landing might be the point of invasion. He went to Mexicali and boarded a Pan-American Airways plane for Mexico City.

As usual, Cárdenas refused to overlook the customary rules and regulations in forwarding his petitions for munitions, authorizations, etc. before the Ministry of War. One must realize that to follow regular procedures in one of the Ministries of Mexico requires lots of time. I have never hesitated, if a matter is urgent, to ask for special treatment, but General Cárdenas detests such practices.

He got more delay than he had bargained for, however, and it took days of waiting in one office after another. Again his worship of democratic principles sacrificed his efficiency. Democracy is his worst weakness and his greatest strength. He feels that the law is law and that he should be the first to observe it—even red tape.

Mexico entered the war when two ships of her small merchant marine were sunk near her shores by German submarines. She was immediately united by war, and politics took a back seat. This fact enabled President Avila Camacho to convince General

Cárdenas that he should take over the post of Minister of Defense. This was in September of 1942. With regrets the General and Amalia gave up their little rented home in Ensenada, for they had enjoyed the isolation.

When they returned to Mexico City, however, they took with them a lad named Alejandro Federenko. His parents were Russian Baptists who had come to Mexico from Russia in 1927 to escape religious persecution. Alejandro, though two or three years older than Cuauhtèmoc, had been a frequent guest and companion at the Cárdenas home in Ensenada. One day Mrs. Cárdenas overheard the boys talking with others at play. Someone asked Alejandro if he was for Stalin, for Churchill, or for Roosevelt. Immediately the Russian boy replied: "I am for Cárdenas. None of those other guys ever did anything for me." He lived with Cuauhtémoc until enlisting as a cadet in the Mexican Air Force.

As Minister of Defense Cárdenas was just as silent as ever on politics and affairs of State, but his being near the center of things revived the talk about his being the power behind the throne. Everything radical about the government was somehow traced to Cárdenas. Still he had nothing to say.

Political enemies said that he ran the president; his old followers complained that he would not steer at all, even to rally them to a strong defense of the revolutionary tenets they thought were in jeopardy. They were particularly discomfited over his failure to understand that he needed to have close friends in many positions of importance throughout the country. He would not support them even when they ran for elective offices. Even in the army Cárdenas reorganized things so that promotions and everything that was tied in with politics came under the jurisdiction of the under-secretary who received instructions directly from the president. He worked hard, but said nothing.

Mr. H. T. Marroquín of the American Bible Society, asked his permission to present pocket New Testaments to the soldiers as the Society was doing for the soldiers of the United States Army. "Why, certainly," replied the general; but someone objected to the president after Mr. Marroquín had had a special military edition prepared and the distribution was well under way. The president had only to speak a word to his obedient minister of defense, and a polite captain was sent to the Bible Society's office requesting that the distribution be halted.

General Marshall and other high officers of the United States Army visited Mexico to explain the cooperation that they wanted from the high command there. Some of the requests made did not appeal particularly to General Cárdenas, but no one ever knew it. He simply referred such details to President Camacho and if the president agreed, Cárdenas carried out his wishes.

Mexico cooperated in the war effort fully, though no contingent was sent overseas to fight until Aviation Squadron No. 201 had been carefully trained and fully equipped. Then it was sent to the Pacific and saw action under General MacArthur. The Mexican aviators were good fliers and good fighters. A captain of the Canadian forces who has intimate contact with Mexican soldiers told me that he holds them in great respect. They are well disciplined, courteous, uncomplaining, and of great endurance.

The Mexican Army under Cárdenas was completely reorganized. Obligatory military service was instituted for eighteen year olds chosen by lot though not without considerable opposition in rural areas. In our state of Morelos some of the opponents took to the hills with guns as they had done in the days when Zapata was their leader. They swooped down on the highway one day, held up some cars, and caused some damage.

No one was exempted. The rich man's son had to serve side by side with the son of the uncouth Indian. Modern barracks were constructed as a part of the reorganization program. Mess halls were substituted for the old private lunch counters run by the soldiers' wives. Modern equipment was brought from the United States, and work was begun on a large plant where Mexico was to manufacture munitions for the allies. It was part of an extensive plan that was dropped by our government as soon as the war was over.

General Cárdenas expressed his disappointment over the change in the following terms, as best I can recall:

Much was said by United States officials about a military bloc composed of the United States, Canada, and Mexico. Part of the plan was for Mexico to erect a large munitions plant with United States help. Mexico was willing to set it up as a contribution to continental defense in accordance with the military bloc idea. Construction was begun near Amecameca, but later was discontinued and the project abandoned because the United States changed its mind when the pressure of war was removed.

Now that the skies are over-cast once more with war clouds, we again seek the cooperation of Latin America. The resolutions to bolster Western Hemispheric defenses adopted by the Council of American Republics' Foreign Ministers in April, 1951, at Washington, D. C. are encouraging, but General Cárdenas must wonder if we will again change our minds when the immediate emergency passes.

Long before the war was over Cárdenas told me he was going to resign from the cabinet the day peace was declared. Too many misinterpretations were being placed upon his presence there. As the time drew near for another presidential election, many people said that he was secretly backing the candidacy of his close friend, General Enríquez Guzmán. The opposition press took it as a foregone conclusion that he would try to pick a successor to Avila Camacho. As long as he was in the president's cabinet there was much more danger of people giving credence to these suppositions, though Avila Camacho had undone to a large extent Cárdenas' painstaking reorganization of the Revolutionary Party by first eliminating the military sector and later instituting a new organization altogether. The public should have recalled that Cárdenas had endeavored to limit the power of the generals in politics.

In April of 1946 Cárdenas told me frankly the attitude he had maintained toward President Avila Camacho in the following terms:

Influence lasts as long as it is talked about but not used. Excessive use wears it out. One man in recent history ran Mexico for a good many years. Three or four presidents were under his influence to such an extent that the authority of the presidential office was undermined. I warned him several times, but to no avail, and finally I had to act.

The president is president! An ex-president should not ask too many favors of him or he will wear out his welcome. Nevertheless, I have accomplished more for the building of schools, dams, hospitals, and similar projects by quietly speaking with President Avila Camacho concerning them than though I had tried to exercise a leadership by speaking to multitudes over loud speakers in the capital.

Even though the president makes blunders, it is better for me to help and not criticize. I know what a president has to handle. The one who knows the weight of a load, as the saying goes, is the one who carries it. I have always been willing to serve President Avila Camacho, but not to criticize. Since people say that he became president because of my friendship, I

have to be very careful, but when his successor goes into office I shall feel
more free to speak my mind.
I cannot ask favors of the cabinet officers, for that would be an usurpation
of presidential prerogatives. Most of the people who want me to come out of
retirement and participate in politics have a personal axe to grind. People
come to me for financial help, jobs, projects, etc. I am not an employment
agency. I have neither authority nor money to help them. It makes it
necessary either for me to hide myself or to explain to those that come that
I am not in a position to do what they want.

As far as party candidates were concerned, Cárdenas had stated
earlier in his political life:
It should be taken into account that in Mexico it will be impossible for any
party to win much of a following if it does not include in its platform
measures for bringing the laboring classes out of the poverty and backwardness in which the privileged class held them for centuries.

That was and is the earnest conviction of Lázaro Cárdenas.
Hence, if he had had to choose for president between a general
and a judge who was outstanding in his defense of the rights of
labor, it is my opinion that he would have chosen the judge. As
a matter of fact, it was the judge, Miguel Alemán, who won the
nomination and election, but Cárdenas apparently had nothing
to do with it. As soon as Japan had surrendered he had presented
his resignation as Minister of Defense and had hurried back to
the tranquillity of farming.

It was not a lack of interest in national or even international
affairs. On the contrary, he continues to be interested in all that
goes on, reading the newspapers and receiving frequent reports
on world affairs from friends in the diplomatic service abroad.
His mind is too active and his concern too great for him not to
be interested, but he believes that he can accomplish the most good
for the cause of democracy in Mexico by non-participation in the
debates of the day.

A writer in the big newspaper, *El Universal* in February of 1945
called him a sphinx, criticizing him severely:
Cárdenas is the political enigma of the century, the impenetrable sphinx
of the Social Revolution of Mexico, the most impassive and hermetical
individual we have contemplated in recent years . . . .
It cannot be denied that the political sphinx to whom I refer has a tremendous power of messianic attraction. Doubtless, anyone who failed to
take this sphinx into consideration would make a serious mistake. Nevertheless, an outburst of the restlessness of our times is only being delayed.
The sphinx makes us to be silent also, and in the silence we seem to like
it, though it may work like a time bomb.

One day in 1947 the people of Mexico City were startled by

an extraordinary announcement that was placarded on the walls and billboards. It was the magazine, *Mañana,* calling the attention of the surprised citizens to a twelve-page article entitled "Cárdenas Speaks". The issue was sold out quickly and people looked with avidity to see what the sphinx had been willing to say after a silence of over six years. They found interesting reading and pictures showing the same energetic manners and friendly face, but those thick lips had said nothing of moment.

Cárdenas may yet speak his mind some day. He has said he would feel free to do so. But the question remains, will he?

My father was a very warm-hearted man who always maintained close contact with us in the home and was intensely interested in all we did or failed to do. Even though he was gone a good deal of the time, and we would have preferred to have had him spend more time at home, we realized that that was his life. In spite of it, he never seemed removed from the little concerns and affections of our home.

At home he was very calm and easy going. He always had time to listen to us and to think things over. He did not act in haste. If there was a problem, he took the time necessary to work it out. He will always be present in everything I do.

—Cuauhtémoc Cárdenas—

XXXVI

PRACTICAL ENGINEER, AND OH, WHAT A FRIEND

When I first went to Mexico in 1933 I was disturbed over the extreme anti-clericalism on the part of revolutionary leaders and wondered what effect this would have on inter-American harmony. Upon investigation, however, I found that leaders such as Cárdenas were not opposed to the faith of religion, but to its frills; not to its mysticism, but to its fanaticism; not to its desire to serve, but to its propensity to command; not to its close adherence to the precepts of the revolutionary Carpenter of Nazareth, but to its all too frequent alliances with the moneyed exploiters of humanity; not, in short, to its spiritual devotion, but rather to its temporal ambition.

Even when Mexico's anti-clericalism was extreme, however, it did not seem to affect her diplomatic relations with her Latin American neighbors. Even when some of the extremists were sent as diplomats to countries where Roman Catholicism is the official religion it did not injure Mexico's prestige in the least. Latin America, I found, considered itself to be mature enough to get along with people of other religious beliefs.

Lázaro Cárdenas was not always sympathetic with the clergy, it is true. But when, during his presidency, I told him of a priest who was directing the construction of a community road in the state of Oaxaca and needed help, he sent him two hundred and fifty each of picks, shovels and wheelbarrows. He likewise extended to Protestant missionaries an invitation to cooperate with his government in various projects among the peasants. Catholics or Protestants, Cárdenas welcomed the cooperation of all if they came to serve. He taught a basic lesson for all of us to learn, viz., that we can be good neighbors in spite of religious differences. In his memoirs he declared himself to be neither a Roman Catholic nor an atheist. As a Freemason he had declared his belief in the Supreme Being and in later years I am convinced that he went farther than that in his personal faith.

The One-America that needs to be forged in this hemisphere must be free from prejudice, whether racial, religious, or social. This means a New America, *Amerinova,* if you please. Privilege, prejudice, exploitation, imperialism — all must go. It must be democratic. How can this be brought about? Does it mean, for example, that we must attempt to eliminate dictators?

Here again we have much to learn from Lázaro Cárdenas. He believed so firmly in the principle of non-intervention that he would not meddle in another country's internal affairs even to overthrow a dictatorship which was oppressing the people. His sympathy was always on the side of the latter, but he had found that the best way to overthrow a dictatorship was to let the people do it. Sooner or later they would. And in the meantime, the more democratic governments should be patient so long as a local dictator cooperated in general in the program of *Amerinova.* Perhaps he too (the dictator) will learn from the example of the Mexican statesman who accepted one term in office and one term only, endeavoring all the time to bring the people to a place where they could work out their own well-being. The dictator may come to reflect on how Cárdenas then retired to his farm, wielding there in silence a powerful influence for democracy. Self-buried politically, he had by his example buried his successors and others who might have sought to be reelected to some position and thus perpetuate themselves in power. They dared not go against the precedent he had established. Patriotic rulers in other countries whose friends would make them believe that they are indispensable can hardly fail to meditate on the man of Mexico who refused to listen to the chant of friends who feared for the revolution or wanted themselves to continue in office. He insisted that his country could produce many to supersede and excel him as well as them.

Lázaro Cárdenas saw that the best way for Mexico to attain the respect of other nations was for her to improve the condition of her people and to help other nations do likewise. Foreigners would not respect her, nor could she respect herself, so long as half her people lived in squalor and ignorance. No man ever tried harder to solve this problem than did Lázaro Cárdenas.

His measure of success may be subject to debate but the magnitude of his endeavors and the loftiness of his motives are not. Nor did he stop with herculean efforts to help his own people. To him, being a good neighbor meant more than just to refrain from interfering in the affairs of others. As president, he extended a helping hand to other nations. Bolivia, for example, appreciated the two Mexican missions he sent to her, one to help in her irrigation system, the other to assist in solving her educational problems. He sent athletic missions also to Cuba and Chile under the capable leadership of Ignacio Beteta.

In 1947 Cárdenas doffed his role of hometown farmer and accepted the responsibility of heading up the biggest engineering and community development project Mexico had ever undertaken. In fact, if all of its features and outreach are taken into consideration, it would outrank the Tennessee Valley Project and most other similar projects in this hemisphere. President Alemán named him Executive Director of the Tepalcatepec River Basin Commission. A large part of the state of Michoacan is drained by the Tepalcatepec River, and all of the areas that were underdeveloped were to benefit from the reclamation program. Dams were to be built to provide electric power. Irrigation systems were to be installed where needed to bring more land under cultivation. Roads were to be opened, hospitals and schools erected, forests planted, beaches developed and a seaport constructed. Cárdenas was delighted over the possibilities and hopeful that the government would find ways of adequately financing the big undertaking.

The limited funds initially assigned to the project however did not permit as large a team as was needed. Nevertheless canyons, hillsides, roadways and a route for train tracks to the Pacific Ocean were surveyed. Cárdenas told the engineers what he wanted, and as the plans took shape, he himself would go over them carefully. He had mastered the engineers' techniques and terminology so well that he was able to discuss every angle with them and often suggest improvements. American engineers at the Tennessee Valley Project became aware of this when Cárdenas visited the valley early in '59. In fact, they told him they would like to have him on their team.

The planning required many exploratory trips by jeep, horseback, on foot, in helicopter and by plane. It seemed that Cárdenas never tired. If he did, after 16 hours of activity, any new demand upon his time worked like an instantaneous battery charger; he would suddenly look refreshed and be ready for whatever the occasion demanded. I saw it happen time and again. He never took exercise for the sake of exercise. He would travel for hours at a time in a jeep or pickup without evidencing fatigue. He could walk for miles, seemingly without weariness, when some unusual occasion called for it.

Once I called on him when he was working out from Apatzingán, the center of one of the first major areas to benefit from the accomplishments of the Tepalcatepec Commission. Lemon orchards had been planted on the *ejidos* and a bottling works established to prepare the lemon juice for shipment. Cantelopes were being harvested by peasants who had never eaten one before and were being shipped to the cities for sale at prices never realized before by back country farmers. The Commission had provided the technical instruction and the financing to bring the juice and melon business into being while the peasants were reaping the profits. I observed that more land was being brought under cultivation through irrigation, many varieties of trees were being planted and cattle introduced.

Cárdenas had been away, so problems were awaiting him. Two other house guests and I were on time for breakfast but the general was out in the yard already, surrounded by commissions of peasants who had heard that he was back. He sent word for us to go ahead and eat, which we did, but he did not leave the peasants until he had listened to them all. By that time the schedule called for him to take us on an inspection tour and he had no time to eat.

His first concern it seemed to us was the village school. He talked informally with the teachers, children and any parents that came running when they saw who it was that had stopped by. The classrooms, the benches, the playground, the number of textbooks — everything interested him. In his diary he wrote: We must judge the greatest wealth of a nation to lie in the intellectual development of its people. The day that the Mexican public rises to its obligations and structures itself in such a way as to ensure that no child will lack schooling, that all of its young people will have the opportunity to develop their capabilities, that each citizen can enlighten his being and become a scientist, a craftsman or an up-to-date farmer, — in that day our invaluable natural resources will be truly mobilized and there will be no reason to fear that there can be anything but a glorious future for our fatherland.

To avoid all appearance of exerting influence on his successors, Cárdenas had made no visits to the presidential office either at the central government building on the main square of the city or at the residential office, *Los Pinos*. He deemed absence to be as important as silence in the central arena. He even tried to avoid the invasion of politics into his isolated reclamation area of the Tepalcatepec River basin. On the 14th of October, 1951, the PRI had chosen Adolfo Ruiz

Cortínes, Minister of Government under Alemán, to be its candidate to succeed Alemán, and it seemed only natural that he should seek an interview with Cárdenas. When the Executive Director of the Tepalcatepec project was in Mexico City for a few days in January 1952, the meeting between the past and the future took place. It was frank and open. The candidate of the PRI was aware of the fact that some of Cárdenas' close friends and relatives were backing Henríquez Guzmán, the competitor of Ruiz Cortínes, and that Cárdenas himself was a personal friend of his and of two other contenders. One of the latter was the leftist labor leader, Lombardo Toledano. They were not mentioned in the conversation but Ruiz Cortínes took pains to show proofs that the accusations made by Gen. Múgica to the effect that he had been of some service to the U.S. military forces which President Woodrow Wilson had sent to occupy Vera Cruz in 1914 were incorrect. He also declared his intention, if elected, to help the peasants solve their problems, especially the agrarian problem in Yucatán where Cárdenas and both his successors had wrestled with baffling situations. He also mentioned the need to improve morals in all sectors of society; to this Cárdenas naturally expressed his most hearty accord.

Early in their conversation, Ruiz Cortínes asked Cárdenas what his impressions were concerning the status of things in general. By way of reply, he stated that people were chafing to be guaranteed the full exercise of their rights as citizens. The candidate grasped what was implied and stated that he too was concerned over certain things which had happened contrary to that principle. He felt that political bosses and authorities were to be blamed. Cárdenas also brought up the problems faced by the farm laborers, so many of whom were going annually to the United States as *braceros* to get away from their difficult local situations and earn ready cash. He felt that this loss of manpower was harmful to Mexico. Both men spoke of the need to protect the forested lands from improper exploitation and the erosion that would ensue. The one point on which they disagreed was how to deal with the Indian problem. Ruiz Cortínes felt that having a special branch of government dedicated specifically to the interests of the three million aboriginal Mexicans, such as a Department of Indian Affairs, gave the Indians a feeling of inferiority or second-class citizenship. Cárdenas, to the contrary, felt that three million speakers of other tongues such as *Nahuatl* (Aztec) would feel encouraged by the existence of a government office to give specialized attention to their very evident special needs.

Less than two months after the interview, Ruiz Cortínes was in the state of Michoacán campaigning. Cárdenas carefully avoided encounters with him as he had done with the other candidates. On the 5th of March the candidate was in Jiquilpan but the most outstanding native of that lovely little city was away in Galeana. When Ruiz Cortínes was in Morelia, the capital of the state, Cárdenas was in Uruapan. Another day the candidate was in Apatzingan where the main office for the Tepalcatepec Commission was located but Cárdenas was in El Mirador and other towns. Finally Ruiz Cortínes flew along the valley from Apatzingan to the Pacific Ocean observing from the air the many projects, including a new port which was being developed by the Commission and was of very special importance to Cárdenas. Ruiz Cortínes even landed in Piedras Blancas to inspect dams and other work the Commission was carrying out along the Tepalcatepec River itself, but Cárdenas by then had gone to Mexico City.

This seeming lack of attention and courtesy was not that at all. He was simply avoiding all appearance of either taking sides in the campaign or of trying to influence a man likely to become president. Possibly he also had in mind helping the assistant director of the big reclamation project, Eduardo Chávez. It would give Chávez a better chance to explain his ideas and to get better acquainted with the important visitor if Cárdenas were not on hand to do the explaining. As a matter of fact, Chávez did such a good job of it he was appointed Minister of Public Works when Ruiz Cortínes became president.

Cárdenas continued as head of the big reclamation-development project. This kept him busy year after year coming and going from town to town and from dam sites to irrigation projects with visits to many other projects sandwiched in. At Playa Azul he attended the inauguration of a new school and then went to the home of one of the peasants for lunch. He might direct personally the building of the first dock for a riverside village or look over a surveyor's plans for a new park, a new town, a road or a railway. He would always take time to inspect a nursery, especially if it were growing a new variety of fruit or perhaps olive trees imported from Portugal. He would certainly take time to look at a herd of cattle if the variety was something new from Holland or a new breed developed by crossing some local variety with Brahman. Hospitals being built at strategic points along the Tepalcatepec and recreation areas being located here and there along the river were not neglected. Nothing was.

One day Cárdenas went from Uruapan to the village of Charapan with two engineers and a friend to look for a site to drill a well so that the women of the village would not have to go so far to get water for their homes. Three weeks later he returned to see if drilling had begun. It had. He felt that the village was important, and his amazing energy enabled him to pay personal attention to little things as well as to planning large hydroelectric plants or the giant steel mill at Las Truchas which would benefit not only the people of the Tepalcatepec but multiplied thousands of Mexicans out beyond also.

If Cárdenas avoided accompanying the future president on a visit to inspect the accomplishments of his Commission, he welcomed the opportunity to accompany the man who within a few days was leaving office. Cárdenas and other anti-successionists were confident that once out of office Alemán would not exert undemocratic pressures on his successor. President Alemán arrived at Uruapan on the 4th of November 1952 to inaugurate the works that were ready. After two active days with Cárdenas in the Tepalcatepec area, the President went by car from Uruapan to Morelia. Cárdenas accompanied him almost to that city. Before arriving there he pulled away but not soon enough to avoid the newspaper reporters. He answered their questions but was unhappy about the way the stories came out. He felt that his statements had been twisted to please political interests. Four days later he visited a farm where he and others looked at some imported bulls. These became wild and attacked the party, wounding two of his companions. It seemed natural to draw a comparison between the bulls and the newspaper reporters.

Fully aware of physical dangers, Cárdenas seldom took customary precautions. He did, however, manifest his awareness of risk before entering an airplane by writing notes that would be helpful to his family should there be a fatal accident. One such note says: "... I feel that there is still some risk in airplane travel. Any important papers connected with my official responsibilities are in the metal cabinet in my office at home . . . any other documents or letters which are in the desk or table drawers in . . . and . . . are not worth saving. Cash and securities: 30,000 or 35,000 pesos, proceeds from the sale of Cebú cattle, are in the desk at . . . Bank deposits: none."

Floating in the breezes of friendship and good understanding, and foreshadowing the peace and union of the Hemisphere as one great spiritual fatherland, the flags of our American nations here assembled present a striking contrast to those which in other lands herald tragedy and destruction . . . I trust that our flags may never be found on opposing fields of battle, but rather, as now, may they ever form a rainbow of goodwill, symbol of the oneness of our aspirations and ideals, and expression of our ardent love of liberty based on mutual respect, international justice and love for humanity.

—*Lázaro Cárdenas*—

From a speech delivered on September 16, 1939, when the twenty two American nations presented their flags to the Military Academy of Mexico to be preserved in a shrine dedicated to inter-American unity.

CHAPTER XXXVII

RUIZ CORTÍNES, THE YAQUIS AND YUCATAN

Cárdenas was greatly disappointed when the government of President Arbenz fell in Guatemala in June of 1954. The *World Book Encyclopedia* comments: "The United States Government, which had begun to fear Communist influences in the Arbenz administration, supported a revolt against him." Cárdenas was not anti-North American but anti-interventionist. He was also opposed to foreign exploitation and control of Latin America's natural wealth and labor. In the case of Guatemala this meant the United Fruit Company, which had a corner on the banana industry and was not very mindful, he was told, of the welfare of the laborers who made the industry possible. Other foreigners as well as wealthy Guatemalans and some North Americans owned large tracts of land which were tilled for their benefit by poverty stricken Indians. The Arbenz administration had followed up the reform government of Prof. Juan José Arévalo and made efforts to do something more to improve the situation of the laborers, but Castillo Armas, with equipment sent from the United States, routed the duly elected government and became President.

Again and again Cárdenas spoke out against the extension of foreign interests and their grasping attitude in his own beloved Mexico. He was not the "sphinx of Jiquilpan" when foreign intervention occurred in other lands or when it appeared likely that Mexico's natural wealth would come under the control of foreigners. On one occasion he wrote:

If foreign interests continue their invasion by investing in movies, hotels, soft drink and personal effects factories, and in buying up whole industries already established, what business enterprises will be left for the Mexican people? Shall they, in their own country, always remain mere employees of foreign-owned companies? That type of situation will never result in a unified nation and will quench patriotic fervor. A spirit of sincere friendship and cooperation with our neighboring country in dealing with mutual problems, rather than the offensive intervention of their wealth in our land, will make for a healthier relationship between our two nations.

One other thing that could cause Cárdenas to speak up was any threat to world peace. The atom bomb was an example. Cárdenas never forgave Truman for dropping the atomic bomb over the defenseless civilians of Hiroshima and Nagasaki. Time and again he urged that nuclear energy be used for the benefit and never for the destruction of mankind. Feeling that selfish interests in the democratic world imperiled peace as much as in totalitarian lands, he wrote:

If the so-called democracies did not resort to dictatorial practices and imperialistic tactics, and if they did not aspire to manipulate the economies of other countries, peace between all nations would be possible. But this is not the way it is, and these very democracies will be the ones responsible for future events that will affect world peace.

In the midst of it all, Cárdenas rejoiced when some of his old dreams came true. A note in his diary for December 24, 1952 reports the final approval of a constitutional amendment that he wanted passed during his own administration, granting equal rights to women. This gave him particular satisfaction. His diary reports other happy developments that he had dreamed of and initiated years before. One such involved the Yaqui Indians. On March 18, 1957 he made a flight over a series of dams and irrigation projects that his administration had initiated in the state of Sonora. From the air he noted the progress that had been made in project after project that he had started two decades before. He wrote:

At 11:15 we flew over the Miguel Hidalgo Dam constructed on the Fuerte River during this administration. It will irrigate 250,000 hectares (517,500 acres). The dam is well located in a favorable canyon.

At 11:40 we flew over the Mocúzari Dam on the Mayo River. The dam is completed except for the dikes, locks in the ports and the spillway, etc.; the canal work is still under construction.

At noon we crossed El Oviachi Dam on the Yaqui River. The dam was constructed during President Aleman's administration and has a capacity of 3 billion cubic meters. It, as well as the Angostura Dam, built on the same river during the period of 1934 to 1940, and the distribution of land to the landless, have brought spectacular prosperity to the entire Yaqui Valley, which includes such important cities as Ciudad Obregón. The Navojoa Dam, which utilizes the water of the Mayo River, has also progressed considerably.

The areas of the Yaqui and Mayo Rivers in Sonora and those which can be irrigated in Sinaloa, form at the present time the most important agricultural development in the country. The only comparable region is the southeastern part of the country with its large hydroelectric resources, its land, forests and petroleum.

At 12:15 we flew over the irrigated lands of the Sierra del Bacatete and observed the plains of Ortiz and Maytorena which formed part of the large La Misa estate. I served here during the Yaqui military campaigns of 1916 and 1917. The Yaqui revolt was justified. They were merely fighting for their lands. Fortunately, with the 1910 Revolution came the Agrarian Reform which protected this dissident group and gave them a large tract of land together with water rights from the Angostura Dam. Fifty percent of the water from the dam, according to the Presidential Decree of 1939, is for the Yaqui tribe.

This flight occurred on the 19th anniversary of the nationalization of the petroleum industry. In April he reported on the Yaqui situation to President Ruiz Cortínes who issued the following decree in May and authorized the General to deliver it personally to the chiefs of the Yaqui tribe gathered in Vícam, Sonora:

The President of the Republic
To the Yaqui Indian People:

Being well aware of the problems you face as a group I am glad to inform you that the Executive Branch of the Federal Government, as always, is pledged to grapple with these problems so that you can continue to till the lands which were returned to you according to the Federal Constitution and the applicable laws. The Government also guarantees your right to irrigate those lands with the water which was authorized at that time by means of canals currently available to you, and other canals which will be built, until your full quota of authorized lands within the Irrigation District has been reached, in accordance with the plan being carried out in the District.

At the same time you will be given loans and other help for clearing the land, for plowing, for fencing, for agricultural equipment and for land development. The Government is also concerned: that your cattle industry be organized to benefit the entire community; that medical and health facilities be established; that educational opportunities be provided; that your fishing industry be organized, and legal means used to develop your lands; that networks of roads be completed, as well as other community work projects, all of this as a cooperative effort with those who are benefited thereby, within the framework of standard national laws in force throughout the Republic; that new comprehensive laws be drawn up to coordinate the specific tasks of each department of government in order to reach in the best possible ways these goals, including coordination of the work to be carried out by the State Government of Sonora in areas in which it is responsible for local and municipal functions.

Yours faithfully,

Adolfo Ruiz Cortínes
PRESIDENT OF THE REPUBLIC
Mexico, D.F. May 6, 1957

Armed with this tremendous document which definitely put on the docket his dreams of comprehensive help for the tribe, Cárdenas went to Guadalajara on the 8th of May and early the next morning flew from there to Vícam in Yaquiland. Before leaving his cottage of Eréndira, however, he had written with great satisfaction in his diary:

With the issuance of this proclamation helping the Yaqui Indian community I feel amply repaid and satisfied for the service which I have tried to give to the indigenous people of our country — the roots of our nationality — and especially to the Yaquis, who have been persecuted and hurt so unjustly.

To him, service to Mexico's three million Indians was service to Mexico. He said: "The solution to the Indian problem is not in allowing the Indian to remain Indian nor to indianize Mexico, but to make Mexicans of the Indians."

A visit to Durango and the La Laguna areas convinced him that the agrarian reforms which his administration had instituted there were also working out for the welfare of the peasants. Even so, he was far from satisfied with the overall situation of the working people. When a visit with President Ruiz Cortínes gave him an opportunity, he was apt to point out some specific problems that confronted the peasants and city laborers, though never anything with political connotations.

The twelve or more long conversations Cárdenas had with Ruiz Cortínes from 1952 to 1958 did not in any way indicate a return to politics; they represented rather the encouragement and suggestions he felt free to give the man who very evidently appreciated his advice in his strong desire to do everything possible for the peasants. From the very initiation of his term, Ruiz Cortínes had expressed real concern over the situation that prevailed in Yucatán. He was glad when Cárdenas was willing to go there to find out why the agrarian reforms had not been more successful. Cárdenas' close friend, Alejandro Carrillo, went along and told me the following:

We went to Yucatan in 1957 because Cárdenas, the author of the Agrarian Reform, wanted to find out why it had not been more successful. We arrived in Mérida and for three days received people, anybody and everybody, at the local theatre "Casa del Pueblo" where Cárdenas would stay for 13 or 14 hours each day without food (once in a while someone would offer him a glass of water) receiving people. I have never seen another man with his capacity to listen. With the most insignificant, trivial affairs they would go to him as to a Father Confessor. They told him not only their economic troubles but family and personal troubles, too. They would discuss the situation of their *ejidos* and he would listen to them, give them a few words of advice, and then say: "I will visit you. I came here to visit you, but I want to hear you first." News of his arrival in Yucatán spread like wildfire. From every corner of the peninsula, the people came.

After three days of constant listening we started visiting. He never liked to announce his arrival in a town. He would go to the main plaza but tell no one he was there. He would just start walking around the plaza, saying hello to the children or the people he would meet. In a few minutes the whole town would be there without using church bells or the town crier. Cárdenas would be at the center with the whole town gathered around him. Soon they would take him to their *ejido* and explain: "Remember, you gave us this *ejido* for 350 people to make a living on it. Now there are 1500 people living here." Naturally, Cárdenas immediately realized that no agrarian reform can be possible if there are 1500 people trying to live on land designated for 350. "You must open up new lands, working cooperatively," was a point he emphasized very much. He would tell people: "As long as you work by yourself, you may be successful as an individual; but the only way to achieve real success is if you work together in a cooperative way."

Cárdenas was a great believer in cooperation. When he was attacked as President of Mexico because he believed in cooperative work on farms, he was called a communist because he was trying to copy the collective farms of Russia. In this regard, Cárdenas drew a very interesting comparison that I shall never forget. He said, "The old Mexican *hacienda* was an organic community. The irrigation canals were well laid out and all the various activities were well organized. The Agrarian Reform wants the old *hacienda* to prevail, bettering its technical organization, but with the one fundamental change being that of ownership. Instead of belonging to one person, it should belong to 400 or 500 heads of families — to the laborers themselves."

In an idealistic way, he offered the following challenge to the oil field workers who had already reached higher levels of living:

I deem it appropriate to urge you who work in the petroleum industry and who have attained improved standards of living, to consider the possibility of giving one more example of patriotism and unity by helping those of your same social class and by taking upon yourselves the complete development of an entire region inhabited by Indian people living close to your oil camps.

In this way, perhaps, those of other social classes will follow your example and take upon themselves the development of areas where Indians live in abject poverty. In spite of their poverty, they contribute, by hard work and productivity, to the food supply of the Nation, even though they are a people who see their economic and cultural improvement as still a long way off.

Grabado por Mariana

It is imperative that we widen the avenues which lead to better understanding between nations, that the doors of all lands be open wide to one another without reserve, so that direct contact between people may put an end to suspicions, may tear down prejudices, may eliminate hatred and may promote the hope of universal brotherhood.

—Lázaro Cárdenas—

Moscow, USSR
November 29, 1958

CHAPTER XXXVIII

WORLD TRAVELER

For a Mexican to accept the Lenin Peace Prize was to declare his independence of attitude toward anti-Soviet pressures. Cárdenas accepted it early in 1956. To critics, however, he pointed out that he was simply conforming to new developments. The United States had invited Khrushchev to visit its cities and farms and he had been well received. Eisenhower had commissioned his Vice-President to visit the USSR, and representatives of both countries had met at Geneva to plan peaceful cooperation. Why should he not accept the peace prize that Soviet friends of world peace felt he deserved? He did accept, and at the ceremony held in Mexico at the Nuevo Ideal Theatre in February 1956, he spoke out against dictatorships, imperialism and the intervention of any nation in the internal affairs of another. To him this is what had happened when the USSR had intervened in Hungary. It also applied, he felt, to the selfish outreach of American big business over Latin America. Certainly it applied to the way the United States had gotten rid of socialist tendencies in Guatemala. Top officials of the Mexican Government did not appear at the ceremony and President Ruiz Cortínes was conveniently out of town. A great crowd of laborers, personal friends and the brother of a past president were present however, and the applause was prolonged when the famed Soviet movie director, Gregory Alexandrov, presented the award.

With the Tepalcatepec project nearing completion, Cárdenas had other projects on his mind for 1957 and 1958. President Ruiz Cortínes had spoken to him about heading up a new commission he would name to develop the vast and needy area drained by the Grijalva River in the states of Chiapas, Tabasco and Campeche. This appealed to Cárdenas and he visited the area with reclamation in mind. However, big possibilities also loomed up in the large area drained by the Las Balsas River, part of it being in his own home state of Michoacán. It seemed wise to leave the decision until after the newly elected president, Adolfo López Mateos, had taken office. Furthermore, Cárdenas wanted to be free to travel to other lands and learn from them better ways of helping in either the Grijalva or Las Balsas project. And then there was Las Truchas with its vast reserve of iron ore. Surely if he visited the Krupp Factories in Germany he would get ideas for the steel mill he hoped would be built there. The Krupp people would help without any risk of their elbowing out Mexican interests as foreign neighbors had done in two earlier instances.

Accordingly, the train that left Mexico City on October 12, 1958 for San Antonio, Texas, carried Amalia and the General. On the stops at Nuevo Laredo, Laredo, San Antonio and St. Louis they were shown many courtesies by Mexican consular officials and people whom the U.S. Ambassador to Mexico, Robert C. Hill, had alerted to their coming.

From the broad cattle ranges of Texas to the corn and wheat fields of the central states, to the neat farms, towns and forests of Pennsylvania, and on to the mass of skyscrapers in New York City, Cárdenas watched and made notes. Inveterate traveler though he was in his own land, he had never been across any of Mexico's borders except for two short sallies that had taken him to Los Angeles. He wrote in his diary:

It is especially noteworthy to see the care which has been given to the preservation and planting of rows of trees which protect the crops and soil from erosion and wind and which, furthermore, lend beauty and protective shade to the countryside. Extensive areas planted to corn and pasture can be seen as a checkerboard and thus give an idea of how the land is divided. Farms located close to one another, irrigation, electricity, roads, pleasant looking houses, a variety of crops planted — all of this can be seen in this part of our trip. This is the way the farm country of Mexico will look some day in the future. There is today the human capability to do it but we lack the economic resources. These will come; it is a question of time and perseverance.

Mexican friends and diplomats and a representative of the U.S. Department of State met them in New York. There they spent two days before boarding the passenger ship *Liberte*. Realizing that he would be approached by newspaper men, Cárdenas had written out the following note and gave it to one of them before the ship sailed:

Mexico, like all the other Latin American nations, fervently hopes that all the countries of the American continent will always be united and will present a single front for peace and harmony not only among themselves but also among the rest of the countries of the world. Such peace and harmony would promote a favorable climate for the creation of many new job opportunities so as to put an end to the poverty in which great masses of people live, not only in Latin America but also in this country, which is so rich in many ways. To keep on trying to be prepared adequately for war is to hasten the destruction of mankind.

When their son Cuauhtémoc had left them a year before to study in Europe, they had promised to join him there when his year was over and this they did on the 24th of October when their ship docked at LeHavre. From then on they had the young engineer as guide and interpreter as they visited Belgium, Holland, West Germany, France and Italy. Part of the trip was made by car with Cuauhtémoc at the wheel. The General was on the alert constantly for everything that might be of help to Mexico. The area 60 miles from Rome called Agro Pontino which had been drained, developed and divided up among war veterans by Mussolini, attracted his attention in a special way.

The European journey was interrupted late in November by a flight to Moscow where Khrushchev and Cárdenas, with the help of interpreters, chatted for two hours in the Kremlin. The same day, November 29, the Lenin Peace Prize Committee gave Cárdenas a reception at which he spoke. He expressed satisfaction that the cold war seemed to be drawing to an end now that the USSR and the U.S.A. were sending commissions back and forth and informing each other through expositions of their respective accomplishments. I must quote three paragraphs from his speech:

The Soviet Union which, in the last war, suffered the loss of millions of its sons, and also staggering material losses, impresses us who visit it as a land whose people, by their own labor, have healed the physical wounds of the war, have increased their economic production and improved the standard of living, have eliminated unemployment, are solicitous in caring for their children and young people, have made remarkable cultural and artistic programs and desire peace, not violence.

We must emphasize that peaceful coexistence among all nations is possible, without regard to differences in the social and economic systems they may have.

Today's most urgent task is the search for peace — a peace which guarantees liberty and social justice, and which overcomes the tragic conditions of poverty against which millions of human beings are struggling. Helping one another in this task should be the primary goal of all men of good will.

From Moscow the party flew to Stalingrad for an overnight visit and then after another day in Moscow they flew to Prague. In Czechoslovakia they visited factories, a hydroelectric plant and a dam. After three days there they drove across Bohemia and Austria to Italy and the historic little Republic of San Marino. In his diary Cárdenas noted on December 15, 1958 that this little land had been established in the year 1253 A.D. by a group of evangelical Christians who were fleeing from religious persecution. Referring to the rugged terrain where they had taken refuge, he wrote: "It is a beautiful place which Amalia, Cuauhtémoc and I visited."

Two weeks were spent visiting Switzerland and France. The trip ended in Paris where Cuauhtémoc had spent the previous year studying. There, on the 16th of January, just three months and four days after they had left Mexico City, the happy party broke up. The General, Alejandro Carrillo and César Buenrostro, as well as Cuauhtémoc, bade farewell to Amalia and the others who were returning to Mexico with her. The General and his companions went back to Moscow and later on to China. In his diary, the General wrote of his courageous wife as follows:

Amalia was perfectly calm as she said good-bye to her son who holds a large place in her life. She preferred that he go with me on the trip to Asia and not accompany her as she returned across the Atlantic. Cuauhtémoc was really looking forward to the trip to China about which we had heard so much. As we bade each other farewell Amalia displayed her calm composure. Actually there were good reasons why she might have felt apprehensive about our trip. We had come to Europe to meet Cuauhtémoc and to return to Mexico with him and so it was difficult that we should return by different routes, and especially when weather made flying insecure. Nevertheless, she felt so strongly that we should fulfill our moral obligation to visit China that she was unperturbed as we separated.

Siberia impressed the group by its vastness and the success with which it was being developed. Omsk was found to be a city of over a million inhabitants. Lake Baikal and the possibilities its waters offered for developing electricity as they tumbled seaward caught Cárdenas' fancy. From Irkutsk to Peking, leaving Siberia and crossing Mongolia into China, the "immense ocean of mountains and valleys covered with snow, forests and cultivated fields", as well as the intense cold, merited a note in the General's diary.

In Peking the party was met at the airport by the Pro-Peace Committee of China and its president Kuo Mo-jo, just as in Moscow they had been met by the president of the Lenin Peace Prize Committee, Dimitri Skobeltzin. This was the 20th of January 1959. On the 23rd, the newspaper *Excélsior* in Mexico City reported that at a reception given him by Chinese leaders, Cárdenas had stated:

"Many have been the victims of the cold war and it has disrupted the progress of the economically underdeveloped nations. These nations are insisting that the politics of war be ended. As regards international conflicts, Cárdenas stated, according to radio reports: 'We have heard many opinions regarding the solution to problems by peaceful means instead of by force. We are convinced that only peaceful coexistence among all nations can open the door to unlimited progress for all humanity.' "

He also drew a parallel between the victories of Francisco I. Madero and Sun Yat-sen in 1911.

On the 24th, the party flew from Peking to Shanghai. On the 26th they continued to Canton and two days later to Hong Kong. In Canton, Cárdenas wrote in his diary:

The work which men, women and children in this country are putting into the task of improving living conditions is without precedent in history. How I wish that all people might become informed of their efforts and sacrifices and could, by their friendship stimulate this redeeming operation which the people of China have taken upon themselves in order to escape from the poverty and backwardness in which they previously lived!

Time and again on the long trip across Europe, the USSR and China, Cárdenas spoke out on behalf of world peace. His various statements are best summarized in the message he sent to the Executive Committee of the World Council of Peace, meeting in Helsinki, Finland in December 1958. He wrote:

We join our voices with those of men and women of all creeds and nationalities which have been heard in the various gatherings of the partisans of peace.
They call for the banning of nuclear experiments, as well as the reduction and control of armaments in general. But it seems essential to insist that if peace is to be lasting and real, there must be not only the elimination of the threat of another war but also the easing of the economic burden imposed on the people by the arms race. It is important to use these huge resources to strengthen domestic economies and the cause of international cooperation.
We must lend our ears to the clamoring voices of the people from all corners of the world, especially from those of little material development and wretched living conditions pleading that the enormous sums being spent on equipment and instruments of war be used to do away with the tragic conditions of poverty in which millions of human beings live — a situation which is, in itself, an outrage for all civilization.

After a day and a half in Tokyo, a city that Cárdenas thought to be more Texan than Asian in appearance, the party flew on to San Francisco. There they were met by several colleagues who had driven up from Mexico City to meet them. The General had collected intriguing articles, especially seeds of various types along the route, and it was convenient to be able to turn over the load and send it to Mexico. Then the party flew on to Knoxville and the Tennessee Valley Project to see how it compared to the Tepalcatepec Valley reclamation. From Tennessee they flew to Pittsburgh to see something of the steel industry. On February 7 they continued on to Texas to observe cattle raising as it was done there. In Nuevo Laredo there awaited them a royal welcome from the working people and every sector of Mexican society. The trip had been a success in gathering very useful information that could be helpful to Mexico such as the protection of her forests and the planning of steel mills. In his public statements, Cárdenas found items on which to comment favorably about each country they had visited. However, in April he opened up the intimate recesses of his heart and wrote in his diary a more profound conclusion to which the trip had brought him. The statement is as follows:

When a trip of 62,000 kilometers is made in just four months, visiting countries of different races, languages, and sociopolitical philosophies, it is not really possible to form a complete judgement of the characteristics of each country. But from the observations that I have been able to make, I give my impressions in general terms.

One of the purposes which persuaded me to make this trip through Central Europe, through the various socialist countries, and finally through the United States of North America, was the desire to see, even though superficially, how the people of these countries live and how they are being developed. Even more, having heard on the one hand either from travelers or writers about the "peace" which the western nations enjoy and, on the other, the disparaging information regarding liberty and progress, both individual and collective, which is frequently spread abroad in our continent against the socialist countries, and in view of the intense anti-communist campaigns which have been carried on in our own countries, I wanted to see for myself if, in reality, as it is alleged, the socialist countries are a threat to liberty, independence and peace among nations in general. This desire took me right to the center of one of the most powerful countries on earth, the Soviet Union, and to another country which is made up of the largest population, namely China. I had already visited Belgium, Holland, France, Western and Eastern Germany, Italy, Switzerland, Poland and Czechoslovakia. Then I visited the United States of America. My conclusion is that the countries with a socialist government are following the path which will inevitably put an end to the capitalist system inasmuch as it slows down and hinders the development of the under-developed nations.

There is no country which can progress under the old feudal land system. It must be completely done away with.

—Lázaro Cárdenas—
Havana, Cuba
July 27, 1959

The ideas expressed by Gen. Lázaro Cárdenas in his speech given in Havana . . . are in complete accord with the ideas which he has always expressed in his public life. They correspond to the ideals of progress and social justice which all Mexicans feel, all of us who have a revolutionary outlook on social problems.

—Alfonso Corona del Rosal—
July 28, 1959

XXXIX

CUBA

Back in August of 1956 Cárdenas had been approached by some educators and a lawyer on behalf of a group of young Cubans who were being exiled from their country due to revolutionary activities. They needed a place of refuge. Mexico was their choice. Would the General intercede with President Ruiz Cortínes on their behalf? Yes, he would, with the result that Fidel Castro Ruiz and several companions were given entrance permits. One of the first things that Castro did upon arriving in Mexico was to ask for an interview with Cárdenas in order to express his gratitude. His host wrote in his diary after the interview: "He is a young intellectual with a vehement temperament and the makeup of a fighter."

While in France on January 1, 1959 Cárdenas had heard over the radio that Castro's revolutionary forces had won out in Cuba. The General wrote in his diary for that day:

May the political and social reforms envisioned by this new regime justify the blood that was spilt rather than result merely in a change of people in power.

Agrarian reform was what he hoped for and when it became evident that this was underway, the General decided to visit Cuba and encourage Castro in that area. It was the only Latin American country he ever visited though he was invited to others time and again. He realized that his presence in lands where social and economic reforms were needed badly would encourage would-be reformers to speak up so loudly that his hosts would be embarrassed. In the case of Cuba he knew that no one could speak out more forcefully or longer than Castro himself. I complained to the General one time about the length of a speech by the Cuban reformer that had lasted for four hours. Cárdenas simply replied with a smile: "Oh, well, Townsend, you must remember that Fidel is Cuban."

The General and his engineer son, Cuauhtémoc, arrived in Havana July 25, 1959 in time for the celebration of the anniversary of the beginning of the Cuban Revolution. Again Antonio Carrillo went with them and he reported five days later when they returned to Mexico that the General was given special honors. Cárdenas himself avoided all mention of such things in his diary, where we find only a tribute to Amalia on the occasion of their leaving her for the Cuban trip. To the news reporters back in Mexico City he simply mentioned that there had been many "eloquent declarations of admiration and friendship for the Mexican people which moved him deeply and, as a Mexican, he appreciated these expressions of affection for our people."

A year later President Eisenhower backed up the oil companies in their heavy-handed objection to Castro's purchases of crude oil from the USSR and cancelled the United States' agreement to purchase Cuba's sugar. Castro turned to the Soviets for help. The survival of his government depended either on giving in to American pressures or on getting in line for Soviet assistance. With a one-crop economy, Cuba simply had to sell its sugar. For a long time the United States had been buying most of it at a special price. After all, a great deal of the industry in Cuba was owned by American capital. Nevertheless the sugar contract was cancelled when the oil companies were confiscated due to their refusal to cooperate. A more cautious man might have given in, but not Castro. He refused to bow to powerful nearby pressure and looked far away. Cárdenas quietly applauded and made it clear that he hoped his own country would continue to maintain diplomatic relationships with Cuba as it did. He chafed when Venezuela and some other Latin American countries severed diplomatic ties.

One of the grave concerns of General Cárdenas during 1959 and 1960 was the group of railroad workers being held in jail by the López Mateos administration. In November 1959 after the President had returned from a brief visit to the U.S.A., Cárdenas called on him and congratulated him for his firm stand in defense of the sovereign rights of Cuba and other lands. The President assured him that foreign investments in Mexico would be carefully controlled and that foreign interests would not be permitted to return to participate in the exploitation of Mexico's petroleum fields. He preferred, however, to leave the problem of the railroad workers in the hands of the courts. At one point López Mateos made reference to hemispheric affairs and his conviction that some reforms were needed in the constitution of the Organization of American States to put it more in accord with the day.

In Cárdenas' diary the following paragraphs dealing with Latin America were written a few weeks later:

Eréndira, Pátzcuaro, Mich., 1960. In the countries of Latin America there is a dearth of political organizations to develop the public spirit of the people.

The working classes live with no one to defend them; they are dominated by the whims of a few individuals who are incapable of organizing laborers in such a way that their own moral strength will defend them from fraud and from being used as pawns in shady schemes.

In the countries of Latin America there are men of science, there are technicians of great ability, industrial entrepreneurs, intelligent businessmen, experienced bankers, men of letters who do honor to their profession, idealistic intellectuals, and distinguished artists, together with hard working laborers who know how to face adversity. But what Latin America lacks is intelligent leaders who are willing to struggle. Latin America has no statesmen to guide its people in the paths of socialism. It lacks political parties to prepare teams of political leaders for the future of the Nation.

Many of the people of Latin America have been deprived of schooling; they are kept in ignorance, and as a result their manual labor is exploited. And this is only to be expected when they have no training for the more highly skilled occupations which could free them from being merely masses of cheap labor who will never rise above abject poverty.

Cárdenas was careful to attend funerals of old friends. Before flying to the funeral of General Triana late in February of 1960 he wrote in his diary:

I leave tomorrow morning at 8 to attend his funeral. Cuauhtémoc will accompany me. I would prefer that he stay because of the possibility of an airplane accident, but he wants to go with me. Whenever I fly with him I think about Amalia, but she, putting her personal feelings aside, agrees that he should go along. And oh, how she idolizes her son! But she has a great and sensitive appreciation of the fact that duty must come before everything else. Cuauhtémoc and I hold a deep and affectionate esteem for her because of her moral strength of character and her unmistakably calm spirit.

This attitude on the part of Amalia made it possible for father and son to be together a great deal the next few years and this meant travel, travel, travel. People wondered how Cárdenas could stand up to his heavy schedule. He himself attributed his good health in part to the mineral baths at Los Azufres. He wrote in January, 1960:

For twenty years I've been coming to this place, generally three times a year, sometimes with Amalia and Cuauhtémoc. The baths in these springs of *Los Azufres* and the hikes that I take in the forests, serve to refresh and restore me in my work. Up until now there have been very few times that I have had to consult a doctor. I feel good. Most of my life is extremely busy. I've been able to keep up this pace of intensive mental and physical activity, 18 hours a day for many years without feeling weariness.

If the year 1960 was one of great concern for Cárdenas because of the railway workers who continued in prison in spite of his earnest appeals to the President, 1961 was also one of concern for Cuba and the rest of Latin America. Eisenhower had left office but Kennedy, the new president, had inherited a secret plan to facilitate an invasion of Cuba by anti-revolutionary Cubans. It took place at the Bay of Pigs in April of 1961 and was a dismal failure. However, it stirred up Cárdenas' anti-intervention convictions so strongly he decided to go to Cuba again. Ostensibly, because of bad weather somewhere along the route, the airline cancelled the flight. Then Cárdenas decided to fly to Mérida, Yucatan, and hope for a way to fly from there to Havana. The scheduled flight to Mérida was cancelled also. So Cárdenas gave up the idea of going altogether. However, at a meeting held April 18 in the *Zócalo* to protest the armed intervention in Cuba, he stated in a speech that lasted twenty-five minutes:

Right here in our America, Cuba is being attacked and it is imperative that all the people of Latin America declare themselves in such a unified way that the entire world will realize the moral strength of our people.

Speaking to a large crowd from atop an automobile he urged the United States to cease its blockade of Cuba and urged Mexican youth to organize protests against the country which thinks that money can dominate everything.

In response to an invitation from President López Mateos, Cárdenas called at his residential office, Los Pinos, on the evening of April 28. The conversation dealt at considerable length with Cuba. The President made it clear that he was going to stand firm in supporting the sovereignty of the island republic but that he was not going to promote a Latin American bloc of nations to try to offset the military and economic pressures that the United States was exerting on its game little neighbor. "Mexico is passing through a difficult situation," he said. "Our income from the tourist trade is down. The campaign outside our borders against Cuba and communism is very hot. I don't like to buy trouble, as it were, by getting tangled up in the problems of others."

Cárdenas pointed out that he felt this was a timely opportunity to let imperialistic forces know that Mexico and Latin America would be united against all such aggression as the Bay of Pigs; that together they were saying to the United States, "Thus far, but no farther!" He did not mention to López Mateos one of the reasons why he had wanted to go to Cuba. Had he done so, the President might have been less opposed to his going. Amalia told me: "The General felt sure that if he could talk with Castro face to face he could get him to stop executing so many prisoners of war."

On the 15th of September 1961 the *chargé d' affaires* of the Cuban Embassy in Mexico City called on Cárdenas and told him of rumors that the President of Guatemala, General Ydigoras, was fostering the training of counter-revolutionary forces at certain secluded points with the thought of attacking Cuba again. Cárdenas was reminded of how three years earlier the Guatemalan President had complained that groups of his antagonists were scheming against him in southern Mexico and had closed the Guatemalan border. At that time Cárdenas had told President López Mateos that he would be willing to accept an assignment as head of the reclamation project that was planned for the Grijalva River basin near the border of Guatemala. As such he would constitute a guarantee that there would be no sheltering of international interventionists in the area. This time he decided to report the rumors to President López Mateos and urge him to put the military on the alert against any possible collaboration that might be emanating from Mexico to the plotters against Cuba. But he himself would accept the post the President had urged upon him to head up the Balsas River Reclamation Project.

Grabado por Guillermo Rodríguez

Amalia lives in my fondest memories. Among them are those memorable days of the 1938 oil crisis when she was a great source of strength to me. She understood the problem which faced me when I told her of the Government's decision to carry out the expropriation. When the decree was actually signed and put into effect, Amalia saw how well the people reacted and she herself worked very hard. She organized committees of women to serve the humble families who wanted to help out from their own modest resources that the Government might meet its promise to pay for the property.

Together we observed moving acts of true patriotism from the hearts of lowly Mexican families.

To Amalia, then, and to the women who put their patriotism to work in the struggle with foreign interests I dedicate the memorial which is being observed throughout the Nation on this anniversary of the Expropriation Decree. Mexico City, 11 p.m., March 17, 1968.

—*Lázaro Cárdenas*—
OBRAS I APUNTES

XXXX

THE BALSAS RIVER PROJECT, AND GRAVE CONCERN
FOR VIETNAM

There were sentimental reasons that must have made it easier for Cárdenas to accept the responsibility for the big Balsas River Project than the one far to the south. The vast area included the part of his home state where he had first met his beloved Amalia. Quite naturally she would feel more like a part of the project and indeed she was a vital part of everything he did. She never chided him over the long hours he kept nor about his constant traveling. Without complaint she had accompanied him to live in Lower California when his assignment during World War II required it. Gladly she had opened her arms to the many children of poor parents he, while President, had brought home to educate. She had tried to get him to take care of himself but this was foreign to his nature. On the rare occasions when he had come down with a fever or excruciating pain, he always found in her his "best doctor".

Amalia certainly would be glad to see the new developments branching out from their home state into Guerrero and other states. These included the nearby state of Morelos where they had spent so many weekends over the years. As a family they had visited the beaches too on each side of where the Balsas River empties into the Pacific Ocean and had dreamt of pleasant tourist resorts along them. Even the spa at Los Azufres where the General went so often to swim in its health-giving waters bordered on the area which the Balsas project would include.

More than this, however, one of the main engineers who had planned the project and gotten it under way was their own son. Back in July 1960 Cuauhtémoc had decided to resign as planner of the huge undertaking but had been dissuaded by his dad. What had brought him to think of quitting was the rough way in which some of his fellow members of the National Liberation Movement had been treated by the government. His father, also a member of the revolutionary group, had advised him not to pull out from the important assignment just because of the way authorities had mistreated his friends. Now the President was offering Cuauhtémoc's father the task of carrying out what his own son had helped plan with skill, vision and diligence. Cárdenas accepted.

The next eight years of his life were spent in close collaboration with Cuauhtémoc and others in developing the extensive Balsas area. It consisted of 43,400 square miles, spread out over parts of eight states and with tumbling streams giving a hydroelectric potential of 2.6 million kilowatts.

It was my privilege to accompany the General on a part of one of his inspection trips that took us into the back country of the states of Mexico and Guerrero. We spent one night in a town back in the mountains where a family lived whose friendship he had formed in the days of the armed revolution. As a young officer he had ridden his mount over a long rugged trail from the state of Michoacán clear to their village. Now we had come by jeep from the Cuernavaca-Acapulco highway. What I saw on this trip was simply a new version of what I had seen ten years before in the Tepalcatepec area. When I told my old friend, Raul Noriega, then editor of *México en la Cultura,* the magazine section of the big newspaper *Novedades,* he requested that I write an article about it. His readers in Mexico City were about as apt to visit the area themselves as the average citizen of New York City was to see the Tennessee Valley reclamation accomplishments, so his magazine would inform them. I tried, but it must have been hard for city folk to really grasp the great importance of such public works for the villagers back in the hinterland.

The railway workers had continued in jail for five years in spite of repeated appeals by Cárdenas on their behalf. In December 1963 Cárdenas had his wife take his year's salary as head of the Balsas Commission and distribute it among the families of the 29 prisoners, including the family of the well known painter Siqueiros. Again on the 11th of May, Cárdenas appealed to the President. The 1964 election was only two months away and it was expected that the candidate of the PRI, Díaz Ordaz, would be elected. López Mateos, Cárdenas felt, would release the prisoners once the election was over so that the act would not carry too much political significance.

The evening before the new president, Díaz Ordaz, took office, Dec. 1, 1964, General Jara notified Cárdenas that Siqueiros and the other prisoners had been released. In his diary Cárdenas made a note in which he withdrew a previous harsh judgment of López Mateos. Later however when he found out that the report had been inexact he had to qualify the retraction. Not all the prisoners had been released.

The railway workers still in prison were said to be communists who had resorted to violence several years earlier. Furthermore, some students who at the time of the Olympic Games in Mexico had clashed with the police were accused of communistic leanings. Tough measures on the part of the authorities had resulted in death to some of the students and the imprisonment of others. Again Cárdenas fretted. In his diary he admitted that it had caused him an unusual feeling of depression that had lasted for weeks. He felt that foreign capitalistic interests were largely to blame for the crusade that classified all clamor for change as communistic. To him the Mexican Revolution had established the right of young people to strive for improvement of their lot, and if the ultimate goal spelled socialism, as he was convinced it would, they should have a right to say so. The same was true, he felt, regarding laborers and peasants. It was not only their right but their duty to seek better living conditions and intellectual progress as well as freedom from foreign exploitation. Such demands, he insisted, were not communism, as foreign investors claimed. He deplored the resort to violence of which both laborers and students were accused. He felt, however, that it was not political, but rather a natural reaction to a violent attitude on the part of the authorities themselves. He believed that it should be pardoned.

In maintaining that the disturbances were not political, he said:

The underlying issue behind what is happening in Latin America as well as on the other continents is that the real problem which troubles people is not just a political tendency, but the difficulty of attaining a decent standard of living. It is imperative that leaders in government not close their ears to the outcry of the common man, deceiving themselves or trying to deceive the people with noisy "anti-communist" campaigns which swindle those who are crying for employment in order to get bread, clothing and shelter for their families.

There were goals that simply had to be attained. These were not for Mexicans alone but for men of every land. Progress toward them was being made he felt in many parts of the world. However, nations were still interfering in the affairs of other nations. When tanks and troops of the USSR thundered into Czekoslovakia in August 1968 he wrote in his diary:

It is a reprehensible act which hurts the principles of self-determination, sovereignty and harmony of the nations . . . The Soviet nation could have used diplomatic means to reach a clear understanding and thus avoid adopting the imperialistic attitude which North America is following. Now, having done this, what moral arguments can the Soviet Union advance against the unjustified and criminal aggression which Vietnam is suffering?

Time and again Cárdenas spoke out and registered complaints in his diary against the war in Vietnam. When in June 1965 Bertrand Russell invited him to become a member of the Tribunal he was organizing to "put President Johnson on trial for his acts of aggression in Vietnam", he accepted without hesitation. He didn't go to the meeting of the Tribunal but in October 1969 wrote in his diary with evident satisfaction:

Today (October 15, 1969) millions of North Americans of all ages and social strata are holding non-violent demonstrations from one end of the United States to the other, in London, in Vietnam, and in other parts of the world, to express their opposition to the Vietnam war.

When Bertrand Russell died in February of 1970, Cárdenas wrote:

His death will be mourned wherever there are those who love peace. Among those most affected are the people of Vietnam who have lost, in this distinguished English humanist scholar, their best and most effective spokesman and defender against the crimes which the imperialistic North American Government is committing against the heroic people of Vietnam.

The cold war, especially as it affected Latin America, was also a cause of grave concern to Cárdenas. On New Year's Day 1958 he wrote in his diary:

If the great powers of the East and West are themselves seeking an end to the cold war, the Latin American countries surely have the right to ask that there be an end to the constant menace of this kind of hostility which is actually more destructive than war itself.

Nearly three years later, October 5, 1961, he was so encouraged in this regard that he was able to say at a gathering held in Mexico City in honor of communist China:

"As we extend greetings to the New China on its tenth anniversary, we look expectantly for progress in all nations, for their independence, and for peace on earth. This hope is, today, nearer realization than ever before. The statesmen of the world's major powers are opening the way for peacefully resolving the most pressing problems threatening world peace. We must all carry out our responsibility to insure peace with liberty and progress with social justice." (*Excelsior*, Oct. 5, 1961)

Most of the General's still incredible energies continued to be dedicated to the securing of progress in social justice for the needy laboring classes of his own land. It was in 1961 that he was appointed Executive Director of the Balsas River Commission so that the following years were to be spent in developing that large and very needy area. Rugged mountain slopes and valleys that drain to the Balsas River and then to the Pacific Ocean were to be the scene of his coming and going. 500,000 Indians, speaking Mixtec, Trique, Nahuatl, Tarascan, Amuzgo, Tlapaneco or some other local tongue, along with five million Spanish speakers inhabit the area. Their basic need, of course, was land to farm and thus secure more adequate food and clothing. When this was too scarce to cope with the increase of population which was resulting from better living conditions and greater availability of medical help, some peasants would migrate to Mexico City to seek employment. This added to subsistence problems there. Some would take advantage of opportunities for seasonal employment in agricultural areas of the United States. This bothered Cárdenas no little. Why could not Mexico herself utilize her laborers and become more prosperous as a result, he would argue.

From time to time he would repeat his desire that much more attention be given to collective farming. He wrote in his diary:

Actually it is on collective farms that the most efficient ways to produce good crops and to handle labor can be utilized. These would prove to be more productive than any other land tenure system now in effect if the State, in addition to giving constant technical help, would really grasp the basic importance of the collective farm to our socio-economic and farming systems and not abandon it to its own fate.

What had been lacking, he declared time and again, was to give the peasants adequate help in getting organized and then providing them technical advice, as well as financial loans properly supervised so as to guard against unwise speculation and fraud.

Back of all this had to be more technical schools for the teaching of soil analysis and conservation, the use of fertilizers, increase in food production per acre for human and cattle consumption — schools which would have adequate equipment and laboratories.

Often, in his diary, mention is made of the need to give the peasants more land wherever it might be available or where irrigation could be introduced to bring more land under cultivation. Where it was not available he urged that some industrialization be introduced to provide productive employment.

For eight long years, until he was seventy-four, Cárdenas spurred on engineers and traveled himself by jeep and occasionally by horseback throughout the mountains of the Mixteca as well as other parts of the Balsas basin. He had done what he could to help the Indians and other peasants of his native state, Michoacan, for years. Now he was anxious to bring more roads, schools and the proper utilization of their forests to people of neighboring states. He spent long hours talking with them. Much impressed by the Indians and other peasants whom most city folks would not have esteemed very highly, Cárdenas wrote on his 74th birthday (May 21, 1969):

Throughout the whole Mixtec area I found the people perceptive, well disposed, courteous, hospitable, and with a deep desire to better themselves. They possess a remarkable spirit of progress, but there is a great lack of helpful programs on the part of the Government to encourage their efforts. In spite of the poverty in which they live, what dignity there is in their bearing! They do not ask help for themselves personally, but for public works which will benefit everyone.

Where was he on the next to his last birthday when he wrote this heartwarming description? Was it written at home in Mexico City after a birthday party? No! He had spent that day alone far back in the Mixtec under the shade of an oak tree three miles from the nearest village. At five o'clock that morning he and the driver of his pickup, Javier Quiñones, had left Mariscala de Juárez to escape the *mañanitas* (birthday serenade) or any other celebration of his birthday. They had driven on and on, hour after hour across the rugged terrain that he hoped would become some day a prosperous area.

At one o'clock, after eight hours of bumpy road, he chose a spot to get out of the pickup while Javier went back to get an engineer, Adolfo Báez, and his assistant. The rest of the day and into the night the Apostle to the Poor remained there alone under the oak tree. The outside world, even his beloved family, faded out of the picture. One thing gripped his soul: how to serve Mexico to his utmost in the building of a better Mixteca. As he meditated upon the situation he wrote:

The Trique people who live in the Oaxaca Mountains are considered the most culturally deprived. They own coffee plantations, but these have done them more harm than good. Alcoholism is rampant; they fight among themselves over land boundaries which the government has not legalized for them.

The communities of the Tlapaneca Mountains do want schools; many villages do not have them. They have also been forced to fight for the preservation of their timber lands which are rapidly being destroyed. I shall continue to insist that they be helped with their problems . . . The villages of the region, even those without either culture or schools, are today asking for educational centers, job opportunities, roads, medical attention, safe drinking water, etc. Something very important that has been attained is the confidence shown by these people in their organized effort to seek the solution of their needs, now that the government has shown an interest in them.

In the Mixteca region the work being done by some priests in giving the people a helping hand in their efforts to improve their situation is very noteworthy. Some of them, like Father Fidencio Rios of Tonalá, are understanding and real humanists. Some, however, make no contribution and are buried in their bigotry.

Nearly a year later, April 29, 1970, we find Cárdenas again in the region of the oak tree. Things were looking up for the Mixtec Indians. Of one of their towns, San Miguel El Grande, Cárdenas wrote with evident satisfaction:

We offer our most cordial congratulations to the personnel of the Brigade for Indian Improvement No. 20 under the command of teacher Evaristo Cruz Mendoza who lives in this town. We have had opportunity to observe the eagerness and concern of the members of the Brigade in carrying out their mission. How much more could they accomplish if they had the proper basic equipment, especially considering the determination of the Indians of these Mixtec communities to follow the training given them! Yesterday at 1 p.m. we went to San Miguel El Grande in Tlaxiaco District of the State of Oaxaca, to be at the meeting called by the people of San Miguel. We witnessed their contribution of 160,000 *pesos* and some of the building materials necessary for the construction of an agricultural high school.

What nobility there is in these Indian groups who, like others in our country, lack so many things in their homes and yet deny themselves even necessary food, clothing, medical attention, and a better place to live, so that they can have a school which will improve the education of their children! The ceremony yesterday was a spiritual feast for us who witnessed the exemplary attitude of this group of Mixtec Indians.

Today we bid them good-bye and we go away encouraged together with our traveling companions and dear friends, the engineers — Victor Bravo Ahuja, Governor of Oaxaca, Norberto Aguirre Palancares, Chief of the Department of Agriculture, and Joaquín Loredo, Director of the National Fund for Development of Collective Farms.

The name of the Indian town where Cárdenas was so encouraged by the fine attitude of the people themselves took me back in my memory over 30 years. San Miguel El Grande was the very town where, in 1936, a young linguist named Kenneth L. Pike had begun to study the dif-

ficult Mixtec language with the encouragement of the then President of
the Republic, General Lázaro Cárdenas. It was a tonal language
Pike discovered, and was to pass on to the thousands of young men and
women whom he was to teach in subsequent years, the basic principles
to follow in the learning of unwritten tongues, especially those in which
tone is phonemic. Pike, after his field experience of several years in San
Miguel El Grande, was to become one of the most outstanding linguists
of the world. Furthermore, the Summer Institute of Linguistics*, of
which he is president, and which Cárdenas helped so much from its very
inception, has extended its linguistic research, literacy work and other
services to over 700 minority language groups in America, Asia, Africa
and Australia.

---

*The Summer Institute of Linguistics holds courses during the school year in connection
with the University of Texas in Arlington and summer courses at the State Universities
of Oklahoma, North Dakota and Washington, as well as in England, Germany,
Australia and Japan.

Grabado por A. Beltrán

The struggle will be maintained to erase illiteracy from Mexico in the shortest time possible, and to bring to our people by constant and tenacious effort a higher standard of living.

It is the duty of all, and especially of the young people, to constantly seek self-improvement; to get organized in such a way as to promote the furtherance of social justice; and to fight that which is barbaric until an era of brotherhood and progress is established in which all mankind can reap the benefits of civilization.

—Lázaro Cárdenas—

XXXXI

LAS TRUCHAS AT LAST

President Díaz Ordaz had visited the work of the Balsas River Reclamation Project by helicopter during three days in November, 1968. He had inaugurated hydroelectric plants, irrigation systems and dam after dam that the Balsas River Commission, under Cárdenas' leadership, had brought into being. He also visited schools, hospitals, offices and housing that had been constructed. Cárdenas had flown with him in the helicopter as they buzzed from project to project in three different states. Governors, mayors, engineers, teachers and peasants were on hand to welcome them and express appreciation for what had been done. To inspect the big Morelos Dam they had taken a bus at one point. The engineer who was on hand to explain what the dam would accomplish was none other than Cuauhtémoc Cárdenas. He told President Díaz Ordaz that one dam would store up water for irrigating 18,000 hectares (44,478 acres) and for developing 300,000 kilowatts of electricity. He also told of the seaport that had been built at the mouth of the Balsas River. This port, as well as the hydroelectric plant, would play a big part in the development of the Las Truchas Steel Mill for which his father had battled a long time. It gave the young engineer great satisfaction to tell the President of the plans for a Mexican steel mill owned by Mexicans for Mexican industry, quite independent of foreign tutelage or danger of plunder by foreign interests.

On July 1, 1969 the *Siderúrgica Las Truchas, S.A.* was formed with the Mexican Government owning over half the stock. General Cárdenas was named chairman of the Board of Directors. By the middle of April the following year, the chairman was able to write in his diary:

Today, April 14, 1970, from 10 a.m. to 1 p.m. I presided over the meeting of the Board of Directors of Las Truchas Steel Mill. I informed its manager, Engineer Adolfo Orive Alba, of the progress of the feasibility study now underway for the installation of a plant at the mouth of the Balsas River and the cost thereof. The report was well received by the members of the Board.

403

Six days later, Cárdenas was back in the Mixteca. Town after town was visited and new bridges, schools and at least one dam inspected. If he had ideas of celebrating his 75th birthday alone under the oak tree on the lonely mountain as the year before, sickness intervened. On the 7th of May at the village of Silacayoapam at three in the morning, he awoke with chills and fever. By eight the fever had gone and he and the engineers who were with him climbed into the pickup again and hit the road. They stopped to eat in Michapa and then went on to Justlahuaca. The fever had returned by then and so travel was halted and lodging secured. The next morning Cuauhtémoc arrived with a doctor. An hour later Amalia and Alicia arrived. The General improved rapidly and two days later he and Amalia traveled by road the 410 kilometers to Mexico City arriving a little before midnight May 11th.

For the 25 years prior to January 1969 Cárdenas had been free from any serious illness. Then for 24 days he was confined at home with bronchial pneumonia. He lived the rest of 1969 however as usual, going and coming, sometimes 15 hours a day over rugged roads, rain or shine. Then on January 10, 1970 he underwent surgery on the esophagus and also for a growth on his neck. Recuperation at home lasted until February 5th when he and Amalia went to Cuernavaca. Two days later they went to Acapulco where they stayed for ten days at the home of their old friend, Adolfo Orive Alba. The latter part of February they were back at their own cottage in Cuernavaca and on the 27th, at their home in Mexico City. On March 3rd the General called on the leading candidate for the presidency, Licenciado Luis Echeverría, who had hoped to celebrate the 32nd anniversary of the nationalization of the petroleum industry with Cárdenas in the Mixteca. Cárdenas preferred to eliminate himself from the festivities and so Cuauhtémoc was with candidate Echeverría back in the mountains among the Indians on the 18th of March.

On the 2nd of April Cárdenas wrote:

Today is Cuauhtémoc and Celeste's wedding anniversary. They were married on April 2, 1963. Their son, Lázaro, is 6 years old today. I dropped in to see my very dear friend, Architect Albert Leduc.

The following day he wrote:

With family and friends we gathered at our home last night to celebrate Cuauhtémoc and Celeste's anniversary; Amalia, as always, waited on everyone with deep affection. There is an article in the newspaper about the situation in Vietnam. World opinion is coming out strongly against that war and against all aggression.

On April 8 came a trip to the state of Vera Cruz that lasted three days, then a hop to the state of Morelos, followed by a brief visit to the state of Querétaro. The last ten days of April and the first ten days of May were spent putting finishing touches on the development projects he and the Balsas River Commission had been carrying out back in the Mixteca and other mountainous areas of the state of Oaxaca. These village visits and project inspections were interrupted by the illness that had brought his family to his side so abruptly in Justlahuaca but were soon renewed and continued into June. That proved to be his farewell to the Mixteca, one of the main scenes of his untiring efforts during the last nine years of his life.

The next three weeks were spent at home except for a brief visit to the medicinal spa at Los Azufres with Amalia. On July fifth he wrote in his diary:

At 11 a.m. today Amalia and I went to the polls (No. 91, Sec. 72) to cast our vote for President of the Republic in favor of Lic. Echeverría. Lic. Ignacio Acosta accompanied us.

Three months later and just six days before his death, he wrote what he desired to see in a chief of state. Like many of the priceless conclusions of a lifetime lived for others that abound in his diary the picture was idealistic. He wrote:

He who would lead a country wisely must seek to eradicate his personal defects, overcoming prejudices and any inclination toward totalitarianism, avoiding in this way the possibility of causing the country to fall into dictatorship. The countries of America and of the world, for their own well-being, need highly motivated statesmen — dedicated, austere, and with an unbiased sense of justice, unyielding in the face of the powerful, but flexible in dealing with the needy; of balanced judgment in adversity, and serene in complex situations, when under attack or when reviled. In making decisions to act he must distinguish clearly between opposition which is made in defense of liberty and that which is subversive.

The day that he voted for presidential candidate Echeverría and the day following, he made extensive notes in his diary regarding agrarian reform, credit for the peasant farmers, the further distribution of land, and the need for more schools as well as training in the techniques suitable for improving farming.

Then the statesman, standing on the threshold of eternity, opened his heart concerning personal attitudes. As though his own example during forty years were not enough, he quoted Leon Tolstoy: "I could never give credence to the Christian, philosophic or humanistic convictions of any person who would make his servant empty his chamber pot."

This was followed by the comment of Vladimir Ilich Lenin concerning Tolstoy's statement:

"A finer recognition of equality and respect for humanity could not be found."

With his customarily practical application of the ideal, he continued writing:

Speaking to a quarter of a million black people at the foot of the Lincoln Monument in Washington, Martin Luther King said: "I have a dream that one day on the red hills of Georgia the sons of former slaves and the sons of former slave owners will be able to sit down together at the table of brotherhood."

As I read these quotations I realized that Cárdenas himself had gone much further than mere equality in his personal practice, he had lived to serve the needy. I was taken back to January 1936 when, as President of Mexico, he had come to the Indian village where my first wife and I were living while we studied beautiful *Nahuatl,* the local tongue. Desirous of bringing linguists who, along with their scientific work, would also translate the Bible into all the local languages of Mexico and, knowing that people quite commonly failed to distinguish between the Bible and religion, I had decided to demonstrate the difference through practical service. President Cárdenas inspected my linguistic and literacy materials and then looked at the vegetable garden that I had planted in the central square with the help of the Indians. He was so pleased with what he saw he asked me if the Bible translators I wanted to bring would help the minority language groups in a practical way as we were doing.

"Yes, Mr. President," I replied. "In the Bible we read that Christ did not come to be served by others, but to serve them and to give His life on their behalf; and we want to follow His example."

The President said, "That's what is needed. Bring all you can." We did, and at every turn we could count on the help of Mexico's remarkable servant of the poor and needy.

On the 19th of October 1970, Mexico was shocked from one end to the other and from top to bottom. The great friend of the common man had breathed his last. He had just returned from a visit to Jiquilpan, his birthplace, a few days before. During August he had been in constant activity in the central part of the Balsas area. September, too, had been a busy month, much of it spent on the road, though he did take time to dictate letters. I received one of these. It was dated September 10 and he expressed his satisfaction that my daughter, Joy Amalia, and her husband, David Tuggy, had begun linguistic studies and Bible translation work among the *Nahuatl* Indians of Tetelcingo. Another of these letters was dated September 30, 1970 and was addressed to the President-elect of Chile, Salvador Allende. The two letters, written at about the same time, revealed his interest in both the small and the great: two unknown linguists in a small village on the one hand and on the other, an important statesman, leader of a republic that was in the limelight. Once again, they revealed Lázaro Cárdenas, master of men, servant of the masses.

Near the center of the great metropolis that Mexico City has become, looking out majestically over the mountain-brimmed plateau that itself towers a mile and a half above sea level, is located the Monument to the Mexican Revolution. It stands on four giant pillars between which people assemble to pay tribute to heroes of the Revolution. In the four pillars themselves, are four mausoleums. One is the final resting place of the father of the Constitution of 1917, Venustiano Carranza; another is that of the military genius of the Revolution, Francisco I. Madero; a third is that of Plutarco Elías Calles; the fourth holds the mortal remains of Lázaro Cárdenas, the conscience of the Revolution, who returned the land to the peasant and dignity to the Indian, defender of Mexico's economic independence and eradicator of both the *caudillaje* (tyrannical rule by political bosses) and the *continuismo* (more than one presidential term for the same man) that had formerly plagued his country.

Relatively few from distant lands will visit his tomb but in Mexico his record will live on and on, inspiring all who strive for a better world.

He ruled without shedding blood. He had no political prisoners. He welcomed home all political exiles. He guaranteed liberty of expression to the press. He restored liberty of worship. He took the government to the people. He exalted the dignity of the common man. He fought against vice, ignorance, selfishness and prejudice. He sought the welfare of the Indians and promoted the utilization of their own exotic tongues for their initial instruction. He respected other nations and secured their respect for his own. He worked for peace and for a Western Hemisphere united as one great spiritual fatherland, free from intervention and exploitation from without. He submitted to his successors while quietly maintaining his own principles. For year after year until well past the three score years and ten, he toiled tirelessly at tasks that developed and paved the way for further development of large areas of Mexico.

President Luis Echeverría has justly requested that the steel mill, Las Truchas, and the city that is taking shape around it, bear the name, "Lázaro Cárdenas — Las Truchas." The official statement reads:

> "It was basically the vision of this great Mexican which set the studies in motion — an inspired vision for the economic independence and industrialization of our country, based on his personal drive and on his own intimate knowledge of the region."

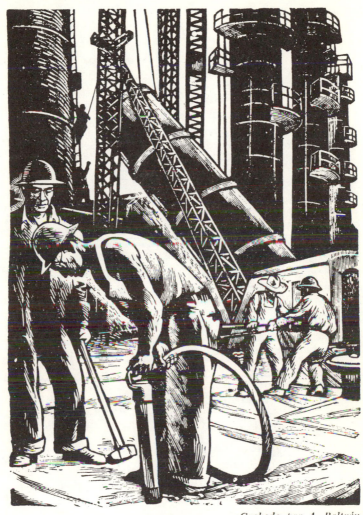

Grabado por A Beltrán

Glossary

agraristas — agrarians
braceros — Mexican Nationals
        under labor contract
        in the U. S. A.
burro — donkey
cacique — chief or boss
caciquismo — bossism
campesinos — peasants
castillo — castle
centavos — pennies
conquistadores — conquerors
cristeros — Catholic revolters
ejido — community land
el chamaco — the kid
equipal — leather chair
frontón — jai alai
guyaba — guava
hacienda — plantation
hectárea — 2.471 acres
juego de avas — a game of keeps
machete — work knife
masa — dough
matador — bull fighter
mecapal — raw hide head band for carrying
mestizos — mixed race
metates — stone for grinding meal
muy macho — he-man
padre — father
peons — day laborers
pueblos — towns
pulquería — saloon
rebozo — shawl
seminario — seminary